ROME
AND HER
NORTHERN
PROVINCES

Sheppard Frere

ROME
AND HER
NORTHERN
PROVINCES

Papers presented to Sheppard Frere in honour of his retirement from the Chair of the Archaeology of the Roman Empire, University of Oxford, 1983

EDITED BY

BRIAN HARTLEY AND JOHN WACHER

ALAN SUTTON
1983

Alan Sutton Publishing Limited
17a Brunswick Road
Gloucester GL1 1HG

First published 1983

Typesetting and origination by
Alan Sutton Publishing Limited
Photoset Bembo 11/13
Printed in Great Britain
by Redwood Burn Limited, Trowbridge

Contents

List of Illustrations   vii

List of Contributors   xiii

List of Abbreviations   xv

Editor's Note   xvii

Sheppard Sunderland Frere, John Wacher   1

A Bibliography of the published works of Sheppard Frere, John Hopkins   4

Foreign Affairs, J.E. Bogaers   13

Some Romano-British Domestic Shrines and their Inhabitants, G.C. Boon   33

Some Research Work on Roman Villas in Italy, 1960–80, M. Alwin Cotton   56

Earth's Grip Holds Them, Barry Cunliffe   67

The Enclosure of Romano-British Towns in the Second Century A.D., Brian Hartley   84

The Internal Planning of Roman Auxiliary Forts, Mark Hassall   96

The Cauldron Chains of Iron Age and Roman Britain, W.H. Manning   132

The Military Origin of Some Roman Settlements in Belgium, J.R. Mertens   155

The Civilized Pannonians of Velleius, A. Mócsy   169

Sacramentum, H. von Petrikovits   179

The First Icenian Revolt, A.L.F. Rivet   202

A Husband for the Mother Goddesses — Some Observations on the *Matronae Aufaniae*, C.B. Rüger   210

The Roman Fortlet at Gatehouse-of-Fleet, Kirkcudbrightshire,
J.K. St Joseph   222

The Roman Fortress at Eining-Unterfeld: a Reconsideration,
Hans Schönberger   235

The Possible Effects on Britain of the Fall of Magnentius,
Graham Webster   240

Romans, Dacians and Sarmatians, J.J. Wilkes   255

The Lower Enclosure at Carisbrooke Castle, Isle of Wight, C.J. Young   290

Index   303

List of Illustrations

J.E. Bogaers: *Foreign Affairs*

Plate I   Altar (90 × 59 × 30 cm.) dedicated to Nehalennia by a *negotiator Cantianus (et?) Geserecanus*, recovered from the Eastern Scheldt estuary off Colijnsplaat.   14

Plate II   The inscription of the altar represented on Pl. I.   15

Plate III   Altar (63 × 41 × 15.5 cm.) dedicated to Nehalennia by the freedman P. Arisenius Marius, *negotiator Britannicianus*, recovered from the Eastern Scheldt estuary off Colijnsplaat.   16

Plate IV   Altar (74.5 × 46 × 21.5 cm.) dedicated to Nehalennia by C. Aurelius Verus, *negotiator Britannicianus*, recovered from the Eastern Scheldt estuary off Colijnsplaat.   18

Plate V   Part of a dedication-slab (63 × 49 × 14 cm.) of L. Viducius Placidus, found at Clementhorpe, York. *(Photo: M.S. Duffy; copyright York Archaeological Trust).*   21

Figure 1   The inscription *R.I.B.* 1322 from Newcastle upon Tyne, drawn by R.G. Collingwood. Scale 1:8. *(By kind permission of the Clarendon Press and R.P. Wright: copyright reserved).*   25

G.C. Boon: *Some Romano-British Domestic Shrines and their Inhabitants*

Plate I   Lower parts of domestic shrines, Verulamium. *(By permission of S.S. Frere).*   34

Plate II   Cupboard surmounted by a *lararium*, Herculaneum. *(By permission of the Soprintendenza alle Antichità delle Prov. di Napoli e Caserta-Napoli).*   35

Plate III   Lower part of a domestic shrine, Silchester. *(By permission of Reading Museum and Art Gallery).*   37

Plate IV   Remains of shrine, Catterick. 4th century A.D. *(Crown Copyright reserved).*   37

Plate V   Alcove serving as a domestic shrine, Dorchester. *(Photograph by M.B. Cookson, Crown Copyright, National Monuments Record).*   39

Plate VI   Monolithic domestic shrine with niche for a figurine. *(By
            permission of the Musée d'Histoire et d'Art, Luxembourg).*   41
Plate VII   Remains of domestic shrine, Rezé, Loire-Atlantique. *(After
            Parenteau, 1869).*   42
Plate VIII Seated Mother-goddess, holding fruit and emblem of eternity
            in the form of a fir-tree, found at Caerwent. *(By permission of
            Newport Museum and Art Gallery).* Inset, obverse of a gold
            stater of the Dobunni, inscribed CORIO *(National Museum
            of Wales).*   44

M. Alwin Cotton: *Some Research Work on Roman Villas in Italy, 1960–80*

Figure 1   Axonometric reconstruction of the villa at San Rocco in
            Period I.   57
Figure 2   Axonometric reconstruction of the villa at San Rocco in
            Period II.   58

Barry Cunliffe: *Earth's Grip Holds Them*

Plate I   Pennant slab flooring of precinct.   71
Plate II   Collapsed masonry of the fallen ambulatory facade and roof
            in the precinct.   73
Figure 1   Plan of reservoir enclosure.   69
Figure 2   Axonometric reconstruction of reservoir enclosure.   70

Mark Hassall: *The Internal Planning of Roman Auxiliary Forts*

Figure 1   Drobeta, after Florescu, 1967, 147, fig. 3.   102
Figure 2   Chesters, after Richmond, 1947, 85.   104
Figure 3   Slǎveni, restored plan after Tudor, 1977, 402, fig. 2.   106
Figure 4   Künzing, after Schönberger, 1969, 163, fig. 17 and 1975,
            Beilage 1, 1.   107
Figure 5   Valkenburg, after Glasbergen and Groenman-van Waateringe,
            1974, 7, fig. 2.   108
Figure 6   Birrens, after Breeze, 1979, 33, fig. 14.   111
Figure 7   Gelligaer II, after Nash-Williams, 1969, fig. 45.   113
Figure 8   Fendoch, after Richmond, 1939, fig. 2 (opposite p. 114).   114
Figure 9   Oberstimm, after Schönberger, 1978, 138, fig. 65.   115
Figure 10   Caerhun, after Nash-Williams, 1969, 58, fig. 25.   117
Figure 11   Pen Llystyn, after Nash-Williams, 1969, 102, fig. 53.   118
Figure 12   Ain Sinu I, after Oates and Oates, 1959, Plate LII.   122
Figure 13   Reconstructed plan of the legionary fortress at Albano after
            Tortorici, 1975, 93, fig. 135.   123

W.H. Manning: *The Cauldron Chains of Iron Age and Roman Britain*

Figure 1   Continental chains: 1. La Tène, 2. La Tène, 3. Attersee.   133

Figure 2   Continental chains: 1. St. Aubin, Jura, 2. Zugmantel, 3.
            Cannstatt.   135
Figure 3   British Iron Age chains: 1. Over Fen, 2. Butley, 3. 'East
            Anglia', unprovenanced, now in Cambridge.   137
Figure 4   Fragments of British chains: 1. Hunsbury, 2. Bigbury, 3.
            Pulborough, 4. Pentyrch.   139
Figure 5   Stanfordbury tripod.   141
Figure 6   Fragments of British chains: 1. Newstead, 2. 'East Anglia',
            unprovenanced, 3. Blackburn Mill, 4. Silchester.   144
Figure 7   Fragments of British chains: 1. Dorn, 2. Silchester, 3.
            Bartlow.   146
Figure 8   British chains: 1. Cirencester, 2. Winchester, 3. Great
            Chesterford.   148
Figure 9   British chains: 1. Appleford, 2. Brandon.   149

J.R. Mertens: *The Military Origin of Some Roman Settlements in Belgium*

Figure 1   Principal Roman roads in the north of Gaul.   156
Figure 2   Tongres: site plan *(after Vanvinckenroye, 1975)* 1. Ditches (A,
            B, C), 2. Distribution of arretine pottery, 3. Distribution of
            coins with the legend AVAVCIA, 4. Tombs, D. Town wall
            in the second century.   157
Figure 3   The site of Tournai: A. Ditches, B. Roman *vicus*.   159
Figure 4   The site of Velzeke *(after M. Rogge 1980)*: A. Augustan base,
            B. Roman settlements.   160
Figure 5   The site of Elewijt: A. Ditch, B. Roman settlement.   161
Figure 6   The site of Asse *(after Graff, 1981)*: A. Roman 'camp', B.
            Roman settlement.   162
Figure 7   Inscription recording Tiberius' visit to Bavay.   163

H. von Petrikovits: Sacramentum

Plate I   Anonymous *denarius*, A.D. 68. *(Photograph: Badisches
            Landesmuseum, Karlsruhe. Bildarchiv)*.(2:1).   180
Plate II   *Denarius* of Trajan. *(Photograph: Hunter Coin Cabinet)* (2:1). 181
Plate III   *Solidus* of Constantine I. *(Photograph: Rheinisches Landes-
            museum, Trier)*. (2:1).   181
Plate IV   *Solidus* of Constantine I. *(Photograph: Rheinisches Landes-
            museum, Trier)*. (2:1).   182
Plate V   Projection of a relief on a gladiator's helmet from Pompeii.
            *(Drawing after Museo Borbonico X, plate 31, provided by G.
            Ulbert (Munich))*.   183
Plate VI   Detail from the reliefs on Trajan's column in Rome (LXXVII
            203). *(Photograph: Deutsches Archäologisches Institut in Rome)*. 184
Plate VII   Detail from the reliefs on Trajan's column in Rome (LXXXV

223). *(Photograph: as VI).*   185

Plate VIII   Detail from the reliefs on the column of Marcus Aurelius in Rome. *(Photograph: as VI).*   186

Plate IX   Detail from the reliefs on the column of Marcus Aurelius in Rome. *(Photograph: as VI).*   187

Plate X   Detail from the relief on the left-hand side of a sarcophagus from Modena. *(Photograph: H. Gabelmann, Bonn).*   188

Plate XI   Detail of a bas-relief from the arch of Constantine in Rome. *(Photograph: Deutsches Archäologisches Institut in Rome).*   189

Plate XII   'Open' hand in a copper alloy found in Nida (Frankfurt-Heddernheim). In private ownership. *(Photograph: Museum für Vor- und Frühgeschichte, Frankfurt am Main).*   194

Plate XIII   A and B   'Open' hand in a copper alloy found at Mauer an der Url (Lower Austria). *(Photograph: Antiquities Department of the Kunsthistorisches Museum in Vienna).* (½)   195

Plate XIV   Relief on a triangular plaque in copper alloy from Mauer an der Url (Lower Austria). *(Photograph: As XIII).*   196

C.B. Rüger: *A Husband for the Mother Goddess*

Plate I   Altar of the *Matronae Aufaniae* of A.D. 164 (Vettius altar). *(Photograph: Rheinisches Landesmuseum, Bonn).*   211

Plate II   Altar to the *Matronae Aufaniae* by Statilius Proculus and Sutoria Pia; A. Front; B. Back. *(Photograph: Rheinisches Landesmuseum, Bonn).*   212

Plate III   Altar to the *Matronae Aufaniae* of Flavia Tiberina; A. Front; B. Back. *(Photograph: Rheinisches Landesmuseum, Bonn).*   216

Figure 1   Altar of Statilius Proculus and Sutoria Pia; scale 1/10. *(Drawn by Margret Sonntag-Hilgers).*   217

J.K. St Joseph: *The Roman Fortlet at Gatehouse-of-Fleet, Kirkcudbrightshire*

Plate I   Roman fortlet, Gatehouse of Fleet. Steep oblique photograph looking north-east. Neg. No. DT 38, taken 11 July, 1949. *(This photograph from the Cambridge University Collection is Crown Copyright and is reproduced by permission of the Ministry of Defence, and of the Controller of Her Majesty's Stationery Office).*   223

Figure 1   Gatehouse of Fleet. The site of the fortlet in relation to the river.   224

Figure 2   Gatehouse of Fleet. Plan of the fortlet.   *facing* 226

Figure 3   Section across the south-east defences.   *facing* 227

Figure 4   Plan of oven.   229

Figure 5   Sections of querns. The numbers are those of the numbered stones in Fig. 4.   230

Figure 6   Sections: water tank and pits. The lines of sections AB, CD
            and EF are marked on Fig. 2.   231

H. Schönberger: *The Roman Fortress at Eining-Unterfeld: a Reconsideration*

Figure 1   The Roman Fortress at Eining-Unterfeld. *(After Beilage 9,
            Germania, xxxxviii, and fig. 2,* Archäologisches Korrespon-   236
            denzblatt, *ix, 425).*

G. Webster: *The Possible Effects on Britain of the Fall of Magnentius*

Plate I   A coin of Magnentius found at Chester. *(Grosvenor Museum,
            Chester).*   242
Figure 1   Map reflecting changes in villa establishments.   246
Figure 2   Plan of villa at Gadebridge Park in Period 5. *(Reproduced by
            permission of David Neal and the Society of Antiquaries).*   248

J.J. Wilkes: *Romans, Dacians and Sarmatians*

Plate I   Marble relief of a horseman clad in Sarmatian scale armour
            and holding a lance *(contus)*; from Tanais in south Russia.
            Set up by Tryphon, son of Andromenos, perhaps in the wall
            of a temple, in the late second or early third century A.D.
            See Latyschev, V., *Inscriptiones Antiquae orae Septentrionalis
            Ponti Euxini Graecae et Latinae. Vol. II.* Petrograd, 1890, 231,
            no. 424. *(Reproduced by kind permission of Thames and Hudson
            Ltd.).*   257
Plate II   Scenes from Trajan's column showing armoured Sarmatians;
&   see p. 258. *(Photograph: Deutsches Archäologisches Institut in
Plate III   Rome, reproduced by kind permission of Thames and Hudson).*   272
Figure 1   Map of Danube lands.   256

C.J. Young: *The Lower Enclosure at Carisbrooke Castle, Isle of Wight*

Plate I   Air photograph of Carisbrooke, from the south-west,
            showing Lower Enclosure wall at base of castle bailey bank.
            (Crown Copyright).   293
Plate II   View of the east gateway of the Lower Enclosure: scale 2m.
            (Crown Copyright).   295
Plate III   Masonry structure possibly associated with the gateway:
            scale 50 cm. *(Crown Copyright).*   295
Figure 1   The Isle of Wight, showing Carisbrooke; inset locating the
            Isle of Wight and Saxon Shore Forts in southern Britain.   291
Figure 2   Carisbrooke Castle showing the Lower Enclosure, the pre-
            sent Castle, excavated sites, possible ringworks and
            seventeenth-century defences.   292

Figure 3   A.   Plan showing Coach House, excavation Site 1, and curtain walls of the Lower Enclosure and medieval castle; B.   South-east corner of Site 1 showing large stone footing as excavated and as traced under east and south walls of the Coach House; C.   possible reconstruction of Lower Enclosure gateway.   296

List of Contributors

J.E. Bogaers, Dr., Professor of Classical, especially Provincial Roman and Dutch, Archaeology, Catholic University, Nijmegen.

G.C. Boon, B.A., F.S.A., Keeper of Archaeology and Numismatics, National Museum of Wales.

M. Aylwin Cotton, O.B.E., M.B., B.S., F.S.A., Sometime Secretary of the Verulamium Excavation Committee.

Barry Cunliffe, M.A., Ph.D., F.B.A., F.S.A., Professor of Prehistoric Archaeology, University of Oxford.

Brian Hartley, M.A., F.S.A., Reader in Roman Provincial Archaeology, University of Leeds.

Mark Hassall, M.A., F.S.A., Senior Lecturer, Institute of Archaeology, University of London.

John Hopkins, M.A., Librarian, Society of Antiquaries of London.

W.H. Manning, Ph.D., F.S.A., Senior Lecturer, Department of Archaeology, University College, Cardiff.

J.R. Mertens, Professor of Archaeology, the Universities of Louvain and President, Department of Archaeology, Catholic University of Leuven.

A. Mócsy, Ph.D., Hon. F.S.A., Professor of Archaeology, University of Budapest.

Harald von Petrikovits, Dr. Phil., Professor and sometime Director of the Rheinisches Landesmuseum, Bonn.

A.L.F. Rivet, M.A., F.B.A., F.S.A., Emeritus Professor of Roman Provincial Studies, University of Keele.

C.B. Rüger, Dr. Phil., Director of the Rheinisches Landesmuseum, Bonn.

J.K.S. St Joseph, O.B.E., M.A., Ph.D., F.B.A., F.S.A., Emeritus Professor of Aerial Photographic Studies, University of Cambridge.

Hans Schönberger, Dr. Phil., Professor and sometime Director of the Römisch-Germanisch Kommission, Frankfurt-am-Main.

John Wacher, B.Sc., F.S.A., Reader and Head of Department of Archaeology, University of Leicester.

Graham Webster, O.B.E., M.A., Ph.D., F.S.A., sometime Reader in Archaeology, Department of Extra-Mural Studies, University of Birmingham.

J.J. Wilkes, B.A., Ph.D., F.S.A., Professor of the Archaeology of the Roman Provinces, Institute of Archaeology, University of London.

C.J. Young, M.A., D.Phil., F.S.A., Principal Inspector of Ancient Monuments, Department of the Environment.

Abbreviations

Antiq. Journ.	*Antiquaries Journal*
Archaeol. Aeliana	*Archaeologia Aeliana*
Archaeol. Cambrensis	*Archaeologia Cambrensis*
Archaeol. Cantiana	*Archaeologia Cantiana*
Archaeol. Journ.	*Archaeological Journal*
B.A.R.	British Archaeological Reports
Proc. Bath Natur. Hist. and Antiq. Field Club	*Proceedings of the Bath Natural History and Antiquarian Field Club*
Trans. Birmingham Archaeol. Soc.	*Transactions of the Birmingham Archaeological Society*
Trans. Bristol and Gloucester. Archaeol. Soc.	*Transactions of the Bristol and Gloucestershire Archaeological Society*
B.M.C.	*Coins of the Roman Empire in the British Museum*, London, 1923 etc.
Proc. Cambridge Antiq. Soc.	*Proceedings of the Cambridge Antiquarian Society*
C.I.L.	*Corpus Inscriptionum Latinarum*
Proc. Devon Archaeol. Soc.	*Proceedings of the Devon Archaeological Society*
Proc. Dorset Natur. Hist. Soc.	*Proceedings of the Dorset Natural History and Archaeological Society*
Trans. Dumfries. and Galloway Natur. Hist. Antiq. Soc.	*Transactions of the Dumfriesshire and Galloway Natural History and Antiquarian Society*
I.L.S.	Dessau, H., *Inscriptiones Latinae Selectae*, 1892–1916
Trans. London and Middlesex Archaeol. Soc.	*Transactions of the London and Middlesex Archaeological Society*
P.I.R.	*Prosopographia Imperii Romani*
Realencyclopädie	von Pauly, A.F., (ed. Wissowa, G.), *Realencyclopädie der classischen Altertumswissenschaft*, Stuttgart, 1894–1980
R.I.B.	Collingwood, R.G. and Wright, R.P., *The Roman Inscriptions of Britain*, Vol. I, Oxford, 1965
R.I.C.	Mattingly, H. and Sydenham, E.A., *The Roman Imperial Coinage*, London, 1923 etc.
Proc. Soc. Antiq. Newcastle upon Tyne	*Proceedings of the Society of Antiquaries of Newcastle upon Tyne*
Proc. Society of Antiquaries of Scotland	*Proceedings of the Society of Antiquaries of Scotland*
Proc. Somerset Archaeol. Natur. Hist. Soc.	*Proceedings of the Somerset Archaeological and Natural History Society*
Proc. University of Bristol Spelaeological Soc.	*Proceedings of the University of Bristol Spelaeological Society*
Wilt. Archaeological Magazine	*Wiltshire Archaeological Magazine*

Editors' Note

This book is presented to Sheppard Frere with all the respect and affection of his colleagues and past and present students, both in Britain and abroad. Many desired to contribute; only few could be accommodated. As far as possible the contributors have been selected to represent those institutions and the areas and places of archaeological interest with which Sheppard Frere has been most closely connected. The editors must take full responsibility for any gaps which, some may think, have been left unfilled.

The editors would like to record their great thanks to the people who have helped in the preparation of this volume and so made its publication possible: David Parsons, Senior Tutor in the Department of Adult Education, University of Leicester, for his accurate translations of the German and Belgian contributions; Susan Osmond, University of Oxford, for the immensely difficult task of standardising all bibliographical references and abbreviations; Susan Vaughan for providing the index; Linda Proud for producing the final typscript, sometimes from much-defaced originals; Julie Kennedy for her rapid production of some of the line illustrations and for standardizing features on others. All the contributors greatly assisted in the remarkably smooth preparation by prompt submission of manuscripts and quick response to queries and proof correction; their conscientiousness may be seen as a further tribute to the recipient of this volume!

Finally, Alan Sutton, first by his generous acceptance of the volume for publication and later by his enthusiastic help and advice, has earned the heartfelt gratitude of both editors and all the contributors for making it possible for them to honour a distinguished scholar and archaeologist in the traditional manner.

Brian Hartley
John Wacher

Sheppard Sunderland Frere

The stature of a great man can often be gauged by the number of humorous stories which circulate about him; they are told with kindly glee, without hint of malice and entirely lack the sharp edge which is sometimes heard in connection with a person who commands less affection. Each new story is added eagerly to the roll by the teller, on whom a little of the reflected glory descends in the telling, until finally a whole saga has grown around the most fortunate and the greatest.

So it is with Sheppard Frere. The more perceptive, many years ago, may have anticipated his rise to the top of any chosen profession, for some of the stories still in circulation date back to his years as a housemaster at Lancing and are still told with animation by those who were then his pupils. From there it seems in retrospect but a series of only comparatively short steps by way of those engendered at Canterbury and Verulamium to Oxford and Strageath. Each place has produced its quota and still the saga grows.

Sheppard Frere's early interest in archaeology took flight while he was at Cambridge, carrying on through his short period as a master at Epsom. His first excavations in Surrey and Norfolk were carried out then and during the war, in short intervals between some grisly experiences serving as a fireman in London. With peace restored in 1945, he went to Lancing as a housemaster and, in the same year, took over direction of the excavations, which had been started in the previous year in the bombed areas of Canterbury, from Audrey Williams (the late Mrs. Audrey Grimes). His remarkable work at Canterbury which lasted with only a few breaks until 1960 greatly increased his reputation, and may be said to have set him firmly on the path to become one of the most respected of British archaeologists. Many of the excavations were carried out in deep trenches and in cramped and confined places, often under appalling or even dangerous conditions, with little money for paid labour, shoring or mechanical aids. But they undoubtedly set an example which was shortly to be copied by excavators in other cities devastated by war damage such as London, Dover, and Exeter, so yielding a harvest of archaeological knowledge, the like of which had never before been seen in Britain, from sites which were soon to be reburied or destroyed for good.

That Sheppard Frere subsequently chose archaeology and not pedagogy as a career was the former's great gain and an undoubted loss for the latter; in 1954 he severed his connections, which had been becoming increasingly unhappy, with Lancing, and for a year became a lecturer in archaeology at Manchester University. A year later he was appointed Reader in the Archaeology of the Roman Provinces at the Institute of Archaeology in London, then still in its old premises at St. John's Lodge. The equivalent chair had been held by Mortimer Wheeler until he left the Institute in 1955. It was not, therefore, entirely surprising that in the same year he should also have been invited to succeed Wheeler as Director of Excavations at Verulamium so as to carry out the extensive rescue operations which were caused by the impending widening of Bluehouse Hill. There, with more money, better support and facilities, and open fields in place of dank basements, he was able to develop to the full the expertise for large-scale excavations which he had acquired from his experiences at Canterbury; they were carried on annually, with only short intermissions, until 1961. Suffice it to say that the reports of these excavations, which are now appearing in print, show his remarkable competence both as an excavator and above all as an interpreter of archaeological remains.

In 1963, Sheppard Frere was promoted professor in the Institute of Archaeology, which had by then moved to its new building in Gordon Square. Meanwhile other sites had also been claiming his time, even though he was still involved with Canterbury and Verulamium: Dorchester (Oxon.), Ivinghoe Beacon, Bignor, Lezoux, Xanten, Bowes; later, Longthorpe, and most recently, Strageath. In addition, there were many rapid forays into Wales and Scotland with Kenneth St Joseph, seeking Roman military installations which had been revealed by aerial photography, and, following this work, by excavations at Trawscoed, Gatehouse of Fleet and Brandon Camp. Yet, while he was doing this, he had begun *Britannia,* his great definitive survey of Roman Britain which was to be published in 1967; it is likely in its later editions to remain the standard source of reference on the subject for many years yet. But before publication could take place Sheppard Frere was to suffer yet another upheaval, following the sudden and unexpected death of Ian Richmond. He was elected in 1966 to succeed Richmond as the second Professor of the Archaeology of the Roman Empire at Oxford, held jointly with a fellowship at All Souls College.

Apart from his many activities in excavation, field survey, teaching and publication, he has been a sympathetic, if sometimes outspoken, yet always invaluable member of many councils and committees, often acting as chairman. He had also served on the Royal Commission on Historical Monuments and the Ancient Monuments Board, as a Vice-President of the Society of Antiquaries, and latterly as President of the Royal Archaeological Institute. His election as a Fellow of the British Academy in 1971 and also the award of a C.B.E. in 1976 for his public services were well deserved. But he is probably best known to several generations of archaeologists for his ever-readiness to visit excavations in order to advise and encourage, and in so doing making his great fund of unparalleled experience available to all who asked, or to give entertaining and informative lectures to undergraduate or local societies. He has travelled many thousands of wearisome miles in this way and his presence on an excavation or in a lecture room was always welcome, despite what some occasionally saw at first sight as an apparently gruff exterior. Yet, as his predecessor at Oxford had done before him, he has endeared himself firmly to many students and colleagues, not only in Britain but also in other European countries. Many, not least the writer, owe him a great debt of gratitude for help generously given; a few of that many, in consequence, have now contributed to this book in what can only be described as a token of respect, appreciation and affection on the occasion of his retirement from Oxford but not, it is to be hoped, from archaeology.

Sheppard Frere has filled his successive chairs at London and Oxford with great distinction. He has proved a worthy successor to Ian Richmond and to those other eminent British romanists who have gone before: Haverfield and Collingwood. In the history of Roman archaeology, he will take his place beside them. It only remains to wish him, and Janet, a long and happy retirement.

John Wacher

A Bibliography of the Published Works of Sheppard Frere

Compiled by JOHN HOPKINS

1939   'Three flint implements from Shrimpling', *Norfolk Archaeology*, xxvii, 29–30.

1940   'A survey of archaeology near Lancing', *Sussex Archaeological Collections*, lxxxi, 140–72.
'A food vessel from Needham, Norfolk', *Antiq. Journ.*, xx, 272–4.

1941   'Roman pottery from Lancing in the British Museum', *Sussex Notes and Queries*, viii, 190–1.
'A Claudian site at Needham, Norfolk', *Antiq. Journ.*, xxi, 40–5.
'An Early Bronze Age burial at Epsom College', *Surrey Archaeological Collections*, xlvii, 92–5.
'A Late Bronze Age hoard from Banstead', *Surrey Archaeological Collections*, xlvii, 95.
'A Medieval pottery at Ashtead', *Surrey Archaeological Collections*, xlvii, 58–66.

1942   'An Iron Age site near Epsom', *Antiq. Journ.*, xxii, 123–8.

1943   'Axe-Hammer from Loddon, Norfolk', *Antiq. Journ.*, xxiii, 154–5.
'A Roman coin from Ewell', *Surrey Archaeological Collections*, xlviii, 154.
'A Roman ditch at Ewell County School', *Surrey Archaeological Collections*, xlviii, 45–60.
'A Romano-British site at Woodmansterne', *Surrey Archaeological Collections*, xlviii, 152–4.
'Beaker sherd from Chanctonbury', *Sussex Notes and Queries*, ix, 156.

1944   'An Iron Age site at West Clandon, Surrey, and some aspects of Iron Age and Romano-British culture in the Wealden area', *Archaeol. Journ.*, ci, 50–67.

1945 'Romano-British finds at Littleton', *Trans. London and Middlesex Archaeol. Soc.*, n.s., ix, 203–4.
'The Romano-British village at Needham, Norfolk', with Clarke, R.R., *Norfolk Archaeology*, xxviii, 187–216.
'The date of the 'Caesar's Camp' pottery', in Lowther, A.W.G., ''Caesar's Camp', Wimbledon, Surrey: the excavations of 1937', *Archaeol. Journ.*, cii, 19–20.

1946 'A Roman coin from Shamley Green, Wonersh', *Surrey Archaeological Collections*, xlix, 112.
'A brooch from the Roman villa, Walton Heath', *Surrey Archaeological Collections*, xlix, 108.
'Polished axe from Bury Hill, Dorking', *Surrey Archaeological Collections*, xlix, 92–3.
'Polished axes from Guildford and Leith Hill, and South Norwood', *Surrey Archaeological Collections*, xlix, 90–2.
'An Iron Age and Roman site on Mickleham Downs', with Hogg, A.H.A., *Surrey Archaeological Collections*, xlix, 104–6.
'Bronze objects from Farnham', *Surrey Archaeological Collections*, xlix, 103.
'Late Bronze Age celt from Betchworth', with Hooper, W., *Surrey Archaeological Collections*, xlix, 102.
'Romano-British pottery from Sanderstead', *Surrey Archaeological Collections*, xlix, 112–3.
'Roman pottery from Betchworth', *Surrey Archaeological Collections*, xlix, 110–111.
'Two Roman coins from Ewell', *Surrey Archaeological Collections*, xlix, 111.
'A Saxon burial on Farthing Down, Coulsdon', *Surrey Archaeological Collections*, xlix, 114.

1947 'The occupation of Sandown Park, Esher, during the Stone Age, the Early Iron Age and the Anglo-Saxon period', with Burchell, J.P.T., *Antiq. Journ.*, xxvii, 24–46.
'A Romano-British occupation site at Portfield gravel pit, Chichester', *Sussex Archaeological Collections*, lxxxvi, 137–40.
Roman Canterbury, 1. Roman Canterbury: city of Durovernum, Medici Society, Maidstone.

1949 'The excavation of a Late Roman bath-house at Chatley Farm, Cobham', *Surrey Archaeological Collections*, 1, 73–98.
'Canterbury excavations 1944–8', *Antiquity*, xxiii, 153–60.
'Canterbury excavations: preliminary reports April, 1948 to April, 1949', *Archaeological News Letter*, ii, 79–80.
Roman Canterbury, 4. Excavations at Butchery Lane, Medici Society, Maidstone.

1950 'The Iron Age pottery from Harting Down huts 1 and 2', in Keefe,

P.A.M., 'Harting Hill hut shelters', *Sussex Archaeological Collections,* lxxxix, 187–91.

1952   'Roman pottery from Oxshott', *Surrey Archaeological Collections,* lii, 82–3.

1953   Review of Aileen Fox, *Roman Exeter (Isca Dumnoniorum): excavations in the war-damaged areas, 1945–7,* 1952, in *Antiq. Journ.,* xxxiii, 232–3.

1954   'Canterbury excavations, Easter, 1953', *Archaeol. Cantiana,* lxvi, 163.
'Canterbury excavations', *Spinks' Numismatic Circular,* lxii, 290 and 490.

1955   'Subterranean chamber at Waddon', *Antiq. Journ.,* xxxv, 90.
'Canterbury excavations, summer, 1946: the Rose Lane sites', *Archaeol. Cantiana,* lxviii, 101–43.
Review of Richmond, I.A., *Roman Britain,* 1955, in *Archaeol. Journ.,* cxii, 137–8.
Review of Baker, F.T., *Roman Lincoln 1945–1954: ten seasons' excavations in Lincoln,* 1955, in *Antiq. Journ.,* xxxv, 252.

1956   'Excavations at Verulamium, 1955: first interim report', *Antiq. Journ.,* xxxvi, 1–10.
'Canterbury', in 'Roman Britain in 1955, I: sites explored', *Journal of Roman Studies,* xlvi, 144–6.
'Verulamium', in 'Roman Britain in 1955. I: sites explored', *Journal of Roman Studies,* xlvi, 134–8.
'Canterbury excavations', *Spinks' Numismatic Circular,* lxiv, 16.
Review of Wheeler, R.E.M., *A Short Guide to Roman York,* 1956, and Webster, G., *The Roman Army,* 1956, in *Archaeol. Journ.,* cxiii, 165.

1957   'Excavations at Verulamium 1956: second interim report', *Antiq. Journ.,* xxxvii, 1–15.
'Bignor Roman villa, 1956', *Sussex Notes and Queries,* xiv, 228–9.
'Late Roman objects from Chalton, Hants.', *Antiq. Journ.,* xxxvii, 218–20.
'Canterbury excavations', *Spinks' Numismatic Circular,* lxv, 299.
Roman Canterbury, the city of Durovernum, second, revised edition, (1957?).

1958   'Excavations at Verulamium 1957: third interim report', *Antiq. Journ.,* xxxviii, 1–14.
'The Camp du Charlat, Corrèze', with Brogan, O., *Antiq. Journ.,* xxxviii, 218–22.
'Lifting mosaics', *Antiquity,* xxxii, 116–9.
Review of Boon, G.C., *Roman Silchester: the archaeology of a Romano-British town,* 1957, in *Antiq. Journ.,* xxxviii, 113.

1959   'Excavations at Verulamium 1958: fourth interim report', *Antiq. Journ,* xxxix, 1–8.

'Roman Canterbury', *South Eastern Naturalist*, liv, 17–21.

'The Iron Age in Southern Britain', *Antiquity*, xxxiii, 183–8.

Review of Scullard, H.H., *From the Gracchi to Nero: a history of Rome from 133 B.C. to A.D. 68*, 1959, in *Antiq. Journ.*, xxxix, 301.

Review of Cotton, M.A. and Gathercole, P.W., *Excavations at Clausentum, Southampton, 1951–1954*, 1958, in *Antiq. Journ.*, xxxix, 114 and *Journal of the British Archaeological Association*, xxii, 79.

Review of Wedlake, W.J., *Excavations at Camerton, Somerset: an account of thirty years' excavations covering the period from Neolithic to Saxon times, 1926–56*, 1958, in *Antiq. Journ.*, xxxix, 303.

Review of Rivet, A.L.F., *Town and Country in Roman Britain*, 1958, in *Surrey Archaeological Collections*, lvi, 163, *Antiquity*, xxxiii, 67–8 and *Past and Present*, xvi, 1–9.

1960   'Excavations at Verulamium 1959: fifth interim report', *Antiq. Journ.*, xl, 1–26.

'Excavations at High Rocks, Tunbridge Wells 1954–1956. Appendix B. The pottery', with Smith, I., *Sussex Archaeological Collections*, xcviii, 207–11.

Review of van der Heyden, A.A.M. and Scullard, H.H. (eds.), *Atlas of the Classical World*, 1959, in *Antiq. Journ.*, xl, 80.

Review of Goodchild, R., *Cyrene and Apollonia, a historical guide*, 1959, in *Antiq. Journ.*, xl, 82.

Review of Copley, G.J., *An archaeology of South East England: a study in continuity*, 1958, in *Surrey Archaeological Collections*, lvii, 104–5.

1961   'Excavations at Verulamium, 1960: sixth interim report', *Antiq. Journ.*, xli, 72–85.

'Some Romano-British sculptures from Ancaster and Wilsford, Lincolnshire', *Antiq. Journ.*, xli, 229–31.

'Civitas — a myth?', *Antiquity*, xxxv, 29–36.

'Late Bronze Age pot from Farnham', *Surrey Archaeological Collections*, lviii, 112.

'Enceintes de l'âge du fer au pays des Lémovices', with Cotton, M.A., *Gallia*, xix, 31–54.

(ed.) *Problems of the Iron Age in southern Britain. Papers given at a C.B.A. conference held at the Institute of Archaeology, December 12–14, 1958*, (Paper 11), London, 1961.

'Some Problems of the Later Iron Age' in above.

Review of Lincoln Archives Committee (ed.), *Lincolnshire Architectural and Archaeological Society. Reports and Papers*, Vol. 8, for 1959 and 1960, in *Antiq. Journ.*, xli, 104–5.

Review of Hartley, B.R., *Notes on the Roman pottery industry in the Nene Valley*, 1960, in *Antiq. Journ.*, xli, 105.

1962   'Excavations at Verulamium, 1961. Seventh and final interim report',
        Antiq. Journ., xlii, 148–59.
        Review of Royal Commission on Ancient and Historical Monuments in
        Wales and Monmouthshire: *An inventory of the ancient monuments in
        Caernarvonshire, Vol. II (Central)*, 1960, in *Antiq. Journ.*, xlii, 104–5.
        Review of Corder, P. (ed.), *The Roman town and villa at Great Casterton,
        Rutland: third report for the years 1954–1958*, 1961, in *Antiq. Journ.*, xlii,
        261–2.
        Review of Clifford, E.M., *Bagendon, a Belgic oppidum: excavations 1954–56*,
        1961, in *Journal of Roman Studies*, lii, 272–3.
        Review of Birley, E., *Research on Hadrian's Wall*, 1961, in *Journal of
        Roman Studies*, lii, 274.
        Review of Royal Commission on Historic Monuments (ed.), *The city of
        York: I. Eboracum, Roman York*, 1962, in *Archaeol. Journ.*, cxviii, 256–7.

1963   'Excavations at Dorchester-on-Thames, 1962', *Archaeol. Journ.*, cxix,
        114–49.
        'A Romano-British relief from Keisby, Lincs.', *Antiq. Journ.*, xliii, 292.
        Review of Baatz, D., *Lopodunum — Ladenburg a.N. Die Grabungen im
        Frühjahr 1960*, 1962, in *Germania*, xli, 153–5.
        Review of Dudley, D.R. and Webster, G., *The rebellion of Boudicca*,
        1962, in *Antiq. Journ.*, xliii, 311–12.
        Review of Clifford, E.M., *Bagendon, a Belgic oppidum: excavations 1954–
        6*, 1961, in *Numismatic Chronicle*, 7 ser., iii, 253–4.
        Review of Allen, D.F., *Sylloge of coins of the British Isles: the coins of the
        Coritani*, 1963, in *Numismatic Circular*, lxxi, 77 and *Journal of Roman
        Studies*, liii, 213–4.
        Review of Ordnance Survey map of southern Britain in the Iron Age, 1962, in
        Journal of Roman Studies, liii, 239–40.
        Review of White, D.A., *Litus Saxonicum: the British Saxon Shore in
        scholarship and history*, 1961, in *Medieval Archaeology*, vi–vii, 350–2.

1964   'Verulamium, three Roman cities', *Antiquity*, xxxviii, 103–12.
        'Ivinghoe', *Records of Buckinghamshire*, xvii, 315.
        'Verulamium — then and now', *Bulletin of the Institute of Archaeology,
        University of London*, iv, 61–82.
        Review of Duval, P.-M., *Paris antique, des origines au troisième siècle*, 1961,
        in *Journal of Roman Studies*, liv, 230–1.
        Review of Grenier, A., *Manuel d'archéologie gallo-romaine. III. L'architec-
        ture: (i) L'urbanisme, les monuments, (ii) Ludi et circenses*, 1958, in *Journal of
        Roman Studies*, liv, 259–60.
        Review of *Victoria History of the County of Essex. III. Roman Essex*,
        1963, in *Antiq. Journ.*, xliv, 256–7.

1965   Comment on Jarrett, M.G., 'Town defences of Roman Britain', in
        Antiquity, xxxix, 137–8.
        Review of Bonsor, W., *A Romano-British bibliography 55 B.C.–A.D. 449*,
        1964, in *Archaeol. Journ.*, cxxii, 246.
        Review of Gardner, W. and Savory, H.N., *Dinorben: a hill-fort occupied in
        Early Iron Age and Roman times*, 1964, in *Journal of Roman Studies*, lv, 296.
        Review of Thomas, E.B., *Römische Villen in Pannonien*, 1964, in
        Antiquity, xxxix, 315–6.

1966   'The end of towns in Roman Britain', in Wacher, J.S. (ed.), *The Civitas
        Capitals of Roman Britain*, 1966, 87–100.
        'Fouilles de Lezoux (Puy-de-Dôme) en 1963', with Hartley, B.R.,
        Cahiers de civilisation Médiévale, ix, 557–63.
        Review of Webster, G. and Dudley, D.R., *The Roman conquest of Britain*,
        1965, in *Antiq. Journ.*, xlvi, 348–9.
        Review of Collingwood, R.G. and Wright, R.P., *The Roman inscriptions
        of Britain. I: inscriptions on stone*, 1965, in *Archaeol. Journ.*, cxxiii, 230–1.
        Review of Lewis, M.J.T., *Temples in Roman Britain*, 1966, in *Antiq.
        Journ.*, xlvi, 352.
        Review of Robertson, A.S., *The Roman fort at Castledykes*, 1964, in
        Journal of Roman Studies, lvi, 269–70.
        Review of Cunliffe, B.W., *Winchester excavations 1949–1960. I.*, 1964, in
        Antiq. Journ., xlvi, 354.
        Review of Merrifield, R., *The Roman city of London*, 1965, in *Antiquity*,
        xl, 158–9.

1967   *Provinces of the Roman Empire. I. Britannia: a history of Roman Britain*,
        London, 1967.

1968   'Excavations in the Iron Age hill-fort at High Rocks, near Tunbridge
        Wells, 1957–1961. Appendix B: the pottery', with Cotton, M.A., *Sussex
        Archaeological Collections*, cvi, 187–93.
        'Ivinghoe Beacon excavations, 1963–5', with Cotton, M.A., *Records of
        Buckinghamshire*, xviii, 187–203.
        'Richmond, Wheeler and Hod Hill', *Antiquity*, xlii, 292–6.

1969   Review of Richmond, I.A., *Hod Hill. II: excavations carried out between
        1951 and 1958 for the Trustees of the British Museum*, 1968, in *Antiq. Journ.*,
        xlix, 154–5.
        Review of Ogilvie, R.M. and Richmond, I.A. (eds.), *Cornelli Taciti: De
        Vita Agricolae*, 1967, in *Antiq. Journ.*, xlix, 155.
        Review of Rivet, A.L.F., *The Iron Age in northern Britain*, 1966, in *Antiq.
        Journ.*, xlix, 153.

1970   'The Roman theatre at Canterbury', *Britannia*, i, 83–113.

'Mould for bronze statuette from Gestingthorpe', *Britannia*, i, 266–7.

'A Romano-British votive relief from Witham', *Britannia*, i, 267.

Review of Nash-Williams, V.E. (2nd ed. M.G. Jarrett), *The Roman frontier in Wales*, 1969, in *Antiq. Journ.*, 1, 381–2.

Review of Rivet, A.L.F. (ed.), *The Roman villa in Britain*, 1969, in *Antiquity*, xliv, 149–50.

Review of the Ordnance Survey, *The Antonine Wall: 2½ inch map*, 1969, in *Antiquity*, xliv, 82–3.

Review of Salway, P. (ed.), *Roman archaeology and art: essays and studies by Sir Ian Richmond*, 1969, in *Britannia*, i, 323–4.

1971 'The urbanization of Roman Britain', in *Britannia Romana*, Accademia Nazionale dei Lincei Quaderno, cl, 3–26.

'The forum and baths at Caistor by Norwich', *Britannia*, ii, 1–26.

1972 *Verulamium excavations: Volume I*, Society of Antiquaries of London Research Report 28, London.

'The Caistor intaglio', *Britannia*, iii, 295–6.

Review of Cunliffe, B.W., *Excavations at Fishbourne 1961–1969. Vol. I: The site; Vol. II: The finds*, 1971, in *Antiquity*, xlvi, 76–8.

1973 'Longthorpe Roman fortress', *Durobrivae*, ii, 20–1.

Review of Schleiermacher, W., *Cambodunum-Kempton: eine Römerstadt im Allgaü*, 1972, in *Britannia*, iv, 354–5.

Review of Hill, D. and Jesson, M. (eds.), *The Iron Age and its hill-forts: papers presented to Sir Mortimer Wheeler on the occasion of his eightieth year*, 1971, in *Britannia*, iv, 431–2.

1974 'The Roman fortress at Longthorpe, England', *Actes du IXe Congrès International d'Études sur les Frontières Romaines*, Mamaia, 351–4.

'The Roman fortress at Longthorpe', with St Joseph, J.K., *Britannia*, v, 1–129,

Review of Gamer, G. and Rüsch, A. from a manuscript of the late Friedrich Wagner, *Corpus Signorum Imperii Romani. Deutschland, I, 1: Raetia (Bayern südlich des Limes) und Noricum (Chiemseegebiet)*, 1973, in *Britannia*, v, 493–4.

Review of Baatz, D., *Kastell Hesselbach und andere Forschungen am Odenwaldlimes*, Limesforschungen 12, 1973, in *Britannia*, v, 494–6.

1975 'The origin of small towns', in *The small towns of Roman Britain: papers presented to a conference, Oxford, 1975*, BAR British Series 15, Oxford, 4–7.

'The Silchester church. The excavation by Sir Ian Richmond in 1961', *Archaeologia*, cv, 277–302.

Principles of publication in rescue archaeology: report by a working party of the Ancient Monuments Board for England, Committee for Rescue Archaeology, Department of the Environment, London.
'Verulamium and the towns of Britannia', in Temporini, H. and Haase, W. (eds.), *Aufstieg und Niedergang der Römischen Welt,* II, 3, 290–327.

1976   Review of Leather, G.M., *Roman Lancaster: some excavation reports and some observations,* (privately produced, no date), in *Britannia,* vii, 402–3.
Review of Cunliffe, B.W., *Excavations at Porchester Castle. Vol. I: Roman,* 1975, in *Antiquity,* li, 163–4.

1977   'The fort at Strageath and the Roman occupation of Scotland', in *Studien zu den Militärgrenzen Roms.* II, Cologne, 1977, 7–12.
'Roman Britain in 1976. I. Sites explored', with Hassall, M.W.C. and Tomlin, R.S.O., in *Britannia,* viii, 356–425.
'Verulamium and Canterbury: continuity and discontinuity', in *Thèmes de Recherches sur les Villes Antiques d'Occident,* Paris, 1977, 185–94.

1979   'Town planning in the western provinces', in *Festschrift zum 75 jährigen Bestehen der Römisch-Germanischen Kommission, Beiheft zum Bericht der Römisch-Germanschen Kommission,* lviii, Mainz, 87–103.
'Verulamium: urban development and the local region', in Burnham, B.C. and Johnson, H.B. (eds.), *Invasion and response: the case of Roman Britain,* BAR British Series 73, Oxford, 273–80.
'The Roman Fort at Strageath', in *Roman Scotland: some recent excavations,* Edinburgh, 1978, 37–41.
Review of Royal Commission on Ancient and Historical Monuments of Scotland, *Lanarkshire: prehistoric and Roman monuments,* in *Britannia,* x, 395–6.

1980   'Hyginus and the First Cohort', *Britannia,* xi, 51–60.
Review of Rivet, A.L.F. and Smith, C., *The place-names of Roman Britain,* 1979, in *Britannia,* xi, 419–23.
Review of the Ordnance Survey, *Map of Roman Britain,* 1978, in *Britannia,* xi, 442–3.

1981   'The Flavian frontier in Scotland', in Kenworthy, J. (ed.), *Agricola's campaign in Scotland,* Scottish Archaeological Forum 12, 89–97.
Foreword to Philp, B., *The excavation of the Roman forts of the Classis Britannica at Dover, 1970–77,* Dover, 1981.
Review of Todd, M., *Roman Britain, 55 B.C.–A.D. 400,* 1981, and Birley, A., *The* Fasti *of Roman Britain,* 1981, in *The Times Literary Supplement,* 4101, 6 November 1981.

1982   *The Archaeology of Canterbury, Vol. I: Excavations at Canterbury Castle,* with Bennett, P. and Stow, S., Maidstone, Kent Archaeological Society for the Canterbury Archaeological Trust.

Foreword to Wacher, J.S. and McWhirr, A.D., *Cirencester Excavations, Vol. I: The early military occupation,* Cirencester Excavation Committee, Cirencester, 1982.

'The Bignor Villa', *Britannia,* xiii, 135–95.

The Archaeology of Canterbury, Vol. II: Excavations of the Roman and medieval defences of Canterbury, with Bennett, P. and Stow, S., Maidstone, Kent Archaeological Society for the Canterbury Archaeological Trust.

Foreign Affairs

by J.E. BOGAERS

I

Pls. I–II. Altar from Ganuenta (-um?),[1] dedicated to Nehalennia, recovered from the Eastern Scheldt estuary off Colijnsplaat (Noord-Beveland), in the territory of the municipality of Zierikzee (Schouwen-Duiveland), province of Zeeland, in August/September 1970 (RMO, inv. no. i 1970/12.7); since 6th December 1978 in the Rijksmuseum Het Catharijneconvent, Utrecht, as a loan. Lotharingian limestone, 90 by 59 by 30 cm. (36 by 24 by 12 in.).

P. Stuart/J.E. Bogaers in *Deae Neh.,* 64, no. 7, and figs. 7a and c.

Date: *c.* A.D. 150–250.[2]

The upper part of the altar is in the form of a niche containing a temple with pediment, and with engaged pilasters and columns supporting a shell canopy.[3] In the shrine the goddess Nehalennia is seated on a bench. In her left hand she has a dish of fruit resting on her left knee; the right hand holds an unknown object. To her left is a large wicker basket filled with fruit; to her right is a dog, partly lying, partly sitting with crossed forelegs.[4] Both sides are decorated with a cornucopia, the left side likewise with a rudder. The back is unadorned, and on top, on the sacrificial table or *mensa,* are two apples (in front) and two pears (at the back).

The monument has been rather heavily affected in the sea, mainly by marine boring organisms and salt. As a result at first only a small part of the inscription could be deciphered; especially, the reading of lines 2–4 remained very unsatisfactory. Now, after a new examination, the text can be read and restored as follows:

DE.. NEHALENNI.. / . VAL·MAR.^{c.6.}. / NEGOT·CAN.^{c.6.}. / . (?)

GESERECAN.^{c.6.}.[5] / .B·MERCES BENE·C.^{c.5.}.

De[ae] Nehalenni[ae] / [.] Val(erius) Mar[......] / negot(iator) Can[tianus] et (?) Gesere(or -i?)can[us ....] / [o]b merces bene c[onser(vatas)[5]].

13

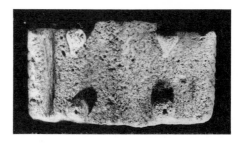

Pl. I   Altar (90 × 59 × 30 cm.) dedicated to Nehalennia by a *negotiator Cantianus (et?) Geserecanus*, recovered from the Eastern Scheldt estuary off Colijnsplaat.

Pl. II The inscription of the altar represented on Pl. I.

To the goddess Nehalennia (.) Valerius Mar(......), merchant trading with Cantia and Gesoriacum, (dedicated this altar) for her good protection of his wares.

L. 2. Before the *nomen gentilicium* Valerius, the *praenomen* (abbreviated to one letter) is missing. The *cognomen* might be restored as, e.g. Mar[cellus], Mar[cianus] or Mar[tialis].[6]

L. 3. Can[tianus]: cf. A.L.F. Rivet and C. Smith, *The Place-Names of Roman Britain* (London 1979) 299 s.v. Cantiaci (Cantii), 300 f. s.v. Cantium and Cantium promontorium. *Negot(iator) Can[tianus]*, merchant trading with Kent; cf. *negotiator Britannicianus,*[7] *Gallicanus*[8] and *Geserecan[us]*.

L. 4. Geserecan[us], perhaps Geserican[us]. This adjective is sure to refer to G(a)esoriacum/Boulogne-sur-Mer.[9] After this word there is still room for four letters, possibly the (abbreviated) name of the place where Valerius was resident, for instance C(olonia) C(laudia) A(ra) A(grippinensium)/Cologne.[10] This merchant seems to have been especially active on either side of the Straits of Dover, in Cantia and in the region of Gesoriacum, in the *civitas* of the Morini.[11]

Pl. III Altar (63 × 41 × 15.5 cm.) dedicated to Nehalennia by the freedman P. Arisenius Marius, *negotiator Britannicianus*, recovered from the Eastern Scheldt estuary off Colijnsplaat.

II

Pl. III. Altar from Ganuenta(-um?), dedicated to Nehalennia, recovered from the Eastern Scheldt estuary off Colijnsplaat in February 1971 (RMO, inv. no. i 1974/9.86 + 89, 145 and 182). Lotharingian limestone, 63 by 41 by 15.5 cm. (25 by 16 by 6 in.).

   J.E. Bogaers in *Deae Neh.,* 35; Hassall 1978, 43, table I, 4; Birley 1979, 127 and 198, s.v. Arisenius Marius; Chastagnol 1981, 66.

   Date: *c.* A.D. 150–250.

This altar was recovered in four fragments, which were only united in 1981, after a petrographical investigation[12] had proved that they belonged together. There is no niche with its representation of the goddess on the front, which is almost completely filled by an inscription. The left side shows a relief of a tree with upright leaves; the right side exhibits an engraved tree. The back is unadorned; on the *mensa* are two apples.

   The inscription runs as follows:

DEAE·NEHALEN/NIAE·P·ARISENIV/SMARIVSLIBERT/VS·PARISENI·

V...⁵/HI·NEGOTIATO/RISBRITANNICIA/NI·OBMERCES /

BENECONS.RVA/TA......L·M

Deae Nehalen/niae P(ublius) Ariseniu/s Marius libert/us P(ubli) Ariseni V(...)/hi, negotiato/ris Britannicia/ni,[13] *ob merces / bene cons[e]rva/ta[s*[14] *v(otum) s(olvit)] l(ibens) m(erito).*

To the goddess Nehalennia Publius Arisenius Marius, freedman of Publius Arisenius V(...)hus, merchant with Britannia, for her protection of his wares fulfilled his vow, willingly and deservedly.

L. 2–3 and 4. The *nomen gentilicium* respectively of the *libertus* and his *patronus* seems to be unique. Perhaps it has been derived from the Celtic *cognomen* Arusenus,[15] which is very rare too: *C.I.L.* XIII, 8066 (Bonn, third century A.D.) on the tombstone of Aurelius Arusenus Turesus (from Turum[16] in Raetia?), veteran of the *Legio I Minervia,* and his son Aurelius Avitianus; cf. *C.I.L.* XIII, 4363 (on a tombstone from Metz).

L. 4–5. The *cognomen* of the *patronus,* V...HVS, points presumably to a Germanic origin, especially on account of the H.[17] This character may stand for the Old Germanic voiceless fricative χ; in the Latin alphabet it was rendered by H, CH or C, and perhaps also by I(J).[18]

Pl. IV   Altar (74.5 × 46 × 21.5 cm.) dedicated to Nehalennia by C. Aurelius Verus, *negotiator Britannicianus*, recovered from the Eastern Scheldt estuary off Colijnsplaat.

III

Pl. IV. Altar from Ganuenta(-um?), dedicated to Nehalennia, recovered from the Eastern Scheldt estuary off Colijnsplaat (RMO, inv. nos. i 1974/9.123 and 154, and i 1981/10.232). Lotharingian limestone, 74.5 by 46 by 21.5 cm. (30 by 18 by 9 in.).

On 17th September 1981 J. Valster, Goes, during diving activities, succeeded in hauling up a large section of this altar, mainly from the front side with its inscription. In January 1982, P. Stuart, keeper of Provincial Roman Antiquities in the RMO, discovered that some other fragments, which had been earlier recovered in February 1971, belonged to the same altar.

Date: *c.* A.D. 150–250.

The upper part of the front shows the goddess sitting in a niche on a seat. In her left hand she holds a dish of fruit, which rests on her lap; in her right hand she has an unknown object. To the left of Nehalennia is a large basket with an upright handle and filled with fruit (apples). To her right a collared dog is sitting on its haunches. The altar is flanked by engaged pilasters decorated with plant motives and crowned by Corinthian capitals. On what remains of the *mensa* an apple is to be seen on the right. On both sides a cornucopia is represented. The back was adorned with a curtain in relief, part of which has been preserved.

The inscription reads as follows:

DEAE / NEHALENNIAE / C·AVRELIVS / VERVS ⁵/ NEGOTIATOR /

BRITANNICIANVS / EX·VOTO·L·M

Deae / Nehalenniae / C(aius) Aurelius / Verus / negotiator / Britannicianus / ex voto l(ibens) m(erito).

To the goddess Nehalennia Caius Aurelius Verus, merchant with Britannia, on account of his vow (dedicated this altar), willingly and deservedly.

The greater part of the text corresponds with an inscription on a slab of black marble which was discovered before 1892 at the St. Pantaleon Church in Cologne and which is now in the Römisch-Germanische Museum in that city: *C.I.L.* XIII, 8164 a (*I.L.S.* 7522):[19]

APOLLINI / C·AVRELIVS·CL / VERVS·NEGOTIATOR /

BRITANNICIANVS ⁵/ MORITEX·D·D / L·D·D·D

Apollini / C(aius) Aurelius Cl(audia tribu) / Verus negotiator / Britannicianus / moritex d(ono) d(edit) / l(oco) d(ato) d(ecreto) d(ecurionum).

To Apollo Caius Aurelius Verus, of the Claudian voting-tribe, merchant with Britannia, moritex (?), gave (this) as a gift, the site being preserved by decree of the town councillors.

L. 2. The letters CL are not separated, either by a stop or by an extra space.[20] There is no reason to read C·L[21] and so to expand *C(ai) l(ibertus)*. C. Aurelius Verus had Roman citizenship; very probably he was living in C(olonia) C(laudia) A(ra) A(grippinensium)/Cologne, and, as a *civis Agrippinensis*, he belonged to the *tribus Claudia*.[22] On the one side in this inscription mention is made of C. Aurelius Verus's *tribus*, but on the other hand the filiation with the first name *(praenomen)* of his father is missing, as well as his *patria*, his *origo* or the name of the town of which the dedicator was a citizen; cf. *C.I.L.* XIII, 12058 (Galsterer 1975, 51, no. 200) on the tombstone, found at Cologne, of *Q. Didius Lemonia (tribu) Euhodianus*, praefectus of the *ala I Thracum*.[23]

There is every reason to presume that the dedicator of the Nehalennia-altar from Colijnsplaat and the man who dedicated an unknown object to Apollo at Cologne are identical. In this connection inquiry is called for into the meaning of *moritex*, a *hapax legomenon*, unless one wishes to believe that this word could also be read on an inscription on a stone coffin, which was discovered in 1579 about a quarter mile west of York/Eboracum, and lost before 1796: *R.I.B.* 678 (*C.I.L.* VII, 248; *I.L.S.* 7062). E. Birley and J.C. Mann suggest the following reading: *M(arcus) Verec(undius) Diogenes IIIIIIvir col(oniae) Ebor(acensis) idemq(ue) morit(ex), cives Biturix Cubus, haec sibi vivus fecit*[24] = Marcus Verecundius Diogenes, *sevir (Augustalis)* of the colony of York and also seafarer, tribesman of the Bituriges Cubi [in Aquitania], set (this) up to himself while alive.

Idemque as a link between *IIIIIIvir col. Ebor.* and *moritex* ('seafarer') makes a somewhat strange impression. It seems preferable to read: (...) *IIIIIIvir col. Ebor. idemq(ue) Mor(inorum) [e]t cives Biturix Cubus* (...). In that case M. Verecundius Diogenes, who was born in the land of the Bituriges Cubi (Bourges and surroundings), would have been *sevir (Augustalis)* not only of the colonia Eboracensis (York) but also of the colonia Morinorum[25] (Taruenna/Thérouanne, in north-west France, dép. Pas-de-Calais), the chief town of the Morini.[26]

Regarding the possible meaning of *moritex* several suppositions have been put forward. This word would indicate an ethnic epithet,[27] a cognomen,[28] an office or a profession,[29] or the object of the dedication to Apollo.[30]

From an etymological point of view there seem to be no objections if one considers *moritex* as a Celtic word.[31] Then it is a *compositum* consisting of the Indo-Germanic > Celtic *i*-stem ★*mori*- 'sea' in first position, and the root noun ★*(s)teigh-s* 'striding, going' in second position. The sound-developments (*tēx* is to be determined with a long *ē*) are regular; the interpretation is straightforward: who strides the sea > navigates the sea > seafarer.[32]

In this way, however, the problem is not solved. It is hardly appropriate that C. Aurelius Verus would have called himself, in an inscription at Cologne, not only *negotiator Britannicianus*, merchant with Britannia, but also *moritex*, seafarer, because this could be a sort of tautology. H. Osthoff and E. Birley have tried to remove this difficulty. The former by presuming that C. Aurelius Verus would have been the *moritex* par excellence, i.e. 'etwa der amtliche Vorstand der Kauffahrer- oder Handelsschiffergilde im alten Köln';[33] the latter by suggesting that *moritex*/seafarer would mean 'shipper perhaps, rather than ship's captain'.[34] Nevertheless it is still highly questionable if the etymology given above can provide the right solution of the problem. 'Die Bedeutung von "moritex" ist unklar';[35] this word at least appears not yet to have been explained in a satis-factory manner.

IV

Pl. V. Part of a gritstone dedication-slab, 63 by 49 by 14 cm. (25 by 20 by 6 in.), found in 1976 at Clementhorpe, York, now in the Yorkshire Museum, York.

R.S.O. Tomlin, *Britannia*, viii, 1977, 430 f., no. 18; id., *Britannia*, ix, 1978, 484 f., corrigenda (c); *A.E.* 1977, 512.

Date: A.D. 221.

Pl. V   Part of a dedication-slab (63 × 49 × 14 cm.) of L. Viducius Placidus, found at Clementhorpe, York. *(Photo: M.S. Duffy; copyright York Archaeological Trust).*

The inscription reads:

[- - -]· ÊT GEN̂IO·LOCI / [- - -]GG·L·VID̂VCIVS / [- - -]CIDVS·DOMO / [-
- -] VELIOCAS[.]IVM ⁵/ [- - -]EGOTIATOR / [- - -]RCV̂M ÊT IANVM / [- -
-] D·[.] GRATO ÊT / [- - -]

Tomlin proposed the following restoration: [I(ovi) O(ptimo) M(aximo)
D(olicheno)] et Genio Loci / [êt nn (= numinibus) Au]gg (= Augustorum) L(ucius)
Viducius / [L(uci) f(ilius) Pla]cidus domo / [civit(ate)] Veliocas[s]ium / [V̅Ivir
n]egotiator / [crêt(arius) a]rcum et ianum / [d(ono) d(edit) l(oco) d(ato)] d(ecreto)
[d(ecurionum)] Grato et / [Seleuco co(n)s(ulibus)].

The writer (1977) agreed, except for some details:
L. 1. [I(ovi) O(ptimo) M(aximo) A(eterno) D(olicheno)] et Genio Loci.
L. 5. [p̂r(ovinciae) Lug(dunensis) n]egotiator.
L. 6. [Br̂it(annicianus) a]rcum et ianum.

Accordingly the translation of the full text could be: 'To Jupiter Best,
Greatest and Eternal, of Doliche, and to the Genius of the Place and to the
Deities of the Emperors (= Elagabalus and Severus Alexander [as Caesar since
10th July 221]), Lucius Viducius Placidus, son of Lucius, of the canton (or the
town: Ratomagus/Rotomagus/Rouen on the northern bank of the Sequana/
Seine) of the Veliocasses, in the province of (Gallia) Lugdunensis, merchant with
Britannia (= a member of a *corpus, collegium,* or *societas* for the trade to
Britannia?)[36] gave arch and covered passage-way (or — as an hendiadys —
arched gateway?) as a gift, the site being given by decree of the town councillors, in the consulship of Gratus and Seleucus (A.D. 221).'

Hassall (1978, 46 f.) proposes quite a different restoration of the inscription,
which is mainly based on his reconstruction of L. 3: [Neptuno] et Genio Loci / [êt
Numin̂ib(us) Au]g(ustorum) L(ucius) Viducius / [Viduci f(ilius) Plac]idus domo /
[civitate] Veliocas[s]ium / [prov(inciae) Lugd(unensis) n]egotiator / [Britann(icianus)
ar]cum et ianuam / [p̂ro se êt suis de]d[it] Grato et / [Seleuco co(n)s(ulibus)].

According to the writer, Tomlin, Hassall and A. Birley[37] the dedicator can be
identified with *Placidus Viduci fil(ius) cives Veliocassinius negotiat(or) Britan-
n(icianus)* known from an inscription on the fragment of an altar dedicated to
Nehalennia and dating from *c.* A.D. 200, which was recovered in 1970 from the
Eastern Scheldt estuary off Colijnsplaat.[38] In Hassall's opinion the dedicator of
the York slab would have been called: L. Viducius Viduci f. Placidus.
'Placidus's filiation in this form [L. 3] occurs on his dedication to Nehalennia
from the shrine near Colijnsplaat, and should be the only possible one since
Viducus, the father, lacked a *praenomen,* or rather the full *tria nomina* of a Roman
citizen'.[39] At first sight it seems, however, hardly probable that the dedicator of
the York inscription would have used the cumbersome and ambiguous patrony-

mic formula 'L. Viducius Viduci f. Placidus.'

In the Gaulish and German provinces frequently patronymic adjectives ending in -*ius* or -*inius* have been formed from the single peregrine name or from the *cognomen* of the father; these were practically functioning as a family-name, a *nomen gentilicium* which, if the person in question did not possess Roman citizenship, may be called better a *pseudo-gentilicium*.

It often happened that, in the north-western continental part of the Roman Empire, the family-name or *(pseudo)gentilicium* changed every generation, since new *(pseudo)gentilicia* were continually formed from the *cognomina* of the fathers. Mostly it is not possible to determine if we are dealing with a *(pseudo)gentilicium* that could change in the next generation, or with a *(pseudo)gentilicium* that had become permanent in a peregrine family, or with a genuine *nomen gentilicium* as characteristic of the Roman citizenship.[40]

In the inscription from the Eastern Scheldt the dedicator has only 'a single name, Placidus, appropriate to a man who lacked Roman citizenship *(peregrinus)*, whereas on the York stone he has the *tria nomina*, Lucius Viducius Placidus, of a Roman citizen.'[41] But in his dedication to Nehalennia, Placidus, according to the above-mentioned practice of nomenclature, might have called himself equally the 'Viducian' Placidus, Viducius Placidus, with a *(pseudo)gentilicium*, instead of Placidus, Viduci fil(ius).

On the other hand it is quite possible that the altar from the Eastern Scheldt dates to the period before the promulgation of the Constitutio Antoniniana (*c.* A.D. 212–213),[42] the edict of Caracalla which granted Roman citizenship to all free-born *peregrini* in the Empire. Placidus may have become *civis Romanus* as a result of that *constitutio*[43] and have formed at that time a *nomen gentilicium* from his father's single, peregrine name, Viducus, which clearly indicates a native, Celtic origin.[44] If Viducus was still alive then, without doubt he too had gained citizenship; on account of the inscriptions from Colijnsplaat and York his full name may have become then: Lucius (?) (+ unknown *nomen gentilicium* formed from his father's single, peregrine name? +) Viducus, whereas his son was called L. Viducius (Luci filius?) Placidus. In case the father of the latter had already died — as *peregrinus* — before *c.* 212–213, the son when taking the *tria nomina* may have attributed a fictitious *praenomen* to his father and called himself *L(uci) f(ilius)*.[45]

In his restoration of the York inscription Hassall suggests, as mentioned above, that the full name of the dedicator would have been L. Viducius Viduci f(ilius) Placidus. If this is right, there would be two possible explanations of the filiation: (a) the father was called L. Viducius Viducus; in that case, in the nomenclature of the son, the father's *praenomen* would have been replaced by his *cognomen*;[46] (b) the father had only a single peregrine name; after the son was granted Roman citizenship he formed, not only his *nomen gentilicium* from his father's name, but also used that name once again in his filiation, and would have given, in that way as it were, a tautological double filiation. It seems to be very difficult to find any more or less exact parallels for such a phenomenon,[47] and even then it is not possible to say if they refer to a *nomen gentilicium* which was only newly-formed from a father's single name or *cognomen,* or to a permanent one already borne by more than one generation of the family in question.[48]

In *A.E.* 1977, 512 is to be found the comment that the dedicator of the York inscription 'paraît à première vue identifiable à *Placidus Viduci fil(ius)*' mentioned on the altar from the Eastern Scheldt. 'Toutefois, la forme plus romanisée peut suggérer qu'il serait plutôt un parent, peut-être même le fils de ce dernier.' In 1981 A. Chastagnol returned to this question. In contrast with the views of others (see above), 'qui ont émis l'opinion qu'il s'agit en fait du même homme, et l'on pourrait songer alors que le pérégrin [*Placidus Viduci fil(ius)*] a été naturalisé romain en application de l'édit de Caracalla, (...) il est beaucoup plus probable, selon une suggestion que nous a faite H.-G. Pflaum, qu'on a affaire ici au fils (ou, à la rigueur, au petit-fils) de Placidus, Viduci filius'.[49]

According to the practice of nomenclature in the Gaulish and German provinces, however, Placidus Viduci fil. might have named himself also the 'Viducian' Placidus, Viducius Placidus. In consequence it is highly improbable that a son of this Placidus Viduci filius or Viducius Placidus would have been called Viducius Placidus. His name undoubtedly was either Placidius, *(pseudo?)-gentilicium* formed from the single name or *cognomen* of his father,[50] followed by a *cognomen,* or possibly Viducius followed by a *cognomen,* but presumably not Placidus, so that his name could be distinguished from his father's. Supposing that Viducius would have become a permanent *nomen gentilicium* of the family in question, a grandson of Placidus Viduci fil. or Viducius Placidus could indeed have been named L. Viducius Placidus, but if the grandson in his turn has formed a *nomen gentilicium* from his father's *cognomen,* then as a matter of course that *nomen gentilicium* can only have been Viducius if his father bore the *cognomen* Viducus. . . .

For the time being it seems to be better to accept the real possibility that Placidus Viduci fil. and L. Viducius [L. f.] Placidus are identical.

V

Fig. 1. Sandstone dedication-slab, 66 by 48 by 5 cm. (26 by 19 by 2 in.), discovered in 1903 in dredging the north channel of the Swing Bridge at Newcastle upon Tyne; in the Museum of Antiquities, Newcastle upon Tyne.
   R.I.B. 1322 (*I.L.S.* 9116).
   Date: A.D. 154/155–158/159.[51]

IMP· ANTONĪ/NO· AVG· PIO· P / PAT· VEX ILATIO / LEG· ĪI· AVG· ET·

LEG [5]/· V̄I· VIC· ET· LEG· /· X̄X· VV· CONR/BVTI· EX· GER· DV/OBVS· SVB·

IVLIO· VE/RO· LEG· AVG· PR· P·

Fig. 1 The inscription *R.I.B.* 1322 from Newcastle upon Tyne, drawn by R.G. Collingwood. Scale 1:8 *(By kind permission of the Clarendon Press and R.P. Wright: copyright reserved).*

Imp(eratori) Antoni/no Aug(usto) Pio p(atri) / pat(riae) vexil(l)atio / leg(ioni) II Aug(ustae) et leg(ioni) / VI Vic(trici) et leg(ioni) / XX V(aleriae) V(ictrici) con(t)r(i)/ buti ex Ger(maniis) du/obus sub Iulio Ve/ro leg(ato) Aug(usti) pr(o) p(raetore).

'For the Emperor Antoninus Augustus Pius, father of his country, the detachment (of men) contributed from the two Germanies for the Second Legion Augusta and the Sixth Legion Victrix and the Twentieth Legion Valeria Victrix, under Julius Verus, emperor's propraetorian legate, (set this up).'

L. 3. In VEX ILATIO one L is missing. The stonemason made two mistakes; after the X he left room for an I, and of the following I he ought to have made an L. *Vexillatio* (= *vexillarii*) . . . (L. 6/7) *contributi* is to be taken as a constructio ad sententiam (ad synesin).[52]

L. 6. CON(t)R(i). The stonemason omitted to make a ligature of N and T, and of R and I, but he could also have cut out the last letter at the beginning of L. 7.

L. 7–8. *ex Ger(maniis) duobus* instead of *ex Ger(maniis) duabus*?

This inscription is generally regarded as recording the arrival at Pons Aelius/ Newcastle upon Tyne of military reinforcements from the legions of the two German provinces, which were destined for all three British legions, in response to an emergency, i.e. a serious rebellion of the Brigantes in the Pennines, that involved the evacuation of the Antonine Wall and much of southern Scotland. Cn. Julius Verus, previously governor of Lower Germany, 'may well have brought the legionary vexillations with him, and the date should not be later than 155.'[53]

Before the publication of *R.I.B.* I in 1965 some abbreviations used to be expanded in another way: (...) *vexil(l)atio leg(ionis)* $\overline{II}$ *Aug(ustae) et leg(ionis)* $\overline{VI}$ *Vic(tricis) et leg(ionis)* $\overline{XX}$ *V(aleriae) V(ictricis) con(t)r(i)buti ex Ger(maniis) duobus* (...)[54] = '(...) a vexillation (draft) of the Second August and Sixth Victorious and Twentieth Valerian Victorious Legions, contributed from the two Germanies (Upper and Lower), (...)'.[55]

It is difficult to decide which view is to be preferred. Both readings seem to be possible, but in inscriptions relating to *vexillationes* (or *vexillarii*) these words are usually followed by a genitive mentioning the parent units from which the detachments had been taken or to which they had belonged.[56]

In 1981 A.R. Birley published another reading: *Imp. Antoni/no Aug. Pio p./ p. vexilatio* [4]*/ leg. II Aug. et leg./ VI Vic. et leg./ XX V. V. con(t)r(i)/buti ex(ercitibus) Ger(manicis) du*[8]*/obus sub Iulio Ve/ro leg. Aug. pr. p.*[57]

The 'expansion *ex(ercitibus) Ger(manicis) duobus* rather than the ungrammatical *ex Ger(maniis) duobus* of RIB and earlier editors' is owed to J.J. Wilkes, and seems to be fortuitous at first sight. It is, however, to be remarked that in this case, on account of the Latin, the inscription would supply information exactly opposite from what is usually inferred. Then the three British legions can have been mentioned only in the genitive dependent on *vexil(l)atio*, whereas *ex(ercitibus) Ger(manicis) duobus* has to refer to *con(t)r(i)buti,* and the translation must read: (...) the detachment (of soldiers) of the Second Legion Augusta and the Sixth Legion Victrix and the Twentieth Legion Valeria Victrix, contributed to the armies of both Germanies (...).[58]

A detachment of soldiers of all three British legions sent to the Continent in A.D. 154–9, as a reinforcement for the armies of both (!) provinces of Lower and Upper Germany, would be very odd, and moreover, with regard to the known history of Britannia as well as that of the *duae Germaniae,* completely inexplicable.

To solve the problem there appears to be only one possibility, viz. to assume that line 7 of the inscription presents a case of haplography.

The text was probably intended to run more or less as follows:

IMP·ANTONÎ/NO·AVG·PIO·P / PAT·VEX<IL>LATÎO / LEG·$\overline{II}$·AVG·

ET·LÊG [5]/·$\overline{VI}$·VIC·ET·LEG·/·$\overline{XX}$·VV·CON⌢T>R⌢I>/BVTI·EX·<EX(*erci-*

tibus)·>GER(*manicis*)·DV/OBVS·SVB·IVLIO·VE/RO·LEG·AVG·PR·P·[59]

In this way the inscription incontrovertibly relates to a detachment sent from the armies of both German provinces. The three British legions mentioned in L. 4–6 may have been referred to either in the genitive dependent on *vexillatio* (this seems to be more probable) or in the dative relating to *contributi.* The stonemason obviously made a serious mistake because he omitted one EX so that the text appears either to present a grammatical blunder or to proclaim precisely the opposite of what was intended.

Finally, there remains another problem: why did the stonemason not correct the mistakes he made in L. 2 and L. 6 by afterwards cutting out or finishing some letters of the words VEXILLATIO and CONTRIBVTI? In so doing he could very easily have retrieved these errors.[60] As a matter of course the constructio ad sententiam *vexil(l)atio . . . con(t)r(i)buti* is not to be taken for an error, as contrasted with the haplography in L. 7, which seems to raise a great difficulty for a correct understanding of the text.

'Twin altars, dedicated respectively to Oceanus and Neptune were dredged from the river [Tyne] in 1875 and 1903.[61] They came from a bridge-shrine erected by the Sixth Legion and intended to protect the structure [of the bridge built by Hadrian, from which Pons Aelius took its name] against tides and floods. In this shrine, too, reinforcements from the German provinces for the three British legions set up an inscription on their arrival in or before A.D. 158.'[62]

One may wonder if the dedication-slab with its inscription recorded in *R.I.B.* 1322 was ever placed in that shrine, or anywhere else. As to lines 3 and 6 the text is apparently incomplete and unfinished. The reason may very well be that the irretrievable omission, the haplography in line 7, caused the slab to have been condemned and thrown away as unsuitable. . . .[53]

ABBREVIATIONS USED IN THE TEXT

A.E. *L'Année épigraphique.*
Deae Neh. *Deae Nehalenniae* — Gids bij de tentoonstelling Nehalennia de Zeeuwse godin, Zeeland in de Romeinse tijd, Romeinse monumenten uit de Oosterschelde, Middelburg/ Leiden, 1971.
RMO Rijksmuseum van Oudheden, Leiden.

NOTES

1. cf. Bogaers, J.E. and Gysseling, M., 'Nehalennia, Gimio en Ganuenta', *Oudheidkundige Mededelingen uit het Rijksmuseum van Oudheden te Leiden*, lii, (1971), 86–92, and *Naamkunde*, iv, (1972), 231–240; *L'Année épigraphique*, (1973), 380 and (1975), 641; Bogaers, J.E. in Chevallier, R. (ed.), *Tabula Imperii Romani, Lutetia — Atuatuca — Ulpia Noviomagus, M 31 Paris*, Paris, 1975, 91. s.v. Ganuent(a?).

2. cf. Bogaers, J.E. in *Deae Nehalenniae — Gids bij de tentoonstelling Nehalennia de Zeeuwse godin, Zeeland in de Romeinse tijd, Romeinse monumenten uit de Oosterschelde*, Middelburg/Leiden, 1971, 34 f.

3. cf. Stuart, P. and Bogaers, J.E., *Jahresberichte aus Augst und Kaiseraugst*, i, (1980), 50 with note 9.

4. On many altars (from Domburg and Colijnsplaat) Nehalennia is shown flanked by a basket of fruit and a dog, but the crossed forelegs are fairly exceptional; cf. *Deae Nehalenniae* (see note 2), no. 11, and Stuart, P. and Bogaers, J.E., *op. cit.* (see note 3).

5. cf. *C.I.L.* XIII, 8793 (from Domburg), *Deae Nehalenniae* (see note 2), nos. 11 (*L'Année épigraphique*, (1973), 370) and 32 (*L'Année épigraphique*, (1975), 646, according to Bogaers, J.E., *Numaga*, xix, (1972), 7–9), and infra, no. II.

6. cf. Kajanto, I., *The Latin Cognomina*, Societas Scientiarum Fennica, Commentationes Humanarum Litterarum, XXXVI, 2, Helsinki, 1965, 399.

7. Bogaers, J.E. in *Deae Nehalenniae* (see note 2), 38 f.; Hassall, M. in du Plat Taylor, J. and Cleere, H. (eds.), *Roman shipping and trade: Britain and the Rhine provinces*, London, 1978, 43 f.; Birley, A.R., *The People of Roman Britain*, London, 1979, 126 f.; infra nos. II–IV.

8. *C.I.L.* X, 7612 and XI, 5068 (*I.L.S.* 7524); Bogaers, J.E. in *Deae Nehalenniae* (see note 2), 39 (and 69, no. 20 = *L'Année épigraphique*, (1973), 374); Hassall, M., *op. cit.* (see note 7), 43 f.

9. For G(a)esoriacum, see Holder A., *Alt-celtischer Sprachschatz*, I, Leipzig, 1896, reprinted Graz, 1961, 1512 f., s.v. Gaesoriacus; Whatmough, J., *The Dialects of Ancient Gaul*, Cambridge, Mass., 1970, 766, s.v. Gaesoriacus portus, and 925, s.v. ?Gaesoriacum; Chevallier, R. (ed.), *op. cit.* (see note 1), 52 f., s.v. Boulogne-sur-Mer. - 'It seems to me (…) likely that your GESERECAN[VS] is related to *G(a)esoriacum* (as though it reflects a form ★G(a)esoricanus as the like errors with vowels [here *E* for *O* before *R*?] are not uncommon)' (D.E. Evans, Oxford, by letter of 29 June 1981). '*Gesoriacum, Geserecanus* (…): dürfte zurückgehen auf ★*gaiso-* > *gaeso-* > *geso-* 'Speer': *Gaiso-rix (Caeso-rix), Gaise-ricus* (…), ★*Gaiso-ricanus*' (K.H. Schmidt, Bonn, by letter of 24 August 1981); see also Schmidt, K.H., *Zeitschrift für celtische Philologie*, xxvi, (1957), 214.

10. cf. *Deae Nehalenniae* (see note 2), no. 1 (*L'Année épigraphique*, (1973), 362): '*M. Exgingius Agricola, cives Trever, negotiator salarius C.C.A.A.*'.

11. cf. Chevallier, R. (ed.), *op. cit.* (see note 1), 52; Delmaire, R., *Etude archéologique de la partie orientale de la cité des Morins (civitas Morinorum)*, Arras, 1976, 51–3 and 309. — N.B.: the *pagus* mentioned by Pliny, *Natural History*, IV, 106, was called *C(h)ersiacus*, not *Gesoriacus*; cf. *L'Année épigraphique*, (1972), 148. It is not at all certain that the *pagus C(h)ersiacus* is 'sans doute le Boulonnais', that 'Le nom de *Cersiacus* est certainement lié à celui de Boulogne: *Gesoriacum*', and that the Cersiaci (*L'Année épigraphique*, (1972), 148) should be identical with the inhabitants of Gesoriacum = Boulogne (Delmaire, R., *op. cit.*, 51 f. and 309).

12. made by C.J. Overweel, Instituut voor Prehistorie, Rijksuniversiteit, Leiden.

13. cf. supra, note 7.

14. cf. supra, p. 000 with note 5.

15. Holder, A., *Alt-celtischer Sprachschatz*, III, Leipzig, 1907, reprinted Graz, 1962, 696; Schmidt, K.H., *op. cit.* (see note 9), 135.

16. Pauly-Wissowa, *Realencyclopädie der*

Classischen Altertumswissenschaft, VII A (1948), 1453, s.v. Turum [P. Goessler].

17. cf. Bogaers, J.E. in *Deae Nehalenniae* (see note 2), 37.
18. Bogaers, J.E., *Helinium*, xi, (1971), 41 ff.
19. Galsterer, B. and Galsterer, H., *Die römische Steininschriften aus Köln*, Cologne, 1975, 13 and pl. 1, no. 4; date: second half of the 2nd/3rd century A.D.
20. cf. Ihm, M. (the first editor of the inscription), *Bonner Jahrbücher*, xcii, (1892), 261: 'Tribusangabe *Cl(audia)*'; *C.I.L.* XIII 8164 a (without expansion of CL) and *ibid.*, pars 5 (indices), p. 134. — Osthoff, H., *Zeitschrift für celtische Philologie*, vi, (1908), 430, and Birley, E., *Yorkshire Archaeological Journal*, xli, (1966), 731 read *Cl.* but wrongly expanded *Cl(audius)*.
21. So can be read in (among others): *I.L.S.* 7522 with note 1: '*Cl. (sine puncto) traditur*'; *C.I.L.* XIII/5 (indices), p. 4: '*C. Aurelius *C. l. Verus*'; Carcopino, J. in *Mémorial d'un voyage d'études de la Société nationale des antiquaires de France en Rhénanie (juillet 1952)*, Paris, 1953, 184; Schoppa, H., *Römische Götterdenkmäler in Köln*, Cologne, 1959, 60; Fremersdorf, Fr., *Urkunden zur Kölner Stadtgeschichte aus römischer Zeit*, second edition, Cologne, 1963, 61; Galsterer, B. and Galsterer, H., *op. cit.* (see note 19), 13, no. 4.
22. cf. Binsfeld, W. in *Mouseion — Studien aus Kunst und Geschichte für Otto H. Förster*, Cologne, 1960, 73; *C.I.L.* XIII/5 (indices), p. 134.
23. In connection with this question, M. Ihm (supra, note 20) refers to *C.I.L.* XIII, 7338 (on an altar from Heddernheim dedicated by *M. Aurel. Cl. Pompeianus* on 13 January A.D. 213) and *C.I.L.* V, 5586 and 6822.
24. Birley, E., *Journal of Roman Studies*, lvi, (1966), 228; *idem, Yorkshire Archaeological Journal*, xli, (1966), 731.
25. cf. *C.I.L.* XIII, 8727, probably from (the neighbourhood of) Nijmegen. See also Byvanck, A.W., *Excerpta Romana*, II, 's-Gravenhage, 1935, 131 f., no. 135; Daniëls, M.P.M. and Brunsting, H.,

Oudheidkundige Mededelingen uit het Rijksmuseum van Oudheden te Leiden, xxxvi, (1955), 49 (no. 81) and 66–70; Wolfs, S.P., *Numaga*, xv, (1968), 110 f. — Already Aem. Hübner (*C.I.L.* VII, 248; cf. *I.L.S.* 7062 and *R.I.B.* 678) supposed MORT to be a corrupt reading of another town-name.
26. cf. *L'Année épigraphique*, (1922), 116; Bogaers, J.E., *Oudheidkundige Mededelingen uit het Rijksmuseum van Oudheden te Leiden*, lviii, (1977), 161, note 12; Hassall, M., *op. cit.* (see note 7), 43, table II, nos. 7–8 and note *.
27. Ihm, M., *op. cit.* (see note 20), 262; Holder, A., *Alt-celtischer Sprachschatz*, II, Leipzig, 1904, reprinted Graz, 1962, 636; *I.L.S.* 7522; Carcopino, J., *op. cit.* (see note 21), 185. cf. Bogaers, J.E. in *Deae Nehalenniae* (see note 2), 84, note 92: '*negotiator Britannicianus Moritex* (...): merchant trading with Britannia and the land of the Morini and/or Aremorica' (= the French coast-land along the Straits of Dover and/or the English Channel); supra, sub I: *negotiator Cantianus (et?) Geserecanus*.
28. cf. Osthoff, H., *op. cit.* (see note 20), 430.
29. *C.I.L.* XIII, 8164 a; Osthoff, H., *op. cit.* (see note 20), 432; Birley, E., *op. cit.* (see note 24) and infra.
30. cf. Schmitz, H., *Colonia Claudia Ara Agrippinensium*, Cologne, 1956, 129 f.
31. See, especially, Osthoff, H., *op. cit.* (see note 20), 430–2.
32. Information kindly supplied in a letter of 14 October 1981 by K.H. Schmidt, Bonn. The latter remarks as well that the root **steigh*- which underlies **(s)teigh-s* is also widespread in the Island-Celtic. cf. Pokorny, J., *Indogermanisches etymologisches Wörterbuch*, I, Bern/Munich, 1959, 1017 f.; Thurneysen, R., *A Grammar of Old Irish translated from the German* by D.A. Binchy and O. Bergin, Dublin, 1946, § 769; Lewis, H. and Pedersen, H., *A Concise Comparative Celtic Grammar*, third edition, Göttingen, 1974, 10. See also: Schmidt, K.H., *Zeitschrift für celtische Philologie*, xxvi, (1957), 245, s.v. Mori-, and 278, s.v. -tex; Birley, E., *op. cit.* (see

note 24), according to J.C. Mann and K. Jackson; Evans, D.E., *Gaulish Personal Names — A Study of some Continental Celtic Formations,* Oxford, 1967, 232 f.; Weisgerber, J.L., *Die Namen der Ubier,* Cologne/Opladen, 1968, 223 and 225; Whatmough, J., *op. cit.,* (see note 9), 585, 726 and 1360.

33. Osthoff, H., *op. cit.* (see note 20), 432.

34. *Yorkshire Archaeological Journal,* xli, (1966), 731; cf. *idem, Journal of Roman Studies,* lvi, (1966), 228.

35. Galsterer, B. and Galsterer, H., *op. cit.* (see note 19), 13, no. 4; cf. G. N(eumann) in von Petrikovits, H. in Jankuhn, H. et al. (eds.), *Das Handwerk in vor- und frühgeschichtlicher Zeit,* I, Göttingen, 1981, 105, s.v. *moritex:* 'Kann *t* aus *f* entstellt sein: *-fex?* Aber das Vorderglied bleibt weiter unklar.'

36. cf. Carcopino, J., *op. cit.* (see note 21), 184; Bogaers, J.E., *op. cit.* (see note 26), 162; Hassall, M., *op. cit.* (see note 7), 45 f.

37. Birley, A.R., *op. cit.* (see note 7), 126 f.

38. *Deae Nehalenniae* (see note 2), 78, no. 45; *L'Année épigraphique,* (1975), 651.

39. Hassall, M., *op. cit.* (see note 7), 46.

40. cf. Hettner, F., *Westdeutsche Zeitschrift für Geschichte und Kunst,* ii, (1883), 7 f.; Mommsen, Th., *Korrespondenzblatt der Westdeutschen Zeitschrift für Geschichte und Kunst,* xi, (1892), 81 f.; Schulze, W., *Zur Geschichte lateinischer Eigennamen,* Berlin, 1904, 56 ff.; Birley, E., *Roman Britain and the Roman Army,* Kendal, 1953, 176 f.; Weisgerber, J.L., *Die Namen der Ubier,* Cologne/Opladen, 1968, 135 ff. and 386 ff.; Weisgerber, L., *Rhenania Germano-Celtica,* Bonn, 1969, 91, 116 f. and 314; *idem,* 'Zu den rheinischen *-inius*-Bildungen', in Ennen, E. and Wiegelmann, G. (eds.), *Festschrift Matthias Zender — Studien zu Volkskultur, Sprache und Landesgeschichte,* II, Bonn, 1972, 931–48.

41. Hassall, M., *op. cit.* (see note 7), 46.

42. Wolff, H., *Die Constitutio Antoniniana und Papyrus Gissensis 40 I,* Cologne, 1976, 12 ff.

43. Bogaers, J.E., *op. cit.* (see note 26), 160 and 164; Hassall, M., *op. cit.* (see note 7), 46.

44. cf. Holder, A., *op. cit.* (see note 15), 292 f.; Schmidt, K.H., *op. cit.* (see note 9), 295.

45. cf. *I.L.S.* 2483 (with note 2; Coptos) and 2247 (Nicopolis near Alexandria) for probable examples of 'bogus' *praenomina* of fathers of legionaries who were likely to be given citizenship on enlistment or when the legion was incorporated in the Roman army (information from J.C. Mann, kindly supplied by M. Hassall).

46. cf. Cagnat, R., *Cours d'épigraphie latine,* fourth edition, Paris, 1914, 61.

47. cf. *C.I.L.* XIII, 8151 (Sechtem near Bonn): *Albania Albani f(ilia) Aspra; C.I.L.* XIII, 1032 (Saintes): *C. Sec[u]nd[i]us Florus Sec[u]ndi (filius); C.I.L.* XIII, 5103 (Avenches): *[T]ib. Sancti[us] Sabucinu[s] Sancti fi[lius].*

48. For doubtless newly formed *nomina gentilicia,* cf. *C.I.L.* XIII, 5100 = Walser, G., *Römische Inschriften der Schweiz,* I, Bern, 1979, no. 85 (Avenches): *Q. Macrius Cluvi Macr(i) fil(ius) Quirin(a tribu) Nivalis; C.I.L.* XIII, 5258 = Walser, G., *Römische Inschriften der Schweiz,* II, Bern, 1980, no. 203 (Kaiseraugst): *M. [et Q. Sa]nuci Atti San[uci fil]i Quir(ina tribu) Messor et Melo; R.I.B.* 67 (Silchester): *T. Tammon[ius] Saeni Tammon[i fil(ius)] Vitalis* = Titus Tammonius Vitalis, son of Saenius Tammonus (not Tammonius!).

49. Chastagnol, A., *Zeitschrift für Papyrologie und Epigraphik,* xliii, (1981) (Gedenkschrift für Hans-Georg Pflaum), 64.

50. cf. Birley, A.R., *op. cit.,* (see note 7), 127.

51. The period in which the Roman governor of Britain was Cn. Julius Verus, mentioned as such in the inscription. cf. Birley, A.R., *Epigraphische Studien,* iv, (1967), 72 f., no. 26; *idem, The Fasti of Roman Britain,* Oxford, 1981, 119; Frere, S.S., *Britannia — A History of Roman Britain,* revised edition, London/Henley/Boston, 1978, 176 f.

52. cf. *R.I.B.* 1322: 'The composer of the text uses *uexillatio* collectively for *uexillarii,* as the subsequent *contributi* plainly shows.' Saxer R., *Epigraphische Studien,* i, (1967), 32, no. 62 with note 170, reads *vexil(l)atio(nes) . . . con(t)r(i)buti,* but his

argument is not convincing.

53. Frere, S.S., *op. cit.* (see note 51), 176 f.; cf. Birley, A.R., *op. cit.*, 1981 (see note 51), 119 f. For another, outdated view, see Saxer, R., *op. cit.* (see note 52), 32, no. 62.

54. Heslop, O. and Haverfield, F., *Proc. Soc. Antiqu. Newcastle upon Tyne,* 3 ser., i, (1903), 73 f.; idem, *Archaeol. Aeliana,* 2 ser., xxv, 1904, 140 and 142; Haverfield, F., *Korrespondenzblatt der Westdeutschen Zeitschrift für Geschichte und Kunst,* xxii, (1903), 202; idem, *Ephemeris epigraphica,* ix, (1913), 583, no. 1163; Ritterling, E. in *Realencyclopädie* (see note 16), XII, (1925), s.v. Legio, 1294; Spain, G.R.B. and Bosanquet, R.C. in *Northumberland County History,* XIII, Newcastle upon Tyne, 1930, 545, no. 3; Saxer, R., *op. cit.* (see note 52), 32, no. 62. cf. Blair, P., *Archaeol. Aeliana,* 3 ser., xvii, (1920), 10, no. 11*b*, and Collingwood, R.G., *Archaeol. Aeliana,* 4 ser., ii, (1926), 78 f., no. 85.

55. *ibid.,* 79, no. 85.

56. cf. among others Saxer, R., *op. cit.* (see note 52), 69, no. 155 (*R.I.B.* 980); 70, no. 172 (*R.I.B.* 2171); 79, nos. 214–215; 93, no. 275; 95, nos. 284–288.

57. Birley, A.R., *op. cit.* (see note 53), 118 and 120, note 11.

58. cf. *Thesaurus Linguae Latinae,* IV, Lipsiae, 1906–1909, 777 f., s.v. *contributio.*

59. cf. Haverfield, F., *Archaeol. Aeliana,* 2 ser., xxv, (1904), 142: '*Duobus* is a blunder for *duabus* — unless some word like *exercitibus* has been omitted —'; idem, *Ephemeris epigraphica,* ix (1913), 583, no. 1163; '*duobus* videtur merus error esse: nimis quaesitum esset *ex* <*ex(ercitibus)*>

Ger(manicis) duobus conicere'; *C.I.L.* VIII, 3157 (*I.L.S.* 2317): *C. Iul(ius) Nestor (...) contributus ex leg(ione) III Augustae* (sic) *in leg(ionem) III Aug(ustam).*

60. cf. Collingwood, R.G., *op. cit.* (see note 54), 79, no. 85: 'the missing letters were no doubt painted in their proper places on the stone'(?).

61. *R.I.B.* 1320 and 1319. Just as *R.I.B.* 1322, both were found in the north channel of the Swing Bridge.

62. Collingwood Bruce, J., *Handbook to the Roman Wall with the Cumbrian Coast and Outpost Forts,* 13th edition, edited by C.M. Daniels, Newcastle upon Tyne, 1978, 62.

63. The writer would like to express his gratitude to the many persons who have so kindly helped him in preparing this article. G.J.M. Bartelink (Nijmegen), J. van den Berg (Middelburg), C.M. Daniels (Newcastle upon Tyne), D.E. Evans (Oxford), J.P. Gillam (Newcastle upon Tyne), M. Hassall, J. Hopkins and Mrs. M.M. Roxan (London), K.H. Schmidt (Bonn), P. Stuart (Leiden), J. Valster (Goes) and J.S. Wacher (Leicester) gave information, comments and suggestions. P.V. Addyman (York) provided the photograph of Pl. V. P. Bersch (Nijmegen) took the photographs of Pl. I and II. P. Stuart generously made it possible to publish here the three Nehalennia-altars from Colijnsplaat and sent the photographs of Pl. III and IV, taken by P.J. Bomhof and M. Vinkesteyn (RMO). J.S. Wacher greatly improved the linguistic quality of the English text of this paper.

BIBLIOGRAPHY

Birley, A.R., 1979, *The People of Roman Britain,* London.

Birley, A.R., 1981, *The Fasti of Roman Britain,* Oxford.

Bogaers, J.E., 1977, 'Bericht uit Britannia', *Oudheidkundige Mededelingen uit het Rijksmuseum van Oudheden te Leiden,* lviii, 159–65.

Carcopino, J., 1953, 'Notes d'épigraphie rhénane', in *Mémorial d'un voyage d'études de la Société nationale des antiquaires de France en Rhénanie (juillet 1952),* Paris, 183–96.

Chastagnol, A., 1981, 'Une firme de commerce maritime entre l'île de Bretagne et le continent gaulois à l'époque des Sévères', *Zeitschrift für Papyrologie und Epigraphik,* xliii (Gedenkschrift für Hans-Georg Pflaum), 63–6.

Chevallier, R., (ed.), 1975, *Tabula Imperii Romani, Lutetia — Atuatuca — Ulpia Noviomagus, M 31 Paris,* Paris.

Collingwood, R.G., 1926, 'Roman Inscriptions and Sculptures belonging to the Society of Antiquaries of Newcastle upon Tyne', *Archaeol. Aeliana,* 4 ser., ii, 52–124.

Frere, S.S., 1978, *Britannia — A History of Roman Britain,* revised edition, London/Henley/Boston.

Galsterer, B. and Galsterer, H., 1975, *Die römische Steininschriften aus Köln,* Cologne.

Hassall, M., 1978, 'Britain and the Rhine provinces: epigraphic evidence for Roman trade', in du Plat Taylor, J. and Cleere, H. (eds.), *Roman shipping and trade: Britain and the Rhine provinces,* Council for British Archaeology Research Report 24, London, 41–8.

Holder, A., 1896–1907, *Alt-celtischer Sprachschatz,* I–III, Leipzig, reprinted Graz 1961–62.

Osthoff, H., 1908, 'Zur keltischen Wortkunde', *Zeitschrift für celtische Philologie,* vi, 395–432.

Saxer, R., 1967, 'Untersuchungen zu den Vexillationen des römischen Kaiserheeres von Augustus bis Diokletian', *Epigraphische Studien,* i, Cologne/Graz.

Schmidt, K.H., 1957, Die Komposition in gallischen Personennamen, *Zeitschrift für celtische Philologie,* xxvi, 33–301.

Stuart, P. and Bogaers, J.E., 1980, 'Augusta Raurica und die Dea Nehalennia', *Jahresberichte aus Augst und Kaiseraugst,* i, 49–58.

Walser, G., 1979–80, *Römische Inschriften der Schweiz,* I–III, Bern.

Whatmough, J., 1970, *The Dialects of Ancient Gaul,* Cambridge, Mass.

Pl. III   Lower part of a domestic shrine, Silchester. *(By permission of Reading Museum and Art Gallery.)*

Pl. IV   Remains of shrine, Catterick. 4th century A.D. *(Crown Copyright reserved).*

Not far away, re-used as a door-sill, the battered remains of a fluted pilaster with feathered capital occurred, and in Mr. Wacher's view might best be explained as part of the shrine. The structure appears to have lasted from about A.D. 300 to 370, when the military occupation was resumed.[12]

Much more important, however, than these examples is the flimsy chamber excavated in 1901 at the extreme east edge of the grounds of XI.7S at Caerwent. This shrine — the description is in this case inescapable — was open to the west, where there was a railing, as in the small chapel at Springhead (Kent); inside, as at Segontium not centrally placed, was a somewhat low-stepped platform of clay and gravel, etc., once faced, doubtless, with boards. On it lay a stone head of deeply native style. Behind, there was a little partitioned area, also as at Springhead.[13] The siting of this shrine suggested to me that it may have been the tolerated place of worship of a pagan *familia* — we remember the strength of rural pagan cults in the fourth century, and fourth-century Caerwent was essentially rural within its walls — whose Christian master kept himself aloof and *purus* in the grand new house across the yard.[14] We shall return to this stone head below.

Almost equally rough, and occupying a position at the rear of a shop or tavern as at Verulamium, was a small shrine belonging to Building XII in Housesteads civil settlement, excavated by Birley and Charlton in 1933. It consisted of a semi-circular wall resting on two huge flagstones set against the side-wall of the next building to the north (IX), and measured about 0.5 m. (1.5 ft.) across; it would have had a flat, or even a corbelled top. Upright, but not fixed, across the front was a fine stone relief of three *Genii Cucullati,* now in Housesteads Museum. Behind this slab, as in a safe, lay a group of five *denarii* running down to Alexander.[15]

So far, we have noticed shrines at a raised level. The last example is an apsidal niche with projecting pilasters, about 60 cm. (27 in.) wide, which rose from the floor in the centre of the south wall of Room 2, Building I, on the Colliton Park site at Dorchester (Pl. V), excavated by Drew and Selby.[16] It was plastered inside, and we need not doubt but that it rose to its full height without there being any intervening shelf; it would have been finished with a rounded head or even a shell-canopy. At Silchester, part of a weathered niche-head of Bath stone, about 80 cm. (32 in.) wide originally, was a stray discovery; but it most likely belonged to an early military tombstone of Rhenish style (as known best in this country from the Facilis monument at Colchester), and not to a structure, for the good carving on the side shows that it was freestanding.[17] The Dorchester niche is illustrated at Pompeii, where one example contained an altar;[18] but at Dorchester, where an entire room seems to have been used as a chapel, a statuette on a pedestal would perhaps be more likely. Such statuettes are known, for example, from Llantwit Major villa (Glamorganshire), where, in the fourth century, they may have been placed for decorative purposes on either side of the doorway into the best room: one was probably a Genius of the half-draped type with *patera* and *cornucopiae,* and the other was a Fortuna with wheel and globe.[19]

Pl. V   Alcove serving as a domestic shrine, Dorchester. *(Photograph by M.B. Cookson, Crown Copyright, National Monuments Record).*

II

The superstructure of such shrines as those at Verulamium and Calleva may next engage attention. Were they *aediculae,* as at Pompeii? Clearly, the excavators thought so at Silchester, for they adduced a Tuscan capital, from a colonnette about 1.2 m. (4 ft.) high; but this object was not found in the same room, and may have come from a half-open corridor somewhere else in the house.[20] In seeking *aediculae,* it will be as well not to insist upon qualificatory reference to the Campanian city, whose climate was different, and whose houses and temples were consequently of a different design, for the most part, from those of the north-west. In the Rhine- and Moselland, for example, house-like shrines are plentiful. The finest, by far, is that from Mainz-Kastel, a monolith about 68.5 cm. (27 in.) square and 76 cm. (30 in.) high, with beautifully carved sides and an arched recess at one end; the pitched roof is a minutely detailed rendering of *tegulae* and *imbrices.*[21] Others, less ambitious but not less interesting, may be seen in the fine collection of the Museum in Luxembourg. The most famous of these is a piece from the Titelberg, which has been taken as a model of a Romano-Celtic temple with lofty central *cella*; but the height of that part is solely due to a niche cut to hold a figurine or some other cult-object.[22] Another important piece, which can be seen restored, is the model monolithic house with a semi-circular window in its gable-end, through which one may see, when the interior is lit, a tiny relief of Epona on the opposite wall.[23] The illustration (Pl. VI) is of yet another in the same collection, also of house-like form and again with a niche for a figurine.[24] Did the Verulamium and Silchester bases support, then, something which to the modern eye would resemble nothing so much as a huge, stately doll's-house? If so, then it must seem that it would have been of timber or other material less enduring than stone, for even in those parts of Britain which possess a good stone for carving, nothing in the shape of such a doll's-house has been found.

But if no miracle has preserved a Romano-British domestic shrine intact for our gaze, we can at least draw attention to an example from another Celtic land. At Rezé, near Nantes, an important discovery was made when the church was being rebuilt in 1863; but it has been almost wholly neglected in France, and has remained unknown in this country. The curator of the Nantes Museum, Fortuné Parenteau, investigated, recorded, and saved this 'laraire' for the collections, and it has been republished by the present curator, M. Dominique Costa.[25] The structure is composed of *tegulae* and fragments set in concrete, and measures some 58 cm. (23 in.) wide and 30 cm. (12 in.) thick; the height is now about 32 cm. (13 in.), but Parenteau makes it plain that there was an arched head, which unfortunately fell victim to the workmen's pick-axes. The shrine was rendered inside and out in a lightly-marbled red stucco. The great interest of the find lies, however, in the disposition of its little denizens, which occupied a niche some 27 cm. (11 in.) wide and 15 cm. (6 in.) deep. According to Parenteau, the 'laraire' had been buried in a deep pit dug expressly to receive it,

Pl. VI   Monolithic domestic shrine with niche for a figurine. *(By permission of the Musée d'Histoire et d'Art, Luxembourg).*

and fine earth had been introduced as a packing-material to retain the five figurines upright and in their proper positions. Now, Parenteau saw the pieces in the ground, and his opinion must therefore be respected: but the fine earth sounds much more like that which would filter down into a void over a long term of years, and the suggestion that the 'laraire' had been bodily removed from a pedestal found against the outer wall of a workshop of the ancient settlement of Ratiatum, some 4.5 m. (15 ft.) away, is not in retrospect very convincing: if danger had arisen, it would surely have been sufficient to carry off the deities to safety. We are put in mind of other discoveries, for example in Champagne where, on the hill of Le Châtelet, J.-Cl. Grignon explored the remains of an unknown Roman town in 1772, and came across a number of underground *sacella*[26] with niches, which must have been something like those later opened at Alise-Ste-Reine.[27] They were, he says, distinguishable from mere cellars because they were approached, from the foot of the steps, through a little antechamber, and had decorated walls. A reconstruction-drawing by Grignon *fils* of one such shrine, with its wall-niche, was published by Grivaud, into whose hands the materials fell.[28]

Pl. VII   Remains of domestic shrine, Rezé, Loire-Atlantique. *(After Parenteau, 1869).*

The engraving (Pl. VII) represents the Rezé figurines as found. All except the boar are of pipeclay. At the back stand two female deities wearing long robes; both are ornamented with a number of solar or stellar symbols, especially the one on the left, whose back is covered with them. The curious band displaying three roundels, which extends from hand to hand — these are stiffly held by her sides — is beyond much doubt a stylised attempt to show the usual lapful of fruits — not an easy thing to manage in a standing posture, either by artist or by a real subject! The figurine is unparalleled, as is her sister, though the latter belongs to a known type. She is standing in a protective attitude, guiding or restraining a small nude figure which, in this case, we should (I think) take as a soul, by a left hand placed on its left shoulder, and a right hand gently rested on its head.[29] Both these deities have traces of gilding on their hair, not a detail which I have previously noted in the case of pipeclay figurines, though common enough on those of marble.[30] The bust standing centrally in front of these two, the focus of attention, is of a well-known type,[31] and so is the seated dog, with a bell round his neck.[32] As for the boar, he is made of yellow-painted stone, and is a little damaged: Parenteau remarks that this erstwhile symbol of Gaulish nationhood has grown fat with idleness since the conquest, and has little sign of tusks! The boar was never a favourite of the Roman terracotta-industry in Gaul; but there is a particularly interesting example which occurs as a bas-relief on the base of a pipeclay figurine of a seated goddess holding a fruit and a cylindrical box.[33]

Who are these three ladies? Or are the two in the background merely there to mark aspects of the *Domina* represented by the imperial-looking bust? They are not servants with hand-washing equipment, like those accompanying the Lady of Naix, who, severe and elderly in mien, yet has her lapful of fruits, and her dog, perhaps here too a chthonic symbol, at her feet.[34] The *Mater*, doubled or tripled, is a commonplace in the statuary of the north-west provinces; what we miss here, as we miss it in many of those carvings, is the explicit sexuality of the Venus and Nurse figurines which, alone of the productions of the terracotta-industry, are common in Britain.[35] In Rezé, probably, we have the Great Mother;[36] and although we may have been accustomed to regard heads like that from Caerwent (p. 38) as male — and the founder of a clan, perhaps — that does not necessarily follow:[37] and there may be less difference between the head and the little seated goddess from Caerwent than we may previously have been prepared to admit. The latter, certainly, has her fruit; and in her right hand holds up-right, worked partly in relief and partly by engraved lines, the fir-tree emblem of eternity seen on Dobunnic staters and a Caerleon antefix, and which answers to the symbols moulded on the Rezé dames (Pl. VIII).[38]

Had the Rezé shrine itself been but a little wider, it would have stood very handsomely on one of the Verulamium bases. Perhaps it gives us as good a glimpse as we are likely to obtain of the superstructure of the initial period, or indeed, if it were duplicated, of the two earlier periods. At Silchester, Fox and Hope had already suggested that the pipeclay figurines of Venus and Nurse might have stood in such shrines as that under notice in XIV.2: there are about ten examples of the Venus, and two of the Nurse, from the town; and in Britain they are virtually always found in domestic (or what can be regarded as domestic) contexts rather than in temples or graves, where they also abundantly occur in Gaul. Had the Silchester excavators known of Rezé, they must inevitably have quoted it: but on a width of 2 m. (6.5 ft.) these figurines, or such small bronzes as have been found at Calleva, would have seemed very forlorn, even when accessories such as the strange little candle-holder carved from chalk, bearing a warrior-god on the front and a serpent and a startled bird on the sides,[39] are included. No; the structures on the Silchester platform, and at Verulamium in its final phase, must have been suitably framed and probably decorated too, perhaps sculptured, and would originally have been coloured:

Pl. VIII   Seated Mother-goddess, holding fruit and emblem of eternity in the form of a fir-tree,
found at Caerwent. *(By permission of Newport Museum and Art Gallery).* Inset, obverse of a gold
stater of the Dobunni, inscribed CORIO *(National Museum of Wales).*

some of the flat-topped bas-reliefs, of which northern and western Britain have yielded such striking specimens, might find a place as backgrounds in shrines, while others, gable-topped, might be set into a wall complete in themselves. The point is best illustrated by reference once more to Pompeii, where the *lararium* in the *atrium* of the 'Casa delle Parete Rosse' contained no fewer than six bronze figurines (Aesculapius, Apollo, Hercules, Mercury, and two flanking Lares, with a good bronze lamp in front); but they scarcely sufficed to fill out the space of only 50 cm. (20 in.) or so between the colonnettes on either side, and would have looked insignificant without the gaily-painted background showing a Genius and dancing Lares on a considerably larger scale.[40]

A group of figurines might have a greater visual effect if spaced around a focal point occupied by a larger or more massive object, such as the Caerwent head, especially if it were mounted on a taller base or plinth: again Pompeii provides an apt example in the curious suite of *imagines majorum,* or ancestor-images — 'little more than puppet heads carved in the traditional materials of wood or wax . . . (representing) . . . symbolic portraits which formed part of the ancestral cult' housed in a niche in an elegant chamber of the House of the Menander.[41] Nearer home, an illuminating find from Vichy conveys a suggestion of the 'supporting cast' which may, perhaps, have surrounded a figure like the Caerwent Mother (Pl. VIII): a pit yielded a similar carving (without the fir-tree); a head from a larger statuette; and a fair number of pipeclay figurines, etc., including eleven of Venus and the Nurse, four busts, four birds, three vases and a rectangular moneybox, all thought to have furnished a shrine close to one of the thermal springs.[42] But it is not *necessary* to people a shrine for the Caerwent Mother: she may have been on her own, inserted into the outer wall of a house, there to watch over the fortunes of the family dwelling within: so, we may conclude, was the place of a seated Mother found in the Yonne.[43]

III

Although we are as far as ever from saying that such *was* the superstructure of the Callevan or Verulamian bases, and that such-and-such *were* the occupants, a good many suggestions of greater or lesser probability can be demonstrated. There remains another source of evidence, which has attracted me before, and to which I return below:[44] the closed groups of figurines, etc. from Devizes (Southbroom), fully published by William Musgrave in 1719; from Felmingham Hall (Norfolk), 1844; and from Lamyatt Beacon, near Bruton (Somerset), 1960. All three offer to tell us something of the position in Romano-British religion occupied by the figurines of *Genius togatus* and Lares, of which perhaps nine and ten or eleven, respectively, have been found in all — no poor record beside that which other transalpine provinces can claim.[45] Roman domestic religion is epigraphically indicated for Spain,[46] Germany[47] and even Pannonia, where remarkable bronzes of the highest quality have been discovered: the Nagydém find, for example, included a superb Lar.[48] The domestic cult, indeed, survived late and widely enough to be the subject of a general prohibitive rescript in A.D. 392, and about the same time was denounced by St. Jerome.[49] The early attempts to implant in Britain Romanised ways, of which we read in the celebrated twenty-first chapter of the *Agricola,* might well have encouraged the adoption of Roman 'Lares and Penates'. How do these finds reflect the possibility?

The concept of guardian family-spirits or Lares, and of the personal guardian angel or Genius (in the case of men, Juno in the case of women), is very well-known, and it would be convenient to leave matters at that,[50] were it not for the doubt which may be felt concerning the character of the ancient cult (or rather cults, as the isolation of Lares and Genius reminds us)[51] when the reforms of Augustus had been implemented. The Lar, on the authority of Servius, was the expression of the continuing vitality of the founder of a family, in remote times interred in the house;[52] in Plautus, reference is usually to a single Lar, as in the prologue to the Aulularia where the Lar states that he has possessed and looked after a particular house since the time of the present owner's grandfather; and he also described himself as the *amicus* of the present head of the household.[53] We might even fancy that he had moved with the grandfather to the house, for he was attached to the family rather than to its place of abode.[54] In addition to looking after the house itself, the Lar also protected the family farm, and was with others duly worshipped at the *compitum* or crossroads, where a number of estates met. It was the public worship of the *Lares Compitales* that Augustus transformed, above all by introducing the veneration of his own Genius,[55] represented as a *paterfamilias* in the act of sacrifice.[56] Pompeian tableaux which show this figure togate, veiled, holding *patera* and *cornucopiae, acerra* or scroll, and flanked by dancing Lares (who to the merest glance seem to have lost their birth-right, as it were, to become mere attendants upon the imperial Genius) are numerous. Equally remarkable is the fact that not every shrine, which retains its painting, exhibits this tableau; but it seems reasonable to conclude (though the reader should be warned that this topic is one where the adage *tot homines, quot sententiae* applies) that the tableaux of Genius flanked by dancing Lares may sometimes represent the introduction of the imperial cult into domestic circumstances, in accordance with Augustus' wish.[57] Genius and Lares are seldom found together as figurines, and except in these tableaux can therefore be regarded as the traditional representatives of the family Lar and the householder's Genius in whatever other company they keep.[58] But in Britain the togate Genius figurines may have had as much to do with the imperial cult as with that of a man's own guardian spirit; and the Lares, which are mostly of the jolly, dancing type of the Pompeian frescoes, pouring libations from the high-held *rhyta* into *situlae* or *paterae,* may indeed have been regarded merely as attendants, of Dionysiac character, just as the charming 'pipe-player' bronze from Silchester may have been a stately little attendant in some domestic shrine.[59] The more reposeful, though still alert, type of Lar, of which a specimen from Silchester was an example, differed in attribute — *cornucopiae* and *patera*;

and according to all ancient belief and practice would have been regarded as a different creature,[60] perhaps indeed as the ancient *Lar familiaris,* whose primitive origin could scarcely have seemed foreign to a Celt.

The occurrence in Britain of as many as nine *Genii togati* is interesting in the light of a suggestion that the type had become obsolete before the end of Julio-Claudian times:[61] Nero's coins inscribed GENIO AUGUSTI show a half-draped figure which itself harks back to the Republic[61] and in imperial times very swiftly became a popular standard type for a wide range of Genii: as a small bronze, for example, he occurs at the Shrine of the Nymphs and *Genius Loci* at Carrawburgh on Hadrian's Wall,[62] and in Bath stone appears in a mosaic-floored *schola* of the legionary headquarters-building at Caerleon.[63] The superficial likeness of the *togati,* however, is really no more than might appear among members of a *type immobilisé*; and so limited a dating is not only stylistically impossible (as Kunckel shows), but in Britain also contends with late occurrences at Devizes and Lamyatt. But although the denizens of a *lararium* were usually cherished — we recollect Juvenal's delightful vignette of 'the little images gleaming with brittle wax' ready to receive their 'tiny chaplets' upon a man's return home[64] — they might sometimes find themselves pawned, or without compunction sold for scrap if long worship had worn and damaged them[65] — the castings were not always of very good quality — or even might be changed, as a Mercury into an Aesculapius![66] The melting-pot, we need not doubt, was the destiny of the Silchester *Genius togatus* found in the Forum bereft of his attributes — and his feet;[67] such, too, was to be the fate of the other broken scraps of statuary, not even excluding the celebrated eagle, now that we know from Fulford's remarkable excavations that the Basilica had been given over to metal-reclamation and the like from the latter part of the third century.[68]

One *Genius togatus* may, however, be attributed to a *lararium* without much hesitation, even though it was found unstratified in the men's quarters of a barrack-block on the sinistral side of the headquarters at Caerleon during the excavations of the Glamorgan-Gwent Archaeological Trust, 1980.[69] From the same excavations came a figurine of a bird, probably an attribute of a deity. But this must have been a private shrine: a *Genius Centuriae,* well-attested (but at Caerleon only by the restored text cut before firing on a wine-jar),[70] is hardly in question, for his shrine would have been in the centurion's quarters, and in form he would have followed the current half-draped fashion, already in evidence elsewhere, and represented for some unknown grade of headquarters staff at Caerleon itself.[71]

We are now in a position to turn briefly to the closed groups of bronzes. Close to the hilltop *fanum* on Lamyatt Beacon, near Bruton (Somerset), a group of figurines was found.[72] It consisted of a small Genius accompanied by Hercules, Mars, Mercury (two) and Minerva, all great Celtic favourites. The propinquity of the Celtic temple, where further fragments have been found,[73] allows us to infer that behind these figures stood Celtic deities, as so well explained by Thevenot. The date lies in the earlier fourth century, as coins —

especially one of Carausius from the floor of a tiny building adjacent to the temple — show. The deposit at Southbroom, Devizes, bears out the hint of an *interpretatio celtica*. Musgrave's detailed account explains that it was discovered with a *denarius* of Alexander beneath a square brick among the remains of ancient buildings. The Penates consisted, in addition to the Genius (that from Lamyatt was first described as a 'priest'; here is unmanned and turned into a '*Virgo Vestalis*'), of Roman deities — Venus, Mars, Jupiter, Mercury, Bacchus, Vulcan — on the one hand, and on the other of a very strange suite of native design, ranging in subject from Jupiter brandishing his thunderbolt, to a Mercury, a passable Minerva, a 'Mars' with raven-crested helmet and serpent-entwined limbs (perhaps a god of healing), and a female clasping her belly with both hands in a typical stance of pregnancy; there were also animals, including a Celtic three-horned bull.[74] Musgrave's plates, however, show that two of the native castings are incomplete, and that other pieces were damaged: the Venus, which was a handsome piece standing 16 cm. (6.5 in.) high, lacks her left arm; the lower half of the Genius has gone; a hand here and there, or an attribute, is missing. On the theory that this group came from a domestic *lararium*, hidden for safety, it is hard to account for these imperfections, and especially for the damage suffered disproportionately by the best pieces. Another explanation, therefore, would see the objects as the stock of a sacred metal-founder — perhaps just as much a wanderer as their latterday finder, the gardener William Cade who travelled the West Country with them as a raree-show. The object would have been to collect old Penates for the melting pot — not indeed to turn Saturn into a cooking-pot and Minerva into a saucepan, as Tertullian proposed,[75] but to use their good and holy metal in moulding other gods anew. The homogeneous style of the native series combines with their especially heavy weight (suggestive of a large admixture of lead to facilitate the casting[76]) to show that some of the products accompanied the scrap, as in many a Late Bronze Age itinerant founder's hoard. To admit the truth of this theory must of course destroy all possibility that the find has something to tell of the part played by a togate Genius in a Celtic milieu, for a figurine obtained for scrap may have come from anywhere.

This leaves the Genius from Lamyatt, which does seem to have come from a temple. Analogous considerations to those which guided our interpretation of the Caerleon example forbid us to recognise in this expression of the *Numen*, or 'divine majesty' of an emperor, which, if seen at all, might likewise be expected to display the half-draped form of a *Genius Augusti* of Neronian or later times: the British inscriptions relating to the emperor's *Genius*, however, are coupled with Jupiter Optimus Maximus, and come from military sites.[77] In short, unless the Lamyatt figurine represented the Genius of the priest or possibly that of a donor, his most likely explanation is still the superficial one: *sacerdos*.

An even more careful mode of burial was observed in the case of the Felmingham Hall deposit (between Aylsham and North Walsham, Norfolk).[78] This is the only closed find from Britain containing a Lar; it lay in a large pottery cauldron sealed with another vessel and standing on two flat bricks; other pots, empty save for one which held a coin thought to be of Severus, were found in the immediate vicinity, but no bones or ashes appear to have accompanied them.[79] The sacred character of the collection, which is dated by a coin of Valerian II, is not in doubt. Apart from the dancing Lar, there was a magnificent hollow-cast male head about 15 cm. (6 in.) high, with hair and beard and worked in a distinctly Celtic manner, but with a fillet (of a different metal?) missing: it was attached at one time to a lay figure, most probably. Besides a head from a statuette of Minerva and a curious terminal exhibiting a head (not of Heliosarapis, as often stated, for there is no point of comparison with that figure, but a syncretised solar-lunar deity),[80] there was a pair of crows with grains in their beaks, one of which is said, in the earliest account of the find, to have been the tip of an iron sceptre. Two other priestly bronze sceptres with spearhead tips were also present, and the three, together with a unique bronze rattle equipped for delivering the *sortes*, distinguish this deposit from that described by Musgrave. Lastly, a wheel from a model chariot may be mentioned[81] as well as pedestals and other relics going to make up a priestly crown of Hockwold type. The broken or damaged state of many of the contents may perhaps find the same explanation as the damaged figurines in the Devizes find, but the extremely careful mode of burial and the possibility that the other, empty vessels had held votive offerings of a perishable nature, urge caution, and may impel us to compare the find with others of a religious character and chthonic significance.[82] The Roman Lar was chthonic too,[83] and the extraordinarily heterogeneous nature of the Felmingham find may certainly encourage us to regard him *in propria persona*.

From old times prolixity has been the privilege of an antiquary,[84] and I fear I am little different from the rest of my colleagues in that respect. To be allowed to range in thought over such problems as are here ventilated is, however, a greater privilege still.

NOTES

1. Frere, S.S., *Antiq. Journ.,* xl, (1960), 9 and Frere, S.S., *Verulamium Excavations, Vol. 1,* Society of Antiquaries of London Research Report, 28, London, 1972, 57–60 and pls. xvii–xix.

2. *Archaeologia,* lv.1, (1896), 237–40 and pl. xv; Boon, G.C., *Silchester: the Roman Town of Calleva,* Newton Abbot/London, 1974, Pl. 24, shows it from the rear.

3. Boyce, G.K., *Memoirs of the American Academy in Rome,* xiv, (1937), nos. 67, 214 and 414 are examples, all illustrated. The finest Romano-British wall-niche remaining is in the so-called bath-house at Ravenglass, about 1.5 m. (5 ft.) from floor-level: Collingwood, R.G., *Transactions of the Cumberland and Westmorland Antiquarian and Archaeological Society,* n.s. xxviii (1928), pl. ivA facing 361.

4. Boyce, G.K., *op. cit.* (see note 3), nos. 189, 207 and 253 (illustrated). There is a triple niche, no. 212.

5. Thevenot, E., *Divinités et sanctuaires de la Gaule,* Paris, 1968, 140, figs. — a little gabled building with two doors or windows below, like a Swiss châlet or for all the world like one of the little 'weather-houses' on sale a few years ago.

6. Maiuri, A., *Ercolano, I nuovi scavi,* Rome, 1958, i, 254.

7. Petronius, 29.

8. See note 2.

9. Boyce, G.K., *op. cit.* (see note 3), no. 385 (pl. 29, 2).

10. *ibid.,* No. 414 (pl. 34, 1).

11. Wheeler, R.E.M., *Segontium and the Roman Occupation of Wales,* London, 1924, 86, fig. 33. Mercury, *ibid.,* 128–9, fig. 50; *Silchester* (see note 2), 333, note 45. *Suum cuique:* Dr. Anne Ross claimed it as a 'horned god of the Brigantes', *Archaeol. Aeliana,* 4 ser., xxxix, (1961), 75, but I think the *caduceus* is plain enough.

12. Unpublished information kindly contributed by Mr. Wacher. On the plan of the excavations in *Civitas Capitals of Roman Britain* (Wacher, J.S. (ed.) London, 1966), fig. 21, the shrine appears, unlabelled, in

Room 3 towards the rear of VIII.5. A monolithic bottom block of the west side-wall, and the central plinth, are drawn immediately below the word 'Stokehole'. The pilaster is shown as the westerly of two blocks forming a gateway-sill adjacent to a mass of fallen voussoirs (marked) between VII.5 and VII.6.

13. *Archaeologia,* lvii.1, (1902), 148–50. John Ward's notes on a re-excavation and my commentary in 'Shrine of the Head', *Welsh Antiquity: Essays presented to H.N. Savory,* National Museum of Wales, Cardiff, 1976, 163–75, with discussion of Springhead IV (Penn, W.S., *Archaeol. Cantiana,* lxxiv, (1960), 114–18).

14. As required by Canon 41 of the Council of Elvira, *c.* A.D. 300, quoted *ibid.,* 175, note 29, from Lauchert, F., *Die Kanones der wichtigsten altkirchlichen Concilien,* Freiburg-i-B., 1896, 20.

15. *Archaeol. Aeliana,* 4 ser., xi, (1933), 190–1, pls. xxvii, 2 and xxviii; the relief, best in Toynbee, J.M.C., *Art in Roman Britain,* London, 1962, pl. 83. Professor Toynbee mentions the relief and the shrine in her 'Genii Cucullati in Roman Britain', *Hommages à Waldemar Deonna,* Collection Latomus, xxviii, 1957, 460, no. 3.

16. *Proc. Dorset Natur. Hist. Archaeol. Soc.,* lix, (1937), 11; *An Inventory of Historical Monuments in the County of Dorset, Vol. 2, South-East, Pt. 3,* Royal Commission on Historical Monuments, 1970, 555–6, pl. 220. The Commission takes the feature to be original, but the excavators regarded it as an addition, the piers being built 'against the plaster'. The point cannot now be determined.

17. *Archaeologia,* lviii.1, (1902), 29–30, fig. 2, with a well-carved acanthus-leaf visible on the side, contrasting with the crude 'man' which the excavators recognised in the spandrel, surely an accidental effect.

18. Boyce, No. 434. (pl. 37, 1). A miniature example from Chedworth is illustrated in Goodburn, R., *The Roman Villa, Chedworth,* National Trust Publications,

London, 1972, pl. 10.2, and Mr. Wacher kindly tells me of an unpublished specimen with shell-headed recess from Cirencester. Several of the Cotswold reliefs of deities, of course, are carved as if standing in such settings, gable-topped or otherwise.

19. Toynbee, J.M.C., *Archaeol. Cambrensis*, cii, (1935), 134–5, pl. xii; Hogg, A.H.A., embodying information from Professor Toynbee, *Britannia*, v, (1974), 242–4, pl. xx,a.

20. *ibid.*, note 2, fig. 3.

21. Oelmann, F., in *Festschrift für August Oxé*, Darmstadt, 1938, 183–91, with some interesting ethnological parallels.

22. Espérandieu, E., *Recueil général des bas-reliefs de la Gaule romaine*, v, Paris, 1913, no. 4193; Thill, G., *Les époques gallo-romaine et mérovingienne . . . Guide illustré*, Luxembourg, 1969, pl. 17.

23. Best in Oelmann, F., *op. cit.* (note 21), Abb. 2; Thill, G. (see note 22), pl. 1, on left (restored). The findspot is unrecorded, but the piece is of course local.

24. Espérandieu, E., *op. cit.* (see note 22), no. 4206; cf. also 4269, with seated mother-goddess carved as part of the object (Thill, G., *op. cit.* (see note 22), pls. 16 and 18).

25. Parenteau, F., *Catalogue du Musée Départmental d'Archéologie de Nantes et de la Loire-Inférieure*, Nantes, 1869, 66–8, no. 128, whence our plate; Lisle du Dreneuc, P. de, (ed.), *Catalogue du Musée archéologique de Nantes*, Nantes, 1903, 44–5, nos. 158–63 (not seen); Costa, D., 'Une chapelle domestique gallo-romaine', *La Revue des Arts — Musées de France*, 10e Année, 1960, iii, 129–32, good photographs of the figurines. I am obliged to Mr. R.W. Lightbown for much help in locating this last, and to M. Costa for a photocopy. The find is barely mentioned by A. Blanchet in his general survey of pipeclay figurines, *Mémoires de la Société des Antiquaires de France*, li, (1890), 211.

26. Grignon, J.-Cl., *Bultin des fouilles faites par ordre du Roi, d'une ville romaine, sur la petite montagne du Chatelet . . . en Champagne, decouverte en 1772*, Bar-le-Duc,

1774, v–viii; *Second Bulletin . . .*, Paris, 1775, ci–cii.

27. Thevenot, E., *op. cit.* (see note 5), 169; Le Gall, J., *Alésia*, (1963), 165, 169 (figs.), 170–2. The shrine with double niche in the house of Pompidius Priscus at Pompeii was also underground (Boyce, G.K., *op. cit.* (see note 3), no. 253).

28. Grivaud de la Vincelle, C.-M., *Arts et Métiers des Anciens*, Paris, 1819–22: pl. lxxxii must be a reconstruction, because Grignon *père* does not give the height of any niche, only the height above the floor and its width. In the plate, it is improbably roofed; and although the fine seated Mercury and the other deity shown were no doubt found in the appropriate circumstances, as was the terracotta lamp, this last is shown suspended in what is, on close inspection, quite indubitably a hipposandal! The same engraving is copied for Tudot, E., *Collection de figurines en argile. Oeuvres premiers de l'art Gaulois*, Paris, 1860, fig. xi.

29. For the first person, cf. the Naix goddess, note 34. For the second, cf. Tudot, E., *op. cit.* (see note 28), fig. xlvii, and fig. xlviii (man and wife, both naked, with child sitting on their linked forearms, in front of the goddess). A protective Venus with five children is shown by Thevenot, E., *op. cit.* (see note 5), 181. A child from some such a representation was found at Caerleon, unpublished. The dressed, rather severe, goddess of the Rezé shrine suggests a *Psychopompé* to me.

30. Costa, D., *op. cit.* (see note 25), 113. cf. the Venus shown in colour in Ward Perkins, J.B. and Claridge, A. (eds.), *Pompeii A.D. 79* London exhibition catalogue, 1977, 83, no. 218.

31. Rouvier-Jeanlin, M., *Les figurines gallo-romaines en terre-cuite du Museé des Antiquités Nationales*, Paris, 1972, 284–5, no. 772.

32. *ibid.*, 345–6, no. 1054. It is of interest that Parenteau, F., *op. cit.* (see note 25), records fragments of moulds 'pour couler nos statuettes' and 'des pains d'argile blanche' which the workmen told him were 'pipeclay to make plates'.

33. Tudot, E., *op. cit.* (see note 28), fig. xliv and pl. 33. A figurine of a boar, pl. 57. The lack of boars is very strange, considering the common occurrence of the animal (admittedly, usually as the object of the chase) in the allied samian industry.

34. Espérandieu, E., *op. cit.* (see note 22), no. 4678; face better shown by Thevenot, E., *op. cit.* (see note 5), 168.

35. F. Jenkin's survey of these two types (not to mention his notes on other, rarer finds) still reveals the general pattern of distribution and offers a useful commentary, although much in need of updating: *Archaeol. Cantiana*, lxxi, (1957), 38–46 and lxii, (1958), 60–76; cf. for later finds: Green, M.J., *Corpus of Religious Material from the Civilian Areas of Roman Britain*, BAR 24, Oxford, 1976 and her *Small Cult-Objects from the Military Areas of Roman Britain*, BAR 52, Oxford, 1978, *passim*.

36. The Gaulish 'Minerva' rather than the 'Venus': Thevenot, E., *op. cit.* (see note 5), chapter 8 on the Mother-Goddesses is especially good, and in this connection see especially 178–80 and 180–4.

37. See my article in *Welsh Antiquity* (see note 13), 171–3 and notes 18–24. I did not know of Rezé then, and there is consequently no realisation that the head might be female — of a deity in the Mother range.

38. *Archaeologia*, lxii.1, (1910), 14–16, from a pit probably belonging to IX.17N. The fir-tree goes right through the range of Dobunnic staters from uninscribed down to Corio, omitting the last, Bodvoc. Antefix, Boon, G.C., *Isca: the Roman Legionary Fortress at Caerleon, Mon.*, National Museum of Wales, Cardiff, 1972, fig. 14c.

39. Boon, G.C., *Silchester* (see note 2), 168, fig. 26.

40. Boyce, G.K., *op. cit.* (see note 3), no. 371, pl. 31, 1. Famous: e.g. in Roscher, W.H., *Ausführliches Lexikon der griechischen und römischen Mythologie*, Leipzig, 1894–97, ii, 2, Abb. 2.

41. Maiuri, A., *La Casa del Menandro*, Rome, 1933, 98–106, fig. 49, tav. xi, for the room itself, in colour. The shrine is also shown in the *Pompeii A.D. 79* London exhibition catalogue, 77; quotation *ibid.*, 76. The heads and accompanying Mercury (?) were found as voids where the wax etc. had melted, and were filled up with plaster-of-Paris.

42. Blanchet, A., *op. cit.* (see note 25), 195–6; Tudot, E., *op. cit.* (see note 28), pl. 48.

43. Thevenot, E., *op. cit.* (see note 5), 167 and 169. Our explanation differs.

44. 'Genius and the Lar in Celtic Britain', *Jahrbuch des Römisch-Germanischen Zentralmuseums, Mainz*, xx, (1973), 265–9, whence Boon, G.C., *Silchester* (see note 2), 162.

45. *Genii Togati*, in general see Kunckel, H., *Der römische Genius, Römische Mitteilungen*, Ergänzungsheft, xx, 1974, map 1 (facing 134), square symbols. Britain: Green, M.J., *Civilian Areas* (see note 35), 185 (Lamyatt, now 2, see note 73)), 187 (Bath), 191 (Cricklade), 195 (Silchester), 231 (Barham); add Devizes (Southbroom, see below), a fine example from Caerleon (see below), and a small specimen from 'North Britain' (Seaby's *Coin and Medal Bulletin* Dec. 1981, A. 393, pl. 40). *Eadem, Military Areas* (see note 35), 67, another from Richborough; —— Lares, all of the dancing type except where marked (★); *Civilian Areas*, 176 (Baston Ford, Worcs.), 187 (nr. Bath), 195★ (Silchester), 205 (Felmingham Hall), 207 (Verulamium), 210 (Harlow Temple), 213★ (Brandon, Norfolk), 216 (Colchester, but two, cf. Pitts, L.F., *Roman Bronze Figurines from the Civitates of the Catuvellauni and Trinovantes*, BAR 60, Oxford, 1979, nos. 87–8), 223 (London), 230 (Hadleigh Castle), and add from *Military Areas*, 46★, the miscalled 'Genius' from Bewcastle, perhaps a *Lar Militaris?* — cf. Dessau, H., *Inscriptiones Latinae Selectae*, nos. 3637–8. I have not been able to check all the Lares.

46. *ibid.*, nos. 3604 and 3605, from Abdera in Baetica, and Tarraco respectively, the first mentioning *Lares et Genius cum aedicula* as the dedication of a bailiff and a freeman — very much the Italian mode,

the second a dedication to the *Lares et Tutela, Genius Luci nostri*. cf. also Tranoy, A., *La Galice romaine*, 1981, 322–4.

47. *ibid.*, no. 3635, *Lares Compitales* (Mainz), but possibly this is to be linked more to the *Lares Viales*.

48. *ibid.*, no. 3607 (Savaria): *Laribus Domesticis sacrum;* Nagydém Lar, Thomas, E.B., *Folia Archaeologica*, xv (1963), 21–42, and *eadem.*, in Lengyel, A. and Radan, G.T.B. (eds.), *The Archaeology of Roman Pannonia*, Lexington, University of Kentucky Press, 1980, 181–2, pls. xxvi–xxviii.

49. *Codex Theodosianus*, xvi, 10.12; Hieronymus, *In Esaiam*, cap. 57 v.8 (Migne, *Patrologia Latina*, xxiv, col. 551). 'The cities of many provinces labour under this error, and even Rome herself in her various *insulae* and homes venerates the statue of a Tutela', etc., cf. Dessau, H., *op. cit.* (see note 45), no. 3605.

50. On the Lares see Waites, M.C., *American Journal of Archaeology*, 2 ser., xxiv, (1920), 241–61; Tabeling, E., *Mater Larum: zum Wesen der Larenreligion*, Frankfurt-a-M., 1932 (repr.), and the standard entries in Roscher, Pauly, and Daremberg-Saglio. On the Genius see these latter and especially Kunckel, H., *op. cit.* (see note 45), for art-forms. Figurines of Juno are everywhere very rare: Mrs. Green, *Military Areas* (see note 35), 75, no. 30, has one from York (it is not a Minerva); for the Juno in a *lararium* see the well-known Avenches example, Cart, W., *Anzeiger für Schweizerische Altertumskunde* n. F., xix, (1917), 78–89, pls. showing a Lar and a Mercury, a mended Victory, and two Minervas.

51. Thus the Lares are painted in one niche, and the Genius in the other, in the underground *sacellum* of the house of Pompidius Priscus (Boyce, G.K., *op. cit.* (see note 3), no. 253, pl. 41, 2) with its double *lararium*. *ibid.*, no. 406, is the only example which he records of Genius and Lares, in figurine form, from a *lararium*; see also under no. 118 for such figures apparently in a cupboard with various

other figurines and miscellaneous objects (*Römische Mitteilungen*, xvi, (1901), 322–3). Kunckel, H., *op. cit.* (see note 45), 85, lists a find from Arezzo (one Lar).

52. Servius, *Ad Aeneid.*, vi, 152: *Apud majores omnes homines in suis domibus sepeliebantur, unde ortum est, ut Lares colerentur in aedibus.*

53. Plautus, *Aulularia*, 2.

54. cf. Plautus, *Trinummus*, 39.

55. Suetonius, *Divus Augustus*, 31, 4; Cassius Dio, li, 19 *ad finem*. Ovid, *Fasti*, v, 143 ff.; cf. Dessau, H., *op. cit.* (see note 45), nos. 3613, 3617, etc.

56. As in the Vatican statue, shown, for example, by Roscher (see note 40), i.2, col. 1626; Kunckel, H., *op. cit.* (see note 45), Taf. 8, 1, and the Vatican relief, Taf. 17 (lower), *Laribus Augustis*; statuettes of *Genius* and *Lares*, carried in procession, Taf. 18.

57. Cassius Dio, *op. cit.* (see note 55).

58. See note 51; Boyce, C.K., *op. cit.* (see note 3), Index for associations — figurines and in paintings.

59. Boon, G.C., *Silchester* (see note 2), 167, pl. 34c.

60. *ibid.*, 161, fig. 23. The attribute distinguished the deity, cf. Minucius Felix, *Octavius*, 24, 8: . . . *ecce ornatur, consecratur, oratur, tunc postremo deus est.*

61. Hill, D.K., *American Journal of Archaeology*, lxxii, (1968), 166; cf. Kunckel, H., *op. cit.* (see note 45), Taf. 4, top two, and next, coin.

62. *Archaeol. Aeliana*, ser. 4, xl, (1962), 66–9, pl. xi.1. In general see Professor Toynbee's note on the type, *Britannia*, ix, (1978), 329–30. Kunckel, H., *op. cit.* (see note 45), 88–9, lists finds at Schwarzenacker (Saarbrücken) and Detzem, Trier, where a half-draped Genius (*Genius Populi Romani* in the one case; Genius of a people or place in the other) were associated with a dancing Lar and various Penates.

63. Boon, G.C. *Isca: the Roman Legionary Fortress at Caerleon, Mon.*, National Museum of Wales, Cardiff, 1972, 71–3, fig. 43.

64. Juvenal, xii, 87 f.

65. Tertullian, *Apologia*, 13. Three of the

four damaged figurines from the Thames at London Bridge are illustrated in the British Museum, *Guide to the Antiquities of Roman Britain,* London, 1951, pl. xvii, 17: note the cuts across the thighs of the Apollo.

66. Noted by Boyce, G.K., *op. cit.* (see note 3), no. 371, in the group mentioned here, p. 00. On change from one god to another, cf. Ramsey Macmullen on 'polyonymy': *Paganism in the Roman Empire,* New Haven/London, 1981, 90–1.

67. Boon, G.C., *Silchester,* (see note 2), 162, pl. 34e.

68. An interim note appears in *Britannia,* xii, (1981), 362.

69. I am grateful to Miss V. Metcalf, the excavator, for an opportunity to examine this figurine and to mention it here, in advance of her own publication. The excavations are mentioned, *Britannia,* xii, (1981), 317, with fig. 4. We should note the occurrence of a Lar at Vindonissa fortress, see Kaufmann-Heinimann, A., *Gesellschaft "Pro Vindonissa', Jahresbericht,* 1981, (1982), 19–22, Abb. 2.

70. Boon, G.C., *Isca* (see note 38), 121, Fig. 80; *Journal of Roman Studies,* xix, (1929), 217, no. 11, which may be expanded [*Genio feli*]*citer > Ael(i) Romuli.*

71. See note 63, and in general von Domaszewski, A., *Die Religion des römischen Heeres,* Trier, 1895, 103–6. Examples are known at Chester of dedications (*R.I.B.* i, nos. 446–8). The cult was managed by *signifer, optio* and *tesserarius* (von Domaszewski, 104; see his Taf. iv, fig. 3 for a half-draped Genius in the side-panel of a dedication).

72. *Journal of Roman Studies,* li (1961), 187, pl. xx; the figurines are in Bristol City Museum. Kunckel (see note 45), 31 uses this group as an indication 'wie lange Statuetten eines Lorariums verehrt werden können', dating the Genius to the end of the first century A.D.(!) and pointing out the different ages of the other components.

73. *Britannia,* v, (1974), 452. See *Fox Review* (ed.) Yeovil, Winter 1982. (illus.) for a second *togatus* (and a Mercury) from here, recently acquired by Castle Cary Museum. This highly important discovery is not at variance with what is said of the other *togatus.*

74. *Musgrave, W., Belgium Britannicum,* 1719, 123–52 and figs. from a large plate of 1717 cut up; Stukeley, W., *Itinerarium Curiosum,* London, 1724, 137: *Wilts. Archaeological Magazine,* i, (1854), 214 for the provenance. Eight of the native figurines are in the British Museum *Guide* (see note 65), pl. xvii, 16. The others are lost. All are reproduced from Musgrave in my paper, 'Genius and the Lar in Celtic Britain' (see note 44), Taf. 58–9.

75. See note 65. The reference to Saturn betrays Tertullian's North African origin, that deity being frequently worshipped there, cf. Leglay, M., *Saturne africain,* Paris, 1966–8.

76. Musgrave suggests that they were filled with lead, but in point of fact this is not true. The extraordinary stalk attaching to the cap of one of the native figurines (Musgrave's no. 2 and last on the right in the British Museum *Guide* (see note 65), pl. xvii, 6) seems unlikely to have been intended for the tip of one of the pointed woven hats affected in Mediterranean regions by both men and women, for it is far too long; it may be a casting-jet.

77. e.g. the Caerwent pedestal, *R.I.B.,* i, 309 for a dedication to the imperial *Numen* and Mars Lenus; and no. 915 from Old Penrith for a dedication to I.O.M. and the Genii (surely?) of Philip I and his son.

78. Hart, R., *The Antiquities of Norfolk, a Lecture,* Norwich, 1844, iii–viii, 2 pls. showing *inter alia* the best sceptre (unbent); Haverfield in *The Victoria County History of Norfolk,* i, 1901, 307–9, with Hart's plates reproduced; British Museum *Guide* (see note 65), 60, pl. xxiv, 2 shows some of the objects. The fine bronze head is well-shown in Toynbee, J.M.C., *Art in Roman Britain,* pl. 47, and the cauldron is shown in the British Museum *Guide,* pl. v, 29. There is very careful study by an undergraduate at the time, Hazel M. Gilbert, in *Bulletin of the Board of Celtic Studies,* xxviii, (1980),

159–86, with good plain drawings. Further examination of the material in the British Museum in 1982 shows that the two bronze hemispheres (rather flat!) joined together, had a bronze rim-binding, and were fitted with the bronze handle (*ibid.*, 180–1, fig. 6c; 180, fig. 8a), the whole making an ensemble very like a baby's celluloid *rattle*. I hope to publish this interesting object after exhibiting it to the Society of Antiquaries. Miss Gilbert was, alas, not quite right in saying that there was no evidence to show that the handle and the hemispheres fitted together: I wish she had made the necessary final observation, instead of myself.

79. *Archaeol. Journ.*, iii, (1846), 246–9. The absence of bones and ashes is stressed.

80. British Museum *Guide* (see note 65), pl. xxiv, 2, bottom, second from right; the mistake was Haverfield's (see note 78), and is continued in the British Museum *Guide* (see note 65), Harris, E. and J., *Oriental Cults in Roman Britain*, Leiden, 1965, 79, and even Kater-Sibbes, G.J.F., *Preliminary Catalogue of Sarapis Monuments*, Leiden, 1973, 159, no. 829, pl. xxviii. Perhaps cf. Boucher, S., *Recherches sur les bronzes figurés de la Gaule pré-romaine et romaine*, Rome, 1976, 137, pl. 50 no. 323 from Cahon (Somme).

81. Hart's pl. 2 no. 18 (see note 78) shows more of a decayed iron axle than now survives. The wheel may stand — secondhand, as it were — as a solar symbol, but I doubt it in view of the manifestly chthonic character of the deposit as a whole.

82. The comparison is with deposits of metalwork ranging from Iron Age to Roman date: cf. Manning, W.H., *Britannia*, iii, (1972), 239, 247, and *passim*. One of the Silchester ironwork 'hoards' contained a bust of Bacchus, from a steelyard.

83. cf. note 52, and the well-known chthonic interest of crossroads which has continued down to modern times.

84. So said the Revd. James Dallaway, *Antiquities of Bristow*, Bristol, 1834, 212.

Some Research Work on Roman Villas in Italy, 1960–1980

by
M. AYLWIN COTTON

When invited to contribute to this *Festschrift*, I remembered that, many years ago, Sheppard Frere had concerned himself with problems relating to the large Roman villa at Bignor, Sussex. He has since resolved some of them by disentangling part of its structural sequence, as he explained in his farewell address as retiring President of the Royal Archaeological Institute, in May 1981. This article is basically about comparable work in Italy.

At the beginning of the 1960s, the Italian scene with regard to *villae rusticae* differed greatly from that which now exists. At that time, the late Dr. John Ward Perkins, then Director of the British School at Rome, and Professor Peter von Blanckenhagen of the Institute of Fine Arts at New York University, backed financially by the then Batchelor Foundation of that Institute, sought a research project in the Mediterannean region. Although large and exciting sites in several countries were visited, it was decided that less seemed to be known about the early development of Roman villas at the heart of the Roman Empire than elsewhere in its provinces. Work in Italy had been, and was being, done on palatial sites, for example at the villa at Piazza Armerina in Sicily, other villa sites were being recorded in increasing numbers, but excavations on stratified sites with structural sequences in small *villae rusticae* were non-existent. For this reason, and for practical logistics, it was decided that two villa sites, which it was hoped would have late-Republican origins, should be chosen for Italy.

With the collaboration of Professor A. de Franciscis, then Soprintendente for Campania, and his Inspector, Professor W. Johannowsky, two platform-villa sites, San Rocco and Posto, at Francolise, Campania, were selected. I was invited to act as Field Director, and, with a team of American and British graduates, and a large team of local workmen (including the resident gypsies), undertook excavations there in the summer seasons from 1962–1966.

The sites were well-chosen. Posto, the smaller of the two farmsteads, yielded a sequence with a small house of Period I, possessing a large walled farmyard dated to *c.* 120–80 B.C. Alterations were made in Period IA, *c.* 50 B.C., but in Period II, *c.* 30 B.C., it was rebuilt on an enlarged platform with more rooms. A bath wing was added in Period III, *c.* A.D. 50.

The San Rocco villa started as a more advanced type of farmhouse, *c.* 75 B.C.

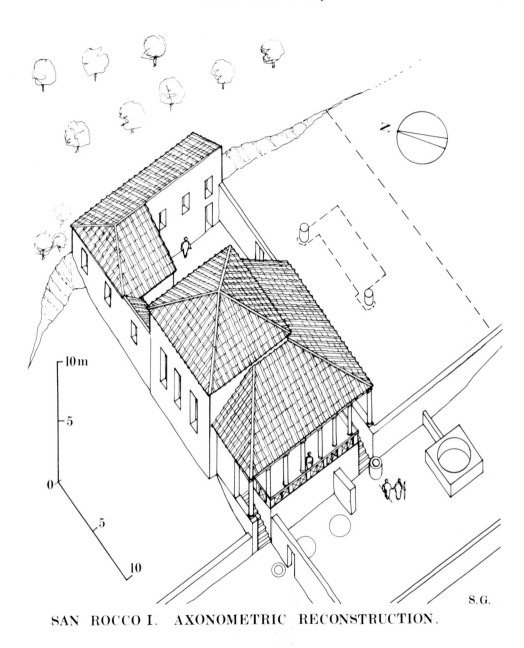

SAN ROCCO I. AXONOMETRIC RECONSTRUCTION.

S.G.

Fig. 1 Axonometric reconstruction of the villa at San Rocco in Period I.

(Fig. 1), and again additions were made in Period IA with further alterations around 50 B.C. But here a great contrast was introduced in the plan of Period II (Fig. 2). On one half of a very large, new platform, a 'gentleman's', many-roomed, peristyled villa was built, which absorbed and partly reused the house of Period I; on the other half a *villa rustica* with two courtyards and slave quarters was laid out. This rebuilding occurred *c.* 30 B.C. In the mid first-century A.D. rooms in one corner of the residence were converted into a bath wing; in the area of the *villa rustica*, rooms were altered to industrial uses and contained oil-presses, separating vats and two kilns for tile-making.

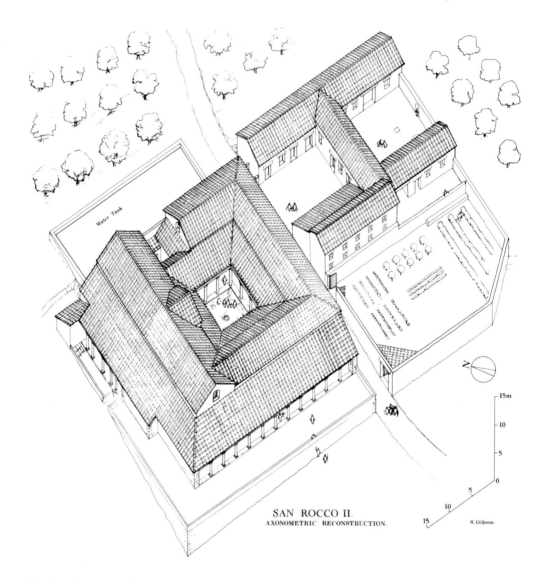

SAN ROCCO II.
AXONOMETRIC RECONSTRUCTION.

S. Gibson.

Fig. 2 Axonometric reconstruction of the villa at San Rocco in Period II.

When interim reports were published[1] the only analogy which could then be quoted, for the simple plan of the Posto I farmhouse, was that of the Sambuco villa, near San Giovenale, South Etruria. It was a small six-room, working farmhouse dated to the late second century B.C., and in use until the first century A.D., and it had been excavated by the Swedish School in Rome.[2]

The plans of Sambuco and Posto I (San Rocco I was only finalised in 1966) appeared, with comments, in works by various authors in the late 1960s and 1970s,[3] and undoubtedly aroused fresh interest in small farmsteads of late Republican type.[4]

A brief account of new work in this field, in the last two decades, is given here under two headings: A. Selected publications (with the reservation that the first two quoted were already in preparation before 1960) and seminars; B. Selected new excavations.

A.   SELECTED PUBLICATIONS

1.   *Jens Erik Skydsgaard, 1961*

It was only after the publication of the interim report on the Francolise villas that I received an off-print from the author and first became aware of his study which seemed to be the first new work on the subject since Carrington's 'Studies in the Campanian "villae rusticae"' of 1931; my gratitude to the author was heartfelt. He emphasised, however, that there was a great lack of information for the late Republican period from excavation results, and hoped that the Francolise reports would do something to remedy this situation.

2.   *John D'Arms, 1970*

Professor John D'Arms, Director of the American Academy in Rome, was working on his monograph *The Romans on the Bay of Naples* at the time of the Francolise excavations. He was concerned with the lovely and luxurious seaside-villas, the 'holiday homes' of the rich Romans on that coast. While this study dealt with an aspect of villa research other than that of the small farmsteads, a point of mutual interest arose. He did not agree with the then prevalent view (not derived from excavation data) that these villas went out of use in the first century A.D., but thought that they were still in occupation in the second century, indeed, well into that century. The Francolise results supported this view.

3.   *The Lancaster University Seminar on Italian Archaeology 1977*

The papers given at this Seminar included an account by Professor Alastair Small on recent evidence for rustic villas in Apulia, Basilicata and Calabria, and their significance for the agrarian history of South Italy.[5] The Monte Irsi Roman building (see below p. 62) is discussed together with the other *villae rusticae* of that area.

4. *Jeremy Rossiter, 1978*

A study of *villae rusticae* had been planned as part of the Francolise project, but was not achieved. The publication of Jeremy Rossiter's *Roman Farm Buildings in Italy* was, therefore, all the more welcome as an addition to our knowledge of these buildings. He lists forty-one sites in Appendix A, with their relevant bibliographies, which are discussed in the text; in Appendix B, there is a further catalogue of excavated, or surveyed, buildings. Of the sites in Appendix A, excluding those mentioned below, very few were actually excavated during the period under review, even though reports on a greater number were published during those years, and none so completely as the exceptions quoted. Additions to this list, not available to Rossiter when his report was written, are: the plans of the San Rocco I farmhouse and the revised plan of Posto I, now available in the definitive reports; a report on a *villa rustica* at Masseria Nocelli, south-east of Lucera, excavated by Barri Jones;[6] and an excavation report on another at Crocicchie, north-west of Rome.[7]

5. *The Colloquium held at the American Academy in Rome on 10 December 1979*

The papers given at this Colloquium on *The Roman Villas in Italy: Current Research* have not, at the time of writing, been published. As they cover wider aspects of studies in the Italian Roman Villa than has been attempted in this article, it seems relevant to reproduce here a list of the subjects chosen and the speakers:

'La villa nel suburbo romano: topografia e urbanistica'. (L. Quilici, Roma).
'The villa at San Rocco: Francolise'. (M.A. Cotton, Roma).
'Maritime villas and their fisheries'. (R.T. Scott, Bryn Mawr College).
'Insediamenti residenziali nelle isole Pontine'. (G.M. Rossi, Roma).
'Sette Finestre 1979'. (A. Carandini, Siena).
'Ricerche sul popolamento rustico nella Cisalpine'. (D. Scagliarini Corlaita, Bologna).
'La villa del Petrarco nell'agro stabiano'. (S. de Caro, Pompeii).
'Luxury villas on the Bay of Naples: Second Thoughts'. (J.H. D'Arms).
'La villa nel surburbio di Pompeii: Nuovi appunti per il rapporto fra città e territorio'. (F. Zevi, Napoli).
'The evil later life of the villa dei Misteri'. (L. Richardson Jr., Duke University).
'La villa dei Papiri di Ercolano: programma decorativo e problemi della committenza'. (M. Wojcik, Perugia).
'San Giovanni di Ruoti: some problems in the Archaeology of the late Roman villa'. (A. Small, Roma).

6. *The British Museum Seminar of 15 February 1980 and its publication.*

The introduction to the published proceedings of this Seminar,[8] held in the Department of Greek and Roman Antiquities of the British Museum, states: 'The purpose of the seminar was to bring together an international group of scholars, currently working in Italy on Roman villas and related topics, in order to discuss current problems in advance of the completion of excavation, study and final publication.'

Papers relevant to five excavation sites are quoted below; one general survey paper is included here, that of 'Villas in South Etruria: some comments and contexts' by T.W. Potter.[9]

B.   SELECTED EXCAVATIONS

As stated above, papers on five villa excavations were circulated and discussed at the British Museum Seminar. These sites vary greatly; all but that of San Rocco have interim reports edited by K. Painter and printed in the British Museum Occasional Paper, No. 24, 1980. Brief notes on some features of special interest are offered here.

1.   *San Rocco, Francolise, Campania*

As described on p. 56, this Anglo-American project was a pioneer effort, the excavations taking place in 1962–6. Superimposed mosaic pavements, and evidence of the technique used in laying them, were then novel finds. The extent to which that part of the *villa rustica* was altered, in its final phase, to accommodate the industrial enterprises of olive-oil processing and tile-making, and the completeness of the different plans were then of importance.[10] Reconstruction drawings of this villa, by Miss Sheila Gibson, are illustrated in Figs. 1 and 2.

2.   *Via Gabina sites, Via Praenestrina, Province of Rome*

The ancient Via Gabina was the subject of a field survey by the British School at Rome.[11] Professors Philip Oliver-Smith and Walter Widrig, of Rice University, Houston, Texas, in collaboration with the Soprintendenza Archeologica di Roma, have been excavating from 1976–82 two of the sites discovered in this survey. The first, Site 11, was that of a villa with a small *hortus,* which showed successive building phases. The first of these, a very simple house with an incomplete plan, is dated to the first half of the third century B.C. and lacks parallels. But this villa is the first to have been excavated which shows, in its later phases, the conversion of a U-shaped plan, open at one end, to that of a closed square plan, complete with *atrium* and *impluvium.* This development had been hypothicated, and disputed, but can now be confirmed.

The second site proved to be a barn of very great size dated to the late fourth or fifth centuries A.D., a find which should be of interest in relation to the economy of Rome at that date.[12]

3.   *Monte Irsi, Basilicata*

Part of the excavations at Monte Irsi, in 1971–2,[13] uncovered a long nine-roomed building with three cisterns in an adjacent yard which should have been fed from its roof. The rooms, except for room 7, were open to the south-west, and must have had an agricultural function. This unique structure has been interpreted as a byre for stalling cattle (possibly oxen), with the closed room being used by the herdsman. The excavator considered it to be but part of a *villa rustica,* datable to *c.*150–100 B.C.

4.   *San Giovanni di Ruoti, Basilicata*

Work on this site, from 1977–81, is a Canadian project, under the Directorship of Professors Alastair Small and R.J. Buck, of the University of Alberta, Edmonton, in collaboration with the Soprintendenza alla Antichità di Basilicata. The site is remote, and consists of an early villa, dated to the first and second centuries A.D., which was rebuilt probably *c.* A.D. 475 and continued in use until *c.* A.D. 525, when it was detroyed in a fire. Small writes that: 'It therefore belongs to the time of Odoacer (479–92) and Theodoric (493–526) and illustrates the kind of building being erected in the Italian countryside under the Germanic kings of Italy. It is not impossible that it was destroyed in the Gothic war, which began in 535 . . .' Its structural features are unusual and are, at the time of writing, still being excavated and interpreted.

5.   *Mura di San Stefano, Anguillara, Lazio*

Research work and excavation on this enigmatic, upstanding monument is a project of the British School at Rome, under the Directorship of Dr. David Whitehouse, with strong support from the British Museum, and in collaboration with the Soprintendenza Archaeologia dell'Etruria Meridonale. Four papers about this site are published in the British Museum Occasional Paper No. 24. Originally described by Dr. Frank Sear and Dr. Margaret Lyttleton,[14] the rectangular building and its function are discussed anew by Dr. Lyttleton;[15] Dr. Anthony Luttrell contributes a paper on Roman Anguillara;[16] Miss Joyce Reynolds discusses the inscriptions found there.[17] Dr. David Whitehouse writes of an earlier knowledge of this monument (notes and a plan were made by Pirro Ligurio in the mid-sixteenth century and were later copied by Palladio), and describes the excavations[18] which took place in 1977 and 1979–81. The findings, at the time of writing, revealed an occupation of the site from the late first century B.C. to the first century A.D.; a large and richly appointed building with an adjacent cistern was erected *c.* A.D. 150; between the mid-second and fourth centuries A.D. this formed part of a larger complex, and finally a church was built over an earlier apsidal structure, in the ninth to tenth centuries A.D.

I am indebted to Dr. David Whitehouse for the following summary of the conclusions reached, up to 1980. He states that:

1. The crux of the problem is that the second century complex is (a) fairly, but not outstandingly, luxurious (plenty of porphyry, flamboyant architecture, etc.), but (b) the building is quite small and in a decidedly *un*spectacular position.
2. The cistern makes sense as part of a bath building, so that this complex has a 'tower' block, a detached bath and other structures. Certainly there is no *villa rustica;* probably there are not enough facilities to make us think that it was lived in permanently. Hence the guess: a country retreat for a rich, but not super-rich Roman.
3. The 'Roman' occupation continues, in one form or another, until at least the fifth century A.D. (on the finding of imported Gaza amphorae) and perhaps to *c.* 600 A.D. (if Dr. Whitehouse's re-dating of Forum ware is correct). As the church is of ninth or tenth century date, the main question posted is whether or not there was continuity of occupation.

6. *Sette Finistre, near Orbetello, South Etruria*

In the seven years of work (1973–81) at this large and imposing Roman villa, a research project of wide-spreading influence has been built up. In the first interim report, printed in the British Museum publication, by the Director, Professor Andrea Carandini then of Siena University and his co-field Director, Mr. Timothy Tatton-Brown, of the Canterbury Archaeological Trust, the origins and development of the project are described.[19] It is now sponsored by two influential committees, one Italian and one British. Visiting the site in 1981 with Dr. David Whitehouse, we saw some hundred and twenty students (of whom twenty-three were British) receiving practical field training in all modern excavation techniques (there was even a special 'ecological trench' in the valley, to relate the local ecology to the changing events on the hill on which the villa is sited). Even so, it is only possible to accommodate about fifty percent of would-be volunteers. This project has helped to revolutionize Italian excavation practice. In May 1981, a four-day conference, held in Siena, on excavation techniques, publication etc., with both British and Italian speakers, attracted an audience of nearly five hundred archaeologists, many of whom were students. In the early 1960s, collaboration on this scale was unheard of.

Plans of the two-period villa are approaching completion. Interim work has been exhibited in several places in Italy, at the Institute of Archaeology, London University and elsewhere. In addition to the fine 'signorile' residential quarters in this villa, the final picture of the *villa rustica* at Sette Finestre is likely to offer a fuller, more detailed and more complete account of its agricultural and industrial functions than any yet available.

Nowadays, excavations of villa sites are accompanied by intensive field surveys. This is especially evident at Ruoti, Anguillara and Sette Finistre. Pioneer work in field survey in Italy started before 1960: one of the best examples, published during the period under review, is that of one of the South Etruria series[20] in the Ager Veientanus. The pattern of 1980 has, therefore, moved a long way from that of 1960 — as it should have done in twenty years — and current studies are (or should be) concerned with the villa in its context, with the economic function, and consequently with the land use. The contrast between Piazza Armerina and Sette Finistre, as investigations, could not be stronger.

NOTES

1. von Blanckenhagen, P., Cotton, M.A. and Ward Perkins, J.B., *Notizie degli Scavi*, (1965), 237–52 and *eadem, Papers of the British School at Rome*, n.s., xx, (1965), 55–69.

2. Macdonald, A.H., *Republican Rome*, London, 1966, 131 and fig. 18 for Östenberg's plan and elevation, and McKay, A.G., *Houses, Villas and Palaces in the Roman World*, London, 1975, 103–4 and figs. 36–7.

3. Macdonald (see note 2); Boëthius, A. and Ward Perkins, J.B., *Etruscan and Roman Architecture*, London, 1970 (San Rocco II preliminary plan); McKay (see note 2); White, K.D., *Farm Equipment in the Roman World*, London, 1975; Percival J., *The Roman Villa: An Historical Introduction*, London, 1976.

4. For the definitive reports of the Francolise excavations: Cotton, M.A., *The Late Republican Villa at Posto, Francolise*, London, 1979 and Cotton, M.A. and Métraux, G., *The San Rocco Villa, Francolise*, London, forthcoming 1983.

5. Small, A., in Blake, H. McK., Potter, T.W. and Whitehouse, D.B. (eds.), *Papers in Italian Archaeology I*, Oxford, 1978, 197–201.

6. Publication forthcoming in *Papers of the British School at Rome*.

7. Potter, T.W., and Dunbabin, K.M., *Papers of the British School at Rome*, n.s., xxxiv, (1979), 19–26.

8. Painter, K. (ed.), *Roman Villas in Italy*, London, 1980.

9. Potter, T.W., in Painter, K. (ed.), *Roman Villas in Italy*, London, 1980, 73–82.

10. Cotton, M.A. and Métraux, G., *op. cit.* (see note 4) for the definitive report.

11. Ward Perkins, J.B. and Kahane, A., *Papers of the British School at Rome*, xl, (1972), 91–126.

12. Widrig, W., in Painter, K. (ed.), *Roman Villas in Italy*, London, 1980, 119–40; Cotton, M.A., *Archeologia Laziale* ii, (1979), 82–5; Oliver Smith, P. and Widrig, W., *Archaeology*, (May/June, 1980), 56–8. Both of the Directors worked with Sheppard Frere at Verulamium, and Walter Widrig was supervisor at San Rocco for the first two seasons.

13. Small, A., *Monte Irsi, Southern Italy*, Oxford, 1977.

14. Lyttleton, M. and Sear, F., *Papers of the British School at Rome*, xlv, (1977), 227–51.

15. Lyttleton, M., in Painter, K. (ed.), *Roman Villas in Italy*, London, 1980, 53–71.

16. Luttrell, A., in *ibid.*, 45–51.

17. Reynolds, J.M., in *ibid.*, 83–9.

18. Whitehouse, D., in *ibid.*, 111–17.

19. Carandini, A. and Tatton-Brown, T., in *ibid.*, 9–43.

20. Kahane, A., Murray-Threipland, L. and Ward Perkins, J.B., *Papers of the British School at Rome*, n.s., xxiii, (1968).

BIBLIOGRAPHY

Boëthius, A. and Ward Perkins, J.B., 1970, *Etruscan and Roman Architecture,* The Pelican History of Art Series, Harmondsworth.

von Blanckenhagen, P., Cotton, M.A. and Ward Perkins, J.B., 1965, 'Francolise (Caserta) — Rapporto provisorio del 1962–64 sugli scavi di due ville romane della Republica e del Primo Impero', *Notizie degli Scavi,* (1965), 237–52.

von Blanckenhagen, P., Cotton, M.A. and Ward Perkins, J.B., 1965, 'Two Roman villas at Francolise, Prov. Caserta. Interim Report on Excavations, 1962–64', *Papers of the British School at Rome,* n.s., xx, 55–69.

Carandini, A. and Tatton-Brown, T., 1980, 'Excavations at the Roman villa of "Sette Finestre" in Etruria, 1975–9. First Interim Report', *British Museum Occasional Paper*, No. 24, 9–43.

Carrington, R.C., 1931, 'Studies in the Campanian "Villae Rusticae"', *Journal of Roman Studies*, xxi, 10–130.

Cotton, M.A., 1979, *The Late Republican Villa at Posto, Francolise*, Papers of the British School at Rome, supplementary volume.

Cotton, M.A., 1979, 'Una villa ed un grande edificio romano lungo la vie Gabina', *Archeologia Laziale, ii, Secondo Incontro di Studio del Comitato per l'archeologia Laziale*, 82–5. Consiglio Nazionale delle Ricerche, Rome.

Cotton, M.A. and Métraux, G., forthcoming 1983, *The San Rocco Villa, Francolise*, Papers of the British School at Rome, supplementary volume.

D'Arms, J.H., 1970, *The Romans on the Bay of Naples*, Loeb Classical Monograph 846, Cambridge, Mass.

Kahane, A., Murray-Threipland, L. and Ward Perkins, J.B., 1968, 'The Ager Veientanus, North and South of Veii', *Papers of the British School at Rome*, n.s., xxiii.

Luttrell, A., 1980, 'Roman Anguillara', in Painter, K. (ed.), 1980, *Roman Villas in Italy*, British Museum Occasional Paper, No. 24, 45–51.

Lyttleton, M., 1980, 'The Muro di Santo Stefano near Anguillara: A roman villa?', in Painter, K. (ed.), 1980, *Roman Villas in Italy*, British Museum Occasional Paper, No. 24, 53–71.

Lyttleton, M. and Sear, F., 1977, 'A Roman Villa near Anguillara Sabazia', *Papers of the British School at Rome*, xlv, 227–51.

McDonald, A.H., 1966, *Republican Rome*, Ancient People and Places series, No. 50, London.

McKay, A.G., 1975, *Houses and Villas and Palaces in the Roman World*, London.

Oliver-Smith, P. and Widrig, W., 1980, 'Excavations on the Via Gabina, Italy', *Archaeology*, (May/June), 56–8.

Painter, K. (ed.), 1980, *Roman Villas in Italy*, British Museum Occasional Paper, No. 24, London.

Percival, J., 1976, *The Roman Villa. An Historical Introduction*, London.

Potter, T.W., 1980, 'Villas in South Etruria: Some comments and contexts', in Painter, K. (ed.), *Roman Villas in Italy*, British Museum Occasional Paper, No. 24, 73–82.

Potter, T.W. and Dunbabin, K.M., 1979, 'A Roman Villa at Crocicchie, Via Clodia', *Papers of the British School at Rome*, n.s., xxxiv, 19–26.

Reynolds, J.M., 1980, 'Mura di San Stefano, Anguillara: The Inscriptions', in Painter, K. (ed.), *Roman Villas in Italy*, British Museum Occasional paper, No. 24, 83–9.

Rossiter, J.J., 1978, *Roman Farm Buildings in Italy*, BAR International Series 52, Oxford.

Skysgaard, J.E., 1961, 'Nuove ricerche sulla *villa rustica* romana fino all'epoca di Traiano', *Analeta Romana Instituti Danici*, v. 25–40.

Small, A. (ed.), 1977, *Monte Irsi, Southern Italy*, BAR Supplementary Series 20, Oxford.

Small, A., 1978, 'The *villa rustica* of the Hellenistic period in South Italy', in Blake, H. McK, Potter, T.W. and Whitehouse, D.B. (eds.), *Papers in Italian Archaeology I*, BAR International Series 41, Oxford, 197–201.

Ward Perkins, J.B. and Kahane, A., 1972, 'The Via Gabina', *Papers of the British School at Rome*, xl, n.s., 91–126.

White, K.D., 1975, *Farm Equipment of the Roman World*, London.

Whitehouse, D., 1980, 'Anguillara: An Introduction', in Painter, K. (ed.), *Roman Villas in Italy*, British Museum Occasional Paper, No. 24, 111–17.

Widrig, W., 1980, 'Two sites on the Ancient Via Gabina', in Painter, K. (ed.), *Roman Villas in Italy*, British Museum Occasional Paper, No. 24, 119–40.

Earth's Grip Holds Them

by

BARRY CUNLIFFE

In 1072, Leofric, the first Bishop of Exeter died, leaving in his will 'one large book of English verse about various subjects' to the Cathedral Library. The *Exeter Book*, as it is now usually called, is composed of 131 leaves thought to have been copied out by a scribe in the second half of the tenth century. Among the miscellany of verse which it contains is a poem called by its editors *The Ruin* written on two leaves scarred by fire or rot to the extent that a number of lines are missing or incomplete. *The Ruin* belongs to a group of Old English poems known as 'Elegies' and is indeed elegiac in tone and subject; the poet describes the awesome magnificence of a decaying city, Roman as we may suppose — 'the work of the giants moulders away. The roofs have fallen, the towers are in ruins, the barred gate is broken. There is frost on the mortar, the gaping roofs are shattered and fallen in, and sapped by old age.'

The content and meaning of the poem has generated a considerable literature which more recently has turned to a consideration of the poet's intent. The fragmentary state of the text of the poem makes it impossible to be sure how it might have ended, though a religious lesson seems likely, and even an allegorical implication has been suggested. Elsewhere, including in Old English verse, ruins are used as symbols of instability, and so they may well be here.[1]

Much of the discussion surrounding *The Ruin* has centred upon the question of whether the poet was writing of a particular city and if so which one. The earliest commentators[2] were led by descriptions of hot springs to the conclusion that the city was Bath (*Aquae Sulis*). This view was further elaborated by Hotchner[3] and was explored in some detail, using the then-available archaeological evidence, by Leslie.[4] Other contenders for the privilege: Hadrian's Wall,[5] and Chester[6] have little to commend them[7] but it ought perhaps to be remembered, as Krapp and Dobbie implied,[8] that the poet need not have had any particular town in mind but may have been generalizing from many.

The arguments in favour of the city being Bath are twofold. First, the names by which the site of *Aquae Sulis* were known to the Saxons: *Hat Bathu, æt Baþum, Baðan* and *Bathonia* all emphasize the baths and may imply a knowledge of the former existence of Roman baths. Second, there are references in the poem which seem to apply specifically to the Roman buildings of Bath. The purpose of the present, brief contribution to the continuing debate is to explore this second contention in the light of evidence from the recent excavations.

The Archaeological Evidence

The central area of Roman Bath was occupied by three public buildings of considerable size and splendour, the temple of Sulis Minerva, the bathing establishment to the south, and a third complex (now largely beneath the Abbey) aligned on the same axis as the temple, which is likely to be either a theatre or a forum. The focus of the complex was the Sacred Spring where hot mineral waters gush out of the ground with some force at the rate of nearly half a million gallons a day. From earliest Roman times the spring was contained within an enclosing wall forming a reservoir from which the flow of water was controlled. The spring now lies beneath the King's Bath. Two lesser springs, no doubt functioning in Roman times, served the Hot Baths and the Cross Bath: all three lie within the walled area of the Roman city.

The Roman baths were cleared of their superincumbent mud and debris in the last two decades of the nineteenth century by the City Engineer, Major Davis, who failed to keep adequate records of his discoveries.[9] There were two campaigns of excavation this century[10] but both were concerned with the structural detail of areas already previously cleared. Thus, although we now understand the development of the bathing establishment reasonably fully, comparatively little evidence survives to indicate the fate of the structure in the post-Roman period.

The spring and reservoir is rather better understood. It was partially cleared by Davis in 1879 but a more extended programme of excavation was undertaken in 1979–80 bringing to light much that is new and relevant to the present discussion.[11]

The reservoir lies in the south-eastern corner of the precinct of the temple of Sulis Minerva. Parts of the temple were briefly observed during building work in the 1790s and again in the 1860s and in trial excavations in the 1960s.[12] A new programme of large scale excavation began in 1981. A reconsideration of the early work in the light of the recent discoveries enables us to give a tolerably full account of the fate of the Roman structure from the fourth to the twelfth centuries. This has some bearing on the possible interpretation of the descriptive passages given in The Ruin.

Sometime during the Roman period the spring and reservoir, which had hitherto been screened by a masonry facade, was completely enclosed with a massive wall, some 2 m. (7 ft.) thick, and was roofed with a barrel vault constructed of brick ribs infilled with hollow box tiles and rendered with pink mortar.[13] On the north side of the reservoir enclosure, facing the sacrificial altar, was constructed an ambulatory, consisting of a screen wall, enlivened by pilasters, supporting a pediment into which the arch of the large central opening intruded (Fig. 1).[14] Access to the spring, from the precinct, lay through this

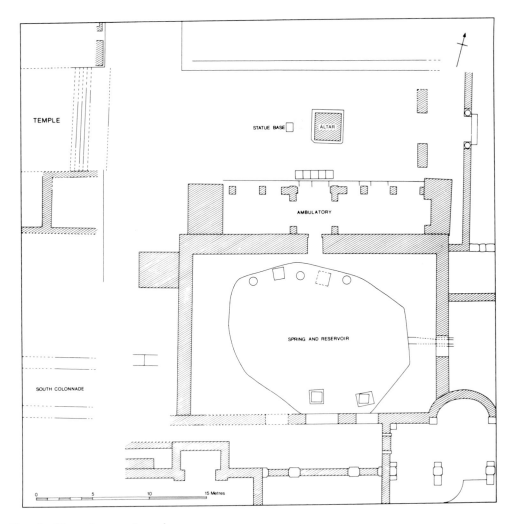

Fig. 1 Plan of reservoir enclosure.

central door, leading to a smaller door set in the north wall of the reservoir: it seems not unlikely that this approach to the sacred waters was reserved for the priests. The principal access for other suppliants was from the south: here the wall dividing the main reservoir enclosure from the baths was perforated by three large windows, a central arched opening flanked by two smaller square-headed apertures (Fig. 2).

A remarkable feature of the enclosure wall is its degree of preservation. The south wall still stands to a height of 4.3 m. (18.5 ft.) above the contemporary floor level and excavation has shown that much of the rest of the enclosure wall remained a dominant feature in the early twelfth century when it was enlivened

THE PRECINCT OF THE TEMPLE OF SULIS MINERVA

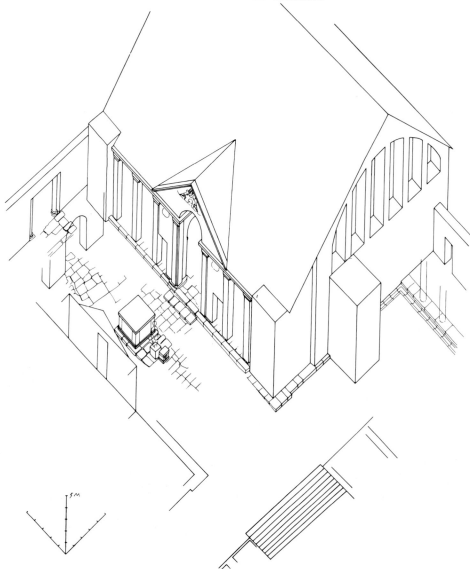

Fig. 2 Axonometric reconstruction of reservoir enclosure.

with arched recesses — a renovation after which it became known as the King's Bath.[15]

The current excavation, of the area immediately to the north of the reservoir, is presenting an unusually detailed picture of the site in the centuries following the last Roman reflooring of the precinct using Pennant slabs (Pl. I). The date of this reflooring has not yet been defined but fourth-century coins and pottery have been found immediately above it. Successive layers of mud and silt clearly demonstrate that in the late or sub-Roman period the precinct was subjected to heavy flooding, either from surface water being unable to escape or from spring water overflowing (perhaps a combination of the two). The result was the continuous formation of a thick black organic mud. Several unsuccessful attempts were made at consolidation by spreading rubble on the surface of the marsh. The last was the most substantial. At this time the ambulatory was reflooored with small stone slabs, many of which were derived from sculptured Roman structures, laid closely together with a gutter provided along the outer face of the ambulatory wall. Beyond this, to the north, a further layer of rubble was spread over the marsh. The reason for the undertaking may well have been that the marsh had risen to such an extent that it was threatening to make the ambulatory impassable.

Pl. I Pennant slab flooring of precinct.

The new arrangement functioned for some while, to judge from the wear on
the paving, before continued flooding led to a further deposit of black mud
beneath which the pavement disappeared from view. In all, three distinct sur-
facings and five layers of mud created a deposit some 0.8 m. (2.8 ft.) in thickness
above the Pennant paving. Given that the Pennant-floored precinct was in active
use during the fourth century, the last phase of stone flagging can hardly be
earlier than the sixth century and may even be as late as the seventh or eighth.[16]
The implications are significant for throughout the many phases of reflooring
and use the superstructure of the ambulatory and the reservoir enclosure must
have been standing largely intact.

The collapse of the standing structure is dramatically demonstrated, in the
precinct excavation, by a scree of massive masonry blocks, representing the
fallen ambulatory facade, together with substantial lumps of concrete from the
roof (Pl. II). The rubble forms a layer sealing the marsh deposits and floors.
What initiated the fall is unclear: gradual subsidence of foundations, deliberate
demolition or earthquake are all possibilities. The fact remains that some time in
the middle Saxon period the ambulatory fell away from the front of the reservoir enclosure and spread, as a sea of rubble, into the old temple precinct. The
fact that very few small stone building blocks were found amongst the rubble is
an indication supporting the view that the reservoir walls remained largely
intact. It is, however, possible that the brick vault had fallen in part or in whole
at this time: its shattered remains were found in the reservoir during excavation
in 1979–80 but no dating evidence for this event has come to light.

By the eighth or ninth century, we can be reasonably sure of the situation in
the centre of Bath. The spring rose through a mass of sand and rubble filling the
old reservoir in the centre of the large chamber represented at this time by a
massive enclosure wall which stood to a considerable height and which may still
have retained much of its brick-vaulted roof. The arched and square-headed
openings in the south wall were readily visible. To the north the marshy
precinct was littered with a scree of fallen masonry.

What the rest of the temple and bathing establishment looked like by the end
of the middle Saxon period is less certain. It is likely, from the surviving
evidence, that the pediment of the temple had fallen at the time of the main
collapse; but this would have left the podium of the temple and possibly part of
its *cella* still standing well above the marsh and rubble level.

To detail the fate of the bathing establishment poses largely insuperable
problems since it was cleared of overburden in Victorian times without adequate
record of the layers removed. It is, however, clear from early accounts that
black mud, representing the growth of marsh conditions, was widely encountered and that parts of the vaulted superstructure lay embedded in it. The walls,
for the most part, have been reduced to a common level of between 1–2 m. (3–7
ft.) above Roman floor level, that is, about equivalent to the level of the marsh
covering the temple precinct before the ambulatory fell. It seems likely, there-

Pl. II   Collapsed masonry of the fallen ambulatory facade and roof in the precinct.

fore, that the superstructure of the baths standing above the marsh had been removed, quite possibly to provide building material. The date of the robbing is unknown but since there is clear evidence of a late Saxon cemetery spreading across the now-buried remains of the east end of the baths[17] the Roman super-structure must have largely disappeared by then.

Although dating is necessarily imprecise the implication of the archaeological evidence, briefly summarized above, is that the reservoir enclosure and its associated structure remained standing and in use well into the middle Saxon period: indeed the walls of the reservoir were still substantial as late as the early Middle Ages. The baths on the other hand, extensively flooded, were probably reduced to marsh level much earlier, and may have been the source of constructional material used in successive rebuildings of the Saxon ecclesiastical structures lying close by. It may be relevant that the Abbey Church of St. Peter was described as 'built with marvellous workmanship' in a mid tenth-century charter and it was here, a few years later (in 973) that Edgar was crowned King of England. The tenth-century building is likely to have been built of re-used Roman stone — so too may have been its predecessors.

If *The Ruin* were composed in the eighth or ninth century, and if the poet was inspired by what he saw at Bath, the most impressive structure at the time of his visit would have been the reservoir enclosure. Its massive walls surrounded a steaming pool, banked with sand, into the centre of which the hot springs bubbled. The enclosure may still have retained part of its vaulted brick roof while the pedimented north ambulatory was either still standing or had recently fallen into a tumble of rubble. Elsewhere the rest of the baths were buried by 1–2 m. (3–7 ft.) of mud and rubble and substantial parts of the superstructure may well have already disappeared.

The Poem

The Ruin comes down to us in an incomplete fragment preserved on two leaves of the Exeter Book.[18] The rendering of the terse Old English into modern English is not easy, partly because of the damaged nature of the manuscript and partly because of the obscurity of the language incorporating, as it does, rare and sometimes unique words.

The transcription here is that of Krapp and Dobbie;[19] the translation is taken from Mackie.[20] Italics indicate editorial emendation.

Wrætlic is þes wealstan,   wyrde gebræcon;
burgstede burston,   brosnað enta geweorc.
Hrofas sind gehrorene,   hreorge torras,
hru*n*geat berofen,   hrim on lime,
5   scearde scurbeorge   scorene, gedrorene,
ældo undereotone.   Eorðgrap hafað
waldend wyrhtan   forweorone, geleorene,
heardgripe hrusan,   oþ hund cnea
werþeoda gewitan.   Oft þæs wag gebad
10   ræghar ond readfah   rice æfter oþrum,
ofstonden under stormum;   steap geap gedreas.
Wonað giet se [................]num geheapen,
fel on [....................................]
grimme gegrunden   [.......................
15   ....] scan   heo[....................
.............]g orþonc   ærsceaft [...........
..............]g[..] lamrindum beag
mod mo[..........]yne swiftne gebrægd
hwætred in hringas,   hygerof gebond
20   weallwalan wirum   wundrum togædre.

Beorht wæron burgræced,   burnsele monige,
heah horngestreon,   heresweg micel,
meodoheall monig · ᛗ · dreama full,
oþþæt þæt onwende   wyrd seo swiþe.
25 Crungon walo wide,   cwoman woldagas,
swylt eall fornom   secgrofra wera;
wurdon hyra wigsteal   westen staþolas,
brosnade burgsteall.   Betend crungon
hergas to hrusan.   Forþon þas hofu dreorgiað
30 ond þæs teaforgeapa   tigelum sceadeð
hrostbeages *h*rof.   Hryre wong gecrong
gebrocen to beorgum,   þær iu beorn monig
glædmod ond goldbeorht   gleoma gefrætwe*d*,
wlonc ond wingal   wighyrstum scan;
35 seah on sinc, on sylfor,   on searogimmas,
on ead, on æht,   on eorcanstan,
on þas beorhtan burg   bradan rices.
Stanhofu stodan,   stream hate wearp
widan wylme;   weal eall befeng
40 beorhtan bosme,   þær þa baþu wæron,
hat on hreþre.   þæt wæs hyðelic.
Leton þonne geotan   [.....................]
ofer harne stan   hate streamas
un[...
45 .]þþæt hringmere   hate [...................
.................]   þær þa baþu wæron.

Splendid is this masonry — the fates destroyed it;
the strong buildings crashed, the work of giants moulders away.
The roofs have fallen, the towers are in ruins,
the barred gate is broken. There is frost on the lime,
5 the gaping roofs are shattered and decayed,
and sapped by old age. The clutch of the grave,
the strong grip of the earth, holds the master-builders,
who have lain in corruption until a hundred generations
of peoples have passed away. Often has this wall,
10 grey with lichen and stained with red, endured one sovereignty after another,
and stood firm under storms; steep and broad, it has perished.
Still [the masonry crumbles; it has been] gashed [by weapons,
.... by files,] ....
fiercely ground ....
15 .... shone
.... the skilfully devised ancient work

.... sank into mud crusts.
[A man made active his] mind, his swift thought;
ingenious and resolute, he bound wondrously together
20   the foundations of the walls, by means of wires, into circles.
There were bright buildings, many bathing-halls,
plenty of tall pinnacles, a great noise of people,
many a banqueting-hall full of revelry
— until Fate the mighty changed everything.
25   Men fell dead all around; there came a time of pestilence;
death destroyed the whole host of the people.
Their fortified positions became waste places,
the citadel crumbled to pieces. The repairers
fell to earth in multitudes. Therefore these courts are dreary,
30   and this arch of red stone. The roof-work, strong and circular,
parts from its tiles. Has fallen in ruins to the ground,
broken into heaps; where once many a man,
glad of heart and bright with gold, splendidly arrayed,
proud and flushed with wine, shone in his armour,
35   looked upon treasure, upon silver, upon intricate gems,
upon wealth, upon possessions, upon the precious stone,
and upon this bright city with its wide dominion.
     There stood buildings of stone; the stream threw forth
a broad surging of hot water. A wall received all of it
40   within its bright bosom, where, in the centre,
were the hot baths: that was convenient.
Then they let the hot streams of water
pour .... over the gray stone
un...
45   until the circular lake .... the hot ....
.... where the baths were;
then it is ....
.... It is a royal thing
how the .... the city ....

The Inspiration

Such is the accuracy of observation that it would be difficult to believe that the poet had not stood among Roman ruins and there contemplated the transience of man. The widely held belief that the ruins were those of *Aquae Sulis* has much to commend it, nor should we forget that an inmate of the monastery at Bath (founded in the seventh century) had one of the most dramatic of surviving Roman ruins literally on his doorstep.[21]

Turning to a detailed comparison between the scene described and what we

now know to have been the situation in Bath at this time, the similarities stand
out with remarkable clarity.

Among several references to hot springs one is particularly relevant:

> the stream threw forth
> a broad surging of hot water. A wall received all of it
> within its bright bosom; there in the centre were
> the hot baths: that was convenient
> (lines 38–41)[22]

The phrase *'stream hate wearp'* is used to signify the force with which the water
gushes out while the words *hat on hreþre* implies heat generated internally.[23] The
general meaning is clear enough: a hot spring gushes up into the centre of a
walled enclosure where the water was at its hottest. This is a very accurate
description of the Roman spring and reservoir: it is a noticeable fact that the
water is, indeed, very hot at the centre of the pool, where the spring emerges,
and cools rapidly towards the periphery. In the seventeenth century the centre of
the King's Bath was provided with a timber structure, known as the Kitchen,
where the heat was so intense that not all could bear it.

The other descriptive passages, though no less dramatic, could be argued to
refer to any Roman buildings not necessarily those of *Aquae Sulis*. Taken
together, however, they could be thought to offer a convincing description of
the reservoir and surrounding structures as we now know them to have been in
the Saxon period. The structural components are clearly drawn. A decaying
brick vault is described thus:

> . . . The roof-work, strong and circular
> parts from its tiles. Has fallen in ruins to the ground,
> broken into heaps; . . .
> (lines 30–32. The meaning of line 30 is obscure in the original)

These are words which could appropriately be used to describe the brick vault
roofing the reservoir enclosure and the tumble of block and tile debris found at
the foot of the north wall after the north ambulatory had collapsed. The fallen
blocks of the central arch of the ambulatory could well have been the direct
inspiration of lines 11 and 12 which Alexander renders:[24]

> . . . high arch crashed —
> stands yet the wallstone, hacked by weapons.

Mackie's translation (above p. 75) does not accept that *gēaþ* is an adjective
meaning 'curved' or 'arched' but Leslie[25] argues the point in detail. Line 12 is a
free reconstruction of a very defective text.

An even more difficult phrase is *hēah horngestrēon* (line 22) variously rendered:
'Plenty of tall pinnacles' (Mackie); 'high, horn-gabled' (Alexander); 'a profusion
of lofty gables' (Leslie). While it would be tempting to allow the phrase to

conjure up visions of sculptured pediments the obscurity of the words should be a warning against too precise an interpretation.[26]

Lines 9 and 10 have led to lively discussion:

> . . . Often has this wall,
> grey with lichen and stained with red endured . . .

Of the various interpretations offered the most convincing is the view originally put forward by Earle[27] that the poet had in mind the iron staining caused by the spring. The brilliant rust-coloured concretion which forms on the stones as the result of fungal action in the hot mineral water is one of the most striking aspects of the stone-work around the spring. It is not at all surprising that it should have been written into the description.

Finally there are two difficult passages of precise description the meanings of which are not immediately apparent. The first appears in lines 19–20.

> . . . he bound wondrously together
> the foundations of the walls, by means of wires, into circles.

The interpretation most frequently given is that the poet was describing the iron cramps with which the Roman masons joined building blocks together. If this is what the poet had in mind he could have seen them in profusion among the tumbled stone of the north ambulatory, if, that is, he had arrived before an enterprising inhabitant had carefully removed them all, together with the lead in which they were set.[28]

Towards the end of the poem, where the manuscript is defective the word *hringmere* is used (line 45) in a context which seems to imply the flowing of the hot mineral waters to this feature. Some commentators have translated the word as 'circular tank' adding the suggestion that it refers to the Circular Bath, lying immediately to the south of the spring in the main bathing establishment. This is most unlikely for the reason that the Circular Bath would, by the mid-Saxon period, have been obscured by between 1–2 m. (3–7 ft.) of mud and debris. The more literal translation 'circular pool' may provide a clue since it is not at all impossible that the overflow of the spring water ponded up somewhere clear of the Roman ruins before finally finding its way to the River Avon. There is no archaeological evidence for this supposition but there exists a remarkable sketch view of Bath drawn between 1568 and 1588.[29] Although highly schematic the map shows a circular pool, called the Mill bath, in an open space east of the King's Bath and south of the Abbey. If the validity of the illustration is accepted then the Mill Bath could be successor of the *hringmere*.

Approaching the poem piecemeal in this manner opens the way for the accusation of wishful thinking and circular argument. But the new archaeological evidence which enables us to reconstruct the physical situation in the centre of Bath in the middle Saxon period throws *The Ruin* into sharper relief. Amid the evocation of a great decaying Roman building, which offers some circumstantial support, there is the central description of what can surely only be the sacred spring rising in the hall of the Roman reservoir enclosure. The clarity and precision of the vision, heightened by metaphor, and its remarkable closeness to the situation demonstrated by the archaeological evidence is, to say the least, striking. It persuades the present writer to the belief that the poet once stood where the excavation is now in progress and gazed in thoughtful wonder at the tumble of great stones which today briefly arrest the attention of the passing tourist.

The Sacred Spring in Dark Age Literature

The phenomenon of nearly half a million gallons of steaming hot water being extruded from the ground every day is hardly likely to have passed unnoticed in Anglo-Saxon Britain. Indeed, in addition to *The Ruin* there are two further mentions of the spring in Dark Age literature.

In Book 1 Chapter 1 of *The History of the English Church and People*, Bede notes 'The Country has both salt springs and hot springs and the waters flowing from them provide hot baths in which the people bathe separately according to age and sex.' Although unlocated, the description fits Bath well.

A more detailed account is given by Nennius in *Historia Brittonum,* a compilation based on sources of varying date put together some time early in the ninth century. In an appendix describing the wonders of Britain we are told:

> 'The third wonder is the Hot Lake, where the Baths of Badon are, in the country of the Hwicce. It is surrounded by a wall made of brick and stone, and men go there to bathe at any time, and every man can have the kind of bath he likes. If he wants, it will be a cold bath; and if he wants a hot bath, it will be hot.'[30]

The reference is clearly to the spring and to the enclosure wall which was, indeed, built in coursed ashlar masonry with tile bonding courses set at intervals (unlike the walls of the baths which had no tile courses). The meaning of the passage, which implies that the water could be made hot or cold according to the wish of the bather, is more obscure, but the possibility remains that the cold water supply to the baths was still functioning at this time.

If the Nennius reference was composed early in the ninth century (rather than just collated then) then it provides corroborative evidence for the archaeological observation that the reservoir enclosure wall remained a dominant feature throughout the Saxon period. The spring was still a notable phenomenon at the beginning of the eleventh century when the biographer of St. Dunstan refers to a place called *Bathum* where hot springs break through the surface from their hiding place in the abyss, in streaming droplets.[31] Sadly there is no reference to the state of the architectural setting at this time.

The arrival of John of Tours in Bath at the end of the eleventh century signifies a new era in the history of the spring. The Roman enclosure wall was still standing to a sufficient height to dominate the medieval and later form of the King's Bath.

This brief contribution, little more than a comment on work in progress, is offered to Sheppard Frere, in recognition of his commitment to the archaeological work at Bath on which Archaeological Trust he serves. He has been a regular visitor to the excavations over the past two decades from the time when he joined the writer there in the early 1960s and crawled, semi-dressed, through the intensely hot, rat-infested space between the temple precinct floor and the Pump Room cellar floor (followed by a trek along the Roman sewer), to the current excavation beneath the Pump Room in its air-conditioned and temperature-controlled splendour. The writer remembers with particular gratitude the many hours of guidance lavished on him in the very early stages of his career (and on many occasions since) in a considerate attempt by SSF to curb some of his worst excesses. At all times cheerful advice, willingly and wisely given, has been a great support to all SSF's many friends and colleagues.

NOTES

1. Keenan (*Tennessee Studies in Literature,* xi, (1966), 109–17) put forward the view that *The Ruin* is allegorical, the description of the city being designed to remind the reader of the fall of Babylon in the Apocalypse. Doubleday (*Journal of English and Germanic Philology,* lxxi, (1971), 369–81), however, dismisses the argument and goes on to argue that the poem is carefully structured to lead the audience to the understanding that great cities, like man, can be destroyed by the three dangerous worldly loves: the pride of life, the lust of the eyes, and the lust of the flesh. In his view *The Ruin* is a religious tract designed to teach that sin arouses the wrath of a righteous God. To make his point the poet uses as a vivid analogy, no doubt easily comprehended by its readers, the crumbling ruins of a Roman city, setting the mood in the very first line 'Splendid is this masonry — the fates destroyed it', the fates in this instance *(wyrd)* being a fatal force serving the Lord's design. Calder also rejects Keenan on the grounds that, since the text is mutilated, 'allegorical speculations based on surmise are futile' (*Neuphilologische Mitteilungen,* lxxii, (1971), 442–5).

2. Leo, H., *Carmen Anglo-Saxonicum in Codice Exoniensi servatum quod vulgo inscribitur 'Ruinae',* Halle, 1865 and Earle, J., *Proc. Bath Natur. Hist. and Antiq. Field Club,* xi, (1870–3), 259–70.

3. Hotchner, C.A., *Wessex and Old English Poetry with special consideration of 'The Ruin',* New York, 1939.

4. Leslie, R.F., *Three Old English Elegies,* Manchester, 1961, 22–8.

5. Herben, S.J., *Modern Language Notes,* liv, (1939), 37–9 and *ibid.,* lix, (1944), 72–4.

6. Dunleavy, G.W., *Philological Quarterly,* xxxviii, (1959), 115–7.

7. Both writers specially plead their cases using selected scraps of archaeological evidence. Neither appear to be in command of the full range of relevant data.

8. Krapp, G.P. and Dobbie, E.V.K., *The Exeter Book,* New York, 1936, lxv.

9. A brief history of this early work is given in Cunliffe, B.W., *Roman Bath,* Oxford, 1969.

10. Knowles, W.H., *Archaeologia,* lxxv, (1926), 1–18 and Cunliffe, B.W., *Britannia,* vii, (1976), 1–32.

11. Cunliffe, B.W., *Antiq. Journ.,* lx, (1980), 187–206.

12. Summarised with references in Cunliffe, *op. cit.* (see note 9).

13. Cunliffe, *op. cit.* (see note 11), 195–6.

14. The axonometric reconstruction must be regarded as tentative. It takes cognizance of all data at present available but since the excavation has not yet been completed it may well be subject to modification.

15. Cunliffe, *op. cit.* (see note 11), 201–4.

16. The crucial levels will be extensively examined in 1982–3. It is possible that dating evidence may be found.

17. Cunliffe, B.W., *Excavations in Bath 1950–1975,* Bristol, 1979, 89–90.

18. Krapp, G.P. and Dobbie, E.V.K., *op. cit.* (see note 8).

19. *ibid.,* 227–9.

20. Mackie, W.S. (ed.), *The Exeter Book: An Anthology of Anglo-Saxon Poetry,* London, 1934, 199–201. There are many translations and several helpful commentaries on the text. Among the fullest may be listed Krapp and Dobbie (see note 8), 364–6 and Leslie (see note 4), 67–76. I am particularly indebted to Professor Eric Stanley for guiding me away from the pitfalls. He has suggested (and I have gladly adopted) modifications to Mackie's translation to render the passages relevant to this discussion closer to their literal meaning.

21. The precise location of the monastic establishment has yet to be identified but it cannot have been many metres from the reservoir. The problem of Osric's monastery and its successors is summarised by Cunliffe: 'Saxon Bath', in Haslem, J. (ed.), *Anglo-Saxon Towns in Southern England,* Chichester, 1983.

22. Line 41 is metrically short: the word þing

is sometimes added making the reading 'that was a convenient thing'. Professor Stanley points out that, in agreement with Dobbie (line 40), the word after the semicolon (for which Dobbie has a comma) should be translated 'where'.

23. Leslie, R.F., *op. cit.* (see note 4), 75.
24. Alexander, M., *The Earliest English Poems,* Harmondsworth, 1966.
25. Leslie, R.F. *op. cit.* (see note 4), 69–70.
26. In discussion Professor Stanley has made the point that, given the context in the poem, the *horn* element *could* even be translated as the musical instrument! *Heah,* 'high, exalted' is, however, not recorded as 'loud' of sounds before the thirteenth century.
27. Earle, J., *op. cit.* (see note 2), 269.
28. Professor Stanley has however stressed that *wirum* is usually used to describe thin metal wire of the kind used in filigree work. Further he accepts Bosworth-Toller's suggestion that *weallwalan* might take with it the connotation of 'ridge, bank'. In view of these doubts the iron cramp explanation is best taken with some reserve.
29. The map is a manuscript quarto volume entitled *The Particular Description of England, with the Portratures of Certaine of the Chieffest Cities and Townes* written by William Smith who died in 1618. It is now in the Sloane Collection of the British Museum (Sloane Mss. no. 2596). First published by Green in *Proc. Bath Natur. Hist. and Antiq. Field Club,* vi, (1866), 58–74.
30. *Nennius,* edited and translated by John Morris, 1980, 40.
31. Stubbs, W., *Memorials of St. Dunstan,* London, 1870, 46.

BIBLIOGRAPHY

Alexander, M., 1966, *The Earliest English Poems,* Harmondsworth.

Calder, D.G., 1971, 'Perspective and Movement in '*The Ruin',* *Neuphilologische Mitteilungen,* lxxii, 442–5.

Cunliffe, B.W., 1969, *Roman Bath,* Society of Antiquaries of London Research Report 24, London.

Cunliffe, B.W., 1976, 'The Roman Baths at Bath: the excavations 1969–75', *Britannia,* vii, 1–32.

Cunliffe, B.W., 1979, *Excavations at Bath 1950–1975,* CRAAGS Excavation Report I, Bristol.

Cunliffe, B.W., 1981, 'The excavation of the Roman sacred spring at Bath 1979: a preliminary description', *Antiq. Journ.,* lx, (1980), 187–206.

Cunliffe, B.W., 1983, 'Saxon Bath', in Haslem, J. (ed.), *Anglo-Saxon Towns in Southern England,* Chichester.

Doubleday, J.F., 1971, '*The Ruin*: Structure and Theme', *Journal of English and Germanic Philology,* lxxi, 369–81.

Dunleavy, G.W., 1958, 'A 'De Excidio' Tradition in the Old English *Ruin',* *Philological Quarterly,* xxxviii, (1959), 115–7.

Earle, J., 1873, 'An Ancient Saxon Poem of a City in Ruins, supposed to be Bath', *Proc. Bath Natur. Hist. and Antiq. Field Club,* xi, (1870–3), 259–70.

Green, E., 1866, 'The Earliest Map of Bath', *Proc. Bath Natur. Hist. and Antiq. Field Club,* vi, 58–74.

Herben, S.J., 1939, 'The Ruin', *Modern Language Notes,* liv, 37–9.

Herben, S.J., 1944, 'The Ruin Again', *Modern Language Notes,* lix, 72–4.

Hotchner, C.A., 1939, *Wessex and Old English Poetry with special consideration of 'The Ruin',* New York.

Keenan, H.T., 1966, '*The Ruin* as Babylon', *Tennessee Studies in Literature,* xi, 109–17.

Knowles, W.H., 1926, 'The Roman baths at Bath; with an Account of the Excavations conducted during 1923', *Archaeologia,* lxxv, 1–18.

Krapp, G.P., and Dobbie, E.V.K., 1936, *The Exeter Book,* Anglo-Saxon Poetic Records III, New York.

Leo, H., 1865, *Carmen Anglo-Saxonicum in Codice Exoniensi servatum quod vulgo inscribitur 'Ruinae'*, Halle.

Leslie, R.F., 1961, *Three Old English Elegies*, Manchester.

Mackie, W.S. (ed.), 1934, *The Exeter Book: An Anthology of Anglo-Saxon Poetry, Part II, Poems ix–xxxii*, Early English Text Society, Original Series 194, London.

Stubbs, W., 1870, *Memorials of St. Dunstan*, Rolls Series 52, London.

The Enclosure of Romano-British Towns in the Second Century A.D.

by

B.R. HARTLEY

Debate about the nature, origins and dates of town defences played a considerable part in Romano-British studies in the 1950s and 1960s.[1] It stemmed originally from discussions at the Great Casterton Summer School which were themselves prompted by the School's excavations at the local small town. A major point from the start, probably first put by Dr. Webster, was the idea that D. Clodius Albinus may have been responsible for ordering the building of town defences (and in the original version of the hypothesis specifically of town walls), because he had realized that sooner or later he would have to take troops away from Britain to fight Septimius Severus. This suggestion, as expounded by Dr. Corder, had immediate and obvious attractions, but it was slowly appreciated over the next few years that many town walls were considerably later than Albinus's governorship. Even so it was still necessary to think of the ditches and banks known to have preceded the walls at many towns as second-century, or potentially so. The attempt to find an historical context for their construction led to various solutions. First, Mr. Wacher drew attention to the possible effect of, not only the presumed Brigantian revolt of the 150s, but also the troubles of A.D. 182, while also taking into account the possibility that there had been problems in Wales. Subsequently, however, he felt that he would prefer to opt for A.D. 196–7, perhaps with some intervention from Wales or Dumnonia, as giving the best tentative hypothesis. That view still prevails in his book on Romano-British towns.[2] In the interval the case for this dating was forcefully argued by Professor Frere in his *Britannia*, and it has been widely accepted.

As with the original Corder hypothesis, the attraction of links with an historical event is undeniable and I was willing to accept it for a considerable time. Gradually, however, doubts set in and a former pupil's questioning of the idea in tutorial discussion led to reconsideration of the evidence.[3] We now have considerably more information about the earlier history of town enclosure in Britain, more evidence bearing on the dates of earthworks and of their presence at particular sites, and here and there some degree of re-interpretation is possible. Curiously enough this applies at Great Casterton itself. In view of all this it seems to be time to reopen the debate, and to start with it is necessary to review the nature and quality of the published evidence. This is done first for the towns certainly or possibly at *caput civitatis* level and then for the lesser towns or enclosed villages with evidence of early banks.

MAJOR TOWNS

Aldborough

Aldborough's bank is dated by two sherds from bowls with decoration assignable to Cinnamus of Lezoux, and in his 'standard' style. A.D. 150 or later.[4]

Brough-Petuaria

If relevant to the small town, the earlier bank at Brough-on-Humber is dated only by a bowl in the style of one of the Quintilianus Group of Lezoux to A.D. 125 or later.[5]

Caerwent

At Caerwent the latest sherd from the early bank in the Nash-Williams excavations may be dated to A.D. 130 or later.[6] Accepting, as surely one must, Professor Frere's reinterpretation of the sections at the eastern gate, the latest material from the bank may be slightly later.[7] No decorated samian later than the Hadrianic-Antonine period was found, but one cup of form 33 was assessed as 'probably Antonine' by Dr. Grace Simpson. Two sherds of imitation samian are strictly undated and probably undatable. The *terminus* is therefore about A.D. 130 or 140.

Caistor-by-Norwich

So far as I know, no dating is available for the early ditches known from aerial photography at Caistor which are assumed, probably rightly, to belong to a civil rather than a military boundary.[8]

Canterbury

No defence existed before the walled circuit of the late-third century.

Carmarthen

At Carmarthen the bank is dated at one point by (unpublished?) early-Antonine samian.[9] If the excavator's interpretation of another site is right, we may add a worn (?) coin of Antoninus Pius, a sherd of decorated samian ware in the Cerialis-Cinnamus style and another which looks more like the 'standard' Cinnamus style.[10] The *terminus* is therefore in the region of A.D. 140–50.

Chichester

In the section which first produced evidence of an early bank at Chichester two 'everted-rim jars, two cavetto-rim jars and a sherd of a poppyhead beaker' gave the evidence of date. In Mr. Holmes's opinion this suggested that the wall was built 'a few years later than A.D. 200, but that the bank was thrown up earlier'.[11] The sherds are not illustrated and further comment is therefore impossible.

Cirencester

At Cirencester the Verulamium and Bath Gates have been shown to be earlier structurally than both the stone wall and the preceding earthwork. Dating evidence from the bank is not yet abundantly published. The latest material seems to be colour-coated ware and a coarse-ware bowl, all certainly later than the beginning of the Antonine period. However, the samian form 81 taken as an indicator of Antonine date is not reliable, since the form was stamped by Trajanic and Hadrianic potters and is rather rare in the Antonine period. A vaguely Antonine date is all that may be deduced.[12]

Dorchester-Durnovaria

At one point Dorchester's rampart was not constructed before A.D. 140, but elsewhere there are complications, since a rampart said to have been constructed after A.D. 150, just possibly with an associated timber tower, was found to be a secondary to a bank 15 m. (50 ft.) wide.[13] A possible retaining wall to the rear of the early bank adds another complication. The pottery offering the *terminus* of A.D. 150 does not seem to have been published.

Exeter

The work at Exeter's south gate in 1964–5 gave a strong hint that the gate went with an earthwork and at the same time gave a *terminus* of A.D. 150 for the rampart, partly from included sherds, partly from the layer sealed by it, which produced decorated vessels in the Cerialis-Cinnamus style, by Albucius, and in the 'standard' Cinnamus style, though with one of the less common ovolos. Nothing that has come to light since the publication of Stanfield and Simpson, *Central Gaulish Potters* suggests a starting date later than A.D. 150 for the normal Cinnamus bowls. This bowl's ovolo could have been a little later, but there is no clear evidence that it was necessarily so, and a *terminus post quem* of A.D. 150 must stand.[14]

Ilchester

Ilchester is included here on the slight possibility that it was a *caput civitatis* in the second century. The bank appears to have been given a palisade in the second phase, before the much-later addition of a town wall. The bank is said to belong to the late second or third century, though the grounds for this statement are not apparent.[15]

Leicester

Although Leicester was a town which developed late, it is still surprising that no bank is known to precede the stone wall.

Silchester

Silchester's defences, although with some problems in the first century, were admirably investigated and published by Mrs. Cotton long ago.[16] Her evidence showed that a bank preceded the town wall on the same circuit, and at least one of the gates is known to have belonged to it.[17] The coarse pottery in the bank goes down to the Antonine period, but there is nothing likely to be mid- or late-Antonine. The samian ware is more helpful. Although the Walters form 81 found below the bank cannot be dated later than Trajan, it should be noted that the dish of form 32 recorded from the bank should be later than A.D. 160 and is consistent with the coin of A.D. 154–5 also in the bank, though without its state of wear recorded.[18] A *terminus* of A.D. 160 seems inevitable.

Verulamium

The Fosse at Verulamium was the first of the British second-century earthworks to be investigated, though at the time it was taken as first-century.[19] The bank itself produced only first-century pottery, but the later identification of the real early earthwork and the realisation that the London and Chester stone gates went with the Fosse allow a re-dating. The gates overlay coins of Trajan and Hadrian respectively (A.D. 103–11 and 118–9, both in good condition). Below the former was a decorated sherd by Criciro of Lezoux which must be later than A.D. 135 and a stamp of Attianus from a die represented in the Castleford shop of A.D. 140–50. The Chester gate overlay a sherd said to have an ovolo 'rather like that of the Trajan-Hadrian pottery Ciriuna of Heiligenberg.'[20] If the sherd was anything to do with Heiligenberg, then an early-Antonine date would be more appropriate. Formally, however, the *terminus* for the Fosse earthwork is A.D. 135.

Winchester

Apart from the early, and possibly unfinished, Winchester earthwork of about A.D. 90–100, there was a second-century bank which has produced Antonine samian ware, though apparently nothing obviously mid- or late-Antonine.[21] Interestingly enough the additions to the bank did contain a sherd by Casurius which should be later than A.D. 160.

Wroxeter

The bank at Wroxeter has produced decorated ware in the 'standard' Cinnamus style and also bowls of the Cerialis-Cinnamus type.[22] (It may be noted here that the wall was later cut into the bank not far from its crest.)

From the bald summaries above it will be seen that the normal *terminus* for the construction of the earthwork circuits is around A.D. 140–50. Only at Silchester is there any compelling reason to think of a date after A.D. 160.

LESSER TOWNS

Towns with no evidence for early banks preceding walled circuits are omitted here.

Alcester

At Alcester a clay bank has been dated to the 'second century or later'.[23] No specific evidence has been published.

Bannaventa

A bank may be inferred for Bannaventa from the presence of a ditch under the town wall, but it seems to be undated, as yet.[24]

Bath

The bank at Bath does not seem to have produced anything necessarily later than the early-Antonine period. A form 37 bowl 'in the style of Paternus' is dated Hadrianic-Antonine and so presumably belonged to one of the earlier Paterni of Lezoux, though it is not illustrated in the report. An example of form Curle 21 which Mr. Dannell thought probably earlier than A.D. 150 is interesting. The form is not yet attested before the Antonine period and only one or two examples reached Antonine Scotland.[25]

Bitterne

The suggested early rampart at Bitterne (Clausentum) is so ill-dated that nothing useful can be said.[26]

Caister-by-Yarmouth

The civil nature of the site is not beyond question. It appears initially to have been enclosed by a palisade.[27]

Chelmsford

A short-lived earthwork is thought to have been built at Chelmsford about A.D. 160–75 and to have been demolished about A.D. 200–20. It would be particularly interesting to have the evidence for these dates in full.[28]

Dorchester, Oxfordshire

At Dorchester the bank and the features below it have produced much evidence which has been fully published.[29] The suggested dating rests rather heavily on some black-burnished ware which should probably now be placed earlier, in view of the changed northern dating, supported by the more recent evidence from Verulamium. In addition one of the samian decorated pieces must also be dated earlier.[30] However, the coin of A.D. 154–5 with little wear and a samian bowl of Advocisus or an associate allow a *terminus* of A.D. 160.

Godmanchester

Although the details are somewhat obscure, there was evidently a second-century ditch around Godmanchester. Presumably this would have had an associated bank, though some of the buildings seem to be extraordinarily close to the ditch. The suggested Hadrianic date of this work needs to be substantiated.[31]

Great Casterton

It is ironic in view of its place in the history of the study that the contemporaneity of the bank and wall at Great Casterton must be open to serious doubt. The wall's foundations fail to penetrate down to the natural subsoil, thus strongly suggesting that the foundation trench was dug into an existing bank not far from its crest. If this is right, the curious step in the bank's profile behind the wall could well be due to the mason's trench for dressing the upper, inner face of the wall from a little below the top of the bank.[32]

Given an early bank, it is firmly dated to the period when colour-coated ware was readily available. However, in this area particularly, there is no need for that to be put later than A.D. 150–60.

Irchester

Though the evidence is not particularly good and consists almost entirely of local coarse pottery, the bank at Irchester was dated to A.D. 150 or later by the excavator. Colour-coated ware was absent here, but the sample of bank was relatively small.[33]

Kenchester

At Kenchester the early bank has yielded black-burnished ware and a fragment of samian form 46. Both point to an Antonine *terminus* but one not necessarily later than A.D. 140 or so.[34]

Margidunum

The recent isolation of the early bank of Margidunum was a considerable step forward in unravelling the history of this difficult site.[35] In the bank the latest sherd was from a samian bowl ascribed to Pugnus, but now known to have been made by Secundus of Lezoux, whose work is akin to the 'standard' Cinnamus style and almost certainly of the same date.[36] The *terminus* is therefore to be put at A.D. 150.

Mildenhall

Although a circuit of defences at Mildenhall earlier than the town wall is well-attested no evidence of its date seems to have been published.[37]

Rocester

Since a sherd of Derbyshire ware from the early bank at Rocester may now be seen as potentially much earlier than the Antonine period,[38] we are reduced to dating by one sherd of colour-coated ware. Dr. Webster put it in the second half of the second century.

Rochester

At Rochester the pottery from the early ditch, filled when the wall was built, was thought to be consistent with a date in the second half of the second century. Pits sealed by the early bank were later given a 'late second-century date', but this cannot be checked, as the pottery is not identified in the report.[39]

Thorpe, Notts.

At Thorpe, as Mr. Wacher kindly tells me, the early ditch was open in the later Roman period, but the date of its bank is unknown.

Wanborough

A defensive ditch at Wanborough has been dated to the late second or early third century. Presumably it once had a bank, but the latter obviously could not be dated by material in the ditch.[40]

Worcester

Worcester apparently also has a ditch without an associated bank surviving. Its dimensions suggest that it belonged to the late (fourth-century) type of defence, though it was dated in preliminary reports to the late second or third century.[41]

York

Since the status of York in the second century is unknown, it is included here. Records made when a communications tunnel cut the *colonia* rampart show a stone wall faced on the inside and a construction trench behind it cutting through what must be an early bank. No dating evidence was recorded.[42]

DISCUSSION

We may now see that the evidence from the lesser towns, though not as abundant as that from the civitas centres, and rarely adequately published, is curiously consistent with it. The *termini* again fall around A.D. 150 or 160 where precision is possible.

The decorated samian ware from the early banks as a whole is now not negligible in quantity. The latest bowls are almost invariably Hadrianic, Hadrianic-Antonine or early- to mid-Antonine. In particular the work of Cinnamus and his associates turns up frequently. Equally impressive is the almost total absence of bowls by common potters whose careers began a little later than Cinnamus's, such as Advocisus, Casurius, Doeccus, Iullinus, Iustus, Mercator and the late Paternus of Lezoux and his associates. Advocisus's work occurs once (at the Oxfordshire Dorchester), but none of the others is represented at all. This is particularly striking for the Paternus Group, because their wares are almost as common in Romano-British towns as the work of Cinnamus. If the banks which we have been considering went up around A.D. 196, the absence of these wares is difficult to explain.

It is, of course, usually very much easier to produce a *terminus post quem* for an earthwork than a *terminus ante quem*. Fortunately, however, one of Miss Jennifer Braund's specific queries involved the unfinished nature of the Fosse at Verulamium, and an examination of the evidence made it clear that the work there was begun before A.D. 160. Failure to complete the Fosse in an emergency in A.D. 196 has always had to be explained by somewhat embarrassing rationalisation. In fact there is a perfectly good context in the history of the town in which the building of an earthwork might have had to be called off, namely the devastation caused by the Antonine fire about A.D. 155–60. The *terminus post quem* arrived at above (p. 87) would be a perfectly reasonable one for work in progress in the 150s. Interruption of work would have been inevitable in view of the need to clear away the debris of the fire, and it is surely significant that a thick layer of burnt material was found by Wheeler dumped on the back of the Fosse bank.[43] Furthermore, the continuing need to rebuild much of the town, presumably at both public and private expense, would mean that resources to continue the Fosse would not be available for a considerable time. In the end, the time never came.

It is now known that at least three towns in Britain had been given enclosure in the first century A.D., namely Verulamium, Silchester and Winchester. The reasons need not concern us, though it may be worth pointing out that the last could have had nothing to do with Cogidubnus, in view of the most recent evidence of date (p. 87). In addition, before the middle of the second century the three existing *coloniae* evidently had walls. In other words Britain already had a considerable tradition of enclosing towns when the Verulamium authorities began the work on the Fosse earthwork, and there were already some major stone gates in existence at the *coloniae*. A possible explanation of the earthworks of the Antonine period is simply that the *municipium* at Verulamium and the unchartered towns elsewhere were acting in the established tradition, and perhaps also copying the colonists, at a time when they had completed their programmes of major public buildings and had both finance and trained labour to hand. Certainly the provision of stone gates at Cirencester, Silchester and Verulamium and their probable use at Caerwent and Exeter would fit well with the kind of emulation envisaged. Moreover, since almost a third of our major towns are now known or suspected to have had such gates, it seems possible that the phenomenon was normal rather than exceptional. All this activity would have been natural enough if the towns wished to enhance their standings while also giving themselves the advantages of controlling traffic (could local taxes have played a part here?), and a means of preventing entry by undesirables after dark.

The evidence for dates discussed above is certainly not inconsistent with the idea of a purely civil impetus behind the enclosures. Verulamium must have been at work before A.D. 160, and possibly before A.D. 155.[44] The other towns could all have been at work then or up to a decade or two later.

Nevertheless, there are some difficulties about this view. For instance, it seems particularly odd that the early bank at Cirencester had stone internal towers, which seem more appropriate to a military defence.[45] Or was it a matter of slavish imitation of the colonial (ex-legionary) defences? Secondly, the apparent tight range of *termini* for the construction of banks obviously might hint at the kind of specific emergency embodied in the original Corder suggestion, though I have always felt that it would have been distinctly sanguine to hope that unarmed and totally untrained Romano-British townsmen, even with the inevitable sprinkling of army veterans, could have held such circuits against anything more than a small party of raiders. However, granting for the moment a catastrophic cause for defences, coupled with an imperial directive to crenellate, it is difficult to point to an incident which would fit. The defences would have to be virtually contemporary and therefore earlier than A.D. 160 or so on the Verulamium evidence. Here the possible Brigantian revolt of the 150s is attractive chronologically, but such a widespread reaction to a northern event seems less likely. Here and there, too, the reaction would have to be thought of as slightly delayed (Silchester and Dorchester). The hints of trouble in Essex in the later second century are interesting and we badly need to see firmer evidence of the date or dates in question, though they are thought to be rather too late to fit with Verulamium.[46] The seeming absence of comparable defences to the British ones in Gallia Belgica does not encourage a connection between the Essex sites and the invasion of north-eastern Gaul by the Chauci in the early 170s. Neither this episode, nor the war in north Britain under Commodus, is likely to have prompted the British earthworks in general and both would be impossible for Verulamium.

The bearing on the subject of the well-known rescripts of Marcus Aurelius is obscure.[47] It may now seem likely that the rescripts are later than the British defences. Could it possibly be the emperor's reaction to reports of widespread crenellation in Britain? After all we do not know what regulation, if any, applied to provincial towns before the rescripts.

On balance, though admitting the problems, I incline towards accepting a purely civilian initiative for the British enclosures, and prefer to think of them as that, rather than as defences in the military sense at this stage of their history. Nevertheless, the history of this particular subject shows only too clearly how the apparent 'facts' can change in a relatively short time. The hypothetical element must be stressed. Even so it does seem clear that the Verulamium evidence will need to be given due weight in future debate.

As so often with Romano-British studies, the subject dealt with above is one to which Sheppard Frere has contributed notably. It is particularly pleasing that a combination of evidence from his own excavations at Verulamium with earlier work offers the key to this chronological problem.

NOTES

1. Corder, P., *Archaeol. Journ.*, cxii, (1956), 20. Wacher, J.S., *Archaeol. Journ.*, cxix, (1964); *The Civitas Capitals of Roman Britain*, Leicester, 1966, 60; *Antiquity*, xxxix, (1965), 225. Frere, S.S., *ibid.*, 137; *Britannia: a history of Roman Britain*, Oxford, 1967, 248. Jarrett, M.G., *Antiquity*, xxxix, (1965), 57.

2. Wacher, J.S., *The Towns of Roman Britain*, London, 1975, 72. See also *idem*, *Roman Britain*, London, 1978, 97–8.

3. I am most grateful to Miss Jenny Braund for making me think about the problems, and particularly about the Fosse at Verulamium.

4. Charlesworth, D., 'The Defences of Isurium Brigantum', in Butler, R.M. (ed.), *Soldier and Civilian in Roman Yorkshire*, Leicester, 1971, 158.

5. Wacher, J.S., *Excavations at Brough-on-Humber 1958–1961*, Society of Antiquaries of London Research Report 25, London, 1969, 22 and 28 with fig. 48, 5.

6. *Archaeologia*, lxxx, (1930), pl. lxxxiv, S96.

7. Frere, S.S., *Britannia* (see note 1), 249, commenting on *Archaeol. Cambrensis*, ciii, (1954), 57, with pottery at 64, nos. 27–38.

8. Note however the pertinent queries in Wacher, J.S., *The Towns of Roman Britain* (see note 2), 234.

9. *Carmarthenshire Antiquary*, vi, (1970), pages not numbered in the offprint.

10. James, H., 'Excavations at Church Street, Carmarthen, 1976', in Boon, G.C. (ed.), *Monographs and Collections. I: Roman Sites*, Cambrian Archaeological Association, Cardiff, 1978, 70–1.

11. *Sussex Archaeological Collections*, c, (1962), 89–90.

12. *Antiq. Journ.*, xxxvii, (1957), 213 with fig. 3, 6; certainly Antonine or later.

13. *Proc. Dorset Natur. Hist. Soc.*, lxxvii, (1955), 129; *Britannia*, ii, (1971), 279 and iv, (1973).

14. *Proc. Devon Archaeol. Soc.*, xxvi, (1968), 1.

15. *Britannia*, ii, (1971), 278.

16. *Archaeologia*, xcii, (1974), 121.

17. *Britannia*, vii, (1976), 368.

18. *ibid.*, 148, no. 6.

19. Wheeler, R.E.M. and Wheeler, T.V., *Verulamium: A Belgic and Two Roman Cities*, Society of Antiquaries of London Research Report 11, London, 1936, 56.

20. *ibid.*, 63, For demonstration that the stone gates were earlier than the stone wall, and thus presumably contemporary with the Fosse, see Frere, S.S., *Verulamium Excavations*, Vol. II, Society of Antiquaries of London Research Report, (forthcoming).

21. *Antiq. Journ.*, l, (1970), 284.

22. *Trans. Birmingham Archaeol. Soc.*, lxxviii, (1962), 34; *Archaeologia*, lxxxviii, (1938), 197 with fig. 3, 14–16.

23. *Journal of Roman Studies*, lvi, (1966), 206.

24. *Britannia*, iii, (1972), 325.

25. Cunliffe, B.W., *Roman Bath*, Society of Antiquaries of London Research Report 24, London, 1969, 169 and 172.

26. Cotton, M.A. and Gathercole, P.W., *Excavations at Clausentum, Southampton 1951–1954*, Ministry of Works Archaeological Reports no. 2, London, 1958, 33–4.

27. *Norfolk Archaeology*, xxxiii, (1963–5), 94; xxxiv, (1966–9), 59.

28. Drury, P.J., 'Roman Chelmsford-Caesaromagus', in Rodwell, W. and Rowley, T. (eds.), *The 'Small Towns' of Roman Britain*, B.A.R. British Series 15, Oxford, 1975, 159.

29. *Archaeol. Journ.*, cxix, (1964), 114; *Oxoniensia*, ii, (1937), 52 with fig. 14, 6.

30. By Cettus, for whom see *Britannia*, iii, (1972), 34..

31. Green, H.J.M., 'Roman Godmanchester', in Rodwell, W. and Rowley, T. (eds.), *op. cit.* (see note 28), 183.

32. Corder, P. (ed.), *The Roman Town and Villa at Great Casterton, Rutland*, Nottingham, 1951, fig. 3 with 13–14.

33. *Archaeol. Journ.*, cxxiv, (1967), 114–15.

34. *Transactions of the Woolhope Club*, xxxv, (1956), 142 and 145.

35. *Transactions of the Thoroton Society*, lxxiii, (1969), 45.

36. *Britannia*, iii, (1972), 35.

37. I have found none in *Wiltshire Archaeo-*

logical *Magazine* or *Britannia*, that is to say.

38. *North Staffordshire Journal of Field Studies*, ii, (1962), fig. 3, 25 with *Antiq. Journ.*, li, (1971), 61.

39. *Archaeol. Cantiana*, lxxviii, (1963), p. liv; lxxxvii, (1972), 124.

40. *Britannia*, viii, (1977), 416.

41. *Journal of Roman Studies*, lvii, (1967), 183.

42. The records are in the Yorkshire Museum, York, Mrs. E.G. Hartley kindly told me about them.

43. Wheeler, R.E.M. and Wheeler, T.V., *op. cit.* (see note 19), pl. xviii.

44. On the date of the fire: Frere, S.S., *Verulamium Excavations Vol. I*, Society of Antiquaries of London Research Report 28, London, 1972, 73.

45. Wacher, J.S., *The Towns of Roman Britain* (see note 2), 302.

46. Rodwell in Rodwell, W. and Rowley, T., *op. cit.* (see note 28), 93. Although this writer is credited with a hand in the dating, it was an unconscious one, in that he did not know that any of the material was from significant burnt groups, and he cannot now isolate the relevant stamps.

47. Frere, S.S., *Britannia* (see note 1), 250. Mr. Wacher has a fuller discussion of the problem of the rescripts in a forthcoming paper, which he has kindly shown me. Our minds seem to have been working independently along somewhat similar lines. I am also grateful to him for references to some recent works.

The Internal Planning of Roman Auxiliary Forts

by

MARK HASSALL

Thirty years ago, Sir Ian Richmond, in a seminal paper on Roman Britain and Roman Military Antiquities,[1] briefly attempted to correlate specific sizes and types of Roman auxiliary units — as known for example from the tract of Hyginus[2] — to a number of British auxiliary forts. Hyginus poses problems including those of date which have recently been discussed by Sheppard Frere,[3] while excavations of the fort at Strageath[4] and the fortress of Longthorpe,[5] and subsequent exercises at interpretation have been carried out by him with characteristic vigour. This short paper then, which takes as its starting point auxiliary unit size and organization (in part based on the evidence of Hyginus), and which is then concerned with the interpretation of fort plans, is offered to him by one of his former pupils as a token of affectionate respect and gratitude.[5]

A. THE STRENGTH AND ORGANIZATION OF AUXILIARY UNITS

The evidence for the theoretical establishment strength and organization of the different types of auxiliary unit in the Roman army has most recently been surveyed by Paul Holder[6] and an extended discussion will not be attempted here. Only in the case of the part-mounted units (cohortes equitatae) are there real problems of interpreting the evidence and these have accordingly been treated at greater length. From Hyginus and other sources we learn that there were six types of auxiliary unit comprising:

1. *Cohors peditata quingenaria*

An infantry regiment containing nominally 500 men. Like nine of the ten legionary cohorts,[7] this consisted of six centuries of eighty, that is 480 men in all. Each century was subdivided into ten sections of eight men who shared a tent or barrack accommodation (contubernium).

2. *Cohors peditata milliaria*

An infantry regiment containing nominally 1,000 men. Like the enlarged first cohort of a legion this comprised 800 men. But unlike the legionary first cohort which was commanded by five centurions each in charge of a double strength century, the auxiliary milliary cohort consisted of ten ordinary sized centuries each under the command of a centurion. Again the smallest sub–unit was the *contubernium* of eight men, there being ten *contubernia,* or eighty men to a century.

3. *Ala quingenaria*

A cavalry regiment containing nominally 500 men. Hyginus states that this type of unit consisted of sixteen *turmae* (troops) of, presumably, about thirty men, probably thirty-two, to give a total of 512. Each *turma* will in that case have consisted of four *contubernia.* The *turmae* were commanded by decurions, who according to Hyginus were provided with separate accommodation.

4. *Ala milliaria*

A cavalry regiment containing nominally 1,000 men. This unit, according to Hyginus, was divided in twenty-four *turmae.* If each *turma* was of the same size as suggested above for the *ala quingenaria,* that is thirty-two men or four *contubernia* of eight men, then the total strength of the unit will have been 768 men if the decurions are not counted.

(Alternatively the *turmae* in the milliary *ala* may have numbered forty men — five *contubernia* of eight — making a total of 960 men).

In addition to the cohorts of infantry and *alae* of cavalry there were "mixed" units, *cohortes equitatae* or "part–mounted" cohorts.[8]

5. *Cohors quingenaria equitata*

A "part-mounted" cohort nominally of 500 men. According to Hyginus this had six centuries and half the number of *turmae* found in a *cohors milliaria equitata.*[9] Unfortunately the figure for the number of *turmae* in this latter type of unit is missing from Hyginus' book. As we shall see, it may have been ten or eight. Most scholars believe that it was eight, in which case there were four *turmae* in the quingenary version. If each *turma* consisted of thirty-two men there would have been 128 troopers in a unit of this sort. Hyginus actually says there were half the number of troopers than were to be found in the *cohors milliaria equitata* (a figure he gives as 240), that is 120 men. If there were ten *turmae* in a *cohors milliaria equitata* and five in a *cohors quingenaria equitata,* then we should probably reckon on only three *contubernia* per *turma,* or, alternatively, of four *contubernia* of six, in both cases giving a *turma* a strength of twenty-four, for a total of precisely 120 men. In addition to Hyginus we also have the evidence of papyri, examined in the next section, and of the fort plans examined in the final part. The annual status reports, *pridiana,* of three part-mounted quingenary cohorts seem to support the figure of four *turmae,* but the rosters of the *Cohors*

XX Palmyrenorum support that of five *turmae*. As regards the fort plans the evidence can be used both ways, and detailed discussion will be found below; here it is enough to state that four *turmae*, each of four *contubernia*, fit into two eight-*contubernia* barrack blocks, but five *turmae* of four *contubernia* fit into two ten-*contubernia* barrack blocks with two and a half *turmae* in each.

Turning to the six centuries, if these numbered eighty men each there would be a total of 480 infantry. Add the cavalry, 128 or 120, and a grand total of 608 (or 600) is arrived at, considerably over the nominal strength of 500. It may be, however, that the strength of the century was reduced. If so, it is tempting to suggest that the century consisted of sixty-four men (eight *contubernia* of eight each) or seventy-two (nine *contubernia* of eight men). In the former case there would be an infantry total of 384, and a grand total of 512 (the same as a quingenary *ala*), or 504, depending on whether there were 128 or 120 cavalry. In the latter case there would be an infantry total of 432 and grand totals of 552 or 560. Another way of reducing the century size would be to retain the number of *contubernia* but reduce the number of men per *contubernium* from eight to six, for a total of sixty per century, an infantry total of 360 and grand totals of 480, or 488 depending on the number of cavalry.

6.   *Cohors milliaria equitata*

Part-mounted infantry cohort nominally of 1,000 men. Hyginus states that it[10] had ten centuries, corresponding to the milliary all-infantry regiment. If each century numbered eighty men there will have been 800 infantry. To this must be added the 240 cavalry that he mentions for a total of 1,040. This total will be correspondingly less depending on whether the century size was less than eighty, i.e. seventy-two, sixty-four or sixty. But how many *turmae* of cavalry were there? Here it will be as well to quote the actual text of Hyginus (27) as it has been transmitted:

> *Habet itaque cohors equitata milliaria centurias X peditum, equites CCXL turmas decuriones.*[10]

It is quite clear that a number has dropped out following *turmas* (or perhaps after both *turmas* and *decuriones*) and since the word *decuriones* occurs again in the next line the suggestion was made over four hundred years ago by R.H. Schele that the original text read *turmas* X or *decem,* And that a tired scribe substituted *decuriones* for it.[11]

As mentioned above there is evidence, both archaeological and, above all, papyrological for the number of *turmae* in the quingenary part-mounted cohort, and since Hyginus tells us that there were half the number of *turmae* in that type of unit, as compared to the milliary version, to solve the problems surrounding the organization of the smaller type is to solve those of the larger. It is time to turn to the papyri.

B. PAPYROLOGICAL EVIDENCE FOR THE ORGANIZATION AND STRENGTH OF *COHORTES EQUITATAE*

Whatever the theoretical establishment strength of auxiliary units, the actual strength is likely to have differed from it, units normally, especially in peace time, being below their nominal strength and in war time possibly above. Roman military papyri, of which a selection are described below, can tell us both something about the actual strength of units and something about the way in which they were organized. They thus, together with inscriptions, provide an invaluable check on the information transmitted by Hyginus and other literary sources. The most important classes of document, for these purposes are muster rolls, i.e. for *Cohors XX Palmyrenorum* from Dura, and the status reports, whether annual *(pridiana)*, monthly, or daily. These last were compiled century by century, as we know from reports written in ink on potsherds at Bu Ngem or wooden writing tablets at Vindolanda.[13]

Muster rolls of *Cohors XX Palmyrenorum*

Four muster rolls, or rosters, were recovered from the archives of the unit in garrison at Dura on the Euphrates. They range in date from A.D. 219 to A.D. 256. Of these the most useful is the earliest which, besides being one of the more complete examples, also gives totals of the men in the six centuries and five *turmae* that comprised the unit. The totals, which survive for three of the centuries only, number between 140 and 150 men, and the evidence of the lists of names themselves show that these figures are true totals. Parts of the totals of all five *turmae* are preserved, though with a single exception, one of 134, all are in a fragmentary state; nevertheless at least one of the other *turmae* had a total of over 140. However these figures do not correspond with the actual numbers in the respective *turmae* which averaged roughly half the nominal totals. No explanation has been advanced for these inflated nominal totals in the *turmae*. Taking the actual strength of the *turmae* to be about seventy, *Cohors XX Palmyrenorum*, consisted, in the early third century, of six centuries of between 140 and 150 men each, and five *turmae* of roughly seventy men each, a total of over 1,200 men or even more if small detachments of camel riders enrolled on the strengths of the centuries are included!

In interpreting these figures there are two connected problems. The first concerns the basic structure of the unit, six centuries and five *turmae*, the second that of the greatly inflated numbers of the centuries and *turmae*. As Mazzarino has pointed out[15] this exactly corresponds to the structure of a *cohors quingenaria equitata* as implied by Hyginus, providing the original statement of Hyginus was correct in attributing ten *turmae* to a *cohors milliaria equitata* and half that number to its quingenary counterpart. He explains inflated numbers as additions made to the cadre of the original unit in the face of the critical situation on the eastern frontier in the early third century. Roy Davies (for whom the *pridiana* appeared to give conclusive support for a *cohors quingenaria equitata* of six centuries and four *turmae,* with its milliary equivalent therefore of eight *turmae*) has proposed an ingenious alternative.[16] Davies suggested that *Cohors XX Palmyrenorum* was originally milliary in size and that a vexillation of four centuries and three *turmae* was detached from it leaving a nucleus of six centuries and five *turmae* for the parent unit. The vexillation never returned, and eventually the original cohort had its establishment increased to something like its original strength, not by recreating new centuries and *turmae* but by doubling the size of those that remained. This is clearly possible, but it must be admitted that Mazzarino's solution is certainly simpler, and despite the evidence of the *pridiana* the theory that, in the case of this cohort, its original strength was actually six centuries and five *turmae* must remain for the moment a viable alternative.

Pridianum of *Cohors I Hispanorum Veterana*

The date of this document[17] which comprises the annual report of a quingenary part-mounted cohort, has long been a matter of debate. Greater precision can now be attained by the find of a new inscription[18] which attests Fabius Justus, the governor mentioned in the document, as present in Moesia Inferior in A.D. 106. His governorship is thought to have run from A.D. 105–8 and the *pridianum* must have been compiled during that period.

This is the most complete of such documents to survive. It begins with the totals of soldiers and officers at the end of the preceding year, 31 December, the day before, *pridie,* the new year; there follow accessions, losses, the strength at the end of the period under review, a list of men on detached service, and the numbers present in camp. It is the two overall totals of officers and men at the beginning and end of the period under review that concern us. At the beginning of the year there were 147 infantry and 119 troopers, six centurions and an uncertain number of decurions. At the end of the year the totals of infantry and cavalry are lost but there were six centurions and four decurions. These figures suggest six centuries of about seventy men, only slightly under strength if in theory it was seventy-two men, and four *turmae* of about thirty, again only slightly understrength if their size was thirty-two. However, if there was one decurion missing at the end of the year one could posit *five* decurions in charge of five *turmae* of twenty-four men each; then the cavalry would be virtually at its full strength of 120. On the whole, however, the first solution seems more likely even though it conflicts with the evidence of the Dura rosters for *Cohors XX Palmyrenorum.*

Pridianum of *Cohors I Augusta Praetoria Lusitanorum Equitata*

This *pridianum*[19] dates to A.D. 156. On 1 January there were 363 infantry and six centurions, and 114 cavalry and three decurions, plus nineteen camel riders who, as is clear from the rest of the document, were enrolled in the *turmae.* The additions follow (perhaps not a full list), which include one decurion. There are no losses listed in the document as it survives and no totals at the end of the period under review. The six centuries average out at about sixty men per century which might suggest strengths of sixty or sixty-four men. The 114 cavalry, ignoring the camel riders, would produce four *turmae* of twenty-eight, compared to a theoretical strength of thirty-two, or five *turmae* of twenty-three, only just below the theoretical strength of twenty-four.

Pridianum of a *cohors quingenaria equitata*

The unit may be identical with the previous one. The *pridianum*[20] dates to *c.* A.D. 215. The totals at the beginning of the year are lost but part of the additions survive, as well as the losses, the full strengths at the end of the period covered and the men on detailed service. The surviving total of infantry works out at 334 with a hundred cavalry and thirteen camel riders; there were six centurions and four decurions.[21] These figures would give six centuries of about fifty-six men, and four *turmae* of twenty-five, or five *turmae* of twenty.

As with the *pridianum* of *Cohors I Hispanorum Veterana,* both list four decurions and strongly support the idea that there were four rather than five *turmae* in the unit(s) concerned.[22]

C. AUXILIARY FORT PLANS

The correlation of fort plan with unit type has attracted the attention of a number of scholars since the appearance of Richmond's paper. In 1969 Michael Jarrett produced a new edition of Nash-Williams' *Roman Frontier in Wales*[23] with its excellent series of fort plans, to coincide with the meeting of the Eighth International Congress of Frontier Studies at Cardiff. At that Congress David Breeze and Brian Dobson gave a paper entitled 'Fort types as a guide to garrisons: a reconsideration',[24] which, as with Richmond's original paper, was confined to the plans of forts in Britain. In a second paper[25] the same two authors looked specifically at Hadrian's Wall, a useful procedure since its forts formed a discrete series as regards both time and place. In that paper they put forward the possibility that Chesters was originally designed for a *cohors milliaria equitata.* However, in 1978 an inscription was found[26] that showed that the Hadrianic garrison was the *Ala Augusta ob virtutem appellata,* a quingenary *ala* as already accepted by Richmond, and this prompted David Breeze to re-examine the whole question of fort types on the Wall.[27] Finally in the course of two recent books on forts in Roman Britain and the Roman army in the province, Roger Wilson and Paul Holder have brought the whole question of fort and garrison types to the attention of a wider audience.[28]

All these studies have been confined to the evidence of forts excavated in Britain and the continental evidence has been relatively neglected, at any rate as far as works of overall synthesis go.[29] The present study has no such geographical limit. Examples of forts have been chosen where complete plans exist or can reasonably be restored, and units in garrison are known. There are six such sites. Five others have been added where the garrisons are not known but where the plans are comparatively well known.[30] Ideally the forts should date to a relatively limited period but this is not yet possible and the examples chosen range from the mid-first century A.D. to the early-third century.

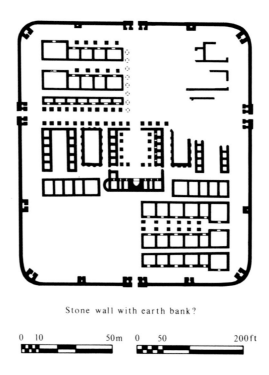

Stone wall with earth bank?

0   10   50m   0   50   200ft

Fig. 1   Drobeta, after Florescu, 1967, 147, fig. 3.

1.   Turnu Severin *(Drobeta)*[31] (Fig. 1)

Constructed in stone in the early second century on the north bank of the Danube, at the point where Trajan's bridge crossed the river below the gorge at the Iron Gates, the fort occupied the site of a turf and timber Flavian predecessor. It enclosed an area of *c.* 1.7 ha. (4.3 acres). The first permanent garrison seems to have been *Cohors III Campestris C(ivium) R(omanorum)*; it was commanded by a tribune instead of a praefect which, despite the *C.R.* title, should mean that it was milliary.[32]

Retentura. There were presumably three barracks in the *sinister* side of the *retentura* corresponding to the three barracks of the *dexter* side, making a total of six arranged *per scamnum*. Each had provision for officers at the end nearest the ramparts and was divided into five large rooms, each large room being equivalent in area to that of the accommodation appropriate to two *contubernia* — so that each barrack could have housed a complete century of eighty men.

Latera Praetorii. The *principia* was flanked by granaries and two identical courtyard buildings each of uncertain use, identified by Florescu as officers' quarters. behind these buildings were two barracks or store rooms each divided into five large rooms like the barracks in the *retentura*.

Praetentura. Two ranges of narrow store rooms each divided into seven compartments flanked the *via principalis*. In front of them were four barrack blocks arranged *per scamnum*, each apparently divided into only four large rooms.

It seems clear that the six barracks in the *retentura* and the four barracks in the *praetentura*, together form the accommodation appropriate to a *cohors milliaria peditata*, which *Cohors III Campestris C.R.* probably was. Puzzles however remain, in particular why the four barracks in the *praetentura* were only divided into four rooms, sufficient for eight *contubernia*, and whether the two buildings towards the rear of the *latera praetorii* housed men, as in the extra barrack accommodation in the *retentura* at Künzing, or were stores or stables as is suggested for the two barrack-like buildings in the *dexter* side of the *retentura* at Caerhun (both discussed below).

2.   Chesters *(Cilurnum)* (Fig. 2)

Constructed in the 120s in stone, in the central sector of Hadrian's Wall, this fort of some 2.35 ha. (5.8 acres), is now known to have been designed from the outset for a quingenary cavalry regiment, the *Ala Augusta ob virtutem appellata*.[33]

Retentura. In the *dexter* side was a barrack block and building identified by Richmond as a stable divided into three aisles, both arranged *per scamnum*. In the *sinister* half were a pair of granaries.

Latera Praetorii. Contained the *principia* and *praetorium* and space perhaps occupied by more granaries and a *fabrica*.

Praetentura. On the *dexter* side were the remains of three obvious barrack blocks and of a building which appeared to have been divided into independent 'chalet-type' accommodation in the fourth century.

Fig. 2 is based on the interpretative restored plan produced by Richmond for the tenth edition of the *Handbook to the Roman Wall*.[34] On Richmond's inter-

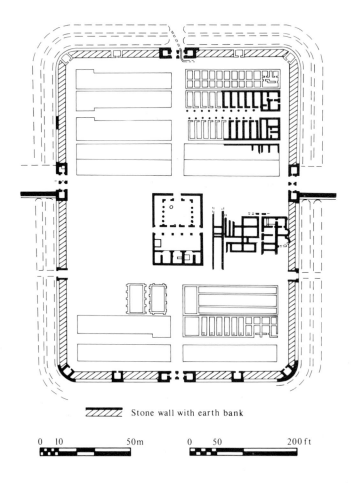

Stone wall with earth bank

0   10   50m   0   50   200 ft

Fig. 2 Chesters, after Richmond, 1947, 85.

pretation, which is accepted here, there were six barrack blocks for twelve *turmae* in the *praetentura* and two barracks for four *turmae* in the *retentura*. Richmond restores the plans of the barracks as having officers' quarters at one end and ten *contubernia,* but it is more likely that there were quarters for the decurions at both ends and only eight *contubernia,* sufficient for two *turmae* of four *contubernia* each. Next to the *via principalis* in the *praetentura* were probably originally two double stable blocks. In the *retentura* besides the barracks of the four remaining *turmae* were two single and one double stable blocks. Altogether there were the equivalent of eight stable blocks, if double blocks are counted as two, each providing stabling for the mounts of two *turmae,* just as each barrack provided accommodation for two *turmae* of troopers.

3. Slǎveni (Fig. 3)

At 3.5 ha. (8.6 acres) this was the largest auxiliary fort in Dacia Inferior.[35] It lay west of the river Olt about 50 km. (31 miles) north of its junction with the Danube and was built on the site of an earlier, somewhat smaller fort. It was surrounded by a defensive wall of brick and the internal buildings were of brick and timber-frame construction. The third century fort was built in A.D. 205 for the *Ala I Hispanorum*.[36] This unit is nowhere described as milliary and presumably in the second century was in fact quingenary in strength, but the large area of the fort suggests that it was increased to milliary size under Severus (compare Stanwix, 3.73 ha. (9.2 acres), on Hadrian's Wall which is known to have been occupied by the milliary *Ala Petriana*, and contrast Chesters, 2.35 ha. (5.8 acres), which was designed for a quingenary *ala*).

Retentura. Remains unexcavated.

Latera Praetorii. The *principia* flanked on the *sinister* side by a granary and a courtyard building[38] and on the *dexter* side by a U-shaped block of rooms,[39] perhaps a hospital.

Praetentura. Parts of six barracks arranged *per scamnum* with, on the *dexter* side, part of another building interpreted as a stable running adjacent to, and parallel with, the rampart.

Fig. 3 is based on Tudor's largely hypothetical plan. If accepted, this would suit the theoretical accommodation required for a milliary cavalry regiment, which *Ala I Hispanorum* probably was, extremely well. There are a total of twelve barrack blocks, six in the *praetentura* and six in the *retentura*, each of which would have held two of the twenty-four *turmae* of an *ala milliaria*, each *turma* of thirty-two troopers being accommodated in four *contubernia*, with the decurions sharing accommodation in the officers' quarters at the end of the barrack nearest the rampart. Stabling is provided by the four large buildings arranged *per strigas* which flank the barracks. It is tempting to take Slǎveni as the type site of an *ala milliaria* fort, and it is very unfortunate that so little is known for certain about the plan and that the suggested milliary strength of the unit is not yet attested epigraphically.

4. Künzing *(Quintana)* (Fig. 4)

This turf and timber fort of about 2 ha. (5 acres)[40] on the Danube frontier in Raetia[41] takes its name from the numerical title of *Cohors V Bracaraugustanorum*, although it was built originally, *c.* A.D. 90, for *Cohors III Thracum C(ivium) R(omanorum) quingenaria equitata*.[42]

Retentura. A single barrack block with officers' quarters set anomalously at the end furthest from the rampart, and four buildings of which the two closest to the rampart are identified by Schönberger as stables, all arranged *per scamnum*.

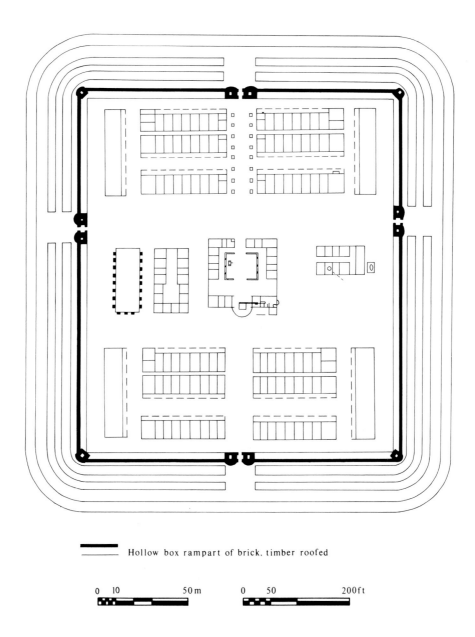

Hollow box rampart of brick, timber roofed

0　10　　　　　　50 m　　　　0　50　　　　200 ft

Fig. 3　Sláveni, restored plan after Tudor, 1977, 402, fig. 2.

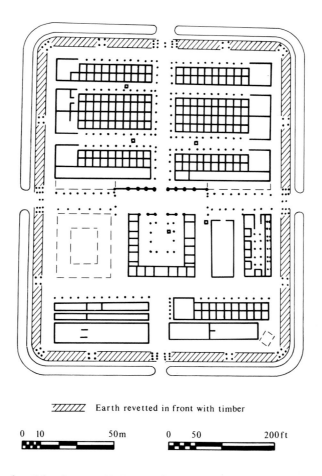

ZZZZZ Earth revetted in front with timber

```
0   10          50m      0    50      200ft
```

Fig. 4   Künzing, after Schönberger, 1969, 163, fig. 17 and 1975, Beilage 1, 1.

Latera Praetorii.   The *principia* was flanked on the *sinister* side by the presumed site of the *praetorium* and on the *dexter* side by a granary and a hospital.

Praetentura.   Eight barrack blocks arranged *per scamnum* and buildings identified by Schönberger as storerooms flanking the *via principalis*.

The barrack accommodation in the *praetentura* is sufficient to house all the soldiers of a *cohors quingenaria equitata*. The six centuries of infantry appear to have consisted of ten *contubernia*, i.e. either eighty men, or sixty if the *contubernia* held only six each. The two remaining barracks in the *praetentura* will have held the cavalry. *Either* two *turmae* were allocated to each barrack, with the men together occupying eight of the ten *contubernia*, the under-officers the remaining two, and with the decurions in the blocks at the ends of the barracks nearest to the rampart, *or* alternatively, if the establishment of the unit consisted of *five turmae* as suggested by the Dura muster rolls, then there would have been two and a half *turmae* per barrack, with each *turma* occupying four of the ten *contubernia* per barrack, and with the number of men in each *contubernium* reduced from eight to six.

The ninth barrack in the *retentura* remains a difficulty. Schönberger has suggested that it may have been for scouts.[43]

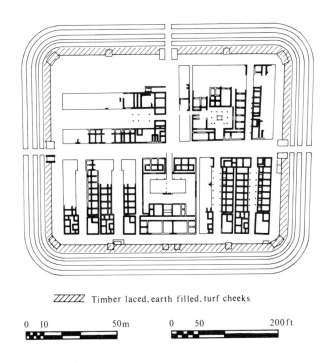

ZZZZZ Timber laced, earth filled, turf cheeks

0   10   50m   0   50   200ft

Fig. 5   Valkenburg, after Glasbergen and Groenman-van Waateringe, 1974, 7, fig. 2.

5.   Valkenburg (Fig. 5)

This famous fort of 1.4 ha. (3.5 acres)[44] was built in earth and wood *c.* A.D. 40 near the mouth of the old Rhine[45] for the *Cohors III Gallorum equitata*.[46] Like some other contemporary forts, Valkenburg has no *retentura* or *porta decumana*.

Latera praetorii.   The *principia* was flanked by eight barracks. They appear to be divided for the most part into only seven *contubernia* with under-officers' quarters at the end facing onto the *via principalis*. Four of these barracks had attached officers' accommodation at the end nearest the rampart, four have detached workshops.

Praetentura. On the *dexter* side of the *via praetoria* there was a large building constructed around a courtyard. This has been identified by Glasbergen as the *praetorium,* an identification that is challenged by Schönberger[47] who suggests that it may have been the *fabrica* on the analogy of a similar building at Oberstimm. This building was flanked by two others of which that closest to the rampart may have been a hospital. On the *sinister* side of the *via praetoria* were two long buildings, one backing onto the *via principalis* and clearly a barrack, the other facing it and probably a stable block divided into five main sections. The space between the latter building and the front rampart of the fort was apparently empty.

Glasbergen and Groenman-van Waateringe believe that the barracks in the *latera praetorii* formed pairs, each pair housing a single century, and with centurions' quarters at the ends of only four. They coin the useful term 'bipartite barracks' for them; such barracks are known elsewhere, notably in fortlets.[48] To account for the fourteen rather than the expected ten *contubernia* in each bipartite barrack, they reserve one for storage and allocate six men to the remaining thirteen, making a total of seventy-eight men for each of the four centuries. They locate two *turmae*, sixty-four men, in the long barrack running parallel to the *via principalis* in the *praetentura*, with their horses in the stables opposite. According to this theory Valkenburg was designed for a unit that was considerably below strength — four centuries and two *turmae,* as compared to an expected six centuries and four (or possibly five) *turmae.*

It seems at least possible, however, that the unit in garrison was at full strength. If each of the *contubernia* in the barracks in the *latera praetorii* held eight men, they would house a total of 448 to which one could add a further sixty-four in the supposed cavalry barrack to give a combined strength of 512. This figure would correspond to a theoretical six centuries of sixty-four men and four *turmae* of thirty-two men, and though the precise way in which these troops and their officers would have been housed in the barrack accommodation at Valkenburg remains not at all clear, this may be the correct answer.

Another solution would be to assume that each of the six centuries was reduced to fifty-six men housed in seven *contubernia*. In this case it is unnecessary to regard pairs of barracks in the *latera praetorii* as forming 'bipartite' barracks at all: six of the eight barracks would contain one century each, and the remaining two, two *turmae* each. The long barrack block in the *retentura* would house supernumerary troops as suggested at both Drobeta and Künzing, where the latter was designed for a quingenary part-mounted unit similar to the third cohort of Gauls at Valkenburg. One difficulty about this theory is the problem posed by the attempt to fit two *turmae* into barracks divided into seven *contubernia*.

A variation on this last solution and one that perhaps surmounts the difficulty raised above, is to assume that there were five *turmae* and not four, as indeed was the case with *Cohors XX Palmyrenorum*.[49] Two of the barracks in the *latera praetorii* appear to have contained respectively more and less *contubernia* than the normal seven. In both cases it was the third barrack along from the *principia*; that on the *sinister* side of the fort may have contained nine *contubernia* while the equivalent barrack on the *dexter* side looks as if it contained only six. It is theoretically possible that the first of these barracks contained three *turmae*, each occupying three *contubernia* with eight men in each, while the second contained two *turmae*, again with each occupying only three *contubernia*. This second barrack may have housed the five decurions, with three in the three rooms nearest the *via principalis* and two, together with living rooms etc., in the 'officers'' block nearest the rampart. As with the decurions, the six centurions will have had to share accommodation in the officers' quarters distributed between three of the six remaining barracks.

The problems posed by Valkenburg may be insoluble, but on the whole a solution which allows for a complete unit in garrison seems preferable to one that requires only part of the unit, unless other evidence is forthcoming to suggest that the unit was in fact divided.

6.   Birrens *(Blatobulgium)* (Fig. 6)

This fort[50] of 2 ha. (5 acres), constructed with turf and timber defences and internal buildings raised on stone foundations, was built in *c.* 140 to the north of the western terminal of Hadrian's Wall on the site of a Hadrianic outpost. Its first garrison was probably *Cohors I Nervana Germanorum milliaria equitata*.[51]

Retentura.   Sixteen narrow buildings arranged *per scamnum*.

Latera praetorii.   The *principia* flanked by three granaries and the *praetorium*.

Praetentura.   Sixteen narrow buildings arranged *per scamnum*.

The whole fort, with the exception of the *latera praetorii*, was occupied by thirty-two long narrow buildings, of which twenty-four were 'paired', each being separated from its immediate neighbour by only a narrow space. Professor Robertson, followed by David Breeze, interpreted these pairs as forming single barrack blocks, twelve in all. They were complemented by eight 'unpaired' blocks, interpreted as sheds and stables. Quite apart from the constructional peculiarity of the supposed barrack blocks with their median eaves drip, David Breeze raised another difficulty about this interpretation; each supposed barrack, or pair of buildings, was divided from its neighbour by a space of 4.9 m. (16 ft.), and, in other words, the 'barrack blocks' were not placed back to back as in most forts, but were evenly spaced 'giving the impression that the narrow

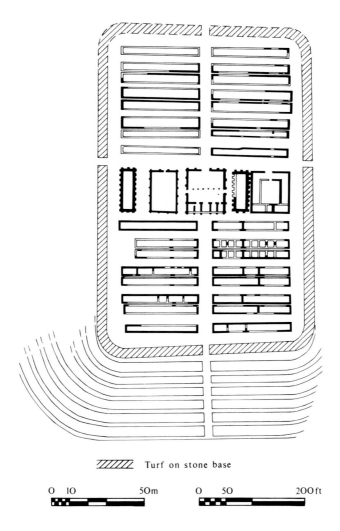

Turf on stone base

0 10   50m   0   50   200ft

Fig. 6   Birrens, after Breeze, 1979, 33, fig. 14.

blocks are separate buildings.' A third problem is that one would expect to find
not twelve but fourteen or perhaps even fifteen barrack blocks for a part-
mounted milliary cohort with ten for the ten centuries and four for the eight
turmae, or possibly five if there were ten *turmae*.[52]

An alternative interpretation to that which argues that the adjacent 'paired'
buildings formed a single barrack, can be made based on the pairing of buildings

facing each other across the intervening access street. Such an arrangement can be seen at the Severan fort of Ain Sinu in Iraq, where the survival of internal walls and of doorways makes a more certain interpretation possible. Something similar existed in the *retentura* of the fortress of *Legio II Parthica* built by Severus at Albano.[53] On this interpretation we have sixteen paired buildings. Of these, fourteen pairs would represent barrack accommodation, ten for the centuries and four for the eight (or five) *turmae*. The remaining two pairs (perhaps the four long buildings closest to the *via principalis*) will be stables, possibly arranged in two rows in each building.[54]

One final point needs to be mentioned. Two of the buildings in the *sinister* side of the *retentura* at Birrens are short, though the buildings that they pair with across the access streets are of normal length. Could these two pairs each have held two *turmae* while the corresponding pair on the other side of the *via decumana* held three so making a total of ten *turmae* rather than eight? It seems at least a possibility.

7.   Gelligaer II (Fig. 7)

This fort of 1.5 ha. (3.7 acres)[55] was built in south Wales under Trajan[56] near the site of a somewhat larger Flavian predecessor. The Trajanic fort had a stone defensive wall backed by an earthen rampart which was retained at the rear by a second stone wall. The internal buildings were of timber-frame construction on stone foundation walls. The garrison is not attested epigraphically.

Retentura.   There were two barrack blocks arranged *per scamnum,* with the centurions' quarters set as normal at the ends of the buildings nearest the rampart, but the wooden internal partitions were not recorded; two long buildings, variously interpreted as sheds or cavalry barracks, of which one is divided into three parts by internal walls and the other into four, were also present.

Latera praetorii.   The *principia* was flanked by the *praetorium* and a granary on the *sinister* side, and by a works-compound and a granary on the *dexter* side.

Praetentura.   There were four barracks similar to those in the *retentura*, and three sheds, stores buildings or stables adjacent to the *via principalis*; all buildings were arranged *per scamnum.*

Most scholars[57] agree that the fort was built for a *cohors quingenaria peditata,* and for Richmond it was the type site of a fort designed for this sort of unit. The possibility has, however, been raised that it was designed for a *cohors quingenaria equitata* with extra barrack accommodation for the cavalry in the two buildings of uncertain use in the *retentura,* and stabling in the three buildings in the *praetentura* which flank the *via principalis*.[58] George Boon, defending the traditional view, interprets these three buildings respectively as a long stable block for baggage animals, a centrally-placed fodder store, and a short stable

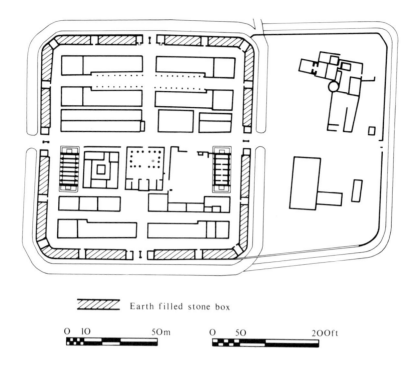

Earth filled stone box

O 10   5Om   O   5O   2OOft

Fig. 7   Gelligaer II, after Nash-Williams, 1969, fig. 45.

block for officers' mounts. He suggests that the tripartite building in the *retentura* was a store with one large room provided per two centuries,[59] and that the other building was a workshop.[60] This detailed analysis carries conviction.

8.   Fendoch (Fig. 8)

This turf and timber fort[61] whose defences enclose an area of *c.* 1.5 ha. (3.7 acres) was built in the early 80s to hold territory won by Agricola in eastern Scotland north of the Forth-Clyde line. Its garrison is not attested epigraphically, but was possibly *Cohors I Tungrorum milliaria.*[62]

Retentura.   Six barracks of ten *contubernia* were arranged *per strigas.*

Latera praetorii.   The *principia* was flanked by the *praetorium* and by two granaries; behind these a hospital and several smaller buildings, probably workshops or cart sheds faced onto the *via quintana.*

Praetentura.   Four barrack blocks were arranged *per strigas,* with two stable blocks for baggage animals flanking the *via praetoria.*

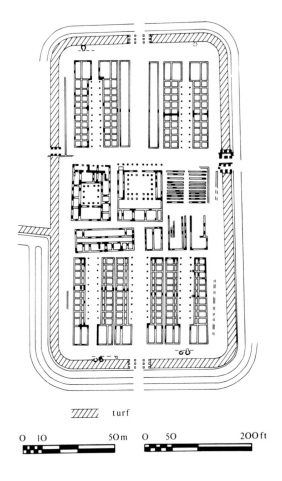

turf

0 10   50m   0   50   200ft

Fig. 8   Fendoch, after Richmond, 1939, fig. 2 (opposite p. 114).

Fendoch is the only one of the eleven fort plans discussed, about which there are no problems of interpretation. The total of ten barracks are appropriate accommodation for a *cohors milliaria peditata*. Doubts[63] about the plan, though possibly justified as far as minor details are concerned, are unfounded as regards the whole. Its arrangement, with the barracks all placed *per strigas,* is very similar to that of Housesteads,[64] though the latter at 2.1 ha. (5.2 acres) is somewhat larger and the exact interpretation of all the buildings in the *praetentura* and *retentura,* whether as stables or barracks, is not always certain.

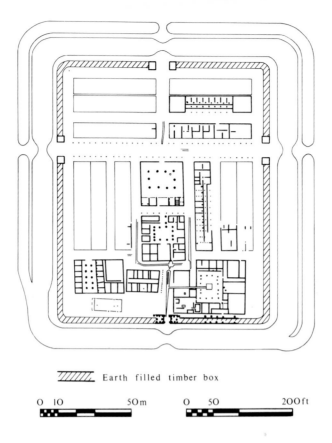

/////// Earth filled timber box

O 10 50m   O 50 200ft

Fig. 9   Oberstimm, after Schönberger, 1978, 138, fig. 65.

9.   Oberstimm (Fig. 9)

This 1.43 ha. (3.5 acres) fort[56] was built *c.* A.D. 50 as part of the Danube defences in the province of Raetia.[66] It was defended by a rampart of earth-filled timber-box construction, while its internal buildings had timber frames infilled with wattle and daub. Their plans are largely conjectural and the existence of many of the barrack buildings is based on the assumption that they were laid out symmetrically about the central axis of the fort. The garrison is not attested epigraphically.

Retentura. Fabrica, placed on the *dexter* side together with a hospital, and accommodation for medical staff and craftsmen.

Latera praetorii. The *principia,* with behind it, the *praetorium,* was flanked probably by six barracks arranged *per strigas,* each containing eight (?) *contubernia,* and with officers' quarters at each end.

Praetentura. Two long storehouses fronted onto the *via principalis,* in front of which were two barracks also divided into eight (?) *contubernia* with officers' quarters at both ends. In front of these barracks was space for two more buildings, which Schönberger suggested were stables.

He also suggested that the six barracks in the *latera praetorii* were for the six centuries of a *cohors equitata.* Each century will have consisted of sixty-four men, giving eight *contubernia* of eight. The centurions will have been quartered in the blocks at each end of these barracks, presumably those fronting onto the *via principalis,* with the under-officers, *principales,* in the blocks at the other ends. The two barracks in the *praetentura* will have accommodated the cavalry element of the unit. If these barracks are correctly restored as having eight *contubernia* apiece, then they should only have housed four *turmae* (contrast Künzing where two ten-*contubernia* barracks can either be thought of as divided between four or five *turmae*).

Certainty is difficult at Oberstimm in view of the greatly restored nature of the plan, but Schönberger's interpretation makes excellent sense of such remains of the fort as were found.

10.   Caerhun *(Kanovium)* (Fig. 10)

Situated on the river Conway in north Wales from which the site derived its name, this 1.97 ha. (4.8 acres) fort[67] was partly converted to stone in the mid-second century, when the original earthen rampart was cut back to allow the insertion of a stone wall and at the same time the internal buildings were given stone footings. There is no independent epigraphic evidence for the garrison.

Retentura. There are barracks on the *sinister* side and, *either* two further barracks, *or* two store rooms (?) or stables (?), both subdivided into three, on the *dexter* side, all arranged *per scamnum.*

Latera praetorii. The *principia* was flanked by the *praetorium* on one side and a pair of granaries, with an enclosed space between them, on the other.

Praetentura. Six barrack blocks and two stables, running alongside the *via principalis,* were all arranged *per scamnum.*

Richmond put forward Caerhun as the type site for a fort designed for a *cohors quingenaria equitata.*[68] He did not go into detail in identifying specific buildings but presumably placed the six centuries of infantry in the six barracks of the *praetentura* and the cavalry in the two obvious barrack blocks in the *sinister* side of the *retentura,* with the two remaining buildings in the *retentura* being for stores and stables.[69]

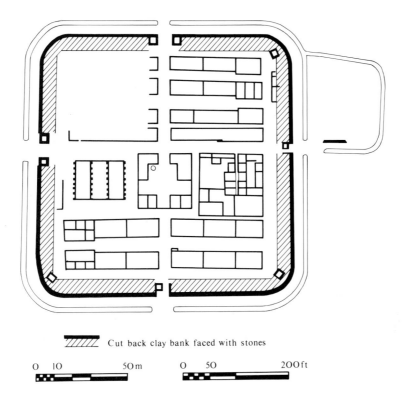

Fig. 10 Caerhun, after Nash-Williams, 1969, 58, fig. 25.

The two long buildings in the *praetentura*, flanking the *via principalis*, will have been for baggage animals. Breeze and Dobson[70] and others have considered the possibility that all the buildings in the *retentura* were barracks, making a total of ten in the fort as a whole, a number appropriate to the ten centuries of a *cohors milliaria peditata*.

On the whole it seems more likely that the buildings on the *sinister* side were the only two barracks in the *retentura,* with the officers' quarters attached at the ends nearest the rampart, and that they were indeed cavalry barracks. If so, the tripartite divisions in the two 'stables' in the *dexter* quadrant opposite is curious. If there were four *turmae,* then four of the divisions in these two buildings could have been for the cavalry mounts, one division per *turma,* and the remainder simply store rooms. However, if there were five *turmae,* then the fifth could have been located in one of the divisions of one of the 'stables' set apart from its fellows on the other side of the *via decumana.*

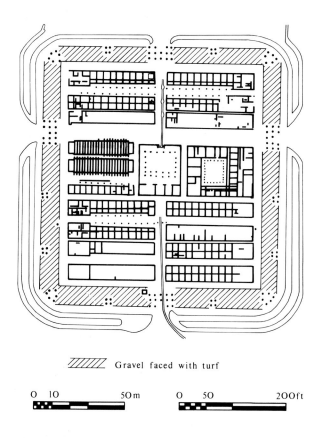

////// Gravel faced with turf

0   10   50m   0   50   200ft

Fig. 11   Pen Llystyn, after Nash-Williams, 1969, 102, fig. 53.

11.   Pen Llystyn (Fig. 11)

This turf and timber fort[71] in north Wales was constructed *c.* A.D. 78. It occupies an area of 1.8 ha. (4.5 acres).

Retentura.   Eight barracks were arranged *per scamnum.*[72]

Latera praetorii. The *principia* was flanked by the *praetorium* and two granaries arranged *per scamnum*. Behind the granaries was a barrack-like building identified as a hospital.

Praetentura. Four barrack blocks and two stores buildings, or stables for baggage animals, flanked the *via principalis*. All the buildings were arranged *per scamnum*.

Pen Llystyn is usually interpreted as having been designed for two quingenary cohorts.[73] If the identification of all the buildings in the *retentura* as barracks,[74] and of the two buildings in the *praetentura* as stores or stables, is correct, then this interpretation will be right. It has been suggested that post holes in the *via decumana* were for a gate separating the rear-most six barracks from the rest of the fort which was consequently divided at this point, as in second-century Newstead, where a transverse wall separated the auxiliary cavalry from the legionary cohorts that formed the joint garrison.[75] Alternatively the fort was divided longitudinally which would mean that the six centuries comprising each cohort could have been housed in facing pairs of barracks as normal, and that one of the stores or stables buildings would then lie in each half of the fort. For such a division compare the situation at Vetera, where the stamped tiles of *Legio V Alaudae* are found exclusively in the *dexter* and those of *Legio XV Primigenia* in the *sinister* side of this double legionary fortress.[76]

CONCLUSIONS

Of the eleven fort plans illustrated and analysed above, one, Gelligaer II probably housed a quingenary infantry cohort; two, Drobeta and Fendoch, milliary infantry regiments; one, Chesters, a quingenary *ala,* and one, Slăveni, perhaps a milliary *ala.* Pen Llystyn may have housed two quingenary infantry cohorts. The analysis of these six fort plans, in so far as it has been possible to make one, has gone some way to confirm the actual existence of the theoretical establishments for the relevant units as outlined at the beginning of this paper.

The remaining five forts probably all housed part-mounted units, Künzing, Valkenburg, Oberstimm and Caerhun *cohortes quingenariae equitatae,* and Birrens, a *cohors milliaria equitata.* This high proportion of forts for part-mounted units to forts for other types of regiment, is reflected in the relative proportion of the unit types themselves. Thus cohorts not only always far outnumbered *alae,* but of, for example, the forty-six quingenary cohorts in Britain, thirty-one were part-mounted, and of the milliary cohorts, five out of seven.[77] What light have the attempted analyses of these five fort plans shed on the internal organization of this type of unit?

First there is the question as to whether there were five or four *turmae* in a quingenary part-mounted cohort, and ten or eight in its milliary equivalent. We have seen how the Dura rosters favour five but the *pridiana,* for at least two separate units of this type, suggest four. At first sight four *turmae,* which fit neatly into two normal century-type barracks, would seem to be supported by the fort plans — and indeed this figure is accepted by most people. However, at Künzing, where all the barracks were divided into ten *contubernia* but where each *contubernium* may have housed only six men, five twenty-four man *turmae* of four *contubernia* each may have been housed in two barracks; at Valkenburg five twenty-four man *turmae* composed of three eight man *contubernia* may have been housed in two barracks and at Caerhun five *turmae* could have been housed in two barracks and one end of a stable block. Only at Oberstimm with its (?) eight-*contubernia* barrack blocks do four *turmae* definitely seem more likely. At Birrens, which housed a milliary part-mounted cohort, ten *turmae* are perhaps slightly more likely than eight.

The second question concerns the strength of the centuries in the part-mounted units. At Künzing and possibly at Birrens, the ten-*contubernia* barracks may have held full strength centuries of eighty men, but if the number in each *contubernium* was reduced to six, then they would have been only sixty strong. At Valkenburg, the barracks, on the assumption that they held complete centuries each and were not 'bipartite', were divided into seven *contubernia* and the centuries may have been of only fifty-six men. At Oberstimm the restored eight-*contubernia* barracks should have been for centuries of sixty-four men.

Perhaps there are no simple answers to these two questions: some part-mounted units may have had five and some four *turmae*; some milliary units ten and some eight. Similarly, though the strength of the centuries could have been reduced by the equivalent of two or three *contubernia,* they could still have remained at ten *contubernia* with or without the number per section being reduced.

There are other points to emerge: the possible recognition of an anomalous type of barrack accommodation at Birrens where the sleeping accommodation and services room are separated by the width of a street; the apparent existence of small detachments of extra troops at Künzing and Drobeta, a phenomenon that is attested epigraphically;[78] the uniting of two different auxiliary units in a single fort, as at Pen Llystyn. We know too that at some sites auxiliaries and legionaries shared the same fort as at Newstead in the second century where an auxiliary *ala* was joined by two legionary cohorts,[79] but whether these mixed garrisons of legionaries and auxiliaries are as common as is sometimes supposed, is not at all certain.[80] The corollary of multiple units in garrison is divided units – particularly the infantry or cavalry elements of *cohortes equitatae,* but an examination of the forts for such bodies of men is beyond the scope of this paper.[81]

Richmond's 1955 summary of the evidence of fort plans was at once wider and narrower than that attempted here. Wider in that he took into account not only excavated fort plans, but also forts which were known only from air photography, about whose internal features little more was known than the plan of the principal roadways and subsidiary access streets. Narrower in that he was concerned only with British examples and none from the continent. Of the six British forts discussed here, only the plan of Pen Llystyn has been recovered since the period in which Richmond wrote, although work at Birrens, both excavation and subsequently of re-interpretation, has greatly clarified the situation. It is a tribute to the work of a great scholar that despite all later discussion surrounding the other five excavated forts, Richmond's interpretations as to the most likely garrisons still stand. The great increase in the last thirty years of knowledge of the internal planning of forts has come not from Britain but principally from abroad, such as at the Rumanian sites of Drobeta and Slăveni; at the site of Valkenburg in Lower Germany where greater precision has been achieved especially in the *praetentura,* and above all in Raetia through the excavations of Hans Schönberger at Oberstimm and Künzing. Yet the dozen or so forts discussed here are but a fraction of those that await proper investigation, even on the European frontiers of the empire, and work has hardly begun on fort sites of the high empire in the eastern and north African provinces.[82] Clearly we can expect a great increase in our knowledge in the next thirty years, even if we find that the more we learn about fort plans the less we in fact know about their interpretation.

APPENDIX

Included here are the plans of two sites whose internal arrangements perhaps throw light on those of the fort at Birrens, even though neither would by themselves come within the scope of this survey. The first is the enigmatic site of Ain Sinu (Fig. 12)[83] in northern Iraq, excavated by David and Joan Oates in 1957. At Ain Sinu, the *Zagurae* of the Peutinger map, are the remains of two adjacent forts, both of which date to the early third century. One was surrounded by a stone wall furnished with external towers, round at the corners and square between (Ain Sinu II). Little is known of its interior. The interior of the other, Ain Sinu I (Fig. 12) was however investigated. It appears to have been entirely taken up with fourteen long buildings arranged *per scamnum,* the four at each end of the fort containing rows of single rooms only, the remaining ten double rows of rooms. These fourteen buildings formed the equivalent of twelve barracks, each *contubernium* being provided with a larger and smaller room as in a conventional fort, but with the one separated from the other by an intervening access street. If each *contubernium* or its equivalent housed eight men, the total force at Ain Sinu I would have numbered something over 2,000 men. Quite apart from the size of the force accommodated in the fort, there is the puzzle about the total lack of officers' accommodation and administrative buildings. The tentative suggestion has been put forward that the barracks may have been an initial training centre for recruits.

The second site is also Severan, the fortress of *Legio II Parthica* at Albano[84]

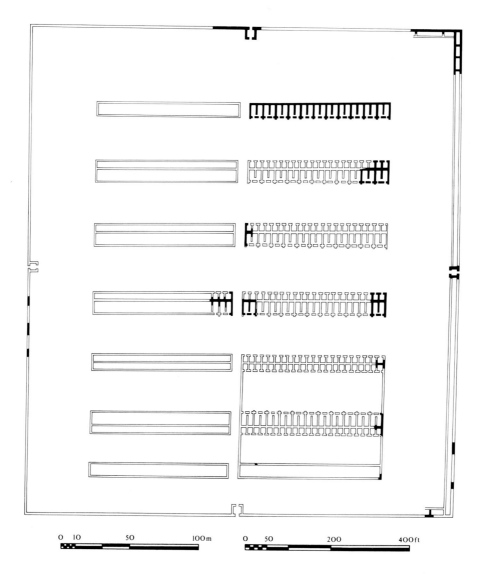

Fig. 12   Ain Sinu I, after Oates and Oates, 1959, Plate LII.

(Fig. 13) on the Via Appia just south of Rome. The fortress is famous for its *porta praetoria,* the best preserved of any such structure at a legionary fortress, but its significance in the present context lies in the barracks in the *retentura.* These, though known only from antiquarian records, appear to be of the same 'divided' type observable at Ain Sinu, the earliest recorded example of which, it has been suggested, may have been at Birrens in the mid-second century A.D.

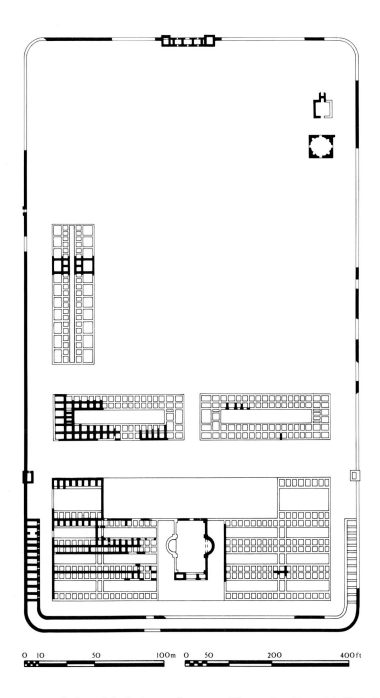

Fig. 13 Reconstructed plan of the legionary fotress at Albano after Tortorici, 1975, 93, fig. 135.

NOTES

1. Richmond, I.A., *Proceedings of the British Academy,* xli, (1955), 304–6.

2. The latest editions of Hyginus are: Grillone, A. (ed.), *Hyginus de Metatione Castrorum,* Leipzig, 1977 and Lenoir, M. (ed.), *Pseudo-Hygin des Fortifications du Camp,* Paris, 1979.

3. Frere, S.S., *Britannia,* xi, (1980), 51–60, arguing for a late-first century date for the composition of the *de munitione castrorum* and a connection with Domitian's Marcomannic War of A.D. 89. *Contra* Birley, E., in *Corrolla memoriae E. Swoboda dedicata,* Graz/Cologne, 1966, 57, arguing for the Danubian Wars of Marcus Aurelius (cf. Birley, E., *Britannia,* xii, (1981), 286). Earlier scholars have preferred an early third century date and an eastern context (e.g. Mommsen, T. and Marquardt, J., *Manuel des Antiquités Romaines,* Paris, 1887–1907, 11, 354–5), partly based on the appearance of camels with Hyginus' field force. For the presence of these animals on the Danube, cf. the bones of three camels at the Lorenzberg: Kellner, H.J., *Die Römer in Bayern,* Munich, 1971, 184.

4. Strageath: Frere, S.S., in Breeze, D.J. (ed.), *Roman Scotland: Some Recent Excavations,* Edinburgh, 1979, 37–41; Longthorpe: Frere, S.S. and St Joseph, J.K., *Britannia,* v, (1974), 1–129.

5. I would like to thank the following for discussing points with me and pointing me in the right direction – even if I have sometimes subsequently lost the way – Alan Bowman, David Breeze, Barri Jones, John Mann, Valerie Maxfield, Margaret Roxan, Hans Schönberger, John Wilkes and, above all, Julie Kennedy, for preparing the plans of the relevant forts.

6. Holder, P.A., *The Auxilia from Augustus to Trajan,* Oxford, 1980, 5–13, working over much the same ground as Cheesman, G.L., *The Auxilia of the Roman Imperial Army,* Oxford, 1914, 25–31.

7. For the strength of the first legionary cohort, see Frere, S.S., *loc. cit.* (see note 3).

8. On these units, see Davies, R.W., *Historia,* xx, (1971), 751–63.

9. Hyginus, Section 27.

10. In fact the text as transmitted also transposes the words *peditum* and *equites.*

11. See the apparatus in Grillone, A., *op. cit.* (see note 2).

12. Lenoir, M., *op. cit.* (see note 2) prints *turmas VI,* following Durry, M., *Les Cohortes Pretoriennes,* Paris, 1938, 83, who bases this restoration on faulty interpretations of the *pridiana* cited below.

13. Bu Ngem: Marichal, M.R., *Comptes Rendus de l'Academie des Inscriptions et Belles-Lettres,* July/October, 1979, 436–52. Twenty-two daily reports give average century-strengths of fifty-seven. Vindolanda: Bowman, A. and Thomas, J.D., *Vindolanda: The Latin Writing Tablets,* (forthcoming, 1983). Q'asr Ibrim may also have produced relevant material, cf. Frend, W.H.C., in Hanson, W.S. and Keppie, L.J.F. (eds.), *Roman Frontier Studies 1979: Papers presented to the 12th International Congress of Roman Frontier Studies, BAR International Series 71,* Oxford, 1980, 927–30; Weinstein, M.E. and Turner, E.G., *Journal of Egyptian Archaeology,* lxii, (1976), 115–30, note esp. No. 34.

14. Fink, R.O., *Roman Military Records on Papyrus,* Cleveland, 1971, No. 1. The other muster rolls are Nos. 2–4. For a discussion of the total number of soldiers in the centuries and *turmae* of the unit, see *ibid.,* 16.

15. Mazzarino, S., *Acta Antiqua,* xix, (1971), 62, note 21. Kennedy, D., *The Auxilia and Numeri raised in the Roman Province of Syria,* (unpublished thesis), 1980, 215, refers simply to the six centuries and five *turmae* as the 'structure of a quingenary cohort' but does not go into the question of the numbers of *turmae* in such a unit. Grillone (see note 2) accepts Mazzarino's arguments and prints X in his restoration of Hyginus' text.

16. Davies, R.W., *Epigraphische Studien,* iv, (1967), 109, note 17.

17. Fink, R.O., *op. cit.* (see note 14), No. 63.

18. Rădulescu, A. and Bărbulescu, M., *Dacia,* n.s., xxv, (1981), 353–8.

19. Fink, R.O., *op. cit.* (see note 14), No. 64. In the translation of this document the figures of the cavalry and camel riders are wrongly given as 145 and 19 respectively. Holder, P.A., *op. cit.* (see note 6), 7 adds the accessions to these totals, without taking the (missing) losses into account.

20. Thomas, J.D. and Davies, R.W., *Journal of Roman Studies,* lxvii, (1977), 50–61.

21. Holder (see note 6), again curiously, adds the losses to the totals without subtracting the additions. If both were taken into account one would arrive at the total for the beginning of the year.

22. Note, however, that in the first total given in the *pridianum* of *Cohors I Augusta Praetoria Lusitanorum,* Fink, No. 64 (quoted above, note 19), at least one decurion is absent, while in the fragmentary *pridianum* of an *ala* from Egypt dated 28 May A.D. 48, only twelve of the sixteen decurions were present. *Chartae Latinae Antiquiores,* Pt. II, 1979, No. 501. Holder's attempt, *op. cit.* (see note 6), 9, to establish the *turma* size in an *ala* from this document is based on the assumption, probably incorrect, that there were only twelve *turmae.* With a total of 434 men this would give a *turma* size of thirty-six men — over strength if there were thirty-two a *turma.* At sixteen *turmae,* however, the figure comes down to an average of twenty-seven men, somewhat under strength. Even if there were only twelve *turmae,* the argument is invalid since the number 434 is restored and 334 would be an equally possible restoration, giving an average *turma* size of twenty-eight.

23. Nash-Williams, V.E., (second edition Jarrett, M.G.) *The Roman Frontier in Wales,* Cardiff, 1969.

24. Breeze, D.J., and Dobson, B., in Birley, E., Dobson, B. and Jarrett, M. (eds.), *Roman Frontier Studies, Eighth International Congress of Limesforschung,* Cardiff, 1974, 13–19.

25. *idem, Archaeol. Aeliana,* 4 ser., xlvii, (1969), 15–32.

26. *Britannia,* x, (1979), 346 no. 7.

27. Austin, P.S. and Breeze, D.J., *Archaeol. Aeliana,* 5 ser., vii, (1979), 114–26.

28. Wilson, R., *Roman Forts: An Illustrated Introduction to the Garrison Posts of Roman Britain,* London, 1980, esp. 22–36. Holder, P.A., *The Roman Army in Britain,* London, 1982, esp. 28–39.

29. An exception is Holder, P.A., *op. cit.* (see note 6), 10–12.

30. Sites that might have been included are Nanstallon (Fox, A. and Ravenhill, W., *Britannia,* iii, (1972), 56–111); Strageath (Frere, S.S., *loc. cit.* (see note 4)) and Wallsend (*Britannia,* xi, (1980), 355–8, figs. 5 and 6). Nanstallon is thought by the excavators to have held a *cohors quingenaria equitata,* while the same type of unit may have served originally in garrison at Wallsend. At Strageath, Frere has suggested that there were two, or parts of two, auxiliary units in garrison in three of its four periods of occupation. I have excluded forts larger than the *c.* 4 ha. (10 acres) appropriate to an *ala milliaria,* such as Hod Hill (Richmond, I.A., *Hod Hill, Volume Two: Excavations carried out between 1951 and 1958,* London, 1968), where, however, large areas remained unoccupied by buildings, and Longthorpe (Frere, S.S. and St. Joseph, J.K., *loc. cit.* (see note 4)). Hod Hill poses problems, cf., for example, Wells, C.M., in Fitz, J. (ed.), *Limes: Akten des XI internationalen Limeskongresses,* Budapest, 1977, 660–1 on the stables. In the case of the forts that have been chosen I have normally discussed the earliest period only.

31. Drobeta: Tudor, D., in *Princeton Encyclopaedia of Classical Sites,* and Florescu, R., in *Studien zu den Militärgrenzen Roms, Vorträge des 6, internationalen Limeskongresses in Süddeutschland,* Cologne/Graz, 1967, 144–51. Fig. 1 is based on Florescu, fig. 3. It does not correspond precisely with that published by

Tudor (*Oltenia Romana,* Bucharest, 1968 and elsewhere).

32. *C.I.L.* III, 14216ˣ. cf. Spiedel, M., *Transactions of the American Philological Association,* cvi, (1976), 345. *L'Année épigraphique,* (1959), No. 309 is a dedication to Trajan by *Cohors I Antiochensium,* but this unit was quingenary cf. *C.I.L.* XVI, 46 (dated A.D. 100) where a praefect is mentioned, and is not thought to have been part of the permanent garrison. In the third century the fort was occupied by *Cohors I Sagittariorum Gordiana milliaria equitata,* cf. *L'Année épigraphique,* (1959), No. 311.

33. Chesters: Daniels, C.M., in *Princeton Encyclopaedia of Classical Sites* (Hadrian's Wall); Daniels, C.M. (ed.), *Handbook to the Roman Wall with the Cumbrian Coast and outpost forts,* Newcastle, 1978, 109–20. For the garrison see note 26 above.

34. Richmond, I.A. (ed.), *Handbook to the Roman Wall,* Newcastle, 1947, 83. The plan is reproduced in the latest edition of the *Handbook,* Daniels, *op. cit.* (see note 33), 110, but without the labels identifying buildings as stables.

35. Slăveni: Tudor, D., in *Princeton Encyclopaedia of Classical Sites* and *idem, Studien zu den Militärgrenzen Roms II, Vorträge des 10 Internationalen Limeskongresses in der Germania Inferior,* Cologne/Bonn, 1977, 399–403, Fig. 3 is based on ibid., fig. 2, and is largely a hypothetical reconstruction based on the scant remains that have actually been excavated. Compare Gudea, N., *Britannia,* x, (1979), 63–87, fig. 12, which distinguishes between planned discovery and restoration. However, in the *latera praetorii,* Tudor's plan appears to be more up-to-date.

36. *C.I.L.* III, 13800.

37. *pace* Roxan, M.M., *The Auxilia of the Roman Army raised in the Iberian Peninsula,* (unpublished thesis), 1973, 142, note 39, where it is suggested that the size of Slăveni is not an argument for its suggested milliary status.

38. Only the external walls of this building are shown on Gudea's plan (*loc. cit.* (see

note 35), fig. 12) — with a single (restored) wall dividing the building in two across the short axis.

39. This building is not shown on Gudea's plan.

40. Künzing: Schönberger, H., in *Princeton Encyclopaedia of Classical Sites* (Limes Raetiae); Schönberger, H., *Kastell Künzing-Quintana,* Berlin, 1975; Breeze, D.J., *Britannia,* viii, (1977), 451–60. Fig. 4 is taken from Schönberger (*Journal of Roman Studies,* lix, (1969), fig. 17), corrected from his 1975 publication, Beilage 1, 1.

41. For the position of Künzing, see Schönberger, H., *Journal of Roman Studies,* lix, (1969), map fig. 20, no. 178.

42. The presence of this unit at Künzing in its first period is attested by three tile stamps reading *Coh(ors) II Thr(acum) C(ivium) R(omanorum).* An inscription of A.D. 144 accords it the additional descriptive epithet *equitata,* as well as the honorific title *bis torquata. Berichte der Römisch-Germanischen Kommission,* 1956–7, (1958), 236, No. 81.

43. Compare the third-century outposts of Hadrian's Wall where milliary *cohortes equitatae* were, in a number of instances, brigaded with detachments of irregular troops (see note 78 below). Note also the extra barrack at Drobeta and the presence of camel riders with both *Cohors XX Palmyrenorum* at Dura in the early third century and *Cohors I Augusta Praetoria Lusitanorum* in the second. The alternative (Hassall, M., *Antiq. Journ.,* lvii, (1977), Pt. 1, 115–7) that the troops quartered in them were part of the regular establishment of the unit, seems on the whole less likely.

44. Valkenburg: De Waele in *Princeton Encyclopaedia of Classical Sites* (with bibliography); Glasbergen, W., *De Romeinse Castella Te Valkenburg Z H: Opgravingen 1962,* Groningen, 1972; Glasbergen, W. and Groenman-van Waateringe, W., *The Pre-Flavian Garrisons of Valkenburg Z.H: fabriculae and bipartite barracks,* Amerstdam/London, 1974; Hassall, M., *Britannia,* v, (1974), 491–3 and *loc. cit.*

(see note 43).

45. For the position of Valkenburg see Schönberger, H., *op. cit.* (see note 41), map fig. 20, No. 4.

46. The name of the unit *C(o)hor(s) III Gallor(um) e(quitata)* is found as part of an address on a wooden writing tablet, Glasbergen, W. and Groenman-van Waateringe, W., *op. cit.* (see note 44), 37.

47. Schönberger, H., *Germania,* lviii, (1979), 135–41. He calls attention particularly to the presence of the large tank or cistern in the centre of the courtyard, a feature regularly found in *fabricae,* but one which also occurs in the courtyards of some *praetoria,* e.g. Lyne (Christison, M.D., *Proceedings of the Society of Anitquaries of Scotland,* 3 ser., xxv, (1901), general plan 169, fig. 8, photo 181, fig. 15), knowledge of which I owe to Leslie Willhite's unpublished London M.A. thesis (*The praetorium: a study of thirty-four select praetoria in Britain and on the German Frontier,* 1976). The correct identification of this building, though important, does not concern the question of barrack accommodation for men and stabling which is the prime importance of this paper.

48. e.g. Barburgh Mill: Breeze, D.J., *Britannia,* v, (1974), 130–62.

49. cf. the possible fivefold division of the stable block in the *sinister* side of the *praetentura.* However, it may be questioned whether each of these large stalls could have contained twenty-four horses for each of the five *turmae.*

50. Birrens: Robertson, A.S., in *Princeton Encyclopaedia of Classical Sites;* Robertson, A.S., *Birrens,* Edinburgh, 1975; Breeze, D.J., *Britannia,* viii, (1977), 451–60.

51. *R.I.B.* 2093, 2097. The unit was succeeded by another milliary part-mounted cohort, *Cohors II Tungrorum,* in 158 (*ibid.,* no. 2110).

52. Ten *turmae,* however, can be accommodated in four barrack equivalents as I attempt to show below. Compare the discussions on Valkenburg and Künzing where it was demonstrated that two

barracks could house either four or five *turmae.*

53. For Ain Sinu and Albano see Appendix, and Figs. 12 and 13. There is a superficial resemblance of the barrack accommodation at these two sites to the layout of the ranges of small rooms ('Kammerbauten') found at the legionary fortresses of Neuss and Bonn, as well as at Asciburgium. Such rooms have in the past been identified as *carceres,* cells. von Petrikovits, H., *Die Innenbauten römischer Legionslager während der Prinzipatzeit,* Opladen, 1975, 87, fig. 22; Bonn: Bechert, T., *Beiträge zur Archäologie des römischen Rheinlandes 3,* Bonn, 1972, 175–80, fig. 16. The barracks at Ain Sinu, Albano and Birrens (?) are all peculiar in having no obvious officers' quarters attached.

54. The long buildings at Birrens are 42 m. (138 ft.) by 4.5 m. (15 ft.). If 240 horses were arranged in two rows in each building, each horse would have a space of about 1.3 m. (4.5 ft.) by 2.3 m. (7.5 ft.), which seems tight, but perhaps just possible.

55. Gelligaer II: Jarrett, M.G. in *Princeton Encyclopaedia of Classical Sites;* Nash-Williams, V.E., *op. cit.* (see note 23), 88–91; Brewer, R.J., *Gelligaer Roman Fort,* Cardiff, 1981; Wilson, R., *op. cit.* (see note 28), 44, 61.

56. *R.I.B.,* 397–9 dating to the period A.D. 103–11.

57. Richmond, I.A., *op. cit.* (see note 1), 304 and Nash-Williams, V.E., *op. cit.* (see note 23), 90.

58. Breeze, D.J. and Dobson, B., *op. cit.* (see note 24), 14.

59. An interesting survival of the Republican maniple system of paired centuries also reflected in the pairing of barracks within forts and fortresses to face each other across a central street, and the *prior* or *posterior* titles of the centurions in legionary cohorts.

60. This building, with its two diminutive wings facing onto a works compound, would be a very simple version of von Petrikovits' 'Wirtschaftsbau *(fabrica)* mit doppelhakenförmigem Grundriss', (*op.*

cit. (see note 53), 92, fig. 25).

61. Fendoch: Steer, K.A., in *Princeton Encyclopaedia of Classical Sites*; Richmond, I.A., *Proceedings of the Society of Antiquaries of Scotland,* lxxiii, (1938–9), 110–54; Wilson, R., *op. cit.* (see note 28), 34.

62. The only certainly attested *cohors milliaria peditata* in the Roman army in Britain, shown as milliary in *C.I.L.* XVI, 48, A.D. 103, and subsequent diplomas, and present at the battle of Mons Graupius in A.D. 84 (Tacitus, *Agricola,* 36).

63. e.g. Holder, P.A., *op. cit.* (see note 6), 11.

64. Housesteads: Daniels, C.M., in *Princeton Encyclopaedia of Classical Sites* (Hadrian's Wall, *Borcovicus*); Daniels, C.M., *op. cit.* (see note 33), 138–55. Plans of the Hadrianic fort: Wilson, R., *op. cit.* (see note 28), 45 and Holder, P.A., *op. cit.* (see note 28), 36.

65. Oberstimm: Schönberger, H., in *Princeton Encyclopaedia of Classical Sites,* (*Limes Raetiae,* no separate entry); Schönberger, H., *Kastell Oberstimm: die Grabungen von 1968 bis 1971,* Berlin, 1978.

66. For the position of Oberstimm see Schönberger, H., *op. cit.* (see note 41), map fig. 20, No. 170.

67. Caerhun: Jarrett, M.G., in *Princeton Encyclopaedia of Classical Sites, (Canovium)*; Nash-Williams, V.E., *op. cit.* (see note 23), 56–9.

68. Richmond, I.A., *op. cit.* (see note 1), 305.

69. cf. Boon, G.C., *Archaeol. Cambrensis,* cxxiv, (1976), 118.

70. Breeze, D.J. and Dobson, B., *op. cit.* (see note 24), 14.

71. Pen Llystyn: Jarrett, M.G., in *Princeton Encyclopaedia of Classical Sites;* Nash-Williams, V.E., *op. cit.* (see note 23), 101–3 and Wilson, R. *op. cit.* (see note 28), 34–5.

72. Note, however, that the identification of one of the buildings in the *retentura* as a barracks is questioned — Nash-Williams, V.E. *op. cit.* (see note 23), 103.

73. e.g. *ibid.,* 11. For the brigading of two auxiliary cohorts together cf. the *duarum cohortium hiberna* of Tacitus' *Histories,* IV, 15.

74. See above, note 72.

75. Richmond, I.A., *Proceedings of the Society of Antiquaries of Scotland,* lxxxiv, (1950), 22 and 20, fig. 5.

76. Lehner, H., *Vetera: die Ergebnisse der Ausgrabungen des Bonner Provinzialmuseums bis 1929,* Berlin/Leipzig, 1930, 38.

77. Davies, R.W., *op. cit.* (see note 8), 751.

78. e.g. at Housesteads, *Cohors I Tungrorum milliaria equitata* with the *Ceneus Frisiorum* (*R.I.B.* 1594) and *Numerus Hnaudifridi* (*R.I.B.* 1567); at Risingham, *Cohors I Vangionum milliaria equitata* with the *Exploratores Habitancenses* (*R.I.B.* 1235) and the *Vexillatio Gaesatorum Raetorum* (*R.I.B.* 216, 217); at High Rochester *Cohors I Vardullorum milliaria equitata* with the *Numerus Bremeniensium* (*R.I.B.* 1262).

79. See note 75.

80. The presence of legionaries is often claimed on the basis of finds of cuirass hinges from *loricae segmentatae,* but it has yet to be shown that this type of body armour was worn exclusively by legionaries. They occur at sites where there is no reason to suppose legionaries were ever stationed, e.g. Oberstimm: Schönberger, H., *op. cit.* (see note 65), Taf. 20. cf. also the 'legionary-type' belt plates from Valkenburg: Glasbergen, W. and Groenman-van Waateringe, W., *op. cit.* (see note 44), plates 12–14.

81. A recently excavated example of such a fort is Bearsden on the Antonine Wall which probably housed the cavalry of *Cohors IV Gallorum,* a quingenary part-mounted cohort stationed at nearby Castlehill: Breeze, D.J., *Current Archaeology,* lxxxii, (1982), 344.

82. Fort sites like Severan Bu Ngem in Libya clearly have great potential. The recent French excavations have concentrated on the *principia* and the baths, Rebuffat, R., *Libya Antiqua,* xi–xii, (1974–5), 189–241, esp. 192, fig. 3, but the outline of barracks, even prior to excavations can be made out clearly from the air. Goodchild, R.G., *Papers of the British School at Rome,* xxii, (1954), 56–68, fig. 1 and plate X. For the *ostraca* from the site, see above p. 99 and Marichal, M.R., *loc. cit.* (see note 13).

83. Ain Sinu: Oates, D. and Oates, J., *Iraq*, xxi, (1959), Part 2, 207–42.
84. Albano: Richardson in *Princeton Encyclopaedia of Classical Sites* (Albano Laziale); Tortorici, E., *Castra Albana*, Rome, 1975, especially 13, fig. 4 (a plan of the nineteenth-century observations on which the restored plan 93, fig. 135 is in part based).

BIBLIOGRAPHY

Austin, P.S. and Breeze, D.J., 1979, 'A New Inscription from Chesters on Hadrian's Wall', *Archaeol. Aeliana*, 5 ser., vii, 114–126.

Bechert, T., 1972, 'Der Stand der Asciburgiumforschung', *Beiträge zur Archäologie des römischen Rheinlandes 3 = Rheinische Ausgrabungen*, xii, 147–97.

Birley, E., 1966, '*Alae* and *cohortes milliariae*', *Corolla memoriae E Swoboda dedicata*, Römische Forschungen in Niederösterreich 5, Graz/Cologne, 54–67.

Birley, E., 1981, 'Hyginus and the First cohort', *Britannia*, xii, 286.

Birley, E., Dobson, B. and Jarrett, M., 1974, *Roman Frontier Studies 1969*, Cardiff.

Boon, G.C., 1976, Review of Birley, E., Dobson, B., and Jarrett, M., 1974, *Archaeol. Cambrensis*, cxxiv, 117–20.

Bowman, A. and Thomas, J.D., 1983, *Vindolanda: The Latin Writing Tablets*.

Breeze, D.J., 1974, 'The Roman Fortlet at Barburgh Mill, Dumfriesshire', *Britannia*, v, 130–62.

Breeze, D.J., 1977, Review Article: 'Birrens (Blatobulgium), Kastell Künzing-Quintana', *Britannia*, viii, 451–60.

Breeze, D.J., 1979, *Roman Scotland: a guide to the visible remains*, Newcastle upon Tyne.

Breeze, D.J., 1982, 'Bearsden', *Current Archaeology*, lxxxii, 343–7.

Breeze, D.J. and Dobson, B., 1969, 'Fort Types on Hadrian's Wall', *Archaeol. Aeliana*, 4 ser., xlvii, 15–32.

Breeze, D.J. and Dobson, B., 1974, 'Fort Types as a guide to garrisons: a reconsideration', in Birley, E., Dobson, B., and Jarrett, M., *Roman Frontier Studies, Eighth International Congress of Limesforschung*, Cardiff, 13–19.

Brewer, R.J., 1981, *Gelligaer Roman Fort*, Cardiff.

Cheesman, G.L., 1914, *The Auxilia of the Roman Imperial Army*, Oxford.

Christison, M.D., 1901, 'Excavations of the Roman Camp at Lyne, Peeblesshire, undertaken by the Society of Antiquaries of Scotland in 1901', *Proceedings of the Society of Scotland*, 3 ser., xxxv, 154–86.

Daniels, C.M., 1978, *Handbook to the Roman Wall with the Cumbrian Coast and outpost forts* (original author, J. Collingwood Bruce), thirteenth edition, Newcastle upon Tyne.

Davies, R.W., 1967, 'A note on a recently discovered inscription from Carrawburgh', *Epigraphische Studien*, iv, 108–11.

Davies, R.W., 1971, '*Cohortes equitatae*', *Historia*, xx, 751–63.

Durry, M., 1938, *Les Cohortes Prétoriennes*, Paris.

Fink, R.O., 1971, *Roman Military Records on Papyrus*, Cleveland.

Florescu, R., 1967, 'Les Phases de Construction du Castrum Drobeta (Turnu Severin)', *Studien zu den Militärgrenzen Roms, Vorträge des 6. internationalen Limeskongresses in Süddeutschland*, Beihefte der Bonner Jahrbucher 19, Cologne/Graz, 144–51.

Fox, A. and Ravenhill, W., 1972, 'The Roman fort at Nanstallon, Cornwall', *Britannia*, iii, 56–111.

Frend, W.H.C., 1980, 'Augustus' Egyptian Frontier', in Hanson, W.S. and Keppie, L.J.F. (eds.), *Roman Frontier Studies 1979: Papers presented to the 12th International Congress of Roman Frontier Studies*, BAR International Series 71, Oxford, 927–30.

Frere, S.S., 1979, 'The Roman Fort at Strageath', in Breeze, D.J. (ed.), *Roman Scotland: Some Recent Excavations,* Edinburgh, 37–41.

Frere, S.S., 1980, 'Hyginus and the First Cohort', *Britannia,* xi, 51–60.

Frere, S.S., and St Joseph, J.K., 1974, 'The Roman Fortress at Longthorpe', *Britannia,* v, 1–129.

Glasbergen, W., 1972, *De Romeinse Castella Te Valkenburg Z H: Opgravingen 1962,* Groningen.

Glasbergen, W. and Groenman-van Waateringe, W., 1974, *The Pre-Flavian Garrisons of Valkenburg Z H: fabriculae and bipartite barracks,* Amsterdam/London.

Goodchild, R.G., 1954, 'Oasis Forts of *Legio III Augusta* on the Routes to the Fezzan', *Papers of the British School at Rome,* xxii, 56–68.

Grillone, A. (ed.), 1977, *Hyginus de Metatione Castrorum,* Leipzig.

Gudea, N., 1979, 'The Defensive System of Roman Dacia', *Britannia,* x, 63–87.

Hassall, M., 1974, Review of Glasbergen, 1972, *Britannia,* v, 491–3.

Hassall, M., 1977, Review of Glasbergen, W. and Groenman Waateringe, W., 1974, *Antiq. Journ.,* lvii, Pt 1, 115–7.

Holder, P.A., 1980, *The Auxilia from Augustus to Trajan,* BAR International Series 70, Oxford.

Holder, P.A., 1982, *The Roman Army in Britain,* London.

Kellner, H.-J., 1971, *Die Römer in Bayern,* Munich.

Kennedy, D., 1980, *The Auxilia and Numeri raised in the Roman Province of Syria,* D.Phil. Oxon. (unpublished thesis).

Lehner, H., 1930, *Vetera: die Ergebnisse der Ausgrabungen des Bonner Provinzialmuseums bis 1929,* Berlin/Leipzig.

Lenoir, M. (ed.), 1979, *Pseudo-Hygin des Fortifications du Camp,* Paris.

Marichal, M.R., 1979, 'Les Ostraca de Bu Njem', *Comptes Rendus de l'Academie des Inscriptions et Belles Lettres,* July–October 1979, 436–52.

Mazzarino, S., 1971, 'La Tradizione sulle Guerre tra Shabuhr I e l'Impero Romano: 'Prospettive' e 'Deformazione Storica', *Acta Antiqua,* xix, 59–82.

Mommsen, T. and Marquardt, J., 1887–1907, *Manuel des Antiquites Romaines,* second edition, Paris.

Nash-Williams, V.E., 1969, *The Roman Frontier in Wales,* (second ed., Jarrett, M.G.), Cardiff.

Oates, D. and Oates, J., 1959, 'Ain Sinu: A Roman Frontier Post in Northern Iraq, *Iraq,* xxi, Pt. 2, 207–242.

von Petrikovits, H., 1975, *Die Innenbauten römischer Legionslager während der Prinzipatzeit,* Opladen.

Rădulsecu, A., and Bărbulescu, M., 1981, 'De Nouveau sur les légats de Trajan en Mésie Inférieure entre 103 et 108 de N.E.', *Dacia,* n.s., xxv, 353–8.

Rebuffat, R., 1974–5, 'Bu Njem 1971', *Libya Antiqua,* xi–xii, 189–241.

Richmond, I.A., 1938–9, 'The Agricolan Fort at Fendoch', *Proceedings of the Society of Antiquaries of Scotland,* lxxiii, 110–54.

Richmond, I.A., 1947, *Handbook to the Roman Wall,* (original author J. Collingwood-Bruce), tenth edition, Newcastle upon Tyne.

Richmond, I.A., 1950, 'Excavations at the Roman Fort of Newstead 1947', *Proceedings of the Society of Antiquaries of Scotland,* lxxxiv, 1–38.

Richmond, I.A., 1955, 'Roman Britain and Roman Military Antiquities', (Albert Reckitt Archaeological Lecture), *Proceedings of the British Academy,* xli, 297–315.

Richmond, I.A., 1968, *Hod Hill, Volume Two: Excavations carried out between 1951 and 1958,* London.

Robertson, A.S., 1975, *Birrens,* Edinburgh.

Roxan, M.M., 1973, *The Auxilia of the Roman Army raised in the Iberian Peninsula,* Ph.D. London, (unpublished thesis).

Schönberger, H., 1969, 'The Roman Frontier in Germany: an Archaeological Survey', *Journal of Roman Studies,* lix, 144–97.

Schönberger, H., 1975, *Kastell Künzing-Quintana,* Limesforschungen 13, Berlin.

Schönberger, H., 1978, *Kastell Obserstimm: die Grabungen von 1968 bis 1971,* Limesforschungen 18, Berlin.

Schönberger, H., 1979, 'Valkenburg Z.H.: Praetorium oder Fabrica', *Germania,* lvii, 135–41.

Speidel, M., 1976, 'Citizen Cohorts in the Roman Imperial Army. New Data on the Cohorts Apula, Campana, and III Equestris', *Transactions of the American Philological Association,* cvi, 339–48.

Thomas, J.D. and Davies, R.W., 1977, 'A New Military Strength Report on Papyrus', *Journal of Roman Studies,* lxvii, 50–61.

Tortorici, E., 1975, *Castra Albana,* Forma Italiae: Regio 1 Vol. II, Rome.

Tudor, D., 1968, *Oltenia Romana,* 3rd edition, Bucharest.

Tudor, D., 1977, 'Le rôle défensif du camp romaine de Slăveni sur le limes Alutanus en Dacie inférieure', *Studien zu den Militärgrenzen Roms II, Vorträge des 10 Internationalen Limeskongresses in der Germania Inferior,* Beihefte der Bonner Jahrbücher 38, Cologne/Bonn, 399–403.

Weinstein, M.E. and Turner, E.G., 1976, 'Greek and Latin Papyri from Qasr Ibrîm', *Journal of Egyptian Archaeology,* lxii, 115–30.

Wells, C.M., 1977, 'Where did they put the horses? Cavalry stables in the early empire', in Fitz, J. (ed.), *Limes: Akten des XI internationalen Limeskongresses,* Budapest, 659–65.

Willhite, L.C., 1976, *The praetorium: a study of thirty-four select praetoria in Britain and on the German Frontier,* M.A. King's College, London (unpublished thesis).

Wilson, R., 1980, *Roman Forts: An Illustrated Introduction to the Garrison Posts of Roman Britain,* London.

The Cauldron Chains of Iron Age and Roman Britain

by

W.H. MANNING

Few pieces of ironwork surviving from Iron Age and Roman Britain are more impressive than the cauldron chains, which makes the absence of a detailed study of their development surprising. The only previous discussion is that by Stuart Piggott in his pioneering study of 'Three Metalwork Hoards of the Roman Period' (1953) where he divided the British chains into the Standford-bury and the Great Chesterford types. Subsequent discoveries have shown that the Stanfordbury type covers too many variant forms to be a meaningful group and the term is not used in this paper.[1] The Great Chesterford type, however, is a distinct form, although it is advisable to restrict the term to chains which are very similar to the type specimen and to exclude a number of less closely related fragments which Piggott originally included in the group.

In Britain such chains first appear towards the end of the Iron Age and are clearly related to those current on the Continent at that time. The story of their later development is of particular interest for it takes them far from their continental ancestors to create forms which are unknown outside England; but it is a story which is confused by gaps in the evidence, and at times by uncertainty on the chronology of surviving pieces.[2]

Continental Cauldron Chains

The idea of suspending a cauldron by a pair of hooked arms at the end of a chain or hooked rod appears in Central Europe before the end of the Hallstatt period, for example from Zárybník, Bohemia[3] and from Salins, Jura[4] and by La Tène I such hangers can be found throughout the Celtic areas of continental Europe.[5] Initially there appear to have been two forms; the simplest having long, hooked arms, linked at their tops by a ring set at the lower end of the hooked rod by which it was hung (Fig. 1.1 from La Tène).[6] Greater length could be obtained by inserting an additional rod between the top hook and the arms, as in the example from Salins mentioned above. The second type was more elaborate, and it was this form which was to become the standard for the remainder of the Iron Age. Here the arms were given a degree of flexibility by making them in two parts, with a lower, hooked rod linked by a ring to an upper rod. The series

132

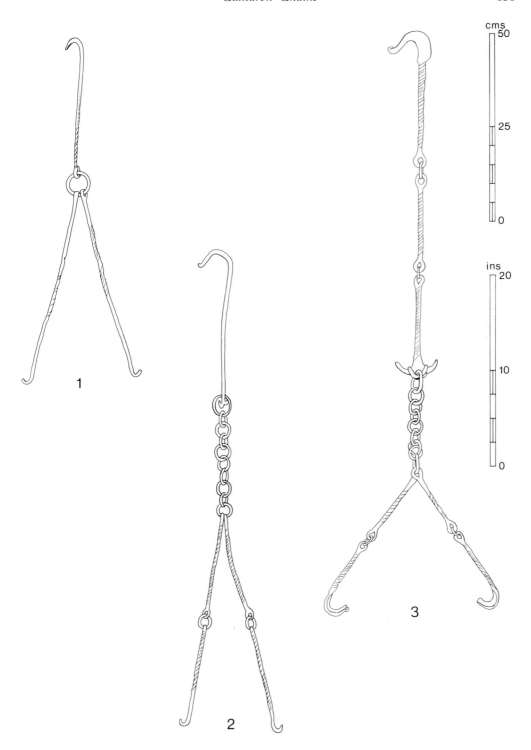

Fig. 1　Continental chains: 1. La Tène, 2. La Tène, 3. Attersee.

of rods by which the arms were suspended in the simpler form was here partly replaced by a chain of round links with a hooked rod at its top; the ring which joined the arms became the final link of this chain. The suspension rod in hangers of this type assumes the form which it was to retain into the Roman period, with a hook at the top and an anchor-shaped double-hook at the bottom, (Fig. 1.2 from La Tène) although in the early examples the top link of the chain was carried not by the anchor-shaped hook, but by an eye set between its arms.[7] The rods in both types usually had spirally-twisted stems.

Although this basic form continued in a few cases almost unchanged into the Roman period, for example from Vertault, Côte-d'Or,[8] the majority show a number of changes. In use they must have hung from a beam above the hearth, the height of which clearly varied, and several techniques were used to give them extra length; the arms or the top rod might be longer, or the links of the chain of larger diameter, or occasionally all three might be used in the same chain (Fig. 1.2 from La Tène). But these rather crude adaptations, which appear mainly in hangers of La Tène C date, were not regarded as satisfactory, probably because they distorted the proportions of the hanger, and by La Tène D they had been largely replaced by the division of the top suspension rod. The simplest way of doing this was to have two interlinked rods, the upper one carrying the suspension hook, the lower one the anchor-shaped hook, for example from Milseburg/Rhön;[9] if still greater length was required, it could be obtained by inserting a third rod between these two (Fig. 1.3 from Attersee).[10] For some reason, what might seem to be the obvious solution, an increase in the number of links of chain, was not used.

A second development was in the way in which the chain was attached to the anchor-shaped hooks. The original method had ignored these hooks and the top link of the chain had been held in an eye between them. This apparently illogical method had largely been superseded in La Tène D by placing a U-shaped link across the arms of the hook, with the top link of the chain passing around it (Fig. 1.3 from Attersee). Such an arrangement made full use of these hooks, and it is surprising to note that this was not their original function; they must instead have carried implements such as flesh-hooks, for it seems improbable that they were originally intended to be entirely decorative.

With this final modification, the continental hangers had reached their apogee, and it is in this form that they usually appear in the Roman period, occurring in the forts of the German *limes* at dates which cannot be earlier than the late first century A.D., for example Fig. 2.2 from Zugmantel;[11] from Gross-Krotzen-burg;[12] Fig. 2.3 from Cannstatt,[13] and from various sites in Gaul, Vertault, Côte-d'Or;[14] Vichy, Allier;[15] St Aubin, Jura (Fig. 2.1).[16] How long this type of chain continued in use on the Continent is uncertain, but it is clear that it never developed into anything resembling the great chains of late Roman Britain.

Hangers of this type were suspended from a beam high above the hearth, suggesting that they were normally used within a house, but, apparently in La Tène C or D, there appeared an alternative method of suspension, the portable

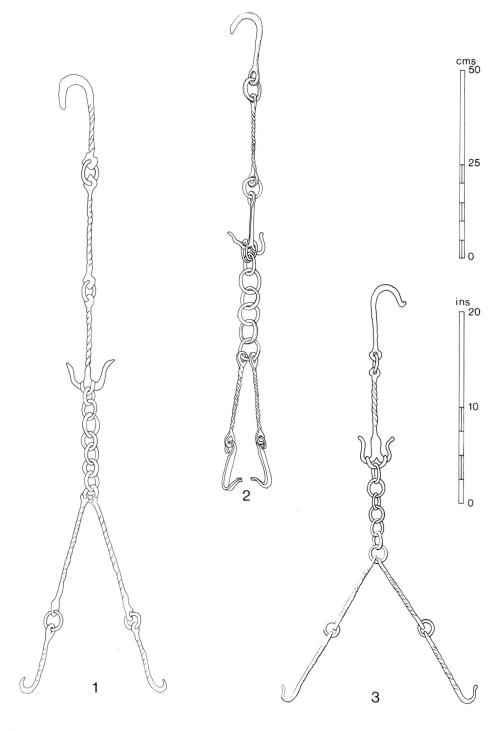

Fig. 2 Continental chains: 1. St. Aubin, Jura, 2. Zugmantel, 3. Cannstatt.

tripod. This had plain legs curving in to meet at a central pivot on which they turned to close the tripod. The usual anchor-shaped hook hung from the bottom of this pivot. In one of the earliest examples, from Dühren,[17] the arms hung on a chain which was carried by an eye set between the double hooks; a similar arrangement existed in a tripod of Roman date from Neuvy-Pailloux, Indre.[18]

British Iron Age Cauldron Chains

Several complete cauldron chains and fragments of others, all from the south of Britain, can either certainly or probably be dated to the Iron Age or early Roman period. The complete ones are from Over Fen, Cambs.; Butley, Suffolk, and from an unknown findspot, most probably in East Anglia. Another, lacking one arm, and a large part of a second come from Bigbury, Kent, and other substantial fragments from Pentyrch, Glam. and Ham Hill, Somerset. Although chains were the normal form of suspension, the tripod was not unknown and a complete example comes from the late Iron Age burial at Standfordbury, Beds., and large parts of another from Bigbury, Kent. Other hangers, which are too fragmentary for the method of suspension to be clear, are known from various sites, including Bigbury, Kent; Hunsbury, Northants; the Caburn, Sussex; Bledlow, Bucks., and Kingsdown Camp, Somerset.

Few of these chains came from dated contexts, and only the hook from Bledlow could be claimed as dating from the early Iron Age. But even this came from an area which had been disturbed in the Roman period, and in view of the general rarity of metalwork on early Iron Age sites, a Roman date is probable. The Hunsbury hooks are certainly Iron Age, but the finds from that site cover almost the whole of the La Tène period and there is no reason to suppose that the hooks are early rather than late; indeed on typological grounds the larger hook (Fig. 4.1) must be late in the series.[19] The Bigbury pieces are almost certainly from one or more hoards dating from the end of the Iron Age.[20] Of the other pieces, a looped rod from Kingsdown Camp is from a deposit which cannot be earlier than the late Iron Age or early Roman period; neither can a rod from the Caburn, although certainly Iron Age, be much earlier, whilst a ring and chain from Pentyrch is from a late Iron Age or early Roman hoard. The fragments from Ham Hill (a hook, fragments of chain and various looped rods) were casual finds from a site which has produced both Iron Age and Roman material and a closer date is not possible.

It is unfortunate that little is known of the contexts of the East Anglian chains. We have no more than an approximate findspot for the pair from Over Fen (Fig. 3.1), although their excellent condition implies that they came from a water-logged deposit. The Butley chain (Fig. 3.2) was found in gravel digging, while the finest of all, that now in Cambridge (Fig. 3.3), is unprovenanced and we can only assume that, since it is in an East Anglian museum, it probably came from that area; its superb condition indicates that it too came from a waterlogged context. Any date for them must be founded, therefore, on other grounds, of

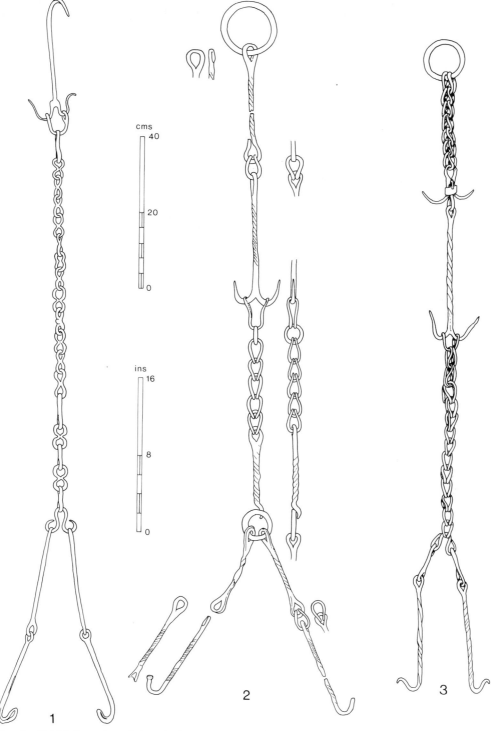

Fig. 3   British Iron Age chains: 1. Over Fen, 2. Butley, 3. 'East Anglia', unprovenanced, now in Cambridge.

which the most important is their stylistic affinity with the continental chains already discussed. Admittedly, all show obvious differences from them but there are also important similarities, including the use of the anchor-shaped double-hooks and twisted rods, as well as the form of the arms, and a detailed comparison of the two groups leaves little doubt that the British examples are derived from ancestors of the continental type. The fact that all of the English chains, which have an anchor-shaped rod, have the chain attached to a U-shaped link rather than to an eye in the end of the rod, probably indicates a relatively late date for them. As we have seen, this method of suspension did not appear until late in the La Tène period on the Continent.

A second argument in favour of a late Iron Age or early Roman date for these pieces is the fact that they were almost certainly intentionally deposited either on their own or as part of hoards, for their excellent condition and value as scrap make it highly improbable that they were casually discarded. In this context we may note that the condition of the Over Fen and 'East Anglian' chains suggests that they came from a waterlogged context, which makes it unlikely that they are from burials but suggests instead deposition in a peat bog or river, a well-authenticated practice in the Iron Age. The deposition of valuable groups of metalwork of this type can only be paralleled in the last phases of the British Iron Age and early Roman period.[21]

Of course such a date can only be accepted as applying to the group as a whole; no doubt there were exceptions with early types continuing late into the Roman period, or being brought from the Continent, where they continued in use long after the conquest period. An example was the discovery of part of an anchor-shaped hook and a simple, hooked arm in a small hoard of bronze and iron objects from Wiggonholt Common, near Pulborough, Sussex (Fig. 4.3). The other objects in the hoard, notably part of a scythe of Great Chesterford type and a bronze pan with a folding handle, leave little doubt that the group was deposited in the late Roman period when the majority of cauldron chains had dispensed with such hooks. Obviously they could have been old when buried, but their occurrence in such a context suggests that individual hangers may have had very long lives indeed, even if they were not still being made in the late Roman period.[22]

As we have seen, the British chains differ in several significant ways from those found on the continent, where there is a striking uniformity of design, which is conspicuously lacking in the British ones. The major differences between the two groups are:

1. The use of a suspension ring rather than a hook.
2. A marked tendency for the number of links of chain to be increased at the expense of rods.
3. The use of various types of link instead of the simple, round links which are normal on the Continent but unusual in Britain.
4. The replacement of a plain ring to hold the arms by a double hook, or a trefoil link as in the Bigbury hanger.

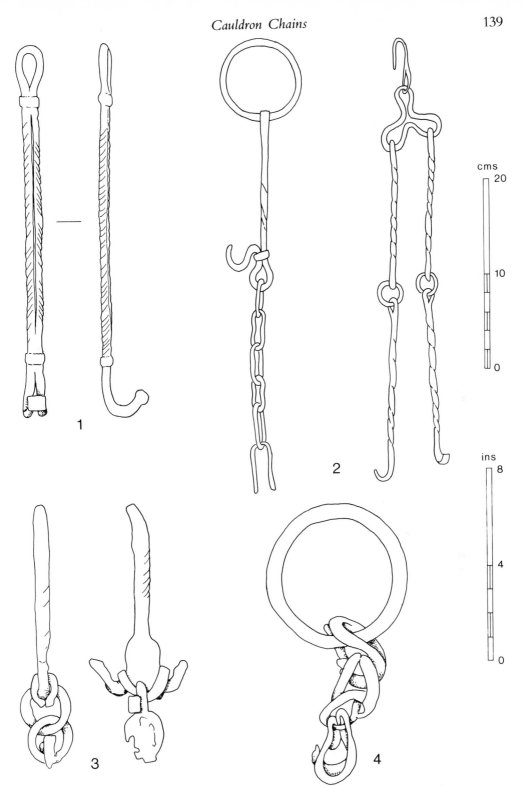

Fig. 4 Fragments of British chains: 1. Hunsbury, 2. Bigbury, 3. Pulborough, 4. Pentyrch.

The British chains have a certain uniformity in their basic structure, no doubt imposed by functional requirements; their diversity appears in the design of individual elements. At the top there is usually a large suspension ring, as in the Butley (Fig. 3.2), Bigbury (Fig. 4.2), Pentyrch (Fig. 4.4) and 'East Anglian' chains (Fig. 3.3); only the Over Fen hanger (Fig. 3.1) has a hook of the continental type. The body of the chain is formed of twisted rods and lengths of chain, with the exact arrangement varying from one to another. In the 'East Anglian' chain (Fig. 3.3) the sequence is a series of links, an elaborate double-junction, a rod with an anchor-shaped hook, a second series of links, and finally a double-hook carrying the arms. The fragment from Pentyrch (Fig. 4.4) is similar to the top of this one, with a ring holding a number of links. The Butley hanger (Fig. 3.2) has a looped rod, connected to an anchor-ended rod, then a series of links, which carry another rod, at the end of which is the ring holding the arms. In the Over Fen chains (Fig. 3.1) the suspension hook has an anchor-shaped hook at its bottom holding the main chain at the end of which is a double hook for the arms. The two Bigbury hangers (Fig. 4.2) are basically similar, each with a looped rod carrying the chain, the main difference being that one has an additional hook at the side of the loop, possibly to hang on a flesh-hook. A loose hook, which may have had a similar function, is fastened to the junction ring of a chain from Emmendingen.[23]

The form of links used in these chains varies, although it is usually uniform within the same chain. The Over Fen chains (Fig. 3.1) have closed figure-of-eight links attached to the anchor-shaped hook by a U-shaped link, as in the continental La Tène D chains. The Bigbury hangers (Fig. 4.2) have links of open hour-glass shape, similar to those on the gang chain from the same site, and so too does a fragment from Ham Hill. The Butley, Pentyrch and 'East Anglian' chains (Fig. 3.2; 4.4; 3.3) all have U-shaped links of the type found in the late Roman cauldron chains discussed below.[24]

The junction which connects the arms to the main chain varies in form. It may be a simple ring of the type used in the Continental chains, as with the Butley and Stanfordbury hangers (Figs. 3.2; 5); it may be a double-hook, as with the 'East Anglian' and Over Fen chains (Figs. 3.3; 3.1), or it may be a trefoil link as on the Bigbury hanger (Fig. 4.2). The upper part of the arms almost always consists of a twisted rod with eyes or loops at its ends, which is attached to the junction, either directly or by means of an intermediate link, as in the Stanford-bury hanger. Only in the 'East Anglian' chain is this arrangement varied (Fig. 3.3); there the looped rod is replaced by a long hour-glass link.

The simplest form of the hook has a twisted stem with a hooked end, as on the Standfordbury (Fig. 5), Ham Hill, Bledlow and 'East Anglian' hangers (Fig. 3.3); in the Butley hanger (Fig. 3.2) the end of the hook is thickened. A more developed form is known from Bigbury where the hook is made by doubling a bar and then twisting the two halves together, with the looped end forming the hook. Something similar is seen in the Over Fen hangers where the hook is also

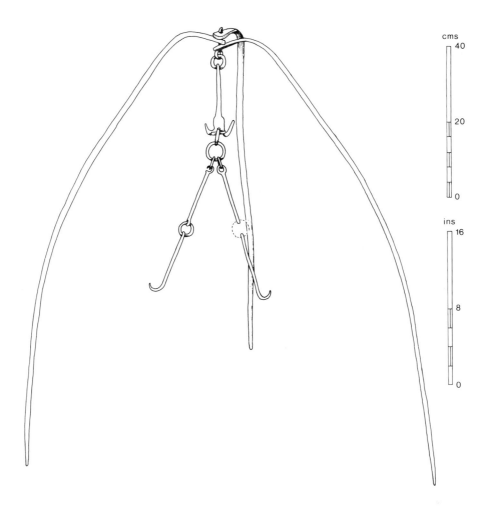

Fig. 5 Stanfordbury tripod.

looped, and the stem formed of a doubled, twisted rod. The most elaborate of these hooks is that from Hunsbury (Fig. 4.1) which is made of a doubled, twisted rod, with a loop at the head and with its ends turned up and slightly parted to form the curve of the hook. Two collars bind the stem and a third the tip of the hook. As will be seen, this type must have formed the prototype for the elaborate hooks of the late Roman chains.

The evidence of both the continental and British finds makes it clear that the normal form of cauldron hanger was the link and rod chain, and that the tripod was a relative rarity, apparently introduced late in the Iron Age. Of the two known from Britain, from Bigbury and Stanfordbury (Fig. 5), only the latter is sufficiently complete for the details of the cauldron hanger itself to be clear. The arms were suspended from an anchor-ended rod which hangs below the pivot, and although these are now separated from this hook there is no reason to doubt that, unlike the Continental ones described above, they were originally attached to it by means of the U-shaped link which still lies across the arms of the anchor.

The evidence does not make it clear when these chains were introduced into Britain. Where they can be given a date it is either late in the Iron Age or early in the Roman period, which might suggest that they were a late introduction probably arriving in the La Tène III period when there was considerable contact between south-eastern England and the Continent. Certainly the use of the U-shaped double-link to hang the chain from the anchor-shaped hooks, a feature which appears in the Continental chains at that time, confirms that British smiths were aware of changes being made in other parts of the Celtic world. But this does not preclude the possibility of such chains being in use in Britain before that date, for the amount of ironwork which can be assigned with certainty to any period before La Tène III is so small that the absence of a particular type is of no significance whatever. Indeed the fact that cauldrons were in use in Britain from the late Bronze Age may be taken as providing indirect support for the supposition that the method of hanging them used throughout the Celtic world will also have been used in this country.

Roman Cauldron Chains

Our knowledge of the evolution of the cauldron chain in Roman Britain is still distinctly incomplete. It is unusually well represented in its final form, but less is known of the stages by which it developed from the late Iron Age types. The main reason is the absence of hoards of the second and third centuries, for most of the late Roman chains, like their Iron Age predecessors, are either known or surmised to be from hoards. Most of the fourth-century chains are of the same, distinctive form: Piggott's Great Chesterford type. A suspension ring is at the top with a swivel and cage below it; next comes the main chain of U-shaped links, with a junction in the form of an elaborate reef-knot at its end which carries the arms, also of U-shaped links, ending in elaborate hooks, formed of a double rod with an ornamental coil at the back.

Complete or almost complete chains of this type come from the Great Chesterford hoard (Fig. 8.3), Winchester (Fig. 8.2) and in a slightly less developed form, from Cirencester (Fig. 8.1); large fragments from Brandon, Suffolk (Fig. 9.2), Appleford, Berks. (Fig. 9.1); and Dorn, Glos. (Fig. 7.1). Only those from Great Chesterford and Appleford in this group are securely dated, both being from fourth-century hoards.

A close examination of the various components of these chains leaves little doubt that they are derived from the Iron Age types. The U-shaped links and suspension ring are seen in the Butley, Pentyrch and 'East Anglian' chains; even the elaborate hooks are presaged in those from Bigbury, Over Fen and, especially, Hunsbury. As none of these are to be found in the Continental chains of similar date it is clear that we are dealing with an insular development.

For a link between these early chains and those of the late empire we must turn to three Scottish hoards (Eckford, Blackburn Mill and Carlingwark Loch), which were deposited around the end of the first century A.D., and which are probably to be associated with the Roman army. But before considering them we may note a fragment of similar date from Newstead which differs from the earlier chains in having its arms formed of links rather than rods (Fig. 6.1), although here its resemblance to the later chains ceases, for the links are of figure-of-eight form. Furthermore the hook which holds the junction is like no other on a cauldron chain, but the trefoil junction is almost identical with that on the Bigbury hanger. The three Scottish hoards contained fragments which together provide a considerable body of information. In particular they show that elaboration of the junction which linked the main chain and arms, had already begun by the end of the first century. The junction from the Carlingwark Loch hoard and one of the two from the Blackburn Mill hoard are fragmentary, but their complete form is shown by an unprovenanced example, probably from East Anglia[25] (Fig. 6.2), and by a less complete fragment from Gestingthorpe, Essex. Here the whole junction was functional, the upper hooks being attached to the main chain, whilst the lower hooks carried the arms. The complete Blackburn Mill junction (Fig. 6.3) differs from them in having an additional pair of coils which reflect in decorative form the hooks themselves. A junction from the Silchester 1900 hoard (Fig. 6.4), which must have been similar, even though it has lost the greater part of both coils and hooks, suggests that this type had a long popularity, for it cannot have been buried much before the middle of the fourth century A.D., although it could have been old at the time of deposition. The diagonal crosses seen on most of these junctions are similar to those decorating the collars on the cages of the Great Chesterford chains; apparently this was a form of decoration which became traditional on cauldron chains. The prototype of such junctions may be the elaborate double-hook which links the chain at the top of the 'East Anglian' cauldron hanger to the anchor-ended rod (Fig. 3.3). That they were used with chains of U-shaped double-links is shown by the one still attached to the Blackburn Mill junction. Whether the terminal hooks were linked to these junctions by rods as in the earlier hangers, or by chains as in the later ones, is an open question, although the fragment of rod attached to the 'East Anglian' junction (Fig. 6.2) suggests the former. Clearly this form of junction was fairly standardised by the end of the first century, but it is not certain when it was replaced by the reef-knot which is so typical of the fourth-century chains.

The development of the elaborate cage and swivel found at the top of the Great Chesterford chains is far from clear. The tops of the Iron Age chains are simple, but a possible prototype may be seen in the device which links the top

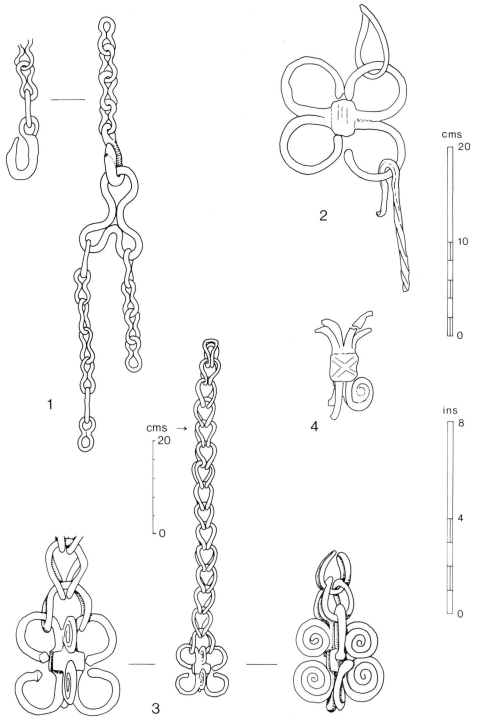

Fig. 6   Fragments of British chains: 1. Newstead, 2. 'East Anglia', unprovenanced, 3. Blackburn Mill, 4. Silchester.

chain to the anchor-ended rod in the 'East Anglian' chain (Fig. 3.3). As with the fragment from Silchester described below, it is made of paired bars bent into loops with their ends turned out as hooks, set head to tail and bound at their midpoint by a collar; all are features which characterise the later cages. A later stage in the development may be represented by a damaged fragment, probably from Bartlow, Essex (Fig. 7.3), which is made of paired, twisted bars, doubled to form loops which hold the suspension ring, with their free ends bent into hooks, only one of which now remains although it was more complete when it was discovered in 1854. The rods are bound at its midpoint, and just above the hooks, with simple collars. A fragment from the fourth-century Silchester 1900 hoard may show a later stage in this development (Fig. 7.2). It too is formed of a pair of doubled rods with loops at their ends, but here the loops are set at opposite ends of the cage so that each is paired with two hooks; the rods are bound by collars just before these loops. The most striking difference between this and the Bartlow piece is that the rods are bowed out in one plane to form a 'cage'. The suspension ring and chain are missing but we may presume that the former was held by the loop at the head of the cage and the latter by the hooks at its bottom. It is possible that it came from the same chain as the Blackburn Mill type of junction, which was found in this hoard (Fig. 6.4), but we cannot be certain, for the same hoard also produced another junction of eccentric design, and fragments of no fewer than four hooked arms, which differ sufficiently to make it clear that they represent at least three separate hangers.

The penultimate stage in this development is probably illustrated by the cage of the Cirencester chain (fig. 8.1), where for the first time we see a broad collar below the suspension ring. It differs from the true Great Chesterford chains in having the suspension ring held by a broad collar which is probably the head of the pivot, rather than by having the pivot pass through the base of the ring itself. As a result the whole pivot would have had to revolve with the ring, instead of the ring turning on the pivot. How the pivot is attached to the cage is concealed by the collar which is immovably corroded. All that is clear is that it has a mushroom-shaped base which would have prevented it being pulled through the collar. Nor is it certain if the cage is made of two rods which have been doubled, as in the Silchester cage, or of four separate rods, as in the Great Chesterford type of cage, although the latter is perhaps more probable. The broad collar is clearly functional for it holds the tops of the rods and the pivot together. At the bottom of the cage the rods are held by a rectangular binding, below which they turn out as simple hooks, two (both now lost) carrying the chain and two being bent back to touch the collar. The remainder of the chain also differs in various ways from the true Great Chesterford type. The U-shaped double-links are tightly closed, and the reef-knot junction is replaced by an S-shaped hook, which carries a second, loose hook. It is most improbable that this was the original arrangement; it appears rather to be a crude adaptation which allowed the arms to be hung from a high beam by the main chain, or be removed from the chain and suspended from a low beam using the spare hook.

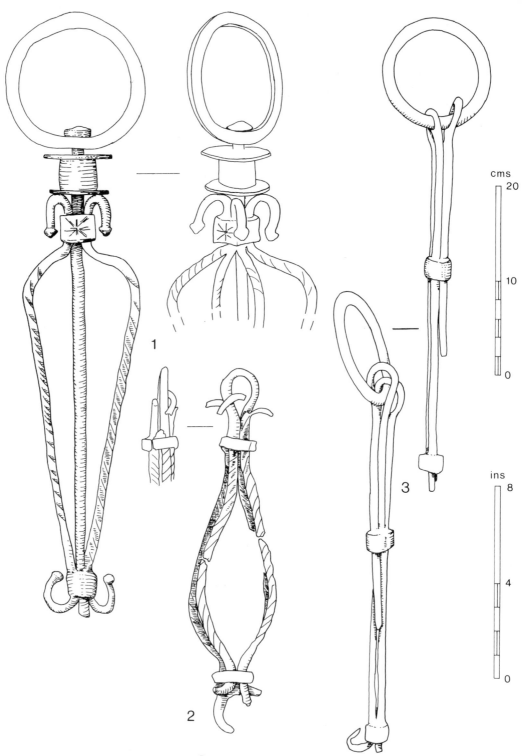

Fig. 7 Fragments of British chains: 1. Dorn, 2. Silchester, 3. Bartlow.

A cage of this type required only one major development to become the true Great Chesterford type: the addition of a bar running through the centre of the cage to emerge at its top where it acted as a pivot for the collar and suspension ring, now perforated to receive the head of the pivot (Fig. 7.1 from Dorn). Here the collar appears to have no real function save perhaps as a spacer between the ring and the cage. The other characteristic of these cages is that the sides are made, not of paired looped rods, but of four separate rods, bound at top and bottom by rectangular collars and with their ends turned out as hooks each ending in conical knobs. Two of those at the bottom carried the chain; the rest were ornamental. It is this form of cage which is found on the Great Chesterford (Fig. 8.3), Brandon (Fig. 9.2) and Winchester chains (Fig. 8.2), and in an isolated example from Dorn, Glos. (Fig. 7.1).

The development of the terminal hooks does not present these problems. The increasing complexity of the Iron Age forms, culminating in the Hunsbury hook (Fig. 4.1), had already almost created the form found on the late chains. All that remained was for the rear bar with its coiled head to be added and the process was complete. We do not know when this occurred, for the hooks which went with early Roman junctions are lost.

The appearance of these elaborate hooks did not lead to the abandonment of the simpler forms. Hangers with twisted rods and simple hooks are known from the late first or second-century Eckford Hoard; from Silchester, where, in addition to an undated pair of linked arms, fragments of others were found in the fourth-century 1900 hoard; and from another fourth-century hoard from Weeting, Norfolk. This last has paired arms which hang from a twisted rod, an arrangement reminiscent of the earlier chains such as that from Butley.

It would obviously be foolish to regard the process outlined here as a simple evolutionary sequence; rather we are seeing stages in a complex development producing many variations, of which the surviving pieces are merely examples. None the less, the general trend is clear, and its final form, the Great Chesterford type of chain, is too uniform in its details to be anything other than the standard cauldron chain of late Roman Britain.

The popularity of these chains, apparently throughout the Roman period in Britain presents an interesting sidelight on the long continuance of Celtic customs and taste even in the most romanised parts of the country. It is inherently improbable that such expensive masterpieces of the blacksmith's craft were intended for the kitchen; rather they suggest the ceremonial cooking which centred around the cauldron and the feast. Yet they come, not from the wilds of Wales or the Pennines where such old customs might be expected to have lingered on, but from some of the major cities of the province, Silchester, Great Chesterford, Winchester and Cirencester. As so often when dealing with Roman Britain one senses that below the veneer of classical culture lay a society which had never really rejected its older values.

Nor was their evolution to stop with the end of the Roman period, as is shown by the great chain from the Sutton Hoo ship burial. Although trans-

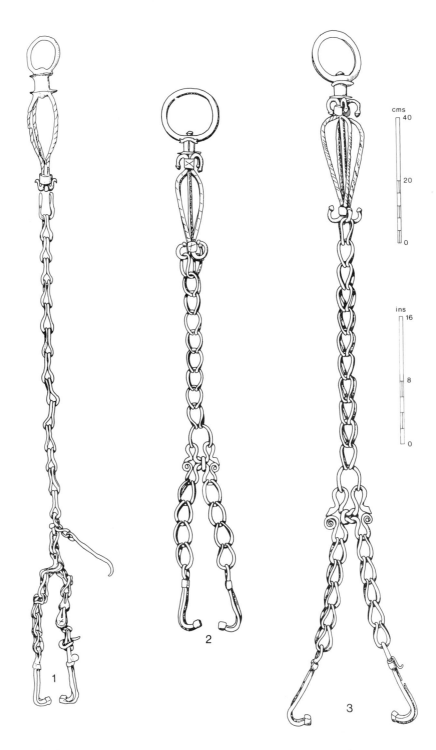

cms
40

20

0

ins
16

8

0

1

2

3

Fig. 8   British chains: 1. Cirencester, 2. Winchester, 3. Great Chesterford.

Fig. 9   British chains: 1. Appleford, 2. Brandon.

formed in many of its details, and grown larger than anything known in the
earlier periods, it is clearly derived from the Romano-British types, with a
terminal ring attached to a now stylised cage, and a more elaborate but still
recognisable reef-knot junction. Indeed in its use of rods in the body of the chain

and U-shaped links hanging from anchor-ended rods, it appears that the typo-logically earlier forms had not entirely lost their influence. As it hung in the hall of the Saxon king it must have formed a fitting end to a thousand years of development.

Acknowledgements

In preparing this paper I have received help from many people. I must thank the curators and staffs of various museums for giving me access to their collections, in particular Miss Joan Liversidge of the Museum of Archaeology and Ethnology, Cambridge; the staffs of the Department of Prehistoric and Romano-British Antiquities of the British Museum; the Corinium Museum, Cirencester; the National Museum of Antiquities, Edinburgh; and Winchester Museum. My former colleague Mr. Christopher Saunders provided much of the information on the British Iron Age chains and some of the original drawings used in that section; without his help that part could not have been written. Information on the Wiggonholt Common chain and a drawing of it was pro-vided by Mr. Ralph Jackson, to whom I am most grateful. The final drawings were the work of Mr. Howard Mason of the Department of Archaeology, University College, Cardiff.

REFERENCES FOR BRITISH CAULDRON CHAINS

Appleford, Berks.	Lower part of a chain. Late Roman. Brown, P.D.C., 'A Roman Pewter Hoard from Appleford, Berks.', *Oxoniensia*, xxxviii, (1973), 193, fig. 5.
Bartlow, Essex	Simple cage. Roman. Museum of Archaeology and Ethnology, Cambridge. Probably that excavated by R.C. Neville in 1854 at Bartlow. 'Description of a remarkable Deposit of Roman Antiquities of Iron, discovered at Great Chesterford, Essex in 1854', *Archaeol. Journ.*, xiii, (1856), 5.
Bigbury, Kent	Fragments of several hangers and a tripod. Late Iron Age. Dawkins, W. Boyd, 'On Bigbury Camp and the Pilgrim Way', *Archaeol. Journ.*, lix, (1902), 215, pl. II, fig. 5; for the tripod cf. Jessup, R.F., 'Bigberry Camp, Harbledown, Kent', *ibid.*, lxxxix, (1932), 107.
Blackburn Mill, Berwicks.	Length of chain and junction, and a fragment of a second junction. Late first or second century A.D. Piggott, S., 'Three Metal-Work Hoards of the Roman Period from Southern Scotland', *Proc. Society of Antiquaries of Scotland*, lxxxvii, (1953), 42, fig. 11, B17 and B18.
Bledlow, Bucks.	Terminal hook. Iron Age or Roman. Head, J.F. and Piggott, C.M., 'An Iron Age site at Bledlow, Bucks.', *Records of Buckinghamshire*, xiv, (1946), 189, fig. 1, 2; Saunders, C., 'The Pre-Belgic Iron Age in the Central and Western Chilterns', *Archaeol. Journ.*, cxxviii, (1971), 15.

Brandon, Suffolk	Fragments of Great Chesterford type of chain; a surface find made in 1948 after ploughing at Fenhouse Farm. Late Roman. Museum of Archaeology and Ethnology, Cambridge. *Proc. Cambridge Antiq. Soc.*, xlv, (1951), 67.
Butley, Suffolk	Complete chain found without associations in gravel digging. Late Iron Age or Early Roman. Ipswich Museum. Information and drawing from C. Saunders.
Carlingwark Loch, Kirkcudbrightshire	Fragment of junction. Late first or early second century A.D. Piggott, S., 'Three Metal-Work Hoards of the Roman Period from Southern Scotland', *Proc. Society of Antiquaries of Scotland*, lxxxvii, (1953), 33, fig. 8, C10.
Cirencester, Glos.	Complete chain found under unknown circumstances at Cirencester. Late Roman. Corinium Museum.
Moreton-in-Marsh, Glos., Dorn Farm	Cage of Great Chesterford type. Late Roman. From a small hoard in a villa. British Museum, Department of Prehistoric and Romano-British Antiquities.
Eckford, Roxburghshire	Fragments of rods and hooked arms. Late first or early second century A.D. Piggott, S., 'Three Metal-Work Hoards from Southern Scotland', *Proc. Society of Antiquaries of Scotland*, lxxxvii, (1953), 24, fig. 5.
'East Anglian' Chain	Complete chain from an unknown provenance. Late Iron Age or early Roman. Museum of Archaeology and Ethnology, Cambridge.
'East Anglian' Junction	Provenance unknown. Roman. Museum of Archaeology and Ethnology, Cambridge. From Braybrooke Collection.
Gestingthorpe, Essex	Junction of East Anglian type. Publication by W.H. Manning and Jo Chaplin, forthcoming.
Great Chesterford, Essex	Complete chain. Late Roman. Neville, R.C., 'Description of a remarkable Deposit of Roman Antiquities of Iron, Discovered at Great Chesterford, Essex in 1854', *Archaeol. Journ.*, xiii, (1856), 4, pl. 3, 32
Hunsbury, Northants.	Two terminal hooks and two looped rods. Iron Age. Northampton Museum. Fell, C., 'The Hunsbury Hillfort, Northants', *Archaeol. Journ.*, xciii, (1936), 67, pl. VII.
Ham Hill, Somerset	Terminal hook and looped rod, looped rod and chain, and two looped rods. Iron Age or Roman. Taunton Museum. Information from C. Saunders.
Kingsdown Camp, Somerset	Looped rod. Late Iron Age or early Roman. Gray, H. St. George, 'Excavations at Kingsdown Camp, Mells, Somerset, 1927-9', *Archaeologia*, lxxx, (1930), 86, fig. 7, I 11.
Newstead, Roxburghshire	Fragment of chain and junction. Flavian. Curle, J., *A Roman Frontier Post and Its People: The Fort of Newstead in the Parish of Melrose*, Glasgow, 1911, 287, pl. LXIV, 3.
Over Fen, Cambs.	Two chains found without associations. Late Iron Age or early Roman. Museum of Archaeology and Ethnology, Cambridge. Piggott, S., 'Three Metal-Work Hoards from Southern Scotland', *Proc. Society of Antiquaries of Scotland*, lxxxvii, (1953), 26, pl. I, left.
Pentyrch, Glam.	Terminal ring and part of the chain. Late Iron Age. Part of a hoard. Savory, H.N., 'A find of early Iron Age metalwork from the Lesser Garth, Pentyrch', *Archaeol. Cambrensis*, cxv, (1966) 38, fig. 3, 2.
Silchester, Hants.	Various fragments in Reading Museum, including a junction of Blackburn Mill type, a cage and several hooks from the fourth cen-

	tury '1900' hoard, and a pair of linked arms from House 1, Insula XIX (*Archaeologia,* lvi, (1899), 24, fig. 3). For the '1900' hoards, cf. *ibid.,* lvii, (1901) and Manning, W.H., 'Ironwork Hoards in Iron Age and Roman Britain', *Britannia,* iii, (1972), 236.
Stanfordbury, Beds.	Hanger and tripod. Late Iron Age. Stead, I.M., 'A La Tène III Burial at Welwyn Garden City', *Archaeologia,* ci, (1967), 55.
Sutton Hoo, Suffolk	Complete chain. Seventh century A.D. Bruce-Mitford, R., *The Sutton Hoo Ship-Burial,* London, 1972, 39, fig. 16 and 17.
Weeting, Norfolk	Gregory, T., 'A Hoard of Late Roman Metalwork from Weeting, Norfolk', *Norfolk Archaeology,* xxxvi, pt. 3, (1977), 265, fig. 4.
Wiggonholt Common, nr. Pulborough, Sussex	Anchor-ended rod and hook. Part of a hoard found with a metal detector. Publication by R.P.J. Jackson, forthcoming.
Winchester, Hants.	Complete chain. Late Roman. The circumstances of its discovery are not recorded but it is a nineteenth-century find almost certainly from the City of Winchester. Winchester Museum.

NOTES

1. Piggott defined the Stanfordbury type as one 'in which looped rods joined by rings form the main components, with lengths of chain adjusted to the height above the fire required'. Unfortunately the Stanfordbury hanger is suspended from a tripod which makes it atypical; in reality Piggott's term has been applied to all hangers or fragments which are unlikely to have come from a Great Chesterford type of chain, a clearly unsatisfactory practice.

2. This study is not intended as a corpus of cauldron chains or of fragments from them, but as a summary of their development. Other pieces are known which have been omitted by intent and no doubt there are more which have been omitted from ignorance. References for the continental chains are given in the footnotes; those for the British ones in the list, arranged alphabetically by site.

3. Déchelette, J., *Manuel d'Archéologie Préhistorique, Celtique et Gallo-Romaine, II ii, Premier Age du Fer,* Paris, 1913, fig. 231, b.

4. *ibid.,* 804, fig. 232, 1.

5. Continental cauldron chains are discussed by Gerhard Jacobi in his report on the ironwork from Manching: *Werkzeug und Gerät aus dem Oppidum von Manching,* Wiesbaden, 1974, 111, where references to other examples may be found.

6. Vouga, P., *La Tène,* Leipzig 1923, 82, pl. XXVII, 4.

7. *ibid.,* 82, pl. XXVII, 5.

8. Déchelette, J., *op. cit.* (see note 3), 807, fig. 323, 3.

9. Jacobi, G., *op. cit.* (see note 5), Abb. 28, La Tène D left.

10. *Mitteilungen der Anthropologischen Gesellschaft Wien,* lvii, (1927), 206, Abb. 1, 1.

11. *Saalburg Jahrbuch,* iii, (1912), 52–3, Taf. 10, 5 and 6.

12. *Der Obergermanisch-raetische Limes des Römerreiches,* Heidelberg, 1914, B II 2, Kastell 23, 25, Taf. V, 1.

13. *ibid.,* B V 1, Kastell 59, 29, Taf. IX, 4.

14. Déchelette, J., *op. cit.* (see note 3), 807, fig. 323, 3.

15. Reinach, S., *Catalogue Illustré du Musée des Antiquités Nationales de Saint-Germaine-en-Laye,* I, Paris, 1923, 277, fig. 281, 25795.

16. *Revue Archéologique de l'Est et du Centre-Est,* xiii, (1962), 167, fig. 61.

17. Lindenschmit, L., *Die Altertümer Unserer Heidnischen Vorzeit, V,* 1912, Taf. 15, 284.

18. *Revue Archéologique,* xiv, (1921), 94, figs. 1 and 2.

19. Fell, C., 'The Hunsbury Hillfort, Northants', *Archaeol. Journ.,* xciii, (1936), 65.

20. Manning, W.H., 'Ironwork Hoards in Iron Age and Roman Britain', *Britannia,* iii, (1972), 230.

21. *ibid.*

22. It may be significant that all of the well-preserved chains which are certainly of fourth-century date are of the Great Chesterford type. The others appear only as dissociated fragments, suggesting that by that date they were being discarded as scrap. That such large and elaborate pieces of ironwork could have had a long life may be accepted as certain, the more so as they are not heavily worn by continual use.

23. Déchelette, J., *Manuel d'Archéologie Préhistorique, Celtique et Gallo-Romaine, IV, Second Age du Fer,* Paris, 1927, 926, fig. 636, I.

24. It was the use of this form of link which led Savory to assign the Pentyrch chain to Piggott's Great Chesterford type, but it is clear that such links cannot be taken as diagnostic of that type whether loosely or closely defined, as the Butley and 'East Anglian' chains show.

25. It is in the Braybrooke Collection in the Museum of Archaeology and Ethnology, Cambridge, a collection which contains material from sites mainly in the area of Great Chesterford, excavated in the mid-nineteenth century by R.C. Neville, later Lord Braybrooke. It is just possible that this piece should be associated with the cage from the same collection which is discussed below.

26. Neville's description of the Bartlow piece differs in a number of ways from the

fragment under discussion (Neville, R.C., *Archaeol. Journ.,* xiii, (1856), 5). He refers to a swivel in the ring and states that the iron 'ropes' were nine inches long with four links of chain attached to their ends. But, despite these discrep-ancies, the two are probably the same, and Neville's reference to nine inches may refer to the length of the cage below the top binding, the upper part being what he calls the swivel.

The Military Origins of some Roman Settlements in Belgium

by

J. MERTENS

(Translation by David Parsons)

It is with great pleasure that I dedicate these few pages to Professor Sheppard Frere, who has on so many occasions drawn attention to the role played by the army in the establishment and development of towns and settlements in Roman Britain.[1] In the following pages we will consider whether the phenomenon also occurs on the continent, more particularly in the northern parts of Belgic Gaul. In these areas urbanization, one of the major achievements of Rome, was actually of late and isolated occurrence; one sometimes has the impression that Romanisation, at least in its urban aspect, was never accomplished there. These largely rural territories enjoyed a peculiar form of government, Rome having recognised for political reasons the old tribal groupings; apart from settling territorial boundaries, the organization of these districts necessitated the establishment of civitas capitals, land management and the creation of a road network.

The road system reflects the strategic aims of the Romans; from Lyon two routes diverge, one in the direction of the Atlantic Coast and Brittany by way of Reims, Thérouanne and Boulogne, the other towards the Rhine and Germania via Metz, Trier and Cologne. The extremities of these two routes are linked by a third road passing through Tongres, Bavay and Cassel (Fig. 1). Practically all the civitas capitals of north Gaul were established, without regard to pre-existing centres of Gaulish population, along these routes, which had been laid out primarily for military purposes. Examples of this are Atuatuca-Tongres *(civitas Tungrorum)*, Bagacum-Bavay *(civitas Nerviorum)*, Castellum-Cassel *(civitas Menapiorum)*, and Tervanna-Thérouanne *(civitas Morinorum)*.

This paper offers some thoughts, resulting from research and excavation carried out in the last few years on settlement sites in Belgium, on the role of the army in this process. First of all, however, a comment on the road system: contrary to what has been implied previously,[2] the road from Bavay to Cologne is an entirely Roman creation. Excavations at Liberchies and Braives have produced most interesting information about the techniques of construction and the date of the roadway. At Liberchies it has been shown that the carriageway was flanked not only by the customary drainage ditches but also by two further ditches about twenty metres from the middle of the road. These ditches, con-

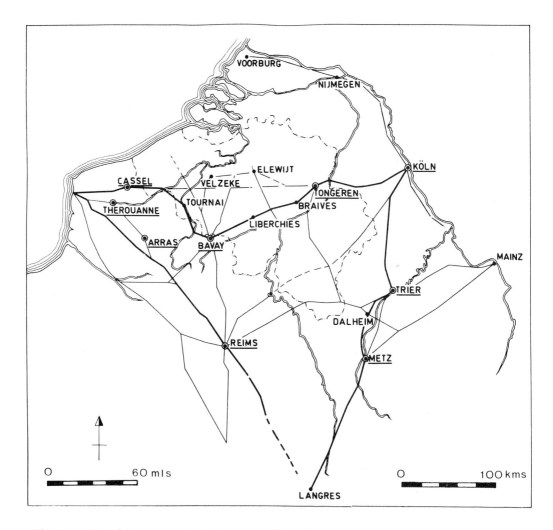

Fig. 1 Principal Roman roads in the north of Gaul.

temporary with the roadway, were disused from the first half of the first century A.D.; their fill contained brooches, fragments of Aco beakers and sherds of arretine, all of which can be dated satisfactorily to the Augustan period.[3] The purpose of these ditches remains obscure: they might be interpreted as the boundaries of a strip of land, either expropriated or kept for public use. Identical ditches were sectioned at Braives on the same road[4] and on the road from Amiens to Senlis.[5] If the layout of these lines of communication was the result of an initiative in the Augustan period, it follows that the settlements

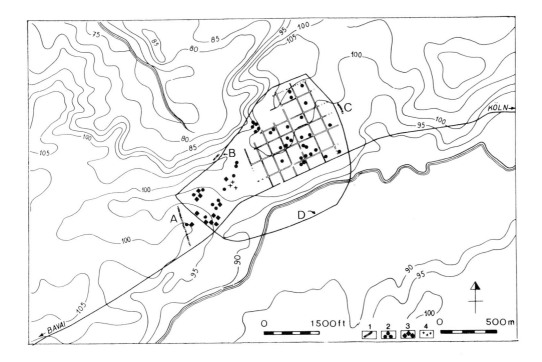

Fig. 2 Tongres: site plan *(after Vanvinckenroye, 1975)* 1. Ditches (A, B, C), 2. Distribution of arretine pottery, 3. Distribution of coins with the legend AVAVCIA, 4. Tombs, D. Town wall in the second century.

which developed alongside them belong to the same programme.[6]

A brief conspectus of some Belgian towns where archaeology has been able to determine their origins may be of interest.

Atuatuca-Tongres

Despite its apparently Gaulish name, the town of Tongres has so far not produced any evidence of pre-Roman occupation. The earliest evidence consists either of pottery or coins, or of archaeological features. Among the latter there are first of all the traces of a ditch located to the west, north and east of the future town;[7] in the present state of research it is difficult to be sure, however whether these fragmentary remains, which are at some distance from each other, belong to the same complex; but if this were the case the ditch would enclose an area of more than 140 ha. (346 acres). The best preserved remains are found in the western area: there is a typical V-shaped ditch, 7.5 m. (25 ft.) wide and 3.6 m. (12 ft.) deep, which can be followed for a distance of approximately 200 m. (500 ft.). On the inner side of this ditch is an earth and timber rampart, of which the palisade posts are still partly preserved. Larger postholes may indicate the site of a gate. To the east, where the nucleus of the town was to develop in the Claudian period, excavation has revealed traces of wooden structures, whose layout, although rectilinear, deviates from the Claudian plan. The dating of these features can be deduced from the finds: the ditches themselves have produced very little material — a coin struck at Lyon between 10 and 3 B.C. and pottery of the 'Augustan-Tiberian' period[8] — but the evidence from the settlement site is much richer: large quantities of arretine[9] and numerous native coins (some with the legend AVAVCIA) or official republican or colonial issues.[10] It is significant that the pottery is widely scattered over the site, while the coins seem to be concentrated in the western sector (Fig. 2). The relative absence of typically military objects is noteworthy. It follows from these data that the site at Tongres was fairly densely settled from the second decade B.C. Further, the excavations appear to show that this early occupation was interrupted and changed its character in the Tiberian period, when they began to bury their dead in the western area[11] and when a purely urban settlement with a rectilinear grid of streets grew up further to the east. The latter, laid out in the Claudian period, reached its final form in the second century at the time of the construction of a massive town wall.

Liberchies

Excavations carried out over the past few years in this small town, which lies on the road from Bavay to Cologne, have produced a vast amount of material proving occupation from the second half of the first century B.C. Among the 114 Gaulish coins, a high proportion are pieces attributed to the Nervii or bearing the legend AVAVCIA.[12] The pottery consists of arretine, thin-walled vessels, amphorae and mortaria.[13] Recently Monsieur Graff, one of the excavators of the site, has announced the discovery of a V-shaped feature 7–8 m. (23–26 ft.) wide and 4.5 m. (15 ft.) deep;[14] it is hoped that future excavations will give more information on the subject.

Braives

This *vicus,* situated on the same road, is currently the subject of exhaustive excavations. A first report has just appeared.[15] It transpires that the occupation there goes back to the last decades B.C., which is proved by the arretine pottery (although this is found in smaller quantities than at Tongres or Liberchies), some Gaulish and Roman coins and brooches of Aucissa type. So far no trace has been discovered of a V-shaped ditch or associated, contemporary features.

Turnacum-Tournai

Between Bavay and Boulogne, Tournai, a mere *vicus* during the early Empire, became a civitas capital during the late Empire. The site seems to have been chosen by military authority: a typical V-shaped ditch was laid out on the heights of La Loucherie, dominating the Escaut and the Roman road, right in the centre of the future town. It was perfectly straight and could be traced for a distance of 55 m. (180 ft.); it makes a right angle to the east[16] and it was filled in before the middle of the first century A.D. (Fig. 3). Cuttings in the vicinity have revealed traces of a second ditch.[17] The material recovered, which indicates the date at which the ditch was abandoned, consists of Nervian bronze coins, a *denarius* of the Republic, and coins with the legend GERMANUS INDUTILLI I, as well as native pottery.[18] All belong to the end of the first century B.C. or the beginning of the first century A.D.; the lack of typical Roman pottery does not allow any closer dating.

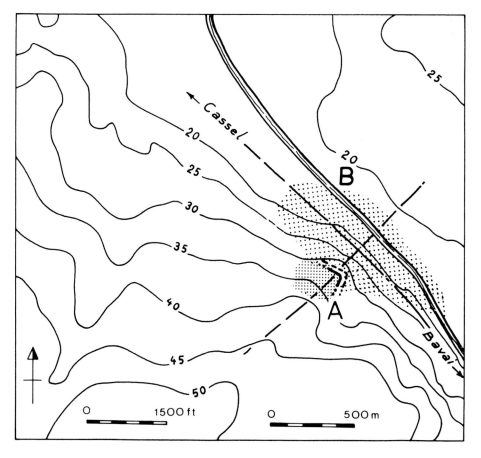

Fig. 3   The site of Tournai: A. Ditches, B. Roman *vicus*.

The places discussed above mark the route Cologne-Bavay-Boulogne. Others lie further north, but are directly linked with this road.

Velzeke

Recent excavations by Monsieur M. Rogge have uncovered an Augustan base with an area of about 5 ha. (12 acres).[19] Although the excavations have not yet revealed any details, it appears that the camp was enclosed by three typical V-shaped ditches, the innermost of which is the most important, measuring 4 m. (13 ft.) in width and 2.4–2.8 m. (8–9 ft.) in depth. On the inner side of this ditch was an earth and timber rampart. The complex is an irregular quadrilateral in plan (Fig. 4). The fill of the ditches contained very little material: amphorae fragments, a *denarius* of Julius Caesar, some arretine and pottery in the La Tène tradition.[20] Gaulish coins were discovered in the vicinity.

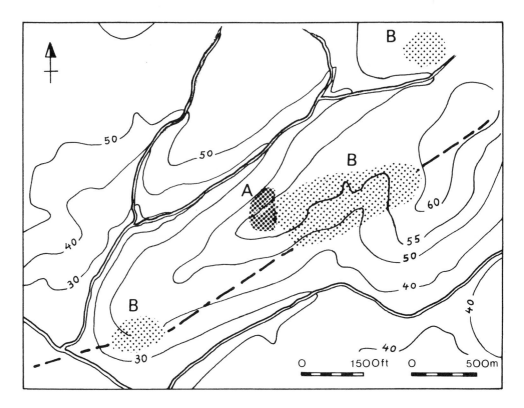

Fig. 4 The site of Velzeke *(after M. Rogge 1980)*: A. Augustan base, B. Roman settlements.

Elewijt

The excavations carried out in this small settlement from 1947 to 1953 revealed part of a V-shaped ditch cut into the sandy soil. It ran east-west, and could be followed for 60 m. (200 ft.), with an interruption of 8 m. (26 ft.) in the centre (Fig. 5). The fill was very homogeneous but sterile, with the exception of one sherd of native pottery, which seems to indicate a short-lived occupation. Indeed, before the middle of the first century, the timber building of a small settlement had covered the entirely deserted, earlier site.[21] Material recovered from the same area indicates occupation from the Augustan period: Gaulish and Roman coins including one with the legend GERMANUS INDUTILLI I, a Republican *denarius* and a *quadrans* of Augustus, dating from 4 B.C.,[22] plus some sherds of arretine.[23]

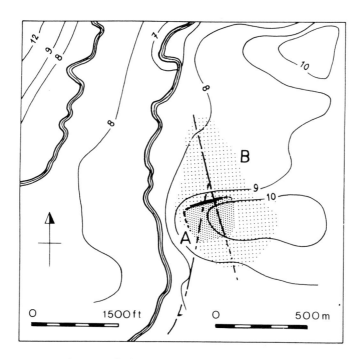

Fig. 5 The site of Elewijt: A. Ditch B. Roman settlement.

Asse

The topography of Asse may be compared with that of Velzeke: a road connects the site directly with Bavay. As at Velzeke and Elewijt, the material found *in situ* is hardly copious, but it proves nevertheless a Roman presence beginning at the

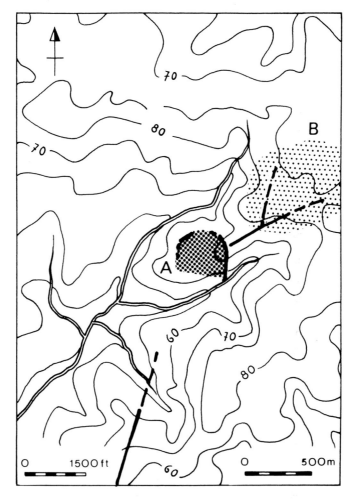

Fig. 6   The site of Asse *(after Graff, 1981)*: A. Roman 'camp', B. Roman settlement.

end of the first century B.C.: arretine, native pottery, Gaulish and Augustan coinage.[24] Surviving topographical evidence as well as recent trial trenches and excavations seem to show the existence of a huge Gaulish *oppidum* some 42 ha. (100 acres) in area, into which a Roman 'camp' of smaller dimensions was later introduced (Fig. 6)[25] Future excavations should make clear the chronological sequence and the nature of this occupation.

Some deductions may be made from this brief survey. Not until three decades after the conquest by Caesar (51 B.C.) was there any effective organization of the occupied territories.[26] It was the work of Augustus and consisted in the first place of the establishment of a road network.[27] Along these routes were series of stations which, in the beginning, had a more military and economic role than a purely administrative one; among these stations the civitas capitals, such as Tongres, Bavay or Thérouanne did not take on their classic urban form until the Claudian period, and the evolution was completed in the second century, the 'century of towns'. At first these centres were mainly supply bases intended for logistical support, run by and for the army, and probably laid out by military engineers. Apart perhaps from some soldiers, their population was made up principally of merchants, *negotiatores* working for the army. It was perhaps one of these *negotiatores* — effectively the local administrators — who greeted Tiberius when he passed through Bavay in A.D. 4 (Fig. 7).[28] The large number of coins and the imported pottery illustrate the scale of the trade: there is no doubt that supplies were of prime importance for the army. Although the army could satisfy its needs in the course of a conquest by extracting contributions from the local populace, it would not be possible thereafter; there would have to have been supply bases, organized collection centres and roads for the rapid distribution of the merchandise. This presupposes the organization of production, since only surplus produce could be sold. In this connection Tongres and its district is an instructive example. Situated in a fertile agricultural area and in the immediate vicinity of the Rhine armies, the town absorbed all the produce of the region; it is hardly surprising that several rural sites have produced evidence for settlements of native type preceding the classic Roman villas.[29] What is more, Tongres continued in its role as a trade centre throughout the Empire.[30]

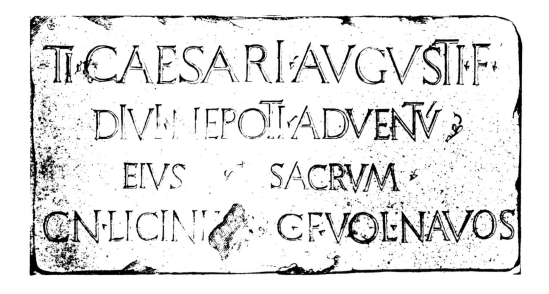

Fig. 7   Inscription recording Tiberius' visit to Bavay.

The waterways also played an important part in this trade, as is shown by the arretine found at Namur, at the confluence of the Sambre and the Meuse.[31] But the great highways were the best means of communication for the army and for the administration. In Belgium, the Rhine-North Sea link via Bavay and Tongres remained the principal route; the settlements that grew along it[32] owed their existence more to these indispensable bases than to the actual presence of strategic units. It is not surprising that these bases sometimes have the appearance of a military camp;[33] one need only refer to the comparable situation in other parts of the Empire, for example at Rödgen. The absence of typically military objects distinguishes these sites from operational camps such as Haltern, Oberaden, Neuss or Nijmegen. It is worthy of note that the stations between Bavay and Tongres are spaced more or less regulaly along the road, which can only be the result of a central administrative control.[34] The forward stations mentioned above — Velzeke, Elewijt and Asse — were part of the same arrangement; they were linked not only directly to the Bavay-Tongres road, but also with each other, even though that may seem to be a secondary connection; a direct route from Tongres to Cassel via Courtai should not be dismissed however,[35] and it would be interesting to discover whether the settlements along this route, such as Tienen or Courtai, had their origin in an identical system.[36]

It would be of some significance if all these elements could be put into a more historical and chronological context. Although they date in general terms from the Augustan period, it would be interesting to be able to relate them to one or other of the military campaigns.[37] As far as Tongres is concerned, the proposed date is the second decade B.C.,[38] as it is at Liberchies.[39] For the other sites the dating remains more fluid despite the presence of arretine[40] or of native coins of AVAVCIA type.[41] Further work will probably lead to greater precision on this subject.[42]

Be all this as it may, it is clear from what has been said above that the role of the army — along with the needs which it created — was a decisive factor in the establishment and early development of many of the Roman settlements, especially those lining the major strategic routes.

Certainly one should not generalize. In the case of certain small towns geographical or economic considerations may have played a significant part. Others developed as secondary administrative or religious centres of a *civitas*, and others again (although they are the exception rather than the rule) grew out of pre-existing settlements. The picture is very diverse.[43] Only in about the second quarter of the first century A.D., when the military administration became concentrated along the frontiers and the hinterland was surrendered to the civilians, can one observe the ultimate flowering of our settlements and towns. In many cases the seed had been sown by the army.

NOTES

1. Frere, S.S., 'The origin of small towns', in Rodwell, W. and Rowley, T. (eds.), *Small Towns of Roman Britain*, Oxford, 1975 and Frere, S.S., 'Verulamium and the towns of Britannia', in Temporini, H. and Haase, T. (eds.), *Aufstieg und Niedergang der Römischen Welt II. 3*, 1975, 290–327.

2. Mertens, J., *Archaeologia Belgica*, xxxiii, (1957), 43.

3. Claes, P., *Helinium*, ix, (1969), 138–50.

4. Brulet, R. *et al.*, *Braives gallo-romain I*, Louvain-la-Neuve, 1981.

5. Agache, R., *Bulletin de la Société des antiquaires de Picardie*, (1968), 258–64.

6. Recent excavations have shown this to be true, particularly in the case of Bavay, Maastricht, Thérouanne (see below) or Dalheim: Krier, J., *Publications de la Section historique de l'Institut grand ducal de Luxembourg*, xciv, (1980), 139–94.

7. Vanvinckenroye, W., *Opgravingen te Tongeren 1963–1964*, Tongeren, 1965 and Vanvinckenroye, W., *Tongeren, Romeinse Stad*, Tongeren, 1975.

8. *ibid.*, 19.

9. Vanderhoeven, M., *De Terra Sigillata te Tongeren, III. De italische terra sigillata*, Tongeren, 1968.

10. Vanvinckenroye, W., *Romeinse Stad*, (see note 7), 17–18.

11. Vanvinckenroye, W., *Opgravingen te Tongeren*, (see note 7), 19–20.

12. Graff, T., *Romana Contact*, ix, (1979), 26–32.

13. Graff, T., *Romana Contact*, vii, (1978), 7–66.

14. *ibid.*, 46.

15. Brulet, R. *et al.*, *op. cit.* (see note 4).

16. Mertens, J. and Remy, H., *Archaeologia Belgica*, clxv, (1974), 29 and plan III, 51.

17. Amand, M., *Helinium*, iii, (1963), 196–204.

18. *ibid.*, 193–204 and Amand, M., *Antiquité Classique*, xxviii, (1959), 108–24.

19. Rogge, M., *Hermeneus*, lii, (1980), 135–9.

20. *ibid.*, and Rogge, M., *Oudheidkundige opgravingen en vondsten in Oost-Vlaanderen*, vii, (1976), 76–8.

21. Mertens, J., *Archaeologia Belgica*, xix, (1954), 26–8 and figs. 7 and 17.

22. Mertens, J., *Revue belge Numismatique*, xciv, (1948), 124–6.

23. Vaes, E. and Mertens, J., *Collection Latomus*, xiii, (1953), 11 and Vanderhoeven, M., *op. cit.* (see note 9), 85.

24. Scheltens, E. *et al.*, *Asse, waar de romeinen thuis waren*. Asse, 1981; Vanderhoeven, M., *op. cit.* (see note 9), 85 and Mertens, J., *Archaeologia Belgica*, iv (1951), 129–44.

25. Graff, T. and Lenoir, P., *Romana Contact*, *xviii*, (1981), 7–72.

26. Wightman, E., *Actes du IX congrès international d'études sur les frontieres romaines*, Bucarest, 1974, 479–82; Wightman, E., *Helinium*, xvii, (1977), 107, 114–16; Wightman, E., 'The pattern of rural settlement in Roman Gaul', in Temporini, H. and Haase, W. (eds.), *Aufstieg und Niedergang der Römischen Welt II, 3*, 1975, 619–34 and Wightman, E., *Akten des XI Internationale Limeskongresses*, Budapest, 1978, 75–86.

27. von Petrikovits, H., *Die Rheinlande in Römischer Zeit*, Düsseldorf, 1980, 54.

28. *C.I.L.* xiii, 3570.

29. Notably at Rosmeer, Valmeer, Haccourt, Donk and Neerharen: De Boe, G., and Van Impe, L., *Archaeologia Belgica*, ccxvi, (1979), 1–44; De Boe, G., *Archaeologia Belgica*, (1981), 37–41 and Van Impe, L., *ibid*, 47–51.

30. In the western area of the Augustan base, but *extra muros*, there was established, around the middle of the first century A.D., a vast complex possibly to be compared with official warehouses: Mertens, J., and Vanvinckenroye, W., *Archaeologia Belgica*, clxxx, (1975), 1–63 and Vanvinckenroye, W., *Een Romeins gebouwencomplex extra-muros te Tongeren*, Tongeren, 1979.

31. Vanderhoeven, M., *op. cit.* (see note 9), 86–87. See du Plat Taylor, J. and Cleere, H. (eds.), *Roman Shipping and Trade: Britain and the Rhine Provinces*, London, 1978. Note also the excavations in the small river port of Pommerœul, which

have revealed an occupation dating from the second half of the first century B.C.: De Boe, G. and Hubert, F., *Archaeologia Belgica,* cxcii, (1977), 1–57 and *Archaeologia Belgica,* ccxlviii, (1982), 13–57.

32. For many sites the archaeological evidence is still patchy. At Thérouanne recent excavations and fieldwork have produced a hypothetical town plan and have proved that the settlement was established on virgin territory; the oldest evidence dates from the period of Tiberius: Bernard, H., *Septentrion,* xliii, (1980), 41–66. At Maastricht a V-shaped ditch was sectioned in 1973; a dating in the Augustan period is possible on the basis of the arretine: Bloemers, J.H.F., *Publications de la Société historique et archéologique dans le Limbourg,* cxi, (1974), 35–46. At Bavay the origins of the town are still obscure, in spite of a fair quantity of representative archaeological material, *inter alia* the unpublished arretine: Will, E., *Gallia,* xx, (1962), 79–101; Pietri, C., *Princetown Encyclopaedia of Classical Sites,* Princetown, 1976, 135–6 and Boucly, J. and Carmelez, J., *L'Archéologie en Hainaut-Cambrésis-Avesnois,* Valenciennes, 1981, 12–13.

33. Ulrix, F., *Kölner Jahrbuch für Vor- und Frühgeschichte,* vi, (1962–3), 58–70.

34. The fact that during the late Imperial period these settlements were converted into military stations proves that they had always been regarded as 'official areas'; most of them collapsed with the Roman administration.

35. Mertens, J. and Despy-Meyer, A., *Cartes archéologiques de la Belgique, 1–2: La Belgique à l'époque romaine,* Brussels, 1968, map.

36. V-shaped ditches, comparable with those at Tournai, were discovered at Coutrai, but the lack of archaeological evidence makes it impossible to date them: Vierin, J., *Archéologie,* (1959), 146–7.

37. Wells, C.M., *The German Policy of Augustus,* Oxford, 1972, map.

38. Vanvinckenroye, W., *Romeinse Stad* (see note 7), 22 and Vanderhoeven, M., *op. cit.* (see note 9), 75–8.

39. Graff, Y., *op. cit.* (see note 13), 46.

40. Wells, C.M., *Rei Cretariae Romanae Fautorum,* (1977), 132–4.

41. Scheers, S., *Traité de Numismatique celtique. II. La Gaule Belgique,* Paris, 1977, 821–30.

42. On this subject see the important study by M. Gechter; *Bonner Jahrbücher,* clxxix, (1979), 1–129.

43. De Laet, S.J., *Mededeelingen van de Koninklijke academie van België,* xxii (1960), 6 and von Petrikovits, H., 'Kleinstädte und nichtstädtische Siedlungen im Nordwesten des römischen Reiches', in *Das Dorf der Einsenzeit und des frühen Mittelalters,* Göttingen, 1977, 86–135.

BIBLIOGRAPHY

Agache, R., 1968, 'Présence de fossés parallèles à certaines voies romaines et particulièrement de fossés-limites situés à une vingtaine de mètres de part et d'autre', *Bulletin de la Société des antiquaires de Picardie,* (1968), 258–64.

Amand, M., 1959 'Céramique pré-claudienne à Tournai', *Antiquité Classique,* xviii, 108–24.

Amand, M., 1963, 'Les véritables origines de Tournai. Travaux préromains à La Loucherie', *Helinium,* iii, 193–204.

Bernard, H., 1980, 'Remarques et hypothèses sur le développement urbain à Thérouanne', *Septentrion,* xliii, 41–60.

Bloemers, J.H.F., 1974, 'Archaeologische Kroniek voor Limburg over de jaren 1973–4', *Publications de la Société historique et archéologique dans le Limbourg,* cxi, 35–46.

Boucly, J. and Carmelez, J., 1981, 'Bavay', *L'Archéologie en Hainaut-Cambresis-Avesnois,* Valenciennes, 12–13.

Brulet, R. *et al.*, 1981, *Braives gallo-romain I. La zone centrale,* Publications d'Histoire, de l'Art et d'Archéologie de l'Université de Louvain, XVI, Louvain-la-Neuve.

Claes, P., 1969, 'Les fossés-limites de la chaussée Bavai-Cologne dans la région de Liberchies', *Helinium,* ix, 138–50.

De Boe, G., 1981, 'Prehistorisch en Romeins te Neerharen-Rekem', *Archaeologia Belgica,* ccxxxviii, 37–41.

De Boe, G. and Hubert, F., 1977, 'Une installation portuaire d'époque romaine à Pommeroeul', *Archaeologia Belgica,* cxcii, 1–57.

De Boe, G. and Van Impe, L., 1979, 'Nederzetting uit de Ijzertijd en Romeinse villa te Rosmeer', *Archaeologia Belgica,* ccxvi, 1–44.

De Laet, S.J., 1960, 'Schets van het ontstaan en de ontwikkeling van stedelijke agglomeraties in Noord-Gallië in de Romeinse tijd', *Mededeelingen van de Koninklijke academie van België,* xxii, 6.

du Plat Taylor, J. and Cleere, H., 1978, *Roman shipping and trade: Britain and the Rhine provinces,* Council for British Archaeology Research Report 24, London.

Frere, S.S., 1975, 'The origin of small towns', Rodwell, W. and Rowley, T. (eds.), *Small Towns of Roman Britain,* BAR British Series 15, Oxford, 4–7.

Frere, S.S., 1975, 'Verulamium and the towns of Britannia', Temporini, H. and Haase, W. (eds.), *Aufstieg und Niedergang der Römischen Welt, II, 3,* 290–327.

Gechter, M., 1979, 'Die Anfänge des Niedergermanischen Limes', *Bonner Jahrbücher,* clxxix, 1–129.

Graff, Y., 1978, 'Liberchies, site Augustéen. Le matériel archéologique', *Romana Contact,* viii, 7–66.

Graff, Y., 1979, 'Les monnaies gauloises de Liberchies (IV)', *Romana Contact,* ix, 23–32.

Graff, Y., and Lenoir, P., 1981, 'Asse-Borgstad. Un *oppidum* gaulois de 42 hectares', *Romana Contact,* xviii, (1980), 7–72.

Krier, J., 1980, 'Zu den Anfängen der römischen Besiedlung auf "Pëtzel" bei Dalheim', *Publications de la Section historique de l'Institut grand ducal de Luxembourg,* xciv, 139–94.

Mertens, J., 1948, 'Monnaies romaines d'Elewijt', *Revue Belge Numismatique,* xciv, 124–6.

Mertens, J., 1951, 'Archeologisch onderzoek van een Romeinse straat te Asse', *Archaeologia Belgica,* iv, 129–44.

Mertens, J., 1954, 'De Romeinse *vicus* te Elewijt', *Archaeologia Belgica,* xix, 21–62.

Mertens, J., 1957, 'Les routes romaines de la Belgique', *Archaeologia Belgica,* xxxiii, 1–44.

Mertens, J. and Despy-Meyer, A., 1968, *Cartes archéologiques de la Belgique, 1–2: La Belgique à l'époque romaine,* Brussels.

Mertens, J. and Remy, H., 1974, 'Tournai. Fouilles à La Loucherie', *Archaeologia Belgica,* xlv, 1–35.

Mertens, J. and Vanvinckenroye, W., 1975, 'Een Romeins gebouwencomplex *extra muros* te Tongeren', *Archaeologia Belgica,* clxxx, 1–63.

von Petrikovits, H., 1977, 'Kleinstädte und nichtstädtische Siedlungen im Nordwesten des römischen Reiches', *Das Dorf der Eisenzeit und des frühen Mittelalters,* Abhandlungen der Akademie der Wissenschaften in Göttingen, 101, 86–135.

von Petrikovits, H., 1980, *Die Rheinlande in Römischer Zeit,* Düsseldorf.

Pietri, C., 1976, 'Bagacum', *Princetown Encyclopaedia of Classical Sites,* 135–6.

Rogge, M., 1976, 'Kataloog van de vondsten uit de Gallo-romeinse nederzettingen van Zottegem-Velzeke', *Oudheidkundige opgravingen en vondsten in Oost-Vlaanderen,* vii, 73–186.

Rogge, M., 1980, 'Een legerplaats uit de vroeg-Romeinse tijd te Velzeke', *Hermeneus,* lii, 135–9.

Scheers, S., 1977, *Traité de Numismatique celtique. II. La Gaule Belgique,* Centre de recherches d'histoire ancienne, 24, série numismatique; Annales littéraires de l'Université de Besançon, 195, Paris.

Scheltens, E. *et al.,* 1981, *Asse, waar de Romeinen thuis waren,* Asse.

Ulrix, F., 1962–3, 'Comparison des plans des villes romaines de Cologne, Trèves et Tongres', *Kölner Jahrbuch für Vor- und Frühgeschichte,* vi, 58–70.

Vaes, E. and Mertens, J., 1953, 'La céramique gallo-romaine en terre sigillée d'Elewijt', *Collection Latomus*, xiii, 1–55.

Vanderhoeven, M., 1968, *De Terra Sigillata te Tongeren. III. De italische terra sigillata*, Publicaties van het Provinciaal Gallo-Romeins Museum te Tongeren, 12.

Van Impe, L., 1981, 'Nederzetting uit de Ijzertijd en Romeinse periode te Donk', *Archaeologia Belgica*, ccxxxviii, 47–51.

Vanvinckenroye, W., 1965, *Opgravingen te Tongeren 1963–1964*, Publicaties van het Provinciaal Gallo-Romeins Museum te Tongeren, 8.

Vanvinckenroye, W., 1975, *Tongeren. Romeins Stad*, Publicaties van het Provinciaal Gallo-Romeins Museum te Tongeren, 23.

Vanvinckenroye, W., 1979, *Een Romeinse gebouwencomplex extra-muros te Tongeren*, Publicaties van het Provinciaal Gallo-Romeins Museum te Tongeren, 26.

Vierin, J., 1959, 'Coutrai: fossés romains en V', *Archéologie*, (1959), 146–7.

Wells, C.M., 1972, *The German Policy of Augustus*, Oxford.

Wells, C.M., 1977, 'Manufacture, Distribution and Date: some methodological considerations on the dating of Augustan *Terra Sigillata*', *Rei Cretariae Romanae Fautorum*, xvii–xviii, 132–40.

Wightman, E., 1974, 'La Gaule chevelue entre César et Auguste', *Actes du IX congrès International d'Etudes sur les frontières romaines*, Bucarest, 473–83.

Wightman, E., 1975, 'The pattern of rural settlement in Roman Gaul', in Temporini, H. and Haase, W. (eds.), *Aufstieg und Niedergang der Römischen Welt*, II, 4, 584–657.

Wightman, E., 1977, 'Military arrangements, native settlements and related developments in early Roman Gaul', *Helinium*, xvii, 105–26.

Wightman, E., 1978, 'Soldier and civilian in early Roman Gaul', *Akten des XI Internationalen Limeskongresses*, Budapest, 75–86.

Will, E., 1962, 'Recherches sur le développement urbain sous l'Empire romain dans le Nord de la France', *Gallia*, xx, 79–101.

The Civilized Pannonians of Velleius

by
András Mócsy
(Translation by David Parsons)

In his description of the Pannonian-Dalmatian revolt in A.D. 6–9 the eye-witness Velleius Paterculus claims nothing less than the complete penetration of Roman culture in Pannonia at all levels of society (II, 110, 5). No wonder this statement has not only fascinated Pannonian scholars but is also quoted as authentic evidence for the general triumph of Romanisation.[1]

In omnibus autem Pannoniis non disciplinae tantummodo, sed linguae quoque notitia Romanae, plerisque etiam litterarum usus et familiaris animorum erat exercitatio.

If this sentence had been written by a late Roman panegyrist, researchers would probably have passed it by. When for example Mamertinus in his panegyric to Maximianus[2] celebrated the *divina generis origo* of a labourer's son[3] and regarded his native province of Pannonia as *gentium domina,* one might think that a few words on the emperor's Roman upbringing or the deeply rooted *romanitas* of his country of origin would have been appropriate in this list of panegyric exaggerations. But in fact all we read about the emperor's *educatio* and *institutio* is that they were sufficient to ensure success in the military context of a frontier province.[4] This is the equivalent, in panegyric form, of what Aurelius Victor meant by *ruris ac militiae miseriae.*[5] The divine ancestry of Herculius Augustus and the honourable nature of his country were not in doubt, but to praise his high culture with equally extravagant language might well have provoked laughter. Indeed the lack of *humanitas* on the part of the Pannonian upstarts became something of a byword.[6]

Velleius's description is thus all the more problematic. It refers to the beginning of Roman control and comes from an eye-witness who was Tiberius's legate during the rebellion,[7] and who regarded himself as sufficiently knowledgeable in Pannonian matters to record the war *iustis voluminibus, ordine*[8] (though he never did). The only justification for rejecting this eye-witness account is that it occurs in the last chapters of the history, in which the work degenerates into rather tasteless flattery of Tiberius. In order to make the most of the qualities of Tiberius as a general, the enemy threat had to be over-emphasised. Thus Velleius assures us directly after the above question that no other people had ever produced such a sophisticated plan of campaign as the Pannonians.[9] Nevertheless the Romans were aware of the danger of the uprising. There can be no doubt about the emperor's warning speech to the Senate, since Velleius himself reports it: in ten days the enemy could be at Rome's gate;[10] Suetonius regarded the campaign as the hardest since the Punic Wars.[11] Velleius's torrent of words consists not only of blatant exaggeration, but of arguments which he could proudly supply from his own experience as a participant in the war.[12] There must therefore be a grain of truth in the claim that the Pannonians had adopted Roman culture. It was nevertheless an obvious exaggeration to say that *every* Pannonian was familiar with Roman *disciplina* and *lingua* and that most of them could write.

Knowledge of Roman discipline, language and writing[13] needs somehow to be made historically credible and interpreted. This has happened in a number of different ways. One explanation attempts to relate the early penetration of Roman culture with Roman-Pannonian trading contacts following the foundation of Aquileia in 181 B.C.: 'such a transformation (i.e. the Romanisation of the Pannonians) seems miraculous, and there must be some cause which has escaped us, for the history of civilizations knows no miracles, a world cannot be completely romanized in less than forty[14] years'. The writer of these words, V. Pârvan,[15] explains away this miracle by arguing that 'the beginning of Roman penetration — using the word in its cultural sense — into the Danubian countries must be placed well back in the second century B.C.' In support of this argument Pârvan calls upon three pieces of evidence: roman settlements on the Adriatic coast of Dalmatia (which actually did not belong to Pannonia[16]), Celtic coins with Latin legends and the flow of Republican *denarii* into the Carpathian basin.[17] Indeed, Velleius himself seems to have known that Roman citizens and merchants were massacred by the insurgents.[18] The question arises whether these Roman immigrants did not live outside the Pannonian area in the Dalmatian towns, which were the subject of attack early in the uprising.[19] It should be noted incidentally that a slaughter of Romans and merchants seems to be a *sine qua non* in the description of all anti-Roman revolts.[20]

Pârvan's rather vague arguments were given more substance by A. Alföldi.[21] He draws attention to *denarii* of the Eravisci (struck according to him in 70–60 B.C.), which bear Latin legends such as RAVIZ, IRAVSCI, ANSA, DVTEVTI, and DOMISA, and to the silver coins of the Boii with Celtic personal names, likewise in Latin script, which he thinks are slightly later.[22] But Alföldi is right to insist that the imitation of Roman coinage and the circulation of Roman *denarii* can have made only a minimal contribution to the spread of the Latin language. However, with the Roman currency came merchants, not only to southern but also, according to him, to northern Pannonia. For south Pannonia he quotes Strabo, who refers to a trade route in the Save valley.[23]

This is a concrete hypothesis and what makes it all the more attractive is the inclusion of non-philological evidence. In the meantime, however, this evidence has become open to question. It has transpired on the one hand that Roman currency began to circulate remarkably late in Pannonia, not in fact before the reign of Augustus; and on the other hand that the Eraviscan *denarii* were minted likewise at a rather late date, probably under Augustus or even later.[24] Roman imports and Roman influences are not to be found in Pannonia in the late La Tène and certainly not in north Pannonia, where Alföldi postulated, with reference to Aquincum, the early appearance of merchants from Aquileia.[25] Even the trade relations in the Save valley have to be interpreted in another way. According to Strabo it was not Roman merchants who crossed the eastern Alps, which is well attested in the case of Noricum; on the contrary, it was the barbarians who offered their wares for sale in the market at Aquileia.[26] No doubt the barbarians who took part in this trade must have learnt some Latin, but this could hardly have led to a knowledge of *disciplina* and *litterae*. Appian's words should also not be forgotten: according to him the Romans took no interest in the barbarian lands east of the eastern Alps before the time of Augustus.[27] Thus an alternative solution becomes more probable.[28] Since there are no traces worth mentioning of Roman penetration into Pannonia before the conquest and since during the Empire the cultural level of the natives is known to have been not very high, Velleius's statement must have limited application. Velleius probably lived mostly in Siscia, where he could mix socially with the upper class of this Pannonian town. Siscia was conquered by Octavian in 35 B.C., and Appian gives evidence for the social division of the inhabitants of the town.[29] E. Swoboda, who previously subscribed to Alföldi's interpretation,[30] has shown[31] that, quite apart from Siscia, the hostages given by the Pannonian upper classes could have become carriers of Roman culture.[32] Augustus in particular took care of the hostages and even introduced some of them to his court. We do not know if the instigators of the rebellion had been hostages with the Romans, but it is highly probable. On their return home they could have passed on anything they had learnt to their fellows. And if Maroboduus, once a favourite of Augustus on the Palatine,[33] had his warriors trained in some aspects of *disciplina*,[34] the same could have happened among the Pannonians.

Thus the problem could be resolved with a high degree of probability by the following hypothesis: like the well-known Celtic and Germanic chieftains of the Julio-Claudian period, the princely Pannonian families were brought up as hostages in the Roman manner and perhaps even trained in Roman *disciplina*. However, there is a serious objection to this theory. It is well known that, after the conquest of Pannonia, Tiberius behaved with a brutality unparalleled even in those days. Prisoners were sold as slaves outside Pannonia.[35] After exacting such drastic retribution, the Romans are hardly likely to have sent home quickly the young princes brought up as hostages, and even less likely to have relaxed their control to the extent that the returning nobles could have given their people military training. If there was to be any such military training for the Pannonian youth at all, then it could only happen under Roman supervision and with the participation of Roman officers.

This conclusion had already been drawn, but it was merely assumed without any argument, as though Velleius had explicitly provided proof for it.[36] '. . . They were led by men who, like Maroboduus and Arminius, had served in the

Roman army as junior officers and knew much about the methods and discipline of their adversaries. Because of this, remarks Velleius, no nation ever followed so quickly the planning of the campaigns . . .'[37] 'Velleius testifies that Pannonian auxiliaries learned Latin and the alphabet.'[38]

A textual critique is necessary here in order to explore these assumptions more thoroughly.[39] It is true that *animorum exercitatio* could perhaps mean 'mental exercise'[40] though the few comparable occurrences[41] do not have exactly this sense, but rather that of 'attention', 'intentness' or 'preoccupation'. Had Velleius wished to emphasise the high intellectual level of the Pannonians, an expression such as *ingenii exercitatio* would have been better.[42] Further, one might also question whether actual knowledge of Latin, the art of writing and the ability to reason would have been the right preparation for the Pannonian people to *tam mature consilio belli bellum iungere*. Velleius lists the virtues of the Pannonians in pairs. On one side are *disciplina* and *lingua*, familiar to everybody *(omnibus)*, on the other writing and *exercitatio*, practised by the majority *(plerique)*. With *lingua* is associated *litterarum usus* and the most suitable pair for *disciplina* is weapon training: *armorum exercitatio*:[43]

	military	civil
knowledge	*disciplina*[44]	*lingua*
skill	*arma*	*litterae*

Our other source, Cassius Dio, seems to provide indirect proof of the military training of the Pannonians:[45] Valerius Messalinus, the Governor of Illyricum, also raised a contingent of troops from the Dalmatians for Tiberius's German campaign. This gathering of warriors was the immediate impetus for the rising. Since it is highly improbable that raw recruits would have been sent in one large mass[46] on a decisive campaign planned to penetrate far to the north,[47] this contingent must have consisted of the *tumultuariae catervae* which were characteristic of many other provinces in the early days of Roman domination.[48] These were admittedly not so *tumultuariae* as Tacitus occasionally implies. It would be pointless to try to establish the organization, service and titles of these troops: *persequi incertum fuit,* as Tacitus says of pre-Claudian auxiliaries in general.[49] It is possible, however, to assume certain generalized characteristics for the Pannonian forces.[50]

The senior officers were probably members of the Pannonian tribal aristocracy, perhaps in fact Pinnes and the two men called Bato who according to Velleius had *maxima auctoritas* and were also *peritissimi*.[51] Cassius Dio implies[52] that the insurrection began with the troops of the Daesidiates under one of the Batos, followed by the soldiers of the Breuci under the other. The people at large joined in only when, under the leadership of the Batos ὀλίγοι τινὲς ἐνεωτέρισαν. Comparable native leaders were Arminius, who was *Romanis in castris ductor popularium,*[53] or Chariovalda, to name only the most famous. In the same capacity the Thracian king Rhoemetalces took part in the suppression of the Pannonian revolt.[54] The chieftains who commanded the troops of their own people are known to us only exceptionally;[55] those who became famous and are named in the sources were either popular freedom fighters or took part in some enterprise outside their country at the head of their troops. As a rule these troops served in their own territory and it was probably regarded as exceptional for them to be employed elsewhere. There seems even to have been an element of risk in using these troops outside their native land. The Thracian revolt in A.D. 26 is a case in point: *aut si mitterent auxilia, suos ductores praeficere nec nisi adversum accolas belligerare,*[56] as are the Batavians[57] and the dreadful affair of the *Cohors Usiporum* in Britain at the end of the period.[58]

Further, the Pannonian revolt was directly provoked by the attempt of the governor of Illyricum to include these native troops in the expeditionary force against Maroboduus.[59] This step was not entirely inappropriate, for these troops had been trained under Roman *disciplina* and with Roman weapons, just like the Thracians under Rhoemetalces *et signis militaribus et disciplina, armis etiam Romanis,*[60] or Florus's Treveri held under *militia disciplinaque nostra*[61] and later the *iuventus* of the Raeti, *sueta armis et more militiae exercita.*[62] Without Roman officers and other ranks this would have been impossible. This training staff had the task not only of *disciplinam tradere,* but of being *exemplum et rectores.*[63] Obviously, they introduced the natives to Roman martial arts by means of Latin rather than the native language. The chieftains, who despite all the courtesy shown them[64] were probably kept politely in the background by these officers, were most in need of learning the language of the Romans.[65] Velleius established contact above all with this hereditary aristocracy and thus was able to find out at first hand what the Pannonians knew of the theory and practice of Roman military skills.

From what has been said it would appear that this 'miraculous transformation' (Pârvan) was not an exception, much less a miracle. The only question is why Velleius did not mention the normality of it straight out, and a glimmer of suspicion begins to appear. As we know from the clear statement by Cassius Dio,[66] and as we may infer from the doubtless intentionally vague description of the rebellion by Velleius,[67] Augustus was by no means satisfied with Tiberius's generalship. On the Palatine the emperor's stepson attracted a great deal of criticism. He may even have been responsible for the outbreak of the insurrection in the first place, for if he had not wanted to use the Pannonian troops against Maroboduus, the revolt would not have broken out at that extremely dangerous moment. Velleius kept quiet about how and why the revolt began[68] because it could have been interpreted as a blunder by Tiberius. His contemporaries, however, were well aware of the circumstances, so the narrative of the rebellion[69] had to take an apologetic tone, skilfully blended with extravagant praise: the incomparable size and danger of the enemy forces (*nulla umquam natio . . .*) as well as the Roman army (*nullo umquam loco post bella civilia*), then a general worthy of this army (*tantum ducem . . ., tanto exercitu*), who was so capable of his task that he had no need of the oversized army (*remisit eo, unde venerant*). A mere quarter century after the rebellion this line of argument provided an answer to the earlier charges that Tiberius was responsible for the revolt and further that he was incapable of putting it down. A chronological contradiction between Velleius and Dio allows one to conclude, in fact, that Tiberius had blundered. According to Dio, the revolt broke out *before* the army set out against Maroboduus but after Valerius Messalinus had arranged the disposition of the troops. Velleius's version is that the revolt first broke out when Tiberius had pressed forward a long way against Maroboduus. Both our witnesses are correct. During the preparations for the German campaign the governor of Illyricum had the task of assembling the Pannonian troops, who were trained in the Roman manner, and to place them at Tiberius's disposal. The troops refused to serve in far-off Germany, which did not worry Tiberius. He set off against Maroboduus without the Pannonian troops, thinking no doubt that the mutiny would have no serious consequences, or could at any rate be sorted out by the provincial administration. Not until the expeditionary force had crossed the Danube did it become clear that Tiberius had miscalculated on this occasion.

Velleius's unremarkable experiences with the Latin-speaking (and perhaps Latin-writing) Pannonians with Roman military training were pressed into service in his apologia: the fact of romanisation was used for emphasis, but its causes were passed over in silence. If the circumstances and causes (Dio) on the one hand and the romanisation (Velleius) on the other had been presented in one single source, they would more easily have led scholars to the conclusion that has been so painstakingly argued here. An apparent contradiction in the two sources has disguised the truth even further. According to Velleius the uprising involved *universa Pannonia* and the Dalmatians merely joined in, while the effects of romanisation were felt not in Dalmatia but *omnibus Pannoniis*. In contrast Dio claims that this contingent of troops was raised in Dalmatia and that the revolt began there. However, it should be noted that Dio's words are very precise and correct: Valerius Messalinus is called 'governor not only of Dalmatia, but also of Pannonia', although in A.D. 6 he could not have been governor of two provinces but only governor of the still undivided Illyricum. Anachronistically but consistently Dio has observed the political divisions of his own day. If the Daesidiates took the initiative in the revolt, as he reports, then in transferring the uprising and the consequential assembling of the troops to Dalmatia, he was strictly correct; the Daesidiates belonged to the province of Dalmatia, while the Breuci — as Dio assumes, equally correctly — were a Pannonian tribe, since their *civitas* was located in the south-western part of Pannonia Inferior. Both tribes, the Daesidiates and the Breuci, belonged nevertheless to the nation of the *Pannonii*,[70] who were divided between two neighbouring provinces only after the subdivision of Illyricum. Velleius was also correct in following the older usage, which was valid in his day. In his text *universa Pannonia* and *omnes Pannonii* mean the tribal group of the Pannonians, not the later province of Pannonia,[71] which did not yet exist in A.D. 6. In short it had been the inhabitants of south Pannonia and north-east Dalmatia who under Augustus had performed their military service for Rome in the usual way on home ground, and so had been in a position to learn the Roman way of fighting, their language and to some extent also their script.

'Originating as they did as territorial units, auxiliary regiments in the early empire were often commanded by the local chieftains who had trained them, and they not infrequently served in the area of their homeland. But this system broke down notably in 69 under the stress of loyalties divided by the civil war.'[72] The bitter experiences of the uprising caused the Romans to abandon the system of local military service very early in Pannonia, not later than A.D. 6–9.[73] It is not known when the many *alae* and *cohortes Pannoniorum, Breucorum, Varcianorum* and *Latobicorum* were established,[74] but at least the eight or more *cohortes Breucorum* imply recruitment soon after the revolt as a form of punishment and as a means of disarming them. In the first century nothing is heard of *tumultuarii* and great care was taken after the revolt not to use Pannonian soldiers in units stationed in Pannonia. Claudius seems to have been the first to break this rule.[75] However, these Pannonians were serving in regular auxiliary units, *disiecti aliisque nationibus permixti.*[76] The time when they could form their own units under their native chieftains was over, and the Pannonians were perhaps the first of all the peoples conquered by Augustus to suffer in this way. The romanisation which began early in Pannonia continued after the break in A.D. 6–9 along new lines.

NOTES

1. Marrou, H.-I., *Geschichte der Erziehung im Klassischem Altertum*, Munich, 1957, 539. (Originally published as *Histoire de l'Éducation dans l'Antiquité*, Paris, 1948 (7th edition 1977), and translated into English by George Lamb as *A History of Education in Antiquity*, London, 1956).

2. Baehrens, W.A., *XII Panegyrici Latini*, Leipzig, 1911, paneg. x, 2.

3. Aurelius Victor, *Epitome de Caesaribus*, 40, 10.

4. Baehrens, W.A., *op. cit.* (see note 2), paneg. c, 2, 4: *an quemadmodum educatus institutusque sis, praedicabo in illo limite, illa fortissima sede legionum inter discursus strenuae iuventutis et armorum sonitus tuis vagitibus obstrepentes?*

5. Aurelius Victor, *Liber de Caesaribus*, 39, 26.

6. Mócsy, A., *Pannonia and Upper Moesia*, London, 1974, 201. There are many references in the fourth century, e.g. Aurelius Victor, *Liber de Caesaribus*, 39, 26; 40, 17. *Epitome de Caesaribus*, 40, 10. Ammianus Marcellinus, xxviii, 1, 6; xxx, 7, 2 etc., including the self criticism contained in the epitaph on a tombstone from Aversa: *me hominem barbarum, nat(um?) Pannunium . . . ignoscatis*: Mancini, G., *Iscrizione sepolcrale di Anversa*, Casalbordino, 1933.

7. Velleius Paterculus, ii, 111, 4.

8. *ibid.*, ii, 115, 4.

9. *ibid.*, ii, 110, 5: *itaque hercules nulla umquam natio tam mature consilio belli bellum iunxit ac decreta patravit.*

10. *ibid.*, ii, 111, 1: *audita in senatu vox principis, decimo die, ni caverentur, posse hostem in urbis romae venire conspectum.*

11. Suetonius Tranquillus, *Divus Augustus*, 16: *gravissimum externorum bellum post Punica.*

12. Especially ii, 111, 4; 113, 3; 114, 1–4.

13. *litterarum usus* cannot, however, mean 'literary education/culture' (*pace* Marrou, H.I., *loc. cit.* (see note 1)).

14. If one reckons from 35 B.C. to A.D. 6. But most properly one should count from 11 B.C. to A.D. 6, i.e. 'less than twenty years'.

15. Pârvan, V., *Dacia. An Outline of the Early Civilisations of the Carpatho-Danubian Countries*, Cambridge, 1928, 151.

16. Apart from Nauportus in the south-west corner of Pannonia, cf. Šašel, J., in Pauly-Wissowa, *Realencyclopädie der Classischen Altertumswissenschaft*, Suppl. xi, 561.

17. Pârvan, V., *op. cit.* (see note 15), 153–4.

18. ii, 110, 6: *oppressi cives Romani, trucidati negotiatores.*

19. Cassius Dio, lv, 29, 4. One might also think of Nauportus, which was threatened as well: Velleius, ii, 110, 4.

20. Frequently after the war against Mithridates, e.g., Tacitus, *Annals*, iii, 42.

21. Alföldi, A., *Zur Geschichte des Karpatenbeckens im 1. Jh. v. Chr.*, Archivum Europae Centro-Orientalis, 8, 1942 = Ostmitteleuropäische Bibliothek, 37, 1942, 44–5. (In Hungarian in *Budapest Története* I, Budapest, 1942, 157).

22. Summarised by Ondrouch, V., *Keltské mince typu Biatec*, Bratislava, 1958.

23. Strabo, iv, 6, 10 (207); vii, 5, 2 (314).

24. Mócsy, A., *Numizmatikai Közlöny*, lx–lxi, 1961–2, 15 f., and *op. cit.* (see note 6), 56.

25. The most important find complex is discussed by Bónis, É.B., *Die spätkeltische Siedlung Gellérthegy-Tabán in Budapest*, Budapest, 1969.

26. Strabo, v, 1, 8, (214).

27. Appian, *Illyrica*, 15.

28. Mócsy, A., *Die Bevölkerung von Pannonien bis zu den Markomannenkriegen*, Budapest, 1959, 123 f.

29. *Illyrica*, 23: δῆμος — πρωτεύοντες.

30. Swoboda, E., *Carnuntum*, (second edition), Graz, 1953, 184. This part is omitted from the third edition (1958); for the new version in the fourth edition, see the following note.

31. Swoboda, E., *Carnuntum*, (fourth edition), Graz, 1964, 296, cf. Swoboda, E., 'Zur Frage der Romanisation', *Anzeiger der Österreichischen Akademie*, (1963), 153 f.

32. Although Swoboda says that there is no literary evidence for Pannonian hostages,

note the tombstone of a boy from the tribe of the Amantini, who died as a hostage in Emona: *C.I.L.* iii, 3224.

33. Strabo, vii, 1, 3 (290).

34. Velleius, ii, 109, 1: *corpus suum custodientium imperium, perpetuis exercitiis paene ad Romanae disciplinae formam redactum.*

35. Cassius Dio, liv, 31, 3.

36. As early as Dessau, H., *Geschichte der römischen Kaiserzeit* I, Berlin, 1924, 428.

37. Wilkes, J.J., *Dalmatia,* London, 1969, 69.

38. Brunt, P.A., *Italian Manpower 225 B.C.– A.D. 14,* Oxford, 1971, 243.

39. I am indebted to Professor I. Borzsák for his important suggestions.

40. Thus translated by, for example, Alföldi, *lóc. cit.* (see note 21), and interpreted in this sense by Mócsy, *op. cit.* (see note 28) and Swoboda.

41. e.g. Ovid, *Amores,* i, 8, 41: *nunc Mars externis animos exercet in armis*; Sallust, *Bellum Catilinae,* 11, 1: *magis ambitio quam avaritia animos hominum exercet.*

42. e.g. Quintilianus, ii, 4, 20.

43. Although this emendation is already noted in the *Thesaurus Linguae Latinae,* s.v. *exercitatio* (p. 1380, 73), the Teubner edition of 1933 by Stegman de Pritzwald omits it. On the problems of the descent of the Velleius text see von der Gönna, G., *Würzburger Jahrbücher,* n. F., iii, (1977); *animorum* on p. 236. According to Beatus Rhenanus the unique, and no longer extant, *Codex Murbacensis* was *'mendosissimus; ausim iurare, eum qui illum descripserat, ne verbum quidem intellexisse, adeo omnia erant confusa . . . nihil erat non depravatum'* etc. as he wrote for the *editio princeps,* 1520.

44. It is not out of the question that the scribe of the *codex Murbacensis* or Beatus Rhenanus (see previous note) took *disciplina* to mean generally 'schooling', or something similar, and derived *animorum* from that: school — language — writing — level of culture (or literature, cf. Marrou, H.I., *op. cit.* (see note 1)). But then the military sophistication of the Pannonians in the next sentence (see note 9) would be meaningless.

45. lv, 29, 1–3.

46. The insurgents had 200,000 infantry and 9,000 cavalry (Velleius, ii, 110, 3). There is no need to question the number of cavalry, which is not a round number (it could in fact represent nine *alae tumultuariae*) but the improbable number of infantry doubtless derives from the customary reckoning whereby the proportion of a nation bearing arms is one quarter (see, for example, Dobiáš, J., *Historica* 2, Prague, 1960, 41, and Caesar, *De Bello Gallico,* i, 29). Velleius knew from some official source, perhaps a tax list, that *omnis numerus amplius DCCC milibus explebat,* and so he arrived at the unlikely number of 200,000.

47. See Birley, E., in *Bonner Historia-Augusta-Colloquium, Antiquitas,* 4, 12, Bonn, 1976, 66.

48. Cheesman, G.L., *The Auxilia of the Roman Imperial Army,* Oxford, 1914, 16. Kraft, K., *Zur Rekrutierung der Alen und Kohorten an Rhein und Donau,* Dissertationes Bernenses, i, 3, Bern, 1951, 39.

49. Tacitus, *Annals,* iv, 5, 4.

50. Apart from Birley, Cheesman and Kraft (*op. cit.* see note 48), see also Forni, G., in *Rhenania Romana,* Atti dei Convegni Lincei 23, Rome, 1976, 103. Saddington, D.B. in Temporini, H. and Haase, W. (eds.), *Aufstieg und Niedergang der Römischen Welt,* ii, 3, Berlin, 1975, 176.

51. ii, 110, 4.

52. lv, 29, 2–3.

53. Tacitus, *Annals,* ii, 10, 3, probably in Pannonia at the same time as Velleius (Velleius, ii, 118, 2) cf. von Petrikovits, H., *Beiträge zur römischen Geschichte und Archäologie,* Bonn, 1976, 427 = *Bonner Jahrbücher,* clxvi, 1966, 177.

54. Velleius, 112, 4. The *frequens eques regius* ii, 113, 1 was probably this Thracian cavalry group.

55. e.g. *C.I.L.* v, 4910.

56. Tacitus, *Annals,* iv, 46.

57. Tacitus, *Histories,* iv, 14.

58. Tacitus, *Agricola,* 28.

59. Cassius Dio talks of the ἡλικία ἀνθοῦσα of the assembled troops, which possibly goes back to the term *iuventus*; cf. Tacitus, *Histories,* i, 68: *Raetorum iuventus,*

iii, 5: *Noricorum iuventus,* also *Annals,* iv, 46: *esse sibi ferrum et iuventutem.*

60. Florus, ii, 27.
61. Tacitus, *Annals,* iii, 42.
62. Tacitus, *Histories,* i, 68.
63. Tacitus, *Agricola,* 28.
64. cf. Dessau, H., *op. cit.* (see note 36), 429.
65. cf. on Arminius, Tacitus, *Annals,* ii, 10, 3. Maroboduus also knew Latin well, cf. Strabo, vii, 1, 3 and Velleius, ii, 109, 1.
66. lv, 31.
67. Especially ii, 111–12, where the chronology is conspicuously not adhered to.
68. ii, 110, 2: *universa Pannonia insolens longae pacis bonis, adulta viribus . . . arma corripuit.*
69. Especially ii, 110–13.
70. Mócsy, A., in Pauly-Wissowa, *Realencyclopädie der Classischen Altertumswissenschaft,* Suppl. ix, 534.
71. For this reason also the 'pre-Roman romanisation' cannot be applied to north Pannonia (as Alföldi, A., *loc. cit.* (see note 21) would have it).
72. Frere, S.S., *Britannia,* London, 1967, 218.
73. cf. Dessau, H., *op. cit.* (see note 36), 279.
74. The earliest evidence assembled by Holder, P.A., *The Auxilia from Augustus to Trajan,* BAR International Series 70, Oxford, 1980, esp. 112, where the *terminus ante quem* for auxiliary recruitment in Pannonia is put at A.D. 9.
75. Tacitus, *Annals,* xii, 29; to the year 50: *ipsaque e provincia lecta auxilia,* see also the epigraphic evidence, e.g. *Acta Archaeologica Hungarica,* xxiii, (1971), 43. On the *cohortes Breucorum,* Bogaers, J.E., *Berichten van de Rijksdienst voor Oudheidkundig Bodemonderzoek,* xix, (1969), 27.
76. Tacitus, *Annals,* iv, 46 on the Thracians A.D. 26.

Sacramentum

by
H. VON PETRIKOVITS
(Translation by David Parsons)

On the Continent of Europe human gestures increase progressively in liveliness and expressiveness from north to south. What can be expressed by gesture is shown by the religious drama of India and south-east Asia. In the study of Graeco-Roman Antiquity relatively little synthesizing work has been done on this subject in comparison with the general research into gestures.[1] The pictorial and literary sources of antiquity have been collected and studied by Carl Sittl, but few scholars have followed in his footsteps.[2] The following pages will deal with only one manifestation of Roman gesticulation, the gesture of the raised 'open' hand. It is a variant of the closed flat hand which is directed towards the person being addressed. The fingers of the 'open hand' are slightly spread and the thumb is more or less strongly bent. The understanding of these gestures of the Roman world was hindered by the fact that antiquarian research 'had not individually investigated every hand or finger gesture, but preferred to pursue the question of which gestures made by votive hands were connected with which gods. From the archaeological record numerous Roman hand and finger gestures must be differentiated: the *benedictio Latina (porrecti digiti tres)*; the hand which holds and displays something usually between thumb and forefinger; the *corna* gesture *(duo . . . medii sub pollicem veniunt)*; the *far la fica (pollicem premere)*; the cursing hand; the raised closed and the raised open hand.

I

Before attempting to demonstrate that the raised open hand which was sometimes mounted at the top of Roman military standards was connected with the swearing of oaths, let us quote some examples of the archaeological and numismatic evidence for such hands. First of all, representations on coins because they may be regarded as the most authentic source.

List 1 Signa *with hands on coins*

Tiberius: a Spanish municipal issue from Caesaraugusta (Saragossa). Heiss,
    A., *Description générale des monnaies antiques de l'Espagne,* Paris, 1870,
    (reprinted Amsterdam, 1966), pl. 25, 32.
Caius (Caligula): *ibid.,* pl. 26, 57.
Galba: *B.M.C.,* 335, no. 156, pl. 58, 2. Martin, P.H., *Die anonymen Münzen*
    des Jahres 68 n. Chr., Mainz, 1974, pl. 5, 60 M2; 61 B; 63 B; 67 Le; pl. 6,
    67P. Herr Martin has kindly told me that hands are shown on these coins.
    B.M.C., 38; *R.I.C.,* 157, 33.
So-called anonymous *denarius,* struck under Galba in A.D. 68. Obv.: Victoria
    with wreath and palm front, on orb, facing left: SALVS GENERIS HYMANI
    Rev.: Eagle facing right above altar between hands. P R to right and left in
    field, SIGNA in exergue (pl. 1).

Pl. I Anonymous *denarius,* A.D. 68. (*Photograph: Badisches Landesmuseum, Karlsruhe.*
Bildarchiv). (2:1).

Domitian: Mazzini, I.G., *Monete imperiali romane I,* Milan, 1957, pl. 88, 94
    (denarius). cf. Franke, P.R. and Paar, I., *Die antiken Münzen der Sammlung*
    Heynen, Cologne, 1976, pl. 12, 19 (municipal issue from Ephesus). *R.I.C.,*
    223.
Nerva: Franke, P.R. and Paar, I., (see previous entry), pl. 12, 20 (municipal
    issue from Asia Minor). *R.I.C.,* 118.
Trajan: *Roman Imperial Coins in the Hunter Coin Cabinet* II, Oxford, 1971,
    pl. 11, 318–19 (*as*); Florescu, F.B., *Die Trajanssäule,* Bucharest/Bonn, 1969,
    133, fig. 69, 10. *R.I.C.,* 294, (*denarius* Rome, Pl. II).
Hadrian: *Roman Imperial Coins in the Hunter Coin Cabinet* (see previous
    entry), pl. 27, 311 and 313 (according to the text, 118, a hand). *R.I.C.,* 546,
    a, b.
Clodius Albinus: *B.M.C.,* pl. 2, 18. *R.I.C.,* 18.
Gallienus: Alföldi, A., *Studien zur Geschichte der Weltkrise des 3. Jahrhunderts*
    n. Chr., Darmstadt, 1967, pl. 2, 7 (*aureus,* struck in Rome). *R.I.C.,* 37.

Pl. II   *Denarius* of Trajan. *(Photograph: Hunter Coin Cabinet)* (2:1).

Postumus: *Antoninianus* of the 14th issue of 265. Elmer, G., 'Die Münz-
prägung der gallischen Kaiser in Köln, Trier und Mailand', *Bonner Jahrbücher,*
cxlvi, (1941), no. 417. Rheinisches Landesmuseum, Bonn, Inv. No. 26616.
Constantine the Great: Alföldi, M.R., *Jahrbuch für Numismatik und Geld-
geschichte,* ix, (1958), 107 and pl. 4, 19. Also 130–1, No. 85. Maurice, J.,
Numismatique Constantinienne, Paris, 1903, 312/13 from Arelate. Issue 2/IX
(solidus). Alföldi, M.R., in Reusch, W. (ed.), *Frühchristliche Zeugnisse im
Einzugsgebiet von Rhein und Mosel,* Trier, 1965, 87, No. 6, and fig. 66,6.

Pl. III   *Solidus* of Constantine I. *(Photograph: Rheinisches Landesmuseum Trier).* (2:1).

Another *solidus, ibid,* 88, No. 14 and fig. 66, 14. *eadem, Die constantinische Goldprägung,* Mainz, 1963, 199, Nos. 507–9.

Solidus of Constantine I. Rev. SPQR OPTIMO PRINCIPI, in exergue PTR. Cohen 556, *R.I.C.* VI Treveri 815 (Fig. 3).

Solidus of Constantine I. Rev. FIDES EXERCITUS in exergue SMT. Cohen, H., *Descriptions historiques des monnaies frappées soue l'empire romain,* Paris, 1880–1892, 156. *R.I.C.* VII, Ticinum, 27, (pl. 3) cf. Maurice, (see above), fig. 17, 17 (from Rome). Fig. 19, 13 (from Ostia). *ibid.* III. fig. 3, 9 (from Nicomedia, Pl. IV).

Pl. IV   *Solidus* of Constantine I. *(Photograph: Rheinisches Landesmuseum Trier).* (2:1).

It is not always easy to discover from the publication what was mounted at the upper end of a standard depicted on a coin: a hand, a half moon, rays, a bundle of hay or even a rising eagle. For this reason only securely identified examples have been quoted. The open hand is more clearly shown on representations of Roman standards found on reliefs or on metalwork than on coins.

List 2 Signa *with hand on reliefs and metalwork*

Relief fragment supposedly from the Arch of Claudius. *Monumenti Inediti,* x, (1874–78), pl. 21. von Domaszewski, A., *Die Fahnen im römischen Heere,* Abhandlungen des Archäologisch-Epigraphischen Seminars der Universität Wien, 5, 1885 (Reprinted in von Domaszewski, A., *Aufsätze zur römischen Heeresgeschichte,* Darmstadt, 1972), 63 fig. 79a. The statement that the fragments illustrated in *Monumenti Inediti* belong to the Arcus Claudii was disproved indirectly by H.P. Laubscher when he and M. Torelli showed that a relief fragment published by G. Mancini, *Notizie degli Scavi,* 1925, 230–31, pl. 3, does not come from the Claudian Arch (Laubscher, H.P., *Arcus Novus*

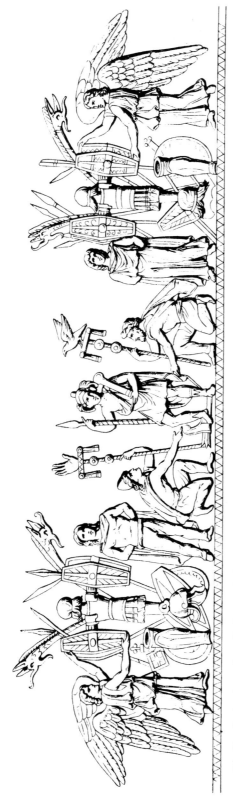

Pl. V Projection of a relief on a gladiator's helmet from Pompeii. (*Drawing after Museo Borbonico X, plate 31, provided by G. Ulbert (Munich)*).

und Arcus Claudii: zwei Triumphbögen an der via Lata in Rom, Nachrichten
der Akademie der Wissenschaften, Göttingen, Phil.-hist. Klasse, 1976, pt. 3,
67–108, esp. 96–97).

Representation on a gladiator's helmet in Pompeii. Literature in Ulbert, G.,
Germania, xlvii, (1969), 104, note 16. Line-drawing fig. 1 on 109. *c.* mid 1st
century A.D. (Pl. V).

Funerary monument from the Forum Livi (Forli). *C.I.L.* xi, 624. Steiner, P.,
Bonner Jahrbücher, cxiv/cxv, (1969), 9, fig. 4. Ubl, Hj., *Die Waffen und
Uniform des römischen Heeres,* (unpublished typescript dissertation, Vienna), 406
and fig. 389. *Dis manibus* spelt out.

Pl. VI   Detail from the reliefs on Trajan's column in Rome (LXXVII 203). *(Photograph: Deutsches
Archäologisches Institut in Rome).*

Decorative shield boss of *Legio VIII Augusta* from the Tyne. Right and left hand. *C.I.L.* vii, 495. von Domaszewski, A., *Die Fahnen im römischen Heere,* (see above) 39, No. 9, fig. 18a, b. Toynbee, J.M.C., *Art in Britain under the Romans,* Oxford, 1967, 299, pl. 69a. Ubl, Hj., *Die Waffen und Uniform des römischen Heeres,* (see above), 406, and fig. 382. *c.* A.D. 119 (Ritterling in *Realencyclopädie,* 12, 1658–9, s.v. *Legio*).

Gravestone from Eburacum (York). *C.I.L.* vii, 243. *R.I.B., 673,* pl. 10. von Domaszewski, A., *Die Fahnen im römischen Heere,* (see above) 37, no. 3, fig. 13. Ubl, Hj., *Die Waffen und Uniform des römischen Heeres* (see above), 405 and fig. 379. Member of *Legio IX Hispana,* so before the third decade of the second century.

Pl. VII   Detail from the reliefs on Trajan's column in Rome (LXXXV 223). *(Photograph: as VI).*

Trajan's Column, scenes 14, 77, 203 (two right hands), 222 (two right hands). Cichorius, C., *Die Reliefs der Trajanssäule,* Berlin, 1896. Lehmann-Hartleben, K., *Die Trajanssäule,* 2 vols., Berlin/Leipzig, 1926. Florescu, F.B., *Die Trajanssäule,* Bucharest/Bonn, 1969. Ubl, Hj., *Die Waffen und Uniform des römischen Heeres* (see above), 405 and fig. 383 (Pl. VI and VII).

Tropaeum Traiani, Adamklissi, Metope 12. Florescu, F.B., *Das Siegesdenkmal von Adamklissi,* Bucharest/Bonn, 1965, 479, fig. 190. Ubl, Hj., *Die Waffen und Uniform des römischen Heeres*(see above), 405 and fig. 388.

Column of Marcus Aurelius. Caprino, C., Colini, A.M. *et al, La Colonna di Marco Aurelio,* Rome, 1955, 83, pl. 5, fig. 11 (= Petersen, E. and von Domaszewski, A., *Die Marcussäule . . . in Rom,* Munich, 1896, Scene 4; 85, pl. 8, fig. 16. (= Petersen, 9) 100, pl. 34, fig. 69 and pl. F (= Petersen 55). Left hand (Pl. VIII and IX).

Pl. VIII   Detail from reliefs on the column of Marcus Aurelius in Rome. *(Photograph: as VI).*

Monument to Marcus Aurelius from the attic of Constantine's Arch. Bianchi-Bandinelli, R., *Rom: Zentrum der Macht,* German edition, Munich, 1970, 317, fig. 336. *c.* A.D. 180–190.

Left side of a sarcophagus from the Piazza Matteotti in Modena. Gabelmann, H., *Die Werkstattgruppen der oberitalischen Sarkophage,* Bonn, 1973, 214, No. 57 (with bibliography) and pl. 25, 2. Two right hands. 'Antonine' (Pl. X).

Pl. IX   Detail from the reliefs on the column of Marcus Aurelius in Rome. *(Photograph: as VI)*.

Pl. X   Detail from the relief on the left-hand side of a sarcophagus from Modena. *(Photograph: H. Gabelmann, Bonn).*

Gravestone of a standard bearer of *Legio V Macedonica* from Sucidava (Celei). *C.I.L.* iii, 14492. Tudor, D., *Oltenia Romana*, Bucharest, 1958, 322, fig. 82. Florescu, G., *I monumenti funerari Romani della Dacia inf.*, Bucharest, 1942, 29, No. 23, fig. 23. Florescu, G. and Petolescu, C.C., *Inscriptiile Daciei Romane 2*, Bucharest, 1977, No. 203. Ubl, Hj., *Die Waffen und Uniform des römischen Heeres* (see above), 405 and fig. 380.

Gravestone from Intercisa. *Archaeologiai Értesitö*, xxxix, (1920–22), 7–9, No. 5, fig. 5. *Budapest Régiségei*, xiv, (1945), 538. *Intercisa*, 285, No. 42, pl. 37, 3. Ubl, Hj., *Die Waffen und Uniform des römischen Heeres* (see above), 380, Cat. No. 128 and fig. 370.

Sarcophagus from Aquincum. *Budapest Régiségei*, xiv, (1945), 537–8, fig. 1. Ubl, Hj., *Die Waffen und Uniform des römischen Heeres* (see above), 388–9, Cat. No. 100 and fig. 369.

Gravestone of a standard bearer of *Legio II Traiana*. *C.I.L.* III, 6592. *I.L.S.*, 2345. von Domaszewski, A., *Die Fahnen im römischen Heere* (see above), 37, No. 4, fig. 14. Reinach, A.J., 4/2, 1313, fig. 6417. Ubl, Hj., *Die Waffen und Uniform des römischen Heeres* (see above), 390, 406 and fig. 373. After 213 because of the legionary title 'Germ'.

Pl. XI Detail of a basal-relief from the arch of Constantine in Rome. *(Photograph: Deutsches Archäologisches Institut in Rome)*.

Representation of a legionary standard bearer on a basal relief of Constantine's Arch. L'Orange, H.P., and von Gerkan, A., *Der spätantike Bildschmuck des Konstantinsbogens,* Berlin, 1939, 116–17 and pl. 25c. Ubl, Hj., *Die Waffen und Uniform des römischen Heeres* (see above), 412 and fig. 396. On the dating to the Constantine period see L'Orange 103–4. One might add the standard with hand *insignium* included in List 3 (Section III) under Mauer an der Url (Pl. XI).

Whether there still exist any original examples of the "open hand" which were mounted on Roman standards does not appear to be altogether clear. It has been thought that this was the purpose of an open hand made of copper alloy and now in the British Museum. It is presumably of Italian provenance. Because its sleeve-like pocket is very long, it is more appropriate to discuss it in Section III. A bronze hand found in Vindonissa is more likely to have functioned as a standard top. It has been discussed in detail by V. von Gonzenbach.[3]

The symbolic meaning of the open hand as the terminal of Roman military standards cannot be readily deduced from the pictorial representations cited above. The examples show that it was mostly the right hand which was depicted, but also sometimes the left, or both hands together, and that the palm of the hand was turned to the viewer. The hands served as a terminal on legionary standards, which were subordinate to the legionary eagle.[4]

Comparative ethnology and folklore have produced a considerable literature suggesting various interpretations of the flat hand: among other things it can serve to ward off an enemy or evil; it can be a gesture of prayer, of oath-giving, or of cursing when the hand of a human is depicted. Or it can represent the hand of a god and signify a gesture of blessing. It is not likely that the Romans' hand insignia represented a divine hand (see below, Section III). It would, of course, be readily comprehensible in the sense of a religious "dynamic" if the troops constantly received new fighting strength from such a symbol. But to the best of my knowledge of Roman military religion it would be difficult to find a god whose naked hand could effect such a blessing (least of all Mars). Of the various meanings of the raised flat hand we can dismiss the cursing hand. The interpretation as a mere protective gesture appears to be too weak for the military aggression of the troops. The category of prayer and oath gestures seems most appropriate for the hand insignia discussed here. For the imperial army of the early period the simple prayer gesture was probably too bland but the oath gesture would make good sense. It is indeed indistinguishable from a gesture of prayer to the extent that the oathmaker calls upon an oath god who is to destroy him if he breaks his promise.[5] V. von Gonzenbach came close to this concept when she emphasised the meaning of the hand for the *fides* of the troops. A remark of Flavius Philostratus, who died under Philip the Arab, is important in connection with prayer and oath gestures of the Roman period. In his biography of Apollonius of Tyana (4, 28; p. 147f. in Kayser's edition) he describes the gesture in the following way: ὀρθοὶ τῆσ χειρὸς . . . οἱ δάκτυλοι καὶ οἷον διείροντες (The fingers of the hand are stretched [straight] and somewhat spread). The oath hand on the military standard should constantly remind the soldier of his *sacramentum* which may be translated as 'oath of loyalty'. In the strict meaning of the word, *sacramentum* is a component part of the *sacramenta militiae*. According to Vegetius (*De Re Militari*, ii, 5), this involved among other things that the recruits after a trial period were tattooed and their names entered in the rolls and they swore an oath. Changes in the *sacramentum* are closely related to the history of the Roman army.

In the consular army of the early republic up to 216 B.C. the oath required by the tribunes was — probably following the Greek model — a mutual oath-giving, or συνωμοσία by the community of soldiers administered by the tribune.[6] Apparently this oath did not yet have a fixed form. According to Livy, M. Fabius, Consul for the year 480 B.C., required an oath from the soldiers whereupon a centurion answered him 'Marcus Fabius, I will return victorious from the battle'. As divine witnesses he called upon Jupiter, Mars Gradivus *aliosque iratos deos*. Then the whole army swore the same oath one to the other. Something similar is described by Livy as current usage up to the year 216 B.C.[7] At this time the previously more or less spontaneous oath was institutionalized. The Italians also knew an oath of this sort as is shown possibly by the literature and certainly by a coin issued by the Italian insurgents in the years 91 to 88.[8] After 216 B.C. the centurions chose suitable recruits who would speak the oath publicly. Each individual soldier had to step forward and declare that he sub-scribed to the same oath. We are ill-informed about the content of this oath. According to Polybios the soldiers swore to be obedient to their superiors and to do whatever they required of them.[9] It would be entirely consistent with the changes which characterized the relationship between the troops and their commander-in-chief in the first century B.C. if the soldiers of that time were sworn-in specifically in the name of the chief of staff. An indication of this, albeit a weak one, could be Caesar's account of his *Civil War* in which Labienus swore an oath as Legate to Pompey *se eum non deserturum eundemque casum subiturum, quemcumque ei fortuna tribuisset*. After him the other legates, officers and men swore the same oath.[10] The personal attachment of the soldier to the Emperor as his supreme commander is also particularly emphasized in the oath. This is shown by a quotation by Suetonius from the *sacramentum*, at the time of C. Caesar (Caligula): *neque me liberosque meos cariores habebo quam Gaium habeo et sorores eius*.[11] A further change in the *sacramentum* formula took place with the triumph of Christianity. Vegetius writes (*De Re Militari*, ii, 5): '(The soldiers) swear by God, Christ and the Holy Ghost and His Imperial Majesty, who should be loved and honoured by mankind next after God'. The content of the oath was clear: *iurant autem milites omnia se strenue facturos, quae praeceperit imperator, numquam deserturos militiam nec mortem recusaturos pro Romana republica* (The soldiers swear to carry out promptly all the Emperor's commands, never to desert, and not to fear death for the Roman state). Several pieces of evidence show that the *sacramentum* was connected with the standards in whose presence the oath was sworn. Such a custom is attested by the representation of the *coniuratio* of the Italians in whose midst a military standard stood and Seneca, Tacitus and Tertullian show the same for the Imperial Roman Army.[12] When Tertullian states *religio Romanorum tota castrensis, signa iurat* etc. he presumably means that the soldier's oath was sworn in front of the standards or at least in their presence. It is hardly a coincidence that both the *rosalia* of the standards and the enrolment of the recruits were celebrated on the same day, 10 May, each year.[13] Thus the hand on the standard constantly reminded the soldiers to fulfil their oath conscientiously.

II

Sacramentum is a noun formed from the verb *sacrare* plus the suffix *-mentum*. *Sacrare* means, according to the Oxford Latin Dictionary 'to set apart for the service or honour of a deity, consecrate', 'to devote to destruction', 'to make (an oath, etc.) subject to religious sanction', 'to bind with an oath'. Further meanings of the word are not important for this discussion. The essence of the *sacramentum* is then that a god is called upon who will injure or destroy the man who has made the oath if he does not keep his promise. The god is addressed with the gesture of prayer which is directed towards heaven or towards a cult picture (or a relic) and it becomes thereby simultaneously an oath gesture. The spirit must be addressed by name. The appeal is particularly effective if it is sung or spoken in rhythmical prose: the Samnite soldiers had to take their oath *diro quodam carmine*. The highpoint of the oath-taking consists of an awe-inspiring enumeration of all that is to happen to the oath breaker: that is implied by Livy's word *dirus* as well as by an account written by Ammianus. Apparently the Samnites did not restrict the curse to the oath-breaker himself but extended it to his family and offspring.[14] Since there is no mention of anything of this sort it can be assumed that the Romans of the Republican period and the early Empire despised this extension of the curse and perhaps it was only an embroidery of the annalist in order to denigrate the Samnites.

The *sacramentum* is also mentioned in an inscription which was found re-used in the Lower Pannonian auxiliary fort at Intercisa (Dunaújváros). This still produces puzzles which will perhaps only be satisfactorily explained if a further lucky find of an inscription reveals the solution. The inscription runs: *iudicio sacramenti cultores,* with each of the three words taking up one line. Since S. Járdányi-Paulovics first published this in 1951 it has been frequently discussed and interpreted in a number of different ways.[15] In order to understand it, one must begin with the fact that between the words *sacramenti* and *cultores* there is a whole line without writing and entirely taken up with small green leaves. The *cultores* must then be regarded as the votaries while the *sacramenti* depends upon *iudicio*. The reader who is uninfluenced by the various attempts at interpretation will regard *sacramenti* as a subjective genitive and translate '*by reason of a judgement of the sacramentum*'. Only if this simple translation were incomprehensible would one need to look for explanations which are less plausible linguistically or practically. Some help in understanding the *sacramentum* as an active and in this case a judging spirit is offered by a Syrian inscription, which Paulovics himself quoted: *Genio sacramenti veterani*.[16] Naturally, the fact that there is a *Genius* of the *sacramentum* in no way implies a numinous character for the *sacramentum* but there is nevertheless a completely personal relationship between the votary and the object whose *Genius* he worships. In this case it is only a short step to the personification of the *sacramentum* in the same way as there was from the Hadrianic period a personification of military discipline. The answer to the question how such a personification could give a judgement is not difficult in the context of the Roman army. Three *immunes* served on the staff of a legionary legate: a *haruspex, a victimarius* and a *pullarius*.[17] The *haruspex* at least was the interpreter of the will of a spirit and so also of the *sacramentum* if it was offended.

Who were the votive *cultores* of the altar? Usually the *cultores* on inscriptions name the god to whose particular devotion they were committed. Because that is not the case here the dedication must have stood either near or in a sanctuary or in a holy precinct of the god so that there could be no doubt in the mind of the reader who was intended. One does not need to assume the *cultores* belonged to a military guild if the original position of the insription was outside the camp. there is no need to prove that various gods both Roman and oriental were worshipped in the auxiliary *vici*. It is my opinion then, that the *cultores* of some god unknown to us fell foul of the *sacramentum* and according to the judgement of the deified *sacramentum* erected by way of expiation a votive stone to a god (perhaps a specifically military god like Mithras, Dolichenus or Iuppiter Heliopolitanus). At the same time one should not exclude the possibility that the *sacramentum* was in this case not the military oath of allegience but the oath of loyalty to his god.[18] This will be dealt with in the next section.

III

Apart from the open hand dealt with above, which presumably symbolized military *sacramentum*, there were identical or similar hands in various cults. Two such hands are dedicated to Iuppiter Dolichenus, and one to a Ba'al of the town Niḥa.[19] Other finds of this kind bear no inscription. We do not know to which gods they were dedicated. Further discussion will be preceded by a provisional list of finds of this sort.

List 3 'Oath-hands' in Rome, Italy and the Provinces behind the limes

Rome, Aventine. Colossal hand in marble. Merlat, P., *Répertoire des inscrip-*

tions et monuments figurés du culte de Iuppiter Dolichenus, Paris/Rennes, 1951, 1, No. 217.

Rome, found during work on the Tiber *presso la Marmorata.* Female hand in almost full relief on a rectangular slab. Five holes in the base suggest that the offering could have been fixed to a wall. Caetani-Lovatelli, E., *Monumenti antichi publicati per cura della R. Academia nazionale dei Lincei,* i, (1889), 169–86.

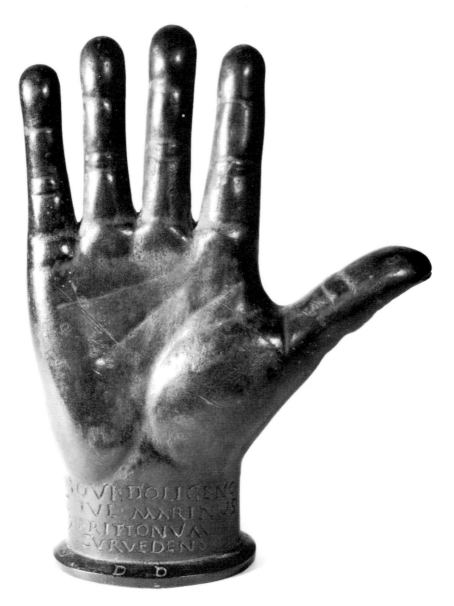

Pl. XII 'Open' hand in a copper alloy found in Nida (Frankfurt-Heddernheim). In private ownership. *(Photograph: Museum für Vor- und Frühgeschichte Frankfurt am Main).*

Three hands from Italy. Straight fingers, thumbs spread, long cuffs. von Gonzenbach, V., *Fides Exercituum, eine Hand aus Vindonissa*, (see note 3) 16–18.

Perhaps from Italy: Becker, J., *Drei römische Votivhände aus den Rheinlanden*, Frankfurt-am-Main, 1862, 9, No. 15 and pl. 2, 3.

Nida (Frankfurt-Heddernheim). Becker, J., (see previous entry), 8, No. 15 and pl. 2, 3. Noll, R., *Das Inventar des Dolichenusheiligtums von Mauer a.d. Url*, 77, with references (Pl. XII).

Mauer a. d. Url (Lower Austria). Undecorated, perhaps female, 'votive hand' and relief on a triangular bronze plaque: military standard with open right hand on either side of Iuppiter and Iuno Dolichenus (-a). Noll, *Mauer a. d. Url* (see above), 1, 45 and 77–8; pls. 16 and 27 (Pl. XIII and XIV).

Forum Claudii (Martigny). von Gonzenbach, V., *Fides Exercituum* (see above), 19–20. Not certain that it belongs to this category, since the thumb and fore-finger may have held some object.

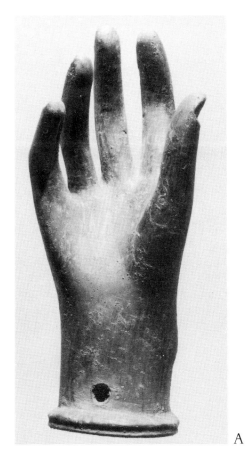 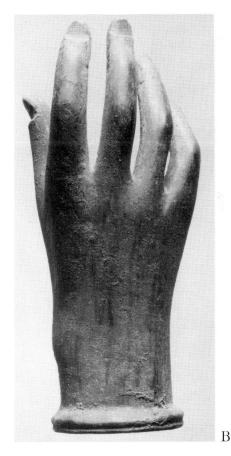

A   B

Pl. XIII A and B 'Open' hand in a copper alloy found at Mauer an der Url (Lower Austria). *(Photograph: Antiquities Department of the Kunsthistorisches Museum in Vienna).* (½).

Ravazd (south of Győr (Raab), NW Hungary). Láng, F., 'Die Dolichenus-Votivhand des Budapester Nationalmuseums.' *Archaeologiai Értesitö*, vii–ix, (1946–8), 183–8 and pl. 35, 1.

Brigetio? (Ó Szöny). Votive inscription to Dolichenus. Merlat, P., *Répertoire des inscriptions et monuments figurés du culte de Iuppiter Dolichenus* (see above), 98, No. 105. Noll, R., *Mauer a. d. Url* (see above), 77.

Gorni Voden (Distr. Plovdiv, Bulgaria). Velkov, I., *Antični Pametnitzi iz Balgarija: Godišnik na narodnija muzej*, iv, (1922–25), 152, fig. 216. Najdenova, V., *Balgarski Istoričeski Pregled*, (Bulgarian Historical Review), (1977), 74 and 82, No. 23.

Naskovo (Bulgaria). Najdenova, V. (see previous entry), 74 and 82, No. 24.

Nīḥa (northern part of the east scarp of the Lebanon). On the palm of the hand an eastern deity between two rams, probably a local Nīḥa god (Jupiter Hadaranēs). Hajjar, Y., *La triade d'Héliopolis-Baalbek*, 2, Études préliminaires aux religions orientales dans l'empire romain, lix, (1977), 474–6. *idem* in *Hommages à M.J. Vermaseren*, 1, Études préliminaires aux réligions orientales dans l'empire romain, lxviii, (1978), 471–2 and pl. 89.

Pl. XIV   Relief on a triangular plaque in copper alloy from Mauer an der Url (Lower Austria). *(Photograph: as XIII).*

Sidon (Saïda). Five hands which apparently resemble the one from Nīḥa. Hajjar, Y., (see previous entry), 2, 482–5. Further similar hands from Syria are mentioned.

'South of France'. On the palm of the (female?) hand an inscription: σύβολον/πρὸς/Ουελλαυνίους. Babelon, E. and Blanchet, J.-A., *Catalogue de bronzes antiques de la Bibliothèque Nationale,* Paris, 1895, 461–2, No. 1065.

Unprovenanced pieces:

   Trau collection (Vienna). Female hand wearing a bracelet above the wrist. On the palm a bullock which carried Dolichenus (broken off).

   Pine-cone balanced above index and middle fingers. Dilthey, K., *Archäologisch-epigraphische Mitteilungen aus Österreich,* ii, (1878), 56–65 and pl. 3, 3 and 4. Noll, R., *Mauer a. d. Url,* (see above), 78.

   Cabinet des médailles, Paris. Babelon, E. and Blanchet, J.-A., *Catalogue de bronzes antiques de la Bibliothèque Nationale,* Paris, 1895, Nos. 1066–7 and Nos. 1074–5. cf. No. 1076.

   Lyon Museum. Two open bronze hands of very different size: one 570 mm., the other 30 mm. high. Bouchet, S. and Tassinari, S., *Bronzes antiques du Musée de la civilisation gallo-romaine à Lyon,* Lyon, 1976, 87, Nos. 76–7. Unlikely for technical reasons that the hands with conical 'cuffs' were attached to statues. Presumably these are the same two hands quoted by Bouchet, S., *Bronzes romains figurés du Musée des Beaux-Arts de Lyon* which are supposed to have come from Asia Minor.

The find spots on the provisional list given above lie with two exceptions behind the military frontiers of the provinces. One exception is Brigetio in Upper Pannonia. Common to all the pieces is that they are connected with a particular god by means of a votive inscription or a divine portrait, or at least that they were not found in a certainly military context. The 'civil' group of open hands should probably be interpreted as an imitation of the military symbols of the oath of loyalty which have already been discussed. It is not necessary to rehearse the evidence quoted in the literature of the history of religion which shows that in the mystery religions of the ancient world the devotee had to swear like a soldier an oath of obedience and loyalty to his god, that is to the principal deity of the particular religion; this oath was similarly known as *sacramentum* (μυστήριον).[19] The first occurrence of this word in the context of the mysteries is in Livy in a fictitious speech of the consul Sp. Postumius Albinus on the occasion of the Bacchanalian scandal in Rome in 186 B.C.: 'O Quirites, is it right that the young people who have been dedicated (into the Bacchic mysteries) with this *sacramentum* should be conscripted as soldiers?'[20] On the question of the equation of devotee and soldier the status of *miles* in the Mithraic religion should be noted.[21] In the first half of the third century A.D. the connection between the military and the mystic oath was well understood as a remark of Herodian shows (viii, 7, 4): 'they kept the soldiers' oath which is the Mystery of the Roman ruling classes.'[22] The close connection between the soldiers' oath and adherence to a Mystery religion is shown not only by the military oath itself but by the branding or tattooing of soldiers and of devotees.[23] However, this indelible identification connects both groups also with the slaves.

If adherents of Mystery cults offered the votive hands at a sanctuary or in a holy precinct, and if the interpretation is correct that such votive gifts signified the oath hand of the devotee, then apparently men and women making the offering intended to express their unconditional commitment to the deity being honoured. The hands were intended to be human and not divine as is shown by the female hands from Rome, from the temple treasure at Mauer an der Url and from the Trau collection. Quintilian (*Institutio oratoria* 11, 3) says this explicitly: *manus leviter pandata voventium est* (the slightly spread hand is that of the donor). It is perhaps surprising that there is such a close pictorial connection between Roman military standards and Syrian Ba'alim so that they become nothing less than military gods. This phenomenon may be regarded in exactly the same light as the frequent worship of Mars in Gaul during the imperial period. In both cases there were dreams of a great military past although the circumstances of the time were quite the reverse. The degree of overlap in Syria between the military and religious spheres is shown by representations from Dura and Mauer an der Url which bear military insignia alongside Ba'alim.[24] From this it is clear that the distinction between the closed and the open raised hand was not a sharp one at least in the Orient. While the closed hand had been a normal form of blessing gesture ever since ancient oriental times, the open hand also occurs occasionally with the same meaning. Examples of this are a Sol relief from the Esquiline and some coins of the 'Sun Emperor' of the second half of the third century.[25] Where two streams of tradition, one Graeco-Roman the other Syrian (eastern), converged, the resulting artefacts were ambivalent, as they frequently are in cultural history where there is a similar hybridisation.

From both spheres, the military and the 'civil', the way leads to the adoption of the word *sacramentum* in early Christian theology. The *militia Christi* as well as the promise of devotion to the one central deity of the eastern mystery cults are symptomatic of the connections. The Church Fathers of Africa, Tertullian and Cyprian, took over the existing vocabulary for the baptism and the Eucharist. Children of their time, they introduced into Christian thinking the available semantically related words of the Latin and Greek languages. Lack of space prevents us from pursuing this development further.[26]

Acknowledgements

I am grateful to the following gentlemen for information:

R. Merkelbach (Cologne), W. Schneemelcher (Bonn), V. Zedelius (Bonn) and A. Zippelius (Kommern). The translation, not always straightforward, was kindly prepared by D. Parsons (Leicester). W. Binsfeld (Trier), H. Gabelman (Bonn), P.H. Martin (Munich), R. Noll (Vienna), H. Schubert (Frankfurt a. M.), G. Ulbert (Munich) and Mrs. I. Huld–Zetsche (Frankfurt a. M.) helped with the preparation of the originals for the illustrations, for which I am most grateful.

NOTES

1. The general literature on hand and finger gestures is given by Lurker, M. (ed.), *Bibliographie zur Symbolik, Ikonographie und Mythologie, II,* Baden-Baden, 1969 and Brilliant, R., *Gesture and Rank in Roman Art,* Memoirs of the Connecticut Academy of Arts and Sciences 14, Connecticut, 1963. The subject is also dealt with in communications research. Of the older literature, von Amira, K., *Die Handgebärden,* Munich, 1905, is recommended.

2. Sittl, C., *Die Gebärden der Griechen und Römer,* Leipzig, 1890 (reprinted 1970); Brandt, E., *Gruss und Gebet: eine Studie zu Gebärden in der minoisch-mykenischen und frühgriechischen Kunst,* Stockholm, 1965; Neumann, G., *Gesten und Gebärden in der griechischen Kunst,* Berlin, 1965; Dölger, F.J., *Die Sonne der Gerechtigkeit und der Schwarze,* second edition, Münster, 1971, 118–19. cf. Kötting, B., 'Geste und Gebärde', *Reallexikon für Antike und Christentum,* x, 898–900.

3. Von Gonzenbach, V., *Fides Exercituum eine Hand aus Vindonissa,* Jahresbericht der Gesellschaft pro Vindonissa, 1951/52, 5–21. I cannot judge how much credence to give the doubts of R. Fellmann in Sahin, S. *et. al.* (eds.), *Studien zur Religion und Kultur Kleinasiens,* 1, Études préliminaires aux religions orientales dans l'empire romain, 66, Leiden, 1978, 288–9. The finds associated with the hand quoted by him need not have anything to do with Sabazios.

4. General literature on standards with open hand: Renel, C., *Cultes militaires de Rome: les enseignes,* Lyon/Paris, 1903, 265–6; Reinach, A.J., 'signa militaria', in Daremberg, C. and Saglio, E., *Dictionnaire des antiquités grècques et romaines d'après les textes et les monuments,* IV, 1909, 1307–25; von Gonzenbach, V., *op. cit.* (see note 3), cf. Brilliant, R., *op. cit.* (see note 1), 23–5; 37 with fig. 1, 59 and 215 with references.

5. Steinwenter, 'Iusiurandum', in Pauly-Wissowa, *Realencyclopädie der classischen*

Altertumswissenschaft 10, 1253–60. On oath gestures, Erler, A., 'Rechtsgebärden', in *Handwörterbuch der Rechtsgeschichte* 1, Berlin, 1971, 1415–17; *idem,* 'Eid', in *ibid.,* 861–3. cf. 'Eid', in *Handwörterbuch des deutschen Aberglaubens,* second edition, Berlin/Leipzig, 1929/30, 663–4. For the ancient world, Sittl, C., *op. cit.* (see note 2), 140–2; 145; 174–5; 189–90 and 193. Schumm, R.W., in *Beiträge der süddeutschen Münzgeschichte,* Stuttgart, 1976, 39.

6. Frontinus, *Strategemata* iv, 1, 4 (216 B.C.). Fiebiger, 'Coniuratio', in *Realencyclopädie* (see note 5), 4, 885. Literature on *sacramentum:* Klingmüller, in *Realencyclopädie* (see note 5), 1A, 1667–8. Seston, W., 'Fahneneid', in *Reallexikon* (see note 2), 277–84 and 'Feldzeichen', in *ibid,* 702–3, Dölger, F.J., *Antike und Christentum 2,* Münster, 1930, 268–80; *ibid.,* 3, 1932, 220. Helgeland, J., in *Aufstieg und Niedergang der Römischen Welt* II, 16/2, Berlin/New York, 1978, 1478–80 and Birley E., in *ibid,* 1509–10. All give further references.

7. Livy, ii, 45, 13–14; xxii, 38, 1–5.

8. Bleicken, J., *Jahrbuch für Numismatik,* xiii, (1963), 51–69. Also Instinsky, H.U., *ibid.,* xiv, (1964), 83–7. Bianchi Bandinelli, R., *Rom: das Zentrum der Macht,* German edition, Munich, 1970, 30, fig. 34 and p. 422. cf. Livy, x, 38, probably embroidering a great deal on the original annal.

9. Polybius, vi, 21; Festus, 250 L 'praeiurationes'.

10. Caesar, *De bello civili,* iii, 13, 3–4.

11. Suetonius, *Caius,* 15, 3; Epictetus, *Dissertationes ab Arriano* 1, 14, 15 and 17 (cf. Schenkl, H., (ed.), second edition, 1916, 58). The difference compared with the second century B.C. is clear from the changed formula. Livy, xxviii, 29, 12, says of the soldiers: *citati milites nominatim apud tribunos militum in verba Scipionis iurarunt,* etc. Tacitus, *Annals* i, 8, 4, on the other hand writes: *renovatum per annos sacramentum in nomen Tiberii.*

12. Seneca, *Epistolae,* 95, 35; Tacitus, *Histories* iv, 31, 8, Tertullian, *Apologeticus,* 16, 8.

13. Fink, R.O., *Roman Military Records on Papyrus,* Princeton, 1971, 425–6 (Feriale Duranum, 10 May); Gilliam, J.F., *Harvard Theological Studies,* xlv, (1954), 187.

14. Livy, ii, 38; Ammianus Marcellinus, xxi, 5, 10–11.

15. Járdányi-Paulovics, S., *Archaeologiai Értesitö,* lxxvii, (1951), 21–3. Further references in Mócsy, A., *Antik tanulmányok,* v, (1958), 91–5 (only in Hungarian); Gáspár, D., *Archaeologiai Értesitö,* c, (1973), 55–8, *L'Année épigraphique,* (1953), 10.

16. *L'Année épigraphique,* (1924), 135.

17. Passerini, A., *Dizionario epigrafico di antichitá romane,* iv, (1949), 604, nos. 10–12; von Domaszewski, A. and Dobson, B., *Die Rangordnung des römischen Heeres,* second edition, 1, Cologne/Graz, 1967, register [index] A1, s. vv.

18. This is how A. Mócsy interprets the *sacramentum* of the inscription. See note 15.

19. Cumont, F., *Die orientalischen Religionen im römischen Heidentum,* fourth edition, Darmstadt, 1959, XII–XIII with notes 5–8, contains further references. Reitzenstein, R., *Die hellenistischen Mysterienreligionen,* third edition, Stuttgart, 1927, reprinted Darmstadt, 1956, index s.v. 'Eid', especially 192–215; on an Orphic oath, 225. Seidl, in *Realencyclopädie* (see note 5), 4A, 1448, 'Συνωμοσία'. cf. Mócsy, A., *op. cit.* (see note 15), and Láng, F., 'Die Dolichenus-Votivhand des Budapester Nationalmuseums', *Archaeologiai Ertesitö,* vii–ix, (1946–8), 186–7. On the designation of soldiers as *consacranei* see Mowat, R., in Daremberg, C. and Saglio, E., *op. cit.* (see note 4), 1/2, 1447.

20. Livy, 39, 15, 13; cf. Apuleius, *De deo Socratis,* 22.

21. Most recently Merkelbach, R., *Mithrasmysterien: Seelenlehre und die Weihegrade;* this will be published in the series Vorträge der Rheinisch-Westfälischen Akademie der Wissenschaften.

22. . . .φυλάσσοντες τὸν στρατιωτικὸν ορκον ὅς ἐστι τῆς Ῥωμαίων ἀρχῆς μυστήριον.

23. Dölger, F.J., *Antike und Christentum 2,* Münster, 1930, 100–16, 271–80.

24. On the evidence from Dura see note 25, on that from Mauer an der Url see List 3.

25. Merlat, P., *Iuppiter Dolichenus. Essai d'interprétation et de synthèse,* Paris, 1960, 180–1 (open hand). cf. L'Orange, H.P., *Der spätantike Bildschmuck des Konstantinsbogens,* 1, Berlin, 1939, 116, 177 and plates 32–3. Babylonian cylinder seal of the time of Hammurabi (closed hand), *ibid,* 179. Relief of Hadad and Atargatis: Baur, P.V.C., in *Excavations at Dura-Europos: Preliminary Report,* 3, New Haven, 1932, 100–39, especially 101 and Plate 14. Láng, *op. cit.,* (see note 19), 186–87. Summary paper by Hildburgh, W.L., *Journal of the Warburg Institute,* xviii, (1955), 67–89. These Syrian blessing gestures even reached the Carthaginians: Horn, G. and Rüger, C.B., *Die Numider,* exhibition catalogue, Bonn, 1979, 568–9; Cintas, P., *Amulettes puniques,* Tunis, 1946, 142–3; Callu, J.P. et al., *Thamusida,* Mémoires de l'École Française de Rome, Supplément 2, Paris, 1965, 102 and plate 67, 1 and 2.

26. The following are selected from a copious literature: Seston, W., *Reallexikon,* (see note 2), vii, 282–4; Bornkamm, G., in Kittel, G. (ed., *Theologisches Wörterbuch zum Neuen Testament,* 4, Berlin, 1942, 809–34 'μυστήριον'; Kopling, A., *Sacramentum Tertullianeum,* Münster, 1948; Kinder, E., 'Sakrament', in *Lexikon für Theologie und Kirche,* ix, (1964), 218–32. Further references: Sieben, H.J., *Voces: eine Bibliographie zu Wörtern und Begriffen aus der Patristica,* supplement 1, 142–3 'μυστήριον'; 324, 'levantes manus puras'; 333 'miles' to 'militia Christi'; 339 'Mysterium'; 389–90, 'sacramentum' to 'sacramentum fidei'.

The First Icenian Revolt

by

A.L.F. RIVET

The only extant account of this curious episode occurs in chapters 31–32 of Book XII of the *Annals* of Tacitus and to understand its full implications it is necessary to pay close attention to the Latin text. For this reason the translation here offered is deliberately literal rather than literary:

'31.   But in Britain a turbulent state of affairs met the governor Publius Ostorius, the enemy having invaded the territory of allies *(agrum sociorum)* the more violently because they did not think that a new general, with an unknown army and with winter already begun, would move against them. He, knowing that fear or confidence is produced by first events, quickly moved his light cohorts and, having killed those who resisted and pursued those who were dispersed, so that they could not band together again and lest an uneasy and uncertain peace should allow no rest to the general or the army, prepared to withdraw arms from suspects *(detrahere arma suspectis)* and to contain with camps everything this side of the Trent and Severn rivers *(cunctaque castris cis Trisantonam et Sabrinam fluvios cohibere)*; which the Iceni were the first to reject, a powerful tribe and people not battered by war because they had entered our alliance *(societatem nostram)* voluntarily. And with these starting it, the surrounding tribes *(circumiectae nationes)* chose a place for battle hedged in by a rough rampart and with an entrance that was narrow so that it could not be penetrated by cavalry. These fortifications the Roman general, although he was leading allied forces *(socialis copias)* without legionary strength, set about breaking through and, having positioned his cohorts, equipped his cavalry too for infantry duties. Then at a given signal they broke through the rampart and routed the enemy entangled in their own defences. And they, conscious of their rebellion and with their escape blocked, performed many notable feats; in which battle the son of the governor, Marcus Ostorius, won the award for saving a citizen's life.

32.   But those who were hesitating between war and peace were quietened by the defeat of the Iceni and the army was led against the Decangi *(inde cangos)*. Their lands were ravaged and booty taken everywhere, the enemy not daring a pitched battle or, if they tried to harrass the column from ambush, their tricks

being punished. And now a point had been reached not far from the sea that looks towards Ireland, when discord among the Brigantes drew the general back, firm in his purpose not to undertake anything new unless his earlier work was consolidated. In fact the Brigantes subsided, those who had taken up arms being killed and the rest pardoned. The tribe of the Silures was persuaded neither by violence nor by clemency to give up the war and had to be repressed by encampments of legions *(castris legionum)*. So that this might come about more quickly, the *colonia* of Camulodunum was founded in conquered lands *(agros captivos)* with a strong band of veterans, to be a defence against rebels and to imbue the allies *(sociis)* with a respect for laws.'

It is evident that the revolt itself was a relatively minor disturbance, not even requiring legionaries for its suppression, and it may well be that Tacitus included it simply because of the distinction gained by Marcus Ostorius, but the account raises a number of questions which demand answers.

The first point to note is that the attack which provoked the new governor was made *in agrum sociorum,* against the territory of allies. It is true that provincials who were not Roman citizens might sometimes be referred to as *socii,* just as the foundation of the *colonia* in chapter 32 was no doubt intended to influence those inside the province as well as those outside it, but if Tacitus had meant that the province proper was invaded he would surely have written not *in agrum sociorum* but *in provinciam.* The territory invaded, then, is likely to have been a client kingdom, and since the attack came almost certainly from Wales the obvious candidate is that of the Dobunni. This probability has long been accepted, especially since the discussion of the Dobunnic coinage by Allen and Hawkes in the Bagendon Report,[1] but whether it was necessarily the territory which they atributed to Bodvoc is another question, to which we shall return later.

Secondly, we must consider the steps taken by Ostorius when he had repelled the attack. As they appear in Tacitus the first was to disarm suspects, the second to control (with camps) everything this side of the two rivers, but since they both fall in the same sentence they should be taken together and the first necessity is to clarify the text. Although the brilliant amendment of Heraeus and Bradley is now almost universally accepted, editors are still divided on the question of whether or not the word *castris* should be retained.[2] On balance, its retention does seem to be demanded, both because sleepy haplography offers the better explanation of the scribe's error and because some innovation is clearly implied and Ostorius was already controlling the area in a general way.[3] Further, the two actions can be seen to be complementary. The bearing of arms (except for hunting) was already illegal in the province proper and to enforce a general ban in the client kingdoms would be virtually impossible.[4] What is implied, surely, is the disbanding of some of the military units of client kings and their replacement by legionary or auxiliary units of the regular Roman army *in castris.* It must also be noted that the withdrawal of arms was not universal but was confined to those whose loyalty was suspect: and the most likely ground for suspicion must be their behaviour during the incursion which had just taken place.

We come now to the crux of the matter, the statement that the Iceni were the first to object, and this raises several difficult questions. First, there is no archaeological evidence for the construction of Roman *castra* (however the term is to be interpreted) in Icenian territory at this time[5] — though that, of course, may simply reflect our limited knowledge. Secondly, the expression 'surrounding tribes' *(circumiectae nationes)* is somewhat odd when applied to the Iceni, seeing that their territory had water on three sides of it — though that may reflect the limitations of Tacitus's knowledge of the political geography of Britain. But thirdly, and most importantly, where was King Prasutagus in all this?

It has sometimes been suggested that Prasutagus may only have been appointed after this uprising,[6] but there are two powerful arguments against this. First, in *Annals* xiv, 31, Tacitus describes him as 'famous for his long-standing wealth' *(longa opulentia clarus)*, which is a strange (and unnecessary) expression to apply to a man who had been installed as king only a dozen years earlier; and that his wealth did come from the Emperor can hardly be doubted, since Dio specifies this when he gives its recall as the main cause of the Boudican Revolt.[7] Secondly, the relationship was one between Emperor as patron and king as client, and a provincial governor was not entitled to make such appointments on his own initiative. The deposition of the reigning monarch, therefore, and his replacement by Prasutagus would have entailed a fairly lengthy interregnum while the Emperor's approval was obtained — just the sort of delay which Ostorius was evidently anxious to avoid: even sons could not succeed their fathers automatically.

There are, then, a number of perplexing aspects of the account. Many of them arise from the omission of specific names of places and people (not only that of Prasutagus but those of the tribes involved in the original incursion too). This is a common feature of Tacitus's writing on Britain, but in deference to him one must remember the nature of the audience for whom the *Annals* were written — upper-class Romans whose interest was in Roman history proper, who mostly knew little about the outlying provinces and who would be confused or bored by the introduction of too many barbarian names; and the same would be true for any other writer whose work Tacitus was here using as a source.[8] Such omissions do not justify the claim of Bury regarding the *Annals,* that 'it may be said with virtual truth that the book ignores the Empire',[9] but it is still legitimate to raise a specifically local question: how much did Tacitus know, or indeed care, about Britain in general and about its political geography in particular?

In all his surviving works there are mentions of seven British tribes, namely the Boresti, Brigantes, Decangi (possibly corrupt), Iceni, Ordovices, Silures and Trinobantes, and each of them could well have been mentioned by Agricola when describing his most interesting experiences in Britain.[10] Agricola certainly did talk to Tacitus about his experiences and it is these (especially the military ones), rather than Britain itself, that Tacitus would have been interested in.[11] But when Agricola died Tacitus had been absent from Rome for four years, so that he had no chance to improve his knowledge as his father-in-law failed and, as the notorious substitution of the name of Brigantes for that of the Iceni in the speech of Calgacus shows,[12] by the time he compiled his laudation he was already a little confused. It is, therefore, not entirely impossible that in this case too he has cited the wrong tribal name — in effect, that his source may have said simply that it was a powerful allied state that started the revolt and that the Iceni were the only such state (disregarding, of course, the Brigantes and loyal Cogidubnus) of which Tacitus had heard. If this were so, the obvious candidates for substitution would be the Dobunni. As the distribution of their coins shows,[13] they were a large tribe and would presumably qualify for the epithet *valida*. If we accept Dio's Bodunni as representing them, as we surely must, they, or at least a part of them, had indeed entered into alliance with the Romans voluntarily and had in fact been the first people to do so. As suggested above, it was almost certainly their territory which had been invaded and they, more than anyone else, would have resented Ostorius's decision to deprive them of their means of self-defence. The archaeological evidence indicates that it was just about this time that new forts were established in their territory, and it was apparently to Gloucester, in that territory, that *Legio XX* was transferred when the *colonia* was established at Camulodunum. Finally, for them the expression 'surrounding tribes' becomes reasonable.

This solution, though somewhat extreme, is not without its attractions, but there is another possibility that is also worthy of consideration. This is that the revolt did not involve the Iceni as a whole, still less their king, but simply a unit of Icenian tribesmen who had behaved suspiciously during the incursion and that the 'surrounding tribes' were similar units, perhaps including some Dobunni, who joined them, in their rebellion — a rebellion directed not only against the Roman governor but also, by implication, against the pro-Roman (and comfortably Roman-endowed) Prasutagus. One argument in favour of this is that the recent excavations at Thetford have demonstrated that a particularly narrow entrance is characteristic of some Icenian fortifications[15] — though in this case the earthwork used should be sought not in East Anglia but more probably in Dobunnic territory. Another is that it offers some explanation of the surprising use of *sociales copiae* by Ostorius to suppress the revolt: to use the notorious divisiveness of the British tribes to combat such indiscipline would be a brilliant stroke of propaganda.[16]

Either of these explanations has the effect of localising the disturbance in Dobunnic territory and this leads on to a consideration of the aftermath, for which we must turn to the other text which, though in extremely contracted form, covers this period of British history. In chapter 14 of the *Agricola* Tacitus writes:

'The first of the consular governors to be appointed was Aulus Plautius, then Ostorius Scapula, each of them a man of military distinction; and the nearest part of Britain was gradually reduced to the form of a *provincia,* with the addition of a *colonia* of veterans. Certain states were presented to king Cogidumnus *(quaedam civitates Cogidumno regi donatae),* who remained most loyal down to our own times, by the old-established custom of the Roman people of using even kings as instruments of servitude. Next Didius Gallus . . .'

The significance of the order in which the events are here presented has been much discussed, most recently by Mr. A.A. Barrett,[17] who conveniently assembles all the proposals but finally decides that it is minimal and that the *donatio* of *civitates* to Cogidubnus probably took place soon after the invasion, during the governorship of Aulus Plautius. But his arguments are not all conclusive,[18] and he does not adequately explain why Cogidubnus (now shorn of his supposed title of *legatus Augusti*) should be singled out for mention (as opposed to Prasutagus and possibly others). An (unusual) extension of his kingdom, however, in the period which we are discussing might offer an explanation not only of his mention but also of an apparent anomaly of Romano-British political geography, the inclusion in the eventual *civitas Belgarum* of what had certainly been Dobunnic territory.

This requires a reconsideration of the position of Bodvoc and the division of the Dobunnic kingdom as it was put forward in the Bagendon report. In reviewing this work the present writer observed:[19]

'Some sort of division might be expected on the general grounds, not mentioned here, that most of the Belgic kingdoms in Britain seem to have had two poles: this is true of the Atrebates, the Iceni, apparently the Coritani, and, at least in Roman times, the Durotriges. But the idea of a complete political split is based solely on the coin evidence, and this is not wholly convincing. Both Mr. Allen and Professor Hawkes agree that the Comux/Catti distributions are too thin to be conclusive, but the former suggests and the latter insists that the Corio/ Bodvoc division is clear-cut, with a frontier in the vicinity of the Stroud valley. Analysis of the map (Fig. 20), however, reveals that while Bodvoc's coins are indeed notably confined, those of Corio have a distribution which could easily be pan-Dobunnic: statistically, out of sixteen find-spots (including Beckford, noted too late to be mapped) three are irrelevant, seven support the argument and six contradict it — in fact a couple of Corio coins from Gloucestershire could upset the whole thesis. The reason for believing Corio and Bodvoc to be contemporary is only slightly stronger — the fact that neither is represented in the Nunney hoard which, from its inclusion of a Claudius of A.D. 41, must be related to the conquest; the Sherborne hoard, lacking Roman coins, is not really relevant. The case is not easy, because on typological grounds, as explained by Mr. Allen, there is little time to play with, but is it not at least possible that Corio was the last king of the Dobunni as a whole and that Bodvoc (or his nominee) led the embassy of the romanising party to Plautius, being rewarded with a *reduced* client kingdom . . .?'

Much of what was said in this review clearly needs revision, but the main point, that Corio and Bodvoc were not necessarily wholly contemporary, still stands; and since we are dealing with a period of only four or five years after the invasion, is it not also possible that the contraction of the Dobunnic kingdom took place not in A.D. 43 but in A.D. 48? The implications of this suggestion are not that Bodvoc was appointed at this later date (for that would raise the same difficulties as the supposed later installation of Prasutagus), but rather that Corio ruled the whole of the Dobunni at the time of the initial invasion; that Bodvoc, having led an embassy of the anti-Catuvellaunian faction to Plautius,[20] was appointed king of the whole tribe by Claudius; but that he failed to control the dissident (pro-Catuvellaunian?) southern part of his kingdom which, after the disruptions we have been considering, was handed over to the more reliable Cogidubnus and so ultimately emerged, after the death of Cogidubnus, as part of the newly-created *civitas Belgarum*.[21] How long Bodvoc himself survived would remain a matter for conjecture, but it is clear from Tacitus's account that Ostorius did not wish to be delayed by unneccessary administrative reforms such as the establishment of direct, truly provincial, control: his aim was to press on into Wales, first in the north, through the territory of the Decangi, then in the south, against the Silures, not only to capture Caratacus but also to carry out his emperor's instructions to Plautius to conquer 'the rest'.[22]

It has not been the purpose of this paper to present indisputable answers to the questions raised (the evidence is too thin for that), but simply to suggest that much that has been generally accepted — that has, so to say, 'got into the works' — is not wholly indisputable either. And it seemed not improper to offer it as a tribute to the most distinguished Romano-British scholar of our generation, who not only began his archaeological career in the territory of the Iceni but is also well known as the iconoclast of Verulamium.[23]

NOTES

1. Clifford, E.M. (ed.), *Bagendon: a Belgic Oppidum,* Cambridge, 1961, especially 56–67.

2. Thus, for example, Jackson (Loeb edition, 1951) omits *castris,* but Koestermann (Teubner edition, 1945) retains it; its retention is also supported by Syme, R., *Tacitus,* Oxford, 1958, 394, note 4.

3. Webster, G., 'The Military Situations in Britain between A.D. 43 and 71', *Britannia,* i, (1970), 179–97, although it is, of course, impossible to establish precise dates within so short a period by archaeology alone.

4. On this see Brunt, P.A., 'Did Imperial Rome Disarm her Subjects?', *Phoenix,* xxix, (1975), 260–70.

5. Webster, G., *op. cit.* (see note 3), but with the same reservations.

6. The strongest argument for this is that put forward by Allen in *Britannia,* i, (1970), 2, 14–16 (arguing for Antedios as the first client king), followed by Wacher, J.S., *Roman Britain,* London, 1978, 37, and others.

7. Cassius Dio, *Epitome,* lxii, 2. The persistent arguments over the part (if any) played by Seneca tend sometimes to obscure the fact that it is the recall of money advanced by Claudius himself that is given as the first cause.

8. cf. Pliny, *Natural History,* iii, 28 (where, in dealing with Spain, he restricts the number of tribal names that can be mentioned *citra fastidium*) and see Syme, R., *op. cit.* (see note 2), 392 and Burn, A.R., in Dorey, T.A. (ed.), *Tacitus,* London, 1969, 40, etc.

9. For a discussion of this, see Syme, R., *op. cit.* (see note 2), 766–7.

10. Of these the Brigantes and the Silures were the tribes most widely known and referred to by Roman authors (see Rivet, A.L.F. and Smith, C., *The Place-Names of Roman Britain,* London, 1979, 46–7, for a full list). Of the rest, Agricola was engaged militarily against the Iceni and the Trinovantes as a tribune, against the Ordovices (and, on the way to them, the Deceangli) as governor and probably also as legionary commander, and the Boresti as governor.

11. Apart from a few references to features like the long summer twilight and the sea-lochs, evidently derived from Agricola, his promise that *quae priores nondum comperta eloquentia percoluere, rerum fide tradentur* (*Agricola,* 10) is not very impressively fulfilled.

12. *Agricola,* 31.

13. Clifford, E.M., *op. cit.* (see note 1), 68, fig. 16.

14. *ibid.,* 61–2.

15. The entrance to the inner enclosure at Thetford is only 2.5 m. (9 ft.) wide. I am most grateful to Mr. Antony Gregory for information on this and for a sight of the draft plans in advance of publication, but it does not follow that he accepts my suggestions.

16. I accept the suggestion of Mr. G.C. Boon (*Archaeologia,* cii, (1969), 37), that the *sociales copiae* were probably those of client kings and included some of the troops of Cogidubnus, against Mr. A.A. Barrett (*Britannia,* x, (1979), 231). The two passages cited by Mr. Barrett (*Annals,* xiii, 38, and Velleius Paterculus, ii, 112) do not really prove his point, since in both cases the author has to vary the language to make it clear that both normal auxiliaries and 'royal' troops were involved. The normal opposite to *legiones* is *auxilia* (as indeed in the passage from Velleius) and there is no reason why Tacitus should not have used it here. On the divisiveness of British tribes see note 20 below.

17. Barrett, A.A., 'The Career of Tiberius Claudius Cogidubnus', *Britannia,* x, (1979), 227–54.

18. The article includes an excellent summary account of client kings (229–30), but the correct interpretation of *regi donatae* (232–3) still remains open; see also note 16 above.

19. *Antiquity,* xxxvi, (1962), 146–7.

20. Cassius Dio, lx, 20, φυγόντων δὲ ἐκείνων

προσεποιήσατο ὁμολογίᾳ μέρος τι τῶν Βοδούννων ὧν ἐπῆρχον Κατουελλανοὶ ὄντες: 'They (sc. Caratacus and Togodumnus) having fled, he (sc. Plautius) won over by agreement (or surrender) a part of the Bodunni whom they ruled over (or commanded), being themselves Catuvellauni.' As Professor Hawkes points out (in Clifford, E.M., *op. cit.* (see note 1), 60), the use of μέρος as a military division is unlikely (which renders the alternative translations here offered in brackets the less probable), but his equation of the word with the Latin *pars* (which almost certainly reflects Dio's source) does not lead inevitably to 'a territorial division'; it could equally well mean a party or faction in the political sense, which might not be reflected territorially. What is evident from the text is that it was anti-Catuvellaunian feeling that led to the agreement; and while for the Romans the appeal of Verica was merely an excuse, the invasion was no doubt presented to most of the Britons as a war against the arrogant Catuvellaunian rulers. For other ideas regarding the implications of this passage and the roles of Corio and Bodvoc, see Wacher, J.S., *The Towns of Roman Britain,* London, 1978, 289–93 (based partly on suggestions of Mr. J. Robinson).

21. The only direct evidence for the westward extension of the *civitas Belgarum* is, of course, Ptolemy's attribution of Bath to it (*Geography*, ii, 3, 13), but the fact that the name *Belgae* is in all other cases applied to a whole people or collection of tribes rather than to a single tribe does suggest an artificial creation and its restriction to the area around Winchester would result in a very small unit by British standards.

22. Cassius Dio, lx, 21, end — though quite what Claudius meant by 'the rest' (τὰ λοιπά) is a little obscure.

23. *Antiq. Journ.*, xxi, (1941), 40–55; the word 'iconoclast' is here used in the dictionary sense of 'one who assails old cherished errors and superstitions'.

A Husband for the Mother Goddesses — Some Observations on the *Matronae Aufaniae*

by
C.B. RÜGER

It is hard to express how much the participants, among them the writer, gained in the hot August days of 1968 and 1969, when Professor Frere was invited to advise an Oxford Institute and Bonn Museum excavation on *insula* XXVII of Colonia Ulpia Traiana at Xanten. Was it the constant comments on sharply-viewed features of the site; was it the profound asides on the topography of the Augustan campaigns and of the Batavian revolt, visited and, hence, seen anew; was it the answers to the numerous questions of young archaeologists? At least it was the iced tea that he, in person, obtained every hot day around eleven o'clock! It restored us to our feet at times and Richard Reece, Roger Goodburn, Martin Henig and others can be remembered gathering round that white-enamelled hospital bucket containing the refreshing liquid.[1]

It is an act of gratitude to the supervising excavator, to the teacher, to the author of the latest history of Roman Britain and to the indefatigable, sometime editor of that provincial forum *Britannia* that makes me raise a topic which was touched upon briefly during the evenings of those days: *curiae* in the Roman North-West and their significance.

After R.G. Collingwood and F.J. Haverfield there was C.E. Stevens' lucid interpretation of the single example from Britain, the *curia Textoverdorum*; there were suggestions on the *curia Arduennae* from Amberloup in Belgium and its meaning. But it was talking to Sheppard Frere that encouraged me to collect all existing evidence, which was published with comments in 1972.[2] It seems that, until now, the arguments on *curiae* have been published in somewhat obscure places. Therefore, they may again be justifiably summarised, with the kind indulgence of those who have read the earlier and fuller accounts:

1. The *curiae* of the Roman north-west can be sharply distinguished from the usual municipal institutions of that name which existed in *coloniae* and *municipia* throughout the empire.

2. All inscriptions of *curiae* in the Rhineland (and some beyond) are building dedications, mostly to a chief tribal god, which in our area is habitually equated with the Roman Mercury.

3. Although there is no reference to the purpose of the buildings, they should have been a kind of club-house *(schola?)*.

Pl. I Altar of the *Matronae Aufaniae* of A.D. 164 (Vettius altar). *(Photograph: Rheinisches Landes-museum, Bonn)*.

B

A

Pl. II Altar to the *Matronae Aufaniae* by Statilius Proculus and Sutoria Pia; A. Front; B. Back.
(Photograph: Rheinisches Landesmuseum, Bonn).

4. *Curiae* are "clubs" for men, perhaps the residue of a tribal Iron Age militia (following C.E. Stevens), which were turned into socio-religious institutions under Roman rule.
5. The dedicating groups bear 'sept'-names. They function below the lowest distinct indigenous level of Roman administration, the *civitas* (e.g. *curia Etratium*). Their equivalent on a territorial level could be that of a *pagus*.[3]
6. The group-names show a relationship with the names of the mother goddesses (e.g. *curia Etra-tium* and *matronae Etra-henae*).
7. Inscriptions from (Mercury-) temples within the sacred precincts of Rhenish *matronae* show that these peasant goddesses of fertility had husband gods.

Agricultural societies of Europe must have known, at least since the first attempts at breeding live-stock in the Neolithic, that a male and a female are needed for procreation. Their Iron Age descendants would hardly have been satisfied with a concept of mother goddesses bearing too close a similarity with later, Christian female saints. In 1972 no example seemed to exist for a clearly-defined relationship between *matronae* and their supposed husbands, so the question was left to be resolved later. In so doing, a most striking example for that relationship was carelessly omitted. It is housed in the Rheinisches Landesmuseum in Bonn, only a few metres away from the finest representation of the mothers, the great altar of the *matronae Aufaniae* by Q. Vettius Severus, *quaestor* of the Claudian colony of Cologne, who set up his dedication in A.D. 164 in the sacred precinct of the matrons at Bonn (Pl. I).[4] With it, and the large series of other sculptured and inscribed representations of the *Aufaniae*, H. Lehner found the following altar (Pl. II, A and B). Its description can be taken from H. von Petrikovits, since it is the most detailed, and its accuracy has been retained since 1962:[5]

'Found in the foundations of a palaeochristian *cella memoriae* under Bonn Minster during excavations in 1928–1930. It was moved there from a sacred precinct, the position of which is hitherto unknown. The altar was made of light Bunter Sandstone, probably from the Trier area: height 1.54 m. (5 ft.); width 1.05 m. (3.5 ft.); depth 0.39 m. (1 ft.). Nesselhauff, H., *Berichte der Römisch-Germanischen Kommission,* xxvii, (1937), no. 151; Espérandieu, E., *Recueil général des bas-reliefs de la Germanie romaine,* Paris/Bruxelles, 1931, no. 7722; Lehner, H., *Bonner Jahrbücher,* cxxv, (1930), no. 7, pl. IV, V).

It has the shape of an altar. Above the profiled foot a wide, but thin, shaft rises which carries an inscription of eight lines. Above it is a cornice with apophyge and a small gable filled by a mask of leaves. On each side of the gable is a half-palmette as a lateral acroterion. On both sides of the small gable lie the rolled-up ends of a cloth covered with scales resembling leaves, such as were used to cover ancient altars. On top, two apples and two pears can be seen.

The altar must have been free standing, as its rear face bears a shallow relief. It shows a rocky landscape, treated with simplicity, in which a firm iconographical tradition requires a rock to rise on one side and form a cave. In the centre of the scene an S-shaped tree grows from a wide root system. Its S-shaped branches end in bunches of leaves. Two or three of the highest branches carry a hemispherical nest, which contains four small, open-mouthed birds. Out of the hole in the middle of the trunk a snake appears. Both under its chin and on top of its head, which is poised to strike, there is a crest. This type of incono-graphical landscape is taken from the late Hellenistic and Augustan tradition and represents nature in the raw. In it the snake threatening the small birds in a nest corresponds to an eagle hunting a hare. Both scenes express the merciless struggle of nature. On the rocky ground behind the tree there is a fabulous creature, a goat consisting of three bodies with a single head. Two of the bodies are standing, the third is lying down. On all three bodies the udders are boldly portrayed. The common head is shown frontally and carries two high horns. It is impossible to decide whether the object under the goat's mouth is part of the surrounding rock or else some other object.

Several dedications to the *matronae* found under Bonn Minster show the tree with the snake creeping out of a hole in the trunk, and there is one other dedication, also from Bonn Minster, depicting a goat. The tree-motif has probably been handed down from earlier observances of the matrons' cult, while their image, representing fertility, was not yet anthropomorphic, but was expressed by a tree-cult, as shown on stones from Upper Italy. The tri-bodied super-goat with her plump udders is likely to have connections with this cult. The snake, an animal that lives on or under the ground, symbolises Earth itself.

When the representations of the cult became anthropomorphic, the older ideas, with connections with nature, retreated and were relegated to occupy the back or the lateral scenes of the altars. Both sides show similar reliefs: from a *cantharos* grows a plant with fleshy acanthus-like leaves. In the centre of the representation, the plant carries a basin from which a similar plant grows; on top of that, there is another basin, in which two birds are sitting on the left side of the altar, while on the right, the basin is filled with three apples and two pears.

The style of the relief is hard to judge. H. Lehner attributed it to the monuments of the second half of the second century. On italianate tombstones and sarcophagi, both the lateral and rear reliefs were less deeply carved than that of the front. But this shallowness should not be seen as a criterion of style. The schematic and stylised representation could be dated to the early third century but, on the other hand, it could simply be due to provincial standards.

The front of the altar carries only an eight-line inscription, which runs:

Matronis/Aufaniabus/T(itus) Statilius/Proculus/praefectus/leg(ionis)I M(inerviae) p(iae) f(idelis) et/Sutoria Pia eius (sic!) */v(otum) s(olverunt) l(ibentes) m(erito).'*

Thus H. von Petrikovits' description. Some similarities, both in theme and style, to a group of altars dedicated to the *Aufaniae*, which was manufactured by the 'Bonn sculpture workshop', enable this altar to be dated to the years around A.D. 185: the altar of Flavia Tiberina, wife of Claudius Stratonicus, which is justifiably dated by G. Alföldy to this time, and other altars with the characteristic leaf-masks in a gable, should belong to this group. It is important for our argument to note that the altar of Flavia Tiberina also had a representation of a goat (Pl. III, B: hind legs to lower left).[6]

At first glance, it seems rather puzzling that two wives of high-ranking officers do not depict the *matronae* in the usual anthropomorphic way, as done for instance by an equally high-ranking civilian like Q. Vettius Severus. Instead, they try to tell their fellow-worshippers, and us, of goats. Who are these women? Sutoria is a rather rare *nomen gentile*. Professor Eric Birley, to whom I am much indebted for another review of the inscription, while on a short visit to the museum in Bonn, even hinted at some ancestral tie of Sutoria Pia to Q. Naevius Cordus Sutorius Macro, that famous *praefectus praetorio* from Alba Fucens, who put Seianus to death in A.D. 37. Considering the short list of Sutorii in *C.I.L.* VI and elsewhere (under ten and mostly belonging to freedmen), the valuable comment of an expert prosopographer is indeed suggestive. The other woman connected with the goat-myth, Flavia Tiberina, wife of Claudius Stratonicus, the legate of *Legio I Minervia* around A.D. 185, was the wife of a senatorial officer and so of senatorial rank herself.

The instructions to the Aufanian sculptors, therefore, came from sophisticated ladies of the highest rank in Bonna. The sculptors can have been left in no doubt as to the way in which the goddesses were to be represented; yet the anthropomorphic example of the matrons had been provided, at least as early as A.D. 164 for Q. Vettius Severus. Why should these high-class women, who enjoyed a thorough education and much privilege in the garrison, openly and alone give way to something of the archaic indigenous myth of the matrons?

As has been shown earlier, the sacred precinct of the *Aufaniae* also contained a temple of *Mercurius Gebrinius*. Its building inscription was found, together with eight other dedications to that god, among the inscriptions to the *Aufaniae* under Bonn Minster.[7] His native name leads us directly, it seems, to the goats: Gebrinius is to be linked to celtic *gabro-*, latin *caper*, he-goat.[8] In other words, at the theriomorphic stage, Gebrinius could be imagined as a divine he-goat. Given our supposition that there should have been sacred husbands for sacred wives, when it came to the fertility of stock and crop, the function of goat-goddesses becomes a little clearer: reputable ancient sources mention that goats reach maturity early and have a life-long ability to bear young. These qualities of the animal must also have been known among the Iron Age peoples of the European North-West.[9]

The lesser, indigenous dedicants to the matrons refrained from depicting the pre-anthropomorphic state of the *Aufaniae* for reasons unknown. Perhaps they could not afford to return to such wild configurations, once the anthropomorphic image of the goddess was in existence. Soldier-worshippers were reluctant even to order human images of the Bonn *Aufaniae* when they dedicated votive inscriptions in the eighty years of *Aufaniae*-worship after A.D. 160. Somewhere around this latter date the humanized cult statues of the *Aufaniae* must, for various reasons, have been created by a competent provincial sculptor in Bonna.

Pl. III Altar to the *Matronae Aufaniae* of Flavia Tiberina; A. Front; B. Back. *(Photograph: Rheinisches Landesmuseum, Bonn).*

Fig. 1   Altar of Statilius Proculus and Sutoria Pia; scale 1/10. *(Drawn by Margret Sonntag-Hilgers).*

But, by about A.D. 185, the myth of the sacred goats was still so vigorous that the cream of noble officers' wives could afford to illustrate the old story on the backs of the altars quite openly, where, if we find anything at all, it is more often a curtain veiling something![10]

To return to the representation of the triple-bodied goat of Bonn, we see the fabulous creature in three varied positions: standing up (left body), lying down (right body), and getting up or kneeling down (front legs first, as ruminants do) or perhaps climbing down the rock (centre body) (Fig. 1). This should remind us of at least two stages of womanhood depicted in the truest copy of the *Aufaniae* cult statues which has survived, the altar of Vettius Severus (Pl. I). There is a young girl in the centre with her hair let loosely down. She is smaller than her two companions, but perhaps higher in rank, as indicated by a foot-stool, on which her feet are placed. On either hand she is accompanied by fully grown women with bonnets on their heads and the amulet of maturity around their necks. Could the different positions of the three bodies of the goats equally represent such stages of life? There is, as yet, no answer to this.

But there is another observation still to add.[11] The object adjacent to the goat's mouth is definitely distinct from the surrounding rock and has a soft and angular shape. The placenta of sheep and goats is of such a shape (zoologically an *uterus* or *placenta bicornis*). While giving birth to their young, goats are described as changing their positions many times, getting up, kneeling or lying down. Furthermore, all zoological literature relating to the animals' behaviour, during and after delivery, seems to agree that goats eat the placenta as soon as the kid has freed itself.[12]

Is it possible that we are viewing a scene of a single she-goat giving birth? If so, it would then be depicted in a rather subtle (Celtic?) way, by showing simultaneously the three movements typical of a goat delivering her kid, with the mother nosing the unbroken placenta immediately after it has slid onto the rocky pastures under the tree. The three positions of the mother would then again have an unlimited significance for the procreation of descendants, and thus for the idea of fertility.

If this is to be believed, the tri-goat is a rather more intricate, albeit archaic, image of an important development in the life of a woman. The sophisticated form of the story being told contrasts successfully with the platitude of the anthropomorphic *Aufaniae,* whose only achievement is the small degree of classical elegance, derived from Mediterranean copy-books, in its provincial styling, and gained only at the expense of lost indigenous religious power and dramatic representation of the myth.

Be that as it may; only two upper class women of the Bonn garrison seem to have taken the opportunity, either for enjoyment or for intellectual liberty, to tell us such an archaic story. Severe criticism may be expected and, indeed, is requested, about the above suggestions. But this must be considered an opportunity to break away from the routine of positivist description, which, as M. Eliade has observed, is most unlikely to generate discussion, and which, in our case, is to get away from 'a fabulous creature', set in a classical landscape.

Perhaps our experiment is as presumptuous as if we were to develop all palaeochristian thought from a single, surviving representation of the crucifix. But it would be a pity neither to have felt the streak of *pensée sauvage* that must have created the archaic matrons, nor to have been challenged by a monument that has not left the author's thoughts since he first saw it with his school-master in the summer of 1952.

May the recipient of this article at least view it with indulgence!

NOTES

1. I should like to thank Mrs. Margret Sonntag-Hilgers, daughter of the owner of the site in *Insula* XXVII, for adding her drawing skill to these lines in vivid memory of those days; Mrs. Marion Eckart, who typed the English manuscript; Mrs. Brigitte Beyer-Rotthoff for her kind help with the Bonn Matronae-Index, and, last but not least, the editors for their efforts in bringing the author's English into shape.

2. Rüger, C.B., 'Gallisch-germanische Kurien', *Epigraphische Studien, 9,* Bonn, 1972, 251. Some comments on the article would have been welcome in Hind, J.G.F., 'The Romano-British Name for Corbridge', *Britannia,* xi, (1980), 165.

3. Following the linguists we proposed, for reasons which are set out in Rüger, *op. cit.* (see note 2), 256: matronae *★Amrahenae* and *★Amrates* to an existing *curia Amratinna.* Following a recent excavation find by W. Gaitzsch (cf. *Ausgrabungen im Rheinland 1979–1980,* Köln/Bonn, 1981, 122) we have now to correct these readings to: matronae *Amfratninae, ★Amfrates, curia ★Amfratnina.* Some thirty inscriptions of the sanctuary at Eschweiler are awaiting publication, the single previous find of *curia Amratnina* (now corrected from the author's *Amratinna*) seems to be the exception.

4. Altar of Vettius: Lehner, H., *Bonner Jahrbücher,* cxxxv, (1930), 11, No. 20: Nesselhauf, H., *Berichte der Römisch-Germanischen Kommission,* xxvii, (1937), No. 163; von Petrikovits, H. (ed.), *Aus rheinischer Kunst und Kultur: Auswahlkatalog des Rheinischen Landesmuseums Bonn,* Düsseldorf, 1963, No. 17.

5. *ibid.,* No. 18, 57.

6. Alföldy, G., 'Die Legionslegaten der römischen Rheinarmeen', *Epigraphische Studien, 3,* Köln/Graz, 1967, 46, No. 54. Altar of Flavia Tiberina: *Bonner Jahrbücher,* cxxxv, (1930), No. 6 = *L'Année épigraphique,* (1930)— No. 30. Its inscription: *Matronis / Aufanibus / pro salute / Fla(via) Tiberina / Cl(audii) Stratonici / legati*

Augusti / leg(ionis) I M(inerviae) p(iae) f(idelis) v.s.l.m.

7. Rüger, C.B., *op. cit.* (see note 2), 258.

8. Holder, A., *Altceltischer Sprachschatz I,* Leipzig, 1891–1913, 1511. H. Birkhan ('Germanen und Kelten bis zum Ausgang der Römerzeit', *Sitzungsberichte der Oesterreichischen Akademie der Wissenschaften,* cclxxii, (1970)) could not decide (cp. No. 559) whether to put Gebrinius to Celtic *★gabros* or indogermanic *★gheimrino,* but he certainly did not take into account the fact that goats are represented on our altars, nor did he realise their connection with Mercurius Gebrinius. In fairness it should be added that Professor K.H. Schmidt (Bonn), whose opinion I sought as an eminent scholar of Celtic, was rather reluctant to agree with my argument, his doubts, resting mainly on the awkward −A− to −E− change (*★gabros— gebrinius*).

9. cf. Will Richter, in *Der Kleine Pauly 5,* Munich, 1975, 1531, s.v. 'Ziege'.

10. For the veiling of altars, its meaning in ancient cult and representations on the backs of altars, cf. Noelke in Bauchhenss, G. and Noelke, P. (eds.), *Die Jupitersäulen der germanischen Provinzen,* Köln/Bonn, 1981. Neither time nor present space permit more ample argument and proof, much of which I should have had to borrow from the current iconographical studies of H.G. Horn (Bonn). We shall deal jointly with the evidence in a forthcoming publication (1984) of the Göttingen Academy of Sciences, which will be devoted to the subject of mother goddesses.

11. I gratefully acknowledge my debt for the following facts to Professor G. Nobis, of the Zoologisches Forschungsinstitut and the Alexander Koenig Museum in Bonn. He is not only an expert on, and longtime collaborator in, the study of archaeological remains of domesticated animals, but was kind enough to encourage me in this part of the paper. He described to me the head of the tri-goat as that of a primitive

European domesticated species of goat ('sabre-horned goat'), often found in archaeological contexts in the Roman North-West.

12. I am most grateful to Professor Nobis for furnishing me with the relevant literature. All facts are taken from Naaktgeboren, C. and Slijper, E.J., *Biologie der Geburt: Eine Einführung in die vergleichende Geburtskunde,* Hamburg/Berlin, 1970, passim.

The Roman Fortlet at Gatehouse of Fleet, Kirkcudbright

by

J.K. ST JOSEPH

The Roman fortlet at Gatehouse of Fleet was discovered during a reconnaissance flight on 11 July 1949.[1] That summer witnessed one of the most severe droughts of this century when parts of the country, and particularly north-west England, appeared from the air to be parched as brown as a desert. The discovery, in Nithsdale, on 6 July of two forts and a camp at Dalswinton, and of two camps at Durisdeer, when considered together with the Roman sites already known in that valley, namely the forts of Carzield and at Wardlaw, pointed to such a strong military presence as to raise the question whether Roman armies had penetrated further west. The lower reaches of the principal rivers, the Cree, the Fleet and the Dee seemed the most profitable places to search, and on 11 July a reconnaissance flight from Silloth airfield, in Cumberland, was accordingly planned for this purpose. After reaching Whithorn, where photography was undertaken, the return route lay along the Galloway coast. Search of the Cree valley between Newton Stewart and the estuary was unrewarding: however, in the valley of the Water of Fleet clear parch marks in a grass field a little north of Gatehouse revealed a rectangular enclosure (Pl. I). The two widely spaced ditches, the well rounded angles, the central gate in the north-east side, and the advantageous position on level ground near the river left little reasonable doubt that this was a small Roman fort. The discovery implied that the much larger valley of the Dee, 15 km. (9.3 miles) east would hardly have been left unguarded, and within some ten minutes flying time, the forts and camps at Glenlochar, north of Castle Douglas had also been discovered.

Two weeks' exploratory excavation at Glenlochar in April 1952[2] showed that there were three superimposed forts, of which the first was associated with Flavian pottery. A still earlier Flavian period was represented by rubbish pits and shacks of a kind that are found outside a garrisoned fort. The Flavian I fort evidently lay outside the excavated area, and presumably a little to the north. The site at Gatehouse was surveyed on 15th August 1956, and, by kind permission of Mrs. Murray Usher on whose estate the fort lies, two short periods of excavation followed in August 1960 and August 1961, the first lasting two weeks, the second twelve days. The object of the work was to determine as far as possible the character and plan of the site, and its date. In the second season

Pl. I Roman fortlet, Gatehouse of Fleet. Steep oblique photograph looking north-east. Neg. No. DT 38, taken 11 July, 1949. (*This photograph from the Cambridge University Collection is Crown Copyright and is reproduced by permission of the Ministry of Defence, and of the Controller of Her Majesty's Stationery Office*).

Sheppard and Janet Frere helped with the work, and I am particularly glad to express my thanks for help not only at Gatehouse and other sites, but also for good company and companionship on field-work over the last twenty-five years, by offering this report for inclusion in a *Festschrift*.

The Water of Fleet, about 20 km. (12.5 miles) in total length is a not very large river fed by streams that rise on the east face of Cairnsmore of Fleet. The river basin lies roughly half-way between two much longer rivers, the Cree on the west, and the Dee to the east. From the Cree, the basin is separated by the high ground that extends southwards from Cairnsmore of Fleet — the 305 m. (1000 ft.) contour reaches to within 1.5 km. (0.9 miles) of the coast. Eastwards, the country between the Fleet and the Dee shows, in its very uneven surface, effects of glaciation, with hillocks that rise here and there to about 152 m. (500 ft.). Only for the lowest 6.5 km. (4 miles) of its course has the Fleet a valley

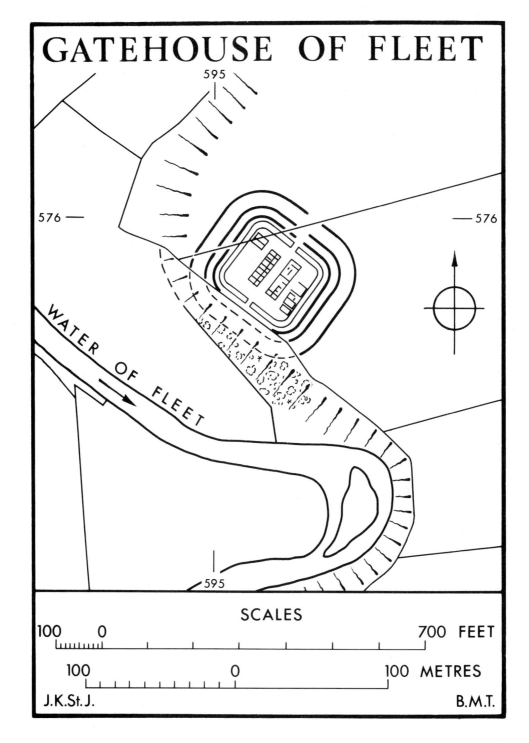

Fig. 1   Gatehouse of Fleet. The site of the fortlet in relation to the river.

floor level enough for cultivation, and even there the floor is hardly more than 1 km. (0.6 miles) wide. The Roman site (Fig. 1) lies on the east bank of the river (at NX 595575), 3.5 km. (2.2 miles) from the head of the estuary, and just above the highest point reached by ordinary Spring tides. The lower ground by the river is liable to flood, but under normal conditions a crossing by bridge or ford would present no difficulty. The fortlet which lies on a gravel terrace some 7.6 m. (25 ft.) above the Fleet, has a good command of the valley both up- and downstream. It is bounded on the west by a steep scarp formed by erosion of the river, for, since Roman times, the Fleet has evidently swung towards the fortlet and then back again.

There seems to be no previous record of this fortlet, but the legend 'ROMAN CAMP (supposed)' is printed on the first edition of the 1:10560 O.S. map (Kirkcudbright XLIII, surveyed in 1849–50) in relation to a small rectangular earthwork beside the Fleet, about 1 km. (0.6 miles) to the north. To judge from the plan, this earthwork was probably a moat. The second edition (1910) carries the same legend, but the earthwork is shown as circular, as indeed it appeared to be in 1956, when it was regarded as a motte. The corresponding O.S. maps of Glenlochar carry the legend 'Roman burying place (supposed)' in relation to a mound about 1 km. (0.6 miles) east of the fort there. Such entries on the early Ordnance Maps may reflect the views of an early antiquary, or merely a tendency for local opinion to assign any unusual earthwork to the Roman period, perhaps on the basis of some casual find. Indeed, the *Statistical Account* of Crossmichael, the parish in which Glenlochar lies, records that 'Farmers in ploughing, and labourers in digging frequently found Roman urns, swords and other implements'.[3] These seem to be the only such entries in this part of the stewartry and both occur close to Roman forts.

With the aid of aerial photographs[4] the position of the fortlet was not difficult to identify on the ground, though the land has been extensively ploughed and no traces are now visible. The photograph (Pl. I) shows that the defences consisted of two widely spaced ditches, and between them a third, narrower feature that appears on photographs as a less conspicuous mark rather closer to the inner ditch than to the outer. The ditches are seen to be continuous along the short, south-east and north-west sides. The angles are turned in curves of large radius. On the south-west, the outer ditch and perhaps much of the central feature of the defensive system have been removed by erosion.

A section dug across the south-east defences (Fig. 3) showed that the outer ditch was V-shaped, 3.8 m. (12 ft.) wide and 1.6 m. (5 ft.) deep, with a square-shaped clearance channel at the bottom. The profile suggests that in this section some slipping of the gravel had occurred on the inner face. The lower 0.7 m. (2.5 ft.) of the filling was of silt and soil washed in from the natural gravel; above came layers of rather coarser gravel, perhaps deliberate infilling, and above this again, at 1 m. (3.3 ft.) from the bottom of the ditch, a layer of black earth with some charcoal, and then more gravel which gave way to modern plough soil.

The distance between the two ditches was 17.3 m. (57 ft.), measured centre to centre. The inner ditch, 2.9 m. (9.5 ft.) wide and 1.35 m. (4.5 ft.) deep also had a small clearance channel. At the bottom, silt had accumulated to a depth of about 20 cm. (8 in.). The filling above this consisted of sandy turfy material with some streaks of peat. This was succeeded by gravel with a few cobbles, and then by a thin layer of clay. An isolated lump of turf-work overlay the outer edge of the clay layer; elsewhere gravelly earth gave place to plough soil. A third feature lay between these two large ditches. It was considerably smaller than either, 1.75 m. (6 ft.) wide and 0.9 m. (35 in.) deep, but the most marked difference was in the character of the filling. This was mostly of packed gravel, not unlike subsoil, but in the centre of the section for a width of 0.3 m. (1 ft.), there was much coarser gravel mixed with black earth. The impression gained was that this feature had been a trench to hold obstacles of some kind.

Some 2.4 m. (8 ft.) beyond the inner ditch, the front of the rampart was encountered. The indications were of the slightest, for traces only of the lowest course of turf-work remained below the plough soil. The width was at least 3.4 m. (11 ft.), a dimension confirmed by a section across the north-west rampart not far from the west angle. This section revealed a layer of stiff, white clay, a few inches thick, lying on the subsoil and the clay had formed a bottoming for turf-work, since there was an extensive deposit of washed turfy material both over the berm, and behind the rampart. Further trenches located the inner ditch on the other three sides and round the south angle. On the north-east, the two squared ends of the ditch were identified, showing that there was an interruption for a causeway 6 m. (20 ft.) wide. The existence of a similar causeway on the south-west was proved when a corresponding squared end of the inner ditch was located there. The obstacle trench was identified on the north-west side, where its dimensions were even smaller than in the main section, no doubt owing to the effects of ploughing.

The information from the various sections together with the evidence of aerial photographs enabled a plan of the defences to be drawn (Fig. 2). The dimensions of the fortlet, measured over the rampart, are 58 m. (190 ft.) from north-west to south-east by 49.5 m. (162 ft.), an area of 0.28 ha. (0.7 acres): the space within the rampart is 51 by 43 m. (169 by 140 ft.), an area of 0.22 ha. (0.52 acres). The area measured over the outer ditch is about 0.9 ha. (2 acres), so that the space occupied by the defences is about three times that enclosed within the rampart. These dimensions compare with an area of 27.4 m. (90 ft.) square within the rampart at the fortlet/signal station at Martinhoe (Devon)[5] constructed under Nero, and with an estimated 44.2 by 32 m. (145 by 105 ft.) for the internal area of the Flavian fortlet at Chew Green.[6]

The rampart was interrupted near the centre of each of the two long sides for a gate, the structure of which consisted of six uprights spaced 1.5 m. (5 ft.) apart, three on either side of a passage 3.5 m. (11 ft.) wide. The timbers measured about 250 mm. (10 in.) square, and were set in post-pits 0.6 to 0.7 m. (23.5 to 27 in.) wide to judge from those that could be measured. The one pit

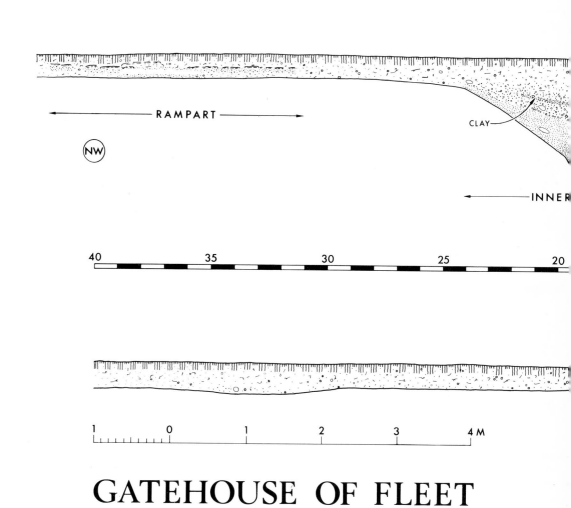

GATEHOUSE OF FLEET

SECTION OF DEFENCES ON SOUTH-EAST SIDE

Fig. 3 Section across the south-east defences.

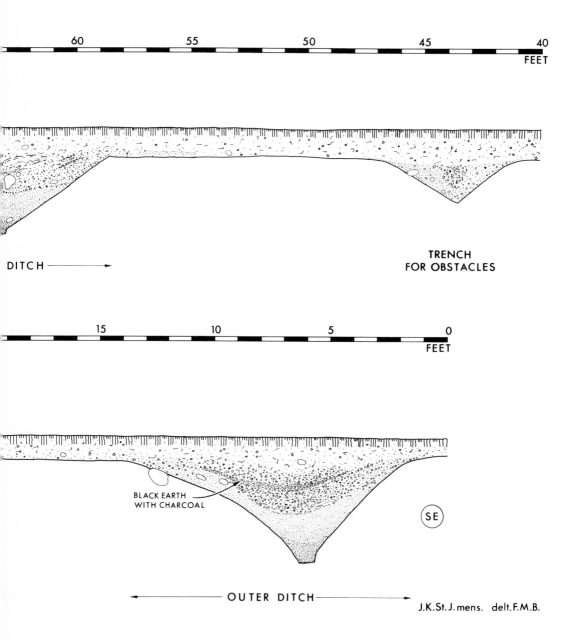

60　　　　　55　　　　　50　　　　　45　　　　　40
FEET

DITCH ⟶

TRENCH
FOR OBSTACLES

15　　　　　10　　　　　5　　　　　0
FEET

BLACK EARTH
WITH CHARCOAL

SE

⟵　OUTER DITCH ⟶

J.K.St.J.mens.　delt.F.M.B.

that was emptied (on the north-west side of the north-east gate) was 520 mm. (20.5 in.) deep. Such timbers would have been strong enough to have carried a rampart-walk across the gateway. No doubt the ends of the rampart were retained by boarding fixed to the uprights. The gates were not precisely opposite each other; the south-west gate lay about 3 m. (10 ft.) further north-west than the other.

The interior was explored in a number of cuttings laid out at forty-five degrees to the axes of the fortlet. The ground within the rampart had been much affected by ploughing which had removed occupation levels except towards the north angle. However, the internal buildings could be planned by tracing their construction-trenches of which there still remained the bottom 150 to 300 mm. (6 to 12 in.) dug into the firm gravel. The buildings were timber-framed, the uprights being set in trenches between 250 and 375 mm. (10 and 15 in.) wide. The few post-holes that could be identified showed that 100 to 125 mm. (4 to 5 in.) posts had been used for the main framework, supporting wattles on to which clay was plastered, to judge from pieces of daub found in the surface soil and in pits. No fragments of tile were found in the surface soil, and the roofs were presumably covered in shingles or thatch. As the plan (Fig. 2) shows, the interior was fairly tightly packed with buildings. The two principal blocks faced each other across a space some 6 m. (20 ft.) wide. This will no doubt have been occupied by a central street that extended from gate to gate. In a parallel street to the north-west a patch of cobbling remained across an area of soft ground, but over the centre of the site, the sub-soil was within a foot of the surface, and there any road-metalling had been scattered by ploughing.

The two largest buildings were not quite parallel, no doubt because, as noted above, the gates were not exactly opposite one another. The longer of the two buildings, that to the south-east, measured 28.3 by 8.2 m. (92.5 by 27 ft.). it was divided into two equal parts by a main cross-wall. The walls within the buildings were often founded in shallow trenches, some of which had been largely removed by ploughing. In the north-east half there seems to have been a central passage with rooms disposed around it; in the south-west half cross-walls were identified, together with a median wall that extended for most of the length of that half. The end section, that most completely defined, was 3.3 m. (11 ft.) wide. The building to the north-west, 25 by 7.6 m. (83 by 25 ft.) was partitioned by cross-walls into seven sections, on average about 3.5 m. (11.5 ft.) wide. Five of these sections were divided into pairs of rooms by a longitudinal wall, and it is reasonable to suppose that the remaining two sections at the south-west end of the building were similarly divided. In each pair, the room facing the street was the smaller of the two.

These two buildings were clearly barrack-blocks. In the larger building, the north-east half 14.2 by 8.2 m. (46 by 27 ft.) provided space for officers' quarters; indeed, the accommodation seems appropriate to a centurion. The plan, with a central passage, resembles in miniature those of some of the centurions' quarters at Inchtuthil. The smaller building, together with the south-westernmost section of the larger, would have accommodated eight *contubernia* of ample size. The remaining space, amounting to a 10.3 m. (34 ft.) length of the larger building, seems to have been divided into four sections, alternately broad 3.2 m. (10.5 ft.) wide, and narrow (2.15 m. or 7 ft.). Whether these should be regarded as the equivalent of two more *contubernia* (the small rooms perhaps housing special equipment), bringing the total to ten, the normal figure for an infantry century, or whether these sections were quarters for junior officers or for men with special duties, remains uncertain. In area 27 sq. m. (32.3 sq. yd.), the *contubernia* compare closely with those at Fendoch (between 21.8 and 27 sq. m. or 26 and 32.3 sq. yd.), but are somewhat larger than those in the Antonine fortlet at Barburgh Mill[7] (22 sq. m. or 26.3 sq. yd.), and three times the size of the equivalent accommodation, consisting of single rooms, at Martinhoe (8.2 sq. m. or 9.6 sq. yd.).[5]

South-east of the larger barrack-block and separated from it by a space of some 5 m. (16.5 ft.), lay three smaller buildings having a common frontage, and respectively 4.2, 7.2 and 7.2 m. (14, 23 and 23 ft.) wide. The walls of the middle building projected slightly beyond the end wall, but this may have been due to an error in laying out the foundations. The buildings were about 8.3 m. (27 ft.) long, with their backs close to the rampart. Their use is uncertain: accommodation of stores or equipment, workshops for carpentry or smithing are among the possibilities. The north-easternmost of the three, which may have been partly open-ended could have provided cover for a cart or similar vehicle.

North-west of the smaller barrack-block was a patch of cobbling that had evidently served as the foundation for a narrow street where this crossed a slight hollow. Beyond were two further buildings: the more complete, which measured 8.4 by 7.1 m. (28 by 23.5 ft.), lay near the north angle of the fortlet, with its north-west end close to the back of the rampart. It was divided by a longitudinal wall into two rooms of nearly equal size. A layer of carbonised grain extended over 2 sq. m. (2.4 sq. yd.) outside the south-west of the building, and within the south-west room. For what the evidence is worth, this might suggest use as a granary or store-house. The second building lay towards the west angle of the fort, where the occurrence of marly soil made the tracing of construction trenches difficult. If the three parallel walls marked on the plan are parts of a single structure, they determine a dimension from north-west to south-east of about 7 m. (23 ft.).

An oven (Fig. 4) was identified at the back of the rampart, about halfway between the west angle and south-west gate. It measured 1.95 m. (6.5 ft.) in diameter, and consisted of a clay wall 0.33 m. (13 in.) thick resting on an uneven stone floor. The hob, now largely destroyed, was on the north-east side. Flat stones that could be used as slabs are not found near the site, and the oven floor was formed of a varied assortment of rocks, including sandstones, igneous rocks and fragments of no less than seven quern-stones, of different types (Fig. 5). Both the floor and the clay wall were heavily burnt and a considerable layer of ash, mixed with burnt clay no doubt from rebuilding of the dome of the oven

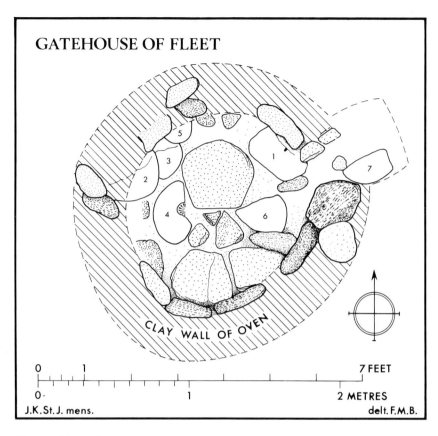

GATEHOUSE OF FLEET

CLAY WALL OF OVEN

0   1   7 FEET

0·   1   2 METRES

J.K.St.J. mens.   delt. F.M.B.

Fig. 4   Plan of oven.

lay to the north. A small fragment of decorated samian was found at the bottom of the projection of the hob, and two more fragments were covered by the pile of ash. No doubt there may have been further ovens along the back of the rampart.

Close to the south-western side of the south-easternmost range of buildings a water tank was identified. The tank (Fig. 6) which had a clay lining 0.175 m. (7 in.) thick, measured 2.4 by 1.75 m. (8 by 6 ft.) in area, and was 1.78 m. (6 ft.) deep, measured from the present surface. The capacity was thus about 7.5 cubic m. (1650 gallons). The filling consisted of earth mixed with lumps of clay, turfy material and large cobbles. The position, not far from the west gate, would be convenient for watering parties drawing water from the Fleet. Outside the east angle of the larger barrack-block there was a rectangular pit about 2.2 m. (7 ft.) from north-west to south-east by 1.1 m. (3.5 ft.) and 1.82 m. (6 ft.) in depth (Fig. 6). A gulley led to it from the direction of the central street. The lowest

SECTIONS OF QUERNS

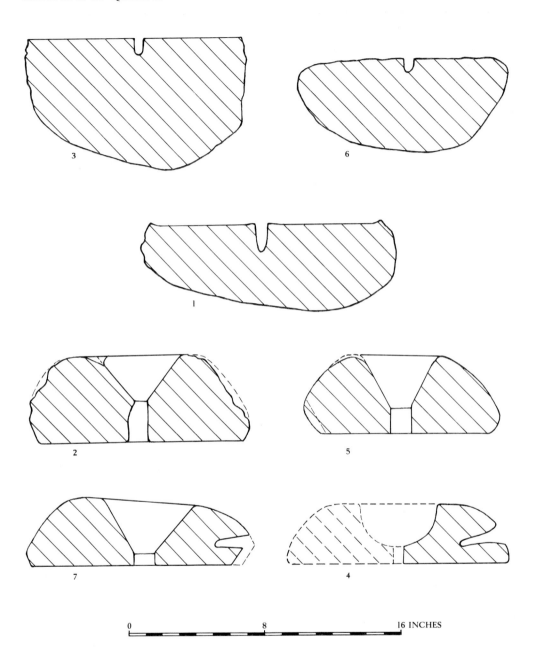

Fig. 5   Sections of querns. The numbers are those of the numbered stones in Fig. 4.

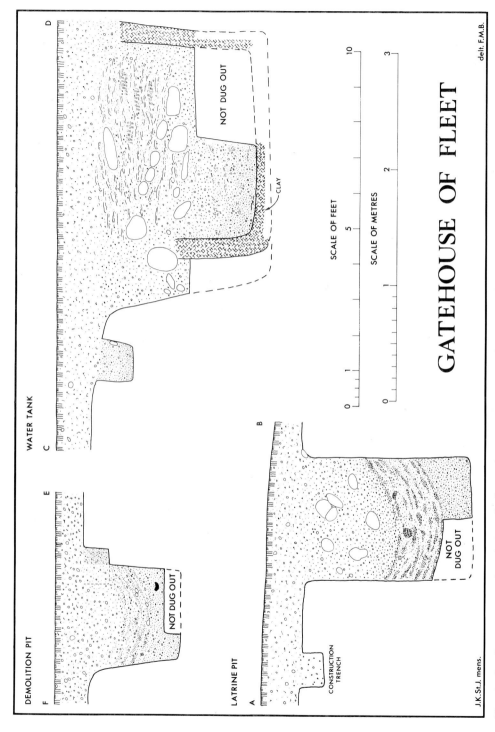

WATER TANK

DEMOLITION PIT

LATRINE PIT

NOT DUG OUT

CLAY

NOT DUG OUT

NOT DUG OUT

CONSTRUCTION TRENCH

SCALE OF FEET

SCALE OF METRES

GATEHOUSE OF FLEET

J.K.St.J. mens.   delt. F.M.B.

Fig. 6   Sections: water tank and pits. The lines of sections AB, CD and EF are marked on Fig. 2.

part of the filling consisted of black earth and silt, above which were several layers of fine gravel and earth, which suggested deliberate infilling. Two small post-holes set a little way out from the corners of the pit remote from the building perhaps supported light boarding in the form of a 'lean-to'. The feature is most likely to have been a latrine pit which would have served the officer's quarters at the end of the barrack-block. A pit in a matching position by the north corner of the smaller barrack-block measured 2 by 1.5 m. (6.5 by 5 ft.) and was 1.4 m. (4.5 ft.) deep. The bottom was covered by a layer of large cobbles and the remainder of the filling was dark earth and gravel. This, too, may have been a latrine pit, and no doubt other latrines existed, for example, close to the inside of the rampart.

Another pit was located close to the north-west rampart, not far from the west angle. It was little more than a shallow scoop 0.4 m. (16 in.) deep, and in plan 2.75 by 1.9 m. (9 by 6.5 ft.). The filling which consisted of black earth with some ash, yielded three nails about 90 mm. (3.5 in.) long, with square shanks. A small pit, 1.4 by 0.92 m. (4.5 by 3 ft.) and 1.1 m. (3.5 ft.) deep, dug through the outer half of the construction trench for the south-east wall of the larger barrack (Fig. 6), must be later than the building. The filling of black earth with patches of clean fine gravel such as might have been thrown in by spadefuls, contained fragments of carbonised wood, lumps of daub and a small nail.

Neither in the defences nor in the buildings was there any evidence for more than one phase of occupation, the date of which is not in doubt. The three small pieces of samian, one incorporated in the base of the oven, the other two buried beneath the adjoining ash heap, have been identified by Mr. Hartley[x] as Flavian South Gaulish ware, but the evidence was insufficient to judge whether the occupation covered both the Flavian and the Flavian-Trajanic periods. The paucity of finds suggest no lengthy occupation. That despite the relatively extensive digging so few objects should have been recovered is a matter for comment: neither the space behind the rampart, nor the ends of the ditch near the north-east gate yielded any finds. Aerial photographs give no hint of rubbish pits near the fortlet, but rubbish might have been dumped or buried on the slope down to the river. The removal by ploughing of all occupation levels, and the erosion of the ground west of the fortlet have evidently limited the chances of recovering objects. Whenever the end of the occupation came, it seems to have been orderly. The water tank and the pits had been filled in (Fig. 6). The small pit dug through the construction trench of the large barrack-block also points the same way, suggesting, slender though the evidence is, removal of the buildings and a tidying up of the site.

If Gatehouse may be accepted as a Flavian fortlet, and, indeed, with as complete a plan as any fortlet of that period known in Britain, the question arises what part did it play in the military strategy for south-west Scotland. At Dalswinton, the Flavian base in Nithsdale, the two forts that lie on a shelf above the river haughs measure respectively 3.2 ha. (7.9 acres) and 4.4 ha. (9.9 acres) within the ramparts. About 29 km. (18 miles) of somewhat broken country separate Dalswinton from the valley of the Dee at Glenlochar, which was chosen as a base in both Flavian and Antonine periods. The precise site of the Flavian I fort is uncertain; the Flavian II fort extended to 2.3 ha. (5.7 acres). From Glenlochar to the lower reaches of the Cree, the next main valley, is about 32 km. (20 miles). Gatehouse, lying in the smaller valley of the Fleet is only 20 km. (12.5 miles) from Glenlochar. The Fleet estuary dries out at low water exposing considerable expanses of muddy foreshore, making that no place for a harbour. Moreover, the position of the fortlet, some 3 km. (2 miles) upstream from the head of the estuary, shows that its main concern was with the river crossing. Few forts in Scotland are known to have, like Glenlochar, as many as seven temporary camps beside them. If these camps are to be taken as evidence of extensive campaigning, the easiest lines of advance lie northwards up the Dee valley, a route that leads through to the Ayrshire plain, and westwards to the Cree and beyond. The fortlet at Gatehouse is most unlikely to have been the end of this carefully planned system of permanent works. The garrison is too small to have formed an effective striking force, but is appropriate to an intermediate post. The system must surely have extended at least as far west as the valley of the Cree, where a fort of some size may be expected. Reconnaissance repeated over several years has provided no clue, but much of the land there is in permanent pasture. The estuary of the Cree, like that of the Fleet, is not by its nature suitable for harbour. At a further distance of 38 km. (23.5 miles) the head of Loch Ryan is reached, a locality that offers the most protected anchorage on the Galloway coast. Such a natural advantage could hardly have been over-looked by the Roman command, whether Loch Ryan was used only for temporary shelter, or on a more permanent basis involving military works on shore.

Notes on the Querns

The numbers given to the sections (Fig. 5) correspond to the numbered stones in the plan of the oven (Fig. 4). Not all the fragments were visible on the surface of the oven floor as there drawn.

1. A nearly complete lower stone, now broken in two pieces. Moderate to coarse-textured igneous rock.
2. About half of an upper stone remains. ? Granite.
3. Almost complete. ? Granite.
4. Two pieces, together forming about half of a lower stone. Coarse grit.
5. Three pieces, nearly complete. Medium to coarse-textured, dark igneous rock.
6. Nearly complete lower stone. Same rock as No. 5.
7. In three pieces, together forming the greater part of a lower stone. Fine-textured granite.

The stones have been deposited in the Burgh Museum, Dumfries.

NOTES

1. St Joseph, J.K., 'Air reconnaissance of north Britain', *Journal of Roman Studies*, xli, (1951), 61.

2. Richmond, I.A. and St Joseph, J.K., 'The Roman fort at Glenlochar, Kirkcudbrightshire', *Trans. Dumfries. and Galloway Natur. Hist. Antiq. Soc.*, xxx, (1953), 1–16.

3. Sinclair, Sir John (ed.), *The Statistical Account of Scotland*, i, Edinburgh, 1791, 182.

4. The site has been reconnoitered on many later occasions, and in the years 1975–8 the fortlet was recorded in terms of crop marks. Some of these photographs show the ditches with slightly greater clarity than the views of 1949, but without adding significantly to the information provided by Plate I.

5. Fox, A. and Ravenhill, W.L.D., 'Early Roman outposts on the North Devon coast, Old Burrow and Martinhoe', *Proc. Devon Archaeol. Soc.*, xxiv, (1966), 1–39, pls. i–xiii, esp. plan, fig. 10.

6. Richmond, I.A. and Keeney, G.S., 'The Roman works at Chew Green, Coquetdalehead', *Archaeol. Aeliana*, 4 ser., xiv, (1937), 129–50, esp. plan, pl. xx.

7. Breeze, D.J., 'The Roman fortlet at Barburgh Mill, Dumfriesshire', *Britannia*, v, (1974), 130–62, esp. plan, fig. 3.

8. Hartley, B.R., 'The Roman occupation of Scotland: the evidence of samian ware', *Britannia*, iii, (1972), 11.

The Roman fortress at Eining-Unterfeld: A Reconsideration

by

HANS SCHÖNBERGER

(Translation by David Parsons)

Some 1.2 km. (0.75 miles) north-east of the well-known auxiliary fort of Eining-Abusina (present-day Stadt Neustadt a.d. Donau (on the Danube), Landkreis Kelheim) there is still visible in the meadowland called Unterfeld a huge ditch which runs from the south-east and meets the Eining-Weltenburg road almost at right angles. Investigation of this feature began about a hundred years ago and in the course of time widely disparate interpretations have been proposed. Following the discovery in 1900 of walling during trial excavations on the land to the south-west of the ditch and the occasional appearance of Roman small-finds, it was assumed that this was a predecessor of the fortress of *Legio III Italica* in Regensburg, completed in A.D. 179. Accordingly on official maps from 1921 at the latest the section of ditch has born the caption *Reste eines röm. Legionslagers* (Remains of a Roman legionary fortress). When in 1966 tiles with the stamp LEG. III. IT.CON were picked up in the Unterfeld, this supposition was strengthened, since the title *con(cors)* or *concordia)* shows that the tiles are among the oldest produced by the Third Legion.

To establish the size of the fortification I conducted an exploratory excavation from 16 September to 23 October 1968.[1] The results were as follows. The site was surrounded by three ditches, behind which the actual defences probably consisted of a turf wall. The average north-east to south-west measurement, taken from the inner edges of the ditches, was 328 m. (359 yd.) and the mean distance from the south-eastern side of the inner ditch to the present edge of the Danube flood plain was approximately 320 m. (350 yd.). The total area was therefore about 10.6 ha. (26 acres). Fig. 1 is based on the information from our limited number of trenches, and it is possible that the ditches did not run as straight as they are shown, so that this calculation may need some minor amendment. Inside the enclosure the excavation also revealed remains of stone walls, which in some cases should probably be interpreted as nothing more than the sleeper walls of wooden-framed buildings. The internal buildings, the most important of which incorporate tiles of *Legio III Italica,* and the ditches, clearly belong together. It can therefore be stated with some confidence that the building of the fortress was probably begun as early as A.D. 171. On the basis of the present small number of finds one may assume also that the site was not occupied for very long.

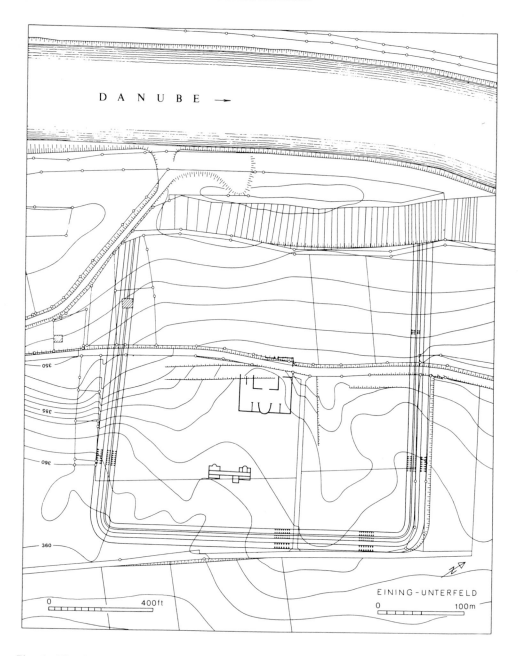

Fig. 1 The Roman Fortress at Eining-Unterfeld. *(After Beilage 9,* Germania, *xxxxviii, and fig. 2,* Archäologisches Korrespondenzblatt, *ix, 425).*

From the south-eastern defences the terrain falls away to the Danube by some 10 m. (33 ft.) or more. The drop is particularly steep north-west of the road. Thus the lower-lying parts by the river are constantly threatened by floodwater and there may not have been any defensive ditches in this area at all, since they would always have been swamped by the slightest rise in the water level. On the other hand, if one assumes that the river bank was fortified in some way and that there was a jetty for ships and barges then the topography, which is apparently so unfavourable, takes on another aspect; the site is extraordinarily appropriate and suitable as a distribution and warehousing centre. The scouring action of the Danube, in the Roman period, so eroded a stretch of the east bank within the fortress area that for about 150 m. (500 ft.) the water reached an estimated depth of 1.5 m. (5 ft.). Thus conditions were favourable for landing and for the transfer of cargoes.

The fort of the *classis Germanica p.f.* in Köln-Alteburg was also built on a slight slope and the site fell some 5–6 m. (16–20 ft.) towards the Rhine. The character of the landscape is even more pronounced at Lympne (Kent), where the late Roman fortification was built on a probable second-century site, which was occupied by units of the *classis Britannica*. It may well have risen to the north as much as 45 m. (150 ft.) above the high water mark.[2]

The fortification at Unterfeld near Eining may owe its existence to the particular requirements of the campaigns against the Marcomanni. In this connection I have drawn attention to an honorific inscription from Zana (Diana Veteranorum), which records the career of M. Valerius Maximianus and is most likely to date from A.D. 171. Maximianus had the responsibility for securing the supplies for the troops in Upper and Lower Pannonia by bringing corn by the waterways from the upper Danube.[3]

Between 1977 and 1979 two buildings were recognised from aerial photographs. We are indebted to R. Christlein and H.T. Fischer for their recent publication of these buildings in a plan.[4] The first is the almost square plan of the *principia* with sides about 60 m. (200 ft.) long. This was built in a topographically favourable position on a spur-like elevation. The other was a building, barely 50 m. (164 ft.) long, in the *retentura,* which on its north-west side had two projections with apses. The authors prefer to interpret this building as the *praetorium*. Although to our present knowledge legionary *praetoria* neither occupied such a position in the *retentura* nor had such a ground-plan (even at Carpow),[5] it is nevertheless not necessary to reject such an interpretation on principle. The particular landscape conditions may have led to the choice of just this position. In any case, the finds so far do not give any reason to date the building to a later period, that is after the abandonment of the fortress.

Christlein and Fischer raised again the question of the purpose of the fortification and argued that the two recently-discovered major buildings are not compatible with the concept of a warehouse for provisions. However, it must be said that the presence of a *principia* does not fundamentally exclude a supply base of whatever kind; the little Augustan site of Rödgen already had an arrangement of this sort.[6] Further, South Shields was rebuilt at the beginning of the third century as a 'defended store base' and was provided with a complete range of *horrea*. But even so the *principia* could not be dispensed with, because it was essential to the administration of the complex in either case.[7]

On the other hand I agree with the authors when they compare the Unterfeld site, of about 10.6 ha. (26 acres), with the vexillation fortresses recognised in Britain; these are between 8 and 12 ha. (20–30 acres) in size and could accommodate about half a legion. They are described as follows: 'although some may have served partly or wholly as store bases, it seems likely that their normal function was as winter-quarters *(hiberna)* for battle groups made up in varying proportions of legionary and auxiliary troops'.[8] The most important comparanda which should be quoted are Longthorpe I and Carpow. Longthorpe I belonged in the Claudio-Neronian period, covered 10.9 ha. (27 acres) and accommodated about half of *Legio IX Hispana* together with its first cohort and an unknown number of auxiliary cavalry.[9] Carpow is datable to the time of Septimius Severus and is 11.16 ha. (28 acres) in size. There are indications of the presence of *Legionis II Augusta, VI Victrix (Britannica) p.f.* and perhaps also *XX Valeria Victrix*.[10]

In the context of this discussion the fact that the three fortresses, Eining-Unterfeld, Longthorpe I and Carpow, belong to quite different periods is not an insuperable difficulty. What they have in common is a closely similar size and the fact that they survived for only a comparatively short time. I, too, previously thought exclusively of a detachment of *Legio III Italica* but considered that the early legionary tiles did not necessarily constitute proof.[11]

Exact proof they are certainly not — but I am grateful to R. Christlein and H.T. Fischer for the reference to vexillation fortresses and for the fruitful discussion. For I now incline to the view that the Eining-Unterfeld site is such a fortress, although naturally the number of cohorts of *III Italica* stationed there remains totally uncertain.[12] It may have changed at short notice according to current needs.

That does not mean that I have undergone a Damascus Road conversion. I am still of the opinion that, even at the time of the establishment of the fortification, a distribution and storage base on the Danube was contemplated. For that reason I have discussed once more in some detail the unsuitability of the terrain from the military point of view and included again on the plan published here (Fig. 1) the division into narrow parcels of the riverside meadows to the north-west. This shows that the land here was previously mostly waterlogged and not cultivated until relatively recently. My interpretation remains the hypothesis it always was, and only future excavation in favourable circumstances can lead to certainty.

NOTES

1. 'Das Römerlager in Unterfeld bei Eining, Bericht über die Grabung im Jahre 1968', *Germania,* xlviii, (1970), 66, with bibliography of previous literature.
2. For Köln-Alteburg and Lympne: *ibid.,* 80, notes 25–6.
3. Pflaum, H.G., 'Libyca', *Archéolog. Épigraph.,* iii, (1955), 135; *idem, Les carrières procuratoriennes équestres sous le Haut-Empire I–IV,* Paris, 1960–1, 476, no. 181; Böhme, H.W., *Kleine Schriften zur Kenntnis der römischen Besetzungsgeschichte Südwestdeutschlands* 16, Stuttgart, 1977, 53.
4. *Archäologisches Korrespondenzblatt,* ix, (1979), 423 and fig. 2. (The scale, 1:2500, is incorrect on this plan.)
5. von Petrikovits, H., *Die Innenbauten römischer Legionslager während der Prinzipatszeit,* Opladen, 1975, 67 and fig. 13.
6. *Limesforschungen,* 15, Berlin, 1976, 18 and fig. 5.
7. Gillam, J.P., *Journal of Roman Studies,* lvii, (1967), 177 and fig. 5; Dore, J.N. and Gillam, J.P., *The Roman Fort at South Shields,* Newcastle, 1979, 61 and fig. 22.
8. Frere, S.S. and St Joseph, J.K., *Britannia,* v, (1974), 6.
9. *ibid.,* 34.
10. *Journal of Roman Studies,* lix, (1959), 202 and fig. 27; Birley, A.R., *Studien zu den Militärgrenzen Roms,* Bonner Jahrbücher Beiheft 19, Bonn, 1967, 1–5; Leach, J.D. and Wilkes, J.J., *Akten des XI Internationalen Limeskongresses,* Budapest, 1977, 47. A remark by Dore and Gillam on the function might be noted in passing, (64, note 7): Carpow . . . probably did not function exclusively as a supply-base, though it may have included this function alongside others.
11. *op. cit.* (see note 1), 81.
12. A "compromise" was also considered by Dietz, K., Osterhaus, U., Rieckhoff-Pauli, S. and Spindler, K., *Regensburg zur Römerzeit,* Regensburg, 1979, 80.

The Possible Effects on Britain of the Fall of Magnentius

by

GRAHAM WEBSTER

It is a privilege to be able to pay tribute to Sheppard Frere whose published works have set a very high standard for us all. Few know of the hard and unremitting labour of editing he has always been prepared to do, and for which there is so often so little proper recognition. Our debt to him, in advancing our studies and placing them in their proper imperial framework, is enormous.

One of the more fascinating aspects of Roman Britain is the interweaving of the evidence recovered from archaeological discovery and that from the surviving historical accounts. The written word always has a special sanctity and more so if it is from a contemporary source, but it needs to be examined with the same ruthless and objective scrutiny as given to the archaeological evidence. This has not always been the case in the past when antiquaries have often blindly accepted accounts as offering established facts and forcing an interpretation of their discoveries to fit. It has even led in extreme cases to a few excavators being so certain of what they would find before they put a spade into the ground, that evidence was selected and rejected in accordance with their predetermined thinking. It is not difficult to interpret archaeological material to fit into a preconceived pattern if one has the determination and mental agility. In 1969, a paper was published which gave some examples of this unfortunate practice. It was my contribution to *The Roman Villa in Britain*[1] and optimistically entitled 'The Future of Villa Studies'. It introduced an attempt to assess the truth of the often reiterated statement that the Great Barbarian Conspiracy of 367 virtually destroyed the villa system in Britain. A clear and detailed historical account of this event is given by Ammianus Marcellinus, who has always been accepted as one of the more reliable of the ancient historians, although it has been recently pointed out by Professor Malcolm Todd[2] that Theodosius I was the patron of Marcellinus, who can hardly be blamed for enlarging on the achievements of the father of the Emperor. It is thus possible that the effect of the Great Conspiracy has been magnified in order to give Count Theodosius greater credibility in his programme of restoration. There is certainly very little archaeological evidence of any serious destruction of property in the countryside at this time.

The examination of the evidence from villas was not as thorough as one would have liked, as in most cases it comes from old accounts and is of

240

extremely poor quality, with very little attempt, if any, at a stratigraphical analysis. The evidence for destruction of buildings is almost non-existent and the human remains of 'the victims' in the majority of cases clearly belong to organised burials in small cemeteries, post-dating the occupation of some of the villa buildings. There are few exceptions where human skulls have been found in wells and which could suggest violence at a later period. The only evidence which seemed at the time to offer any reliable dating was that of the coins which were of sufficient interest to the nineteenth-century antiquarians for them to be recorded, although rarely in detail. But even here it was surprising how few coins were found in extensive clearance and in some cases scarcely more than half-a-dozen were recorded. Whether this is the result of the 'coarse' digging of earlier decades, or that the proportion of coins varies considerably, is a matter which deserves study.[3] A suitable break-point was taken on the death of Magnentius in 353, and of the reports examined from 334 buildings, no less than 199 offered no satisfactory evidence and it could be argued that the remaining 135 hardly offer a sufficient quantity for any serious statistical study. It could be improved by including all the results of excavations since 1961, but this has not been possible for various reasons, the most important of which is that it is no longer the intention to study the results of 367, but to turn to another event recorded by Ammianus which can be illuminated by this old study and by more recent work. The one fact which seems to emerge was that changes were taking place in British villas round about 360 and this was reflected in the two maps, figs. 6.1 and 6.2, included in this 1969 study.

The event which affected Britain at this time was the fall from power of Magnentius. His origins are obscure,[4] but he seems to have been a German from one of the tribes which were allowed to settle within the Empire, and for which privilege they were liable for military service, a practice going back to the late third century. His promotion through the army ranks had been rapid and by 350 he commanded a select corps of *Ioviani* and *Herculiani,* the new type of legion earlier created by Diocletian. Constans, the emperor of the west, had become unpopular in the western provinces through his oppression, and he had neglected to maintain that essential bond which bound the army to him. A conspiracy between Magnentius and Marcellinus, the *comes rei privatae,* overthrew Constans, who fled towards Spain, but he was sought out and killed by Gaiso, dispatched for this purpose by Magnentius, now established as *Augustus.* A clash with Constantius II was inevitable and Magnentius prepared for this immediately by raising a large army with substantial aid obtained from and freely given by the provincials, especially those in Gaul and Britain. But he also had strong support from the barbarian peoples, the Franks, Saxons and Germans. An attempt was made to secure the acceptance of Constantius to the *fait accompli,* and if accepted, it was to be followed by dynastic marriages. But the Emperor remained steadfast in his determination to avenge the murder of his brother, urged, as he told his council of advisors, by his father, the great

Pl. I   A coin of Magnentius found at Chester. *(Grosvenor Museum, Chester).*

Constantine, who appeared to him in a dream. The eventual battle took place at Mursa, where the river Drave joins the Danube. It was a long and bitter struggle with great losses on both sides, causing a serious weakening of the imperial army. Magnentius was forced to flee, but he attempted to hold the Alpine passes, failed, and, after admitting defeat at Lyons, committed suicide.

It is the aftermath of these events from 353 which is recorded by Ammianus (xiv. 5). He reveals the character of Constantius, his cruelty, his instant acceptance of any vague suspicion whispered by his numerous spies and court sycophants. The narrow-minded and mean-spirited Emperor was specially severe on any who injured the name of his father, or any member of his imperial family. Magnentius had caused deep offence in the first place merely by being a barbarian and a pagan, but above all, by murdering Constans, also, no doubt, for receiving such widespread popular support from the peoples of the western provinces. Constantius set out on a determined course of retribution, seeking out all the followers of Magnentius and exacting punishment by execution, imprisonment and confiscation of their estates and wealth. The imperial treasury had been seriously reduced by the war and substantial funds were needed to fill the depleted ranks in the army as rapidly as possible. The Emperor had many precedents to follow from earlier times. But there was an additional element; Constantine the Great had embraced the Christian faith and his sons followed with blind intolerance. Magnentius may have been a pagan, but it was his acceptance and tacit encouragement of paganism which Constantius regarded as an offence against the imperial house. Behind the mean, suspicious mind of the Emperor, there was a total conviction tenaciously held, of a trust descended upon him from Constantine. He raised the status and majesty of the royal household beyond even the limit set by Diocletian, which included an acceptance of Christianity in a purely formal sense, since it is very doubtful if he understood its true meaning. Any outward indications of paganism in the form of monuments and shrines were natural targets for attack, as symbols of the barbarian pagan world of the usurper.[5]

The retribution exacted by Constantius on the Britons is recorded by Ammianus (xiv, 5, 6). The agent selected for this task was a Spaniard called Paulus, a trusted servant of the Emperor, described as a *notarius*. Although this rank was that of a clerk, in the Constantian period it was applied to those officials who were responsible for the minutes of the imperial consistory and some of them rose to the highest ranks. Constantius found them useful as informants and spies, not only in the Court, but also to send on special confidential or delicate missions.[6] Paulus had acquired the soubriquet, *Catena*: the chain, not only for his wanton use of this means of fettering large numbers of suspects, but also for the tangled web of intrigue and innuendo he wove round his victims. He was, acording to Ammianus, especially skilled at extracting information by forced confessions by torture or any other means. Nor was he concerned with justice, but treated the innocent and guilty alike, until he had collected together a large number of wealthy suspects, who could have been associated with Magnentius, to satisfy the suspicious-minded Emperor. He seized the assets of all those he held, doubtless exceeding his authority in cases of the very wealthy. His progress in Britain was marked by slaughter, destruction and imprisonment, putting many freeborn men *(ingenuorum)* in irons and handcuffs. This impious crime, wrote Ammianus, forever stained the reign of Constantius.

The *vicarius* of Britain was Martinus, serving in a temporary capacity, the officers under Magnentius doubtless having been quickly removed as collaborators. Martinus, a just man, protested to Paulus, who promptly threatened him with instant imprisonment for his interference. The governor, fearing for his life, drew his sword and attacked Paulus, but his aim was either too feeble or misdirected to be effective, so he plunged it into his own body. Paulus delivered his large batch of suspects to Constantius. After further torture and forced confessions, they were tried, which in effect meant execution, imprisonment or exile. As Ammianus ironically remarks, there are few who can remember any acquitals under Constantius.

Allowing for a certain amount of exaggeration, it would be reasonable to assume that most of the wealthy landowners and business men would have suffered in this ruthless purge. Their estates and assets were seized for the imperial treasury, and one can only speculate on the possible consequences. Surrounded as he was by flatterers and sycophants, Constantius may have disposed of some of the land as rewards for service and information, but he needed money to recoup the heavy losses in his army. One can only assume that some estates and businesses were sold to his wealthy followers. The general effect must have been a serious breaking-up of the great landed estates of Britain and their redistribution to absentee landlords, apart from those who preferred to move to Britain and take up residence.

There is little doubt about the richness of the British countryside in the first half of the fourth century. The large villas with their elaborate pavements reflect a degree of ostentation, which could only be associated with a well-to-do land-owning or farming class. How such prosperity came about, however, cannot easily be explained. Britain has always acquired its wealth, until the Industrial Revolution, through its agriculture. There are important by-products such as wool and flax, leading to cloth production, milling, tanning etc. It is possible also that viticulture was practiced in the southern limestone and chalk areas, and this may help to explain the particular wealth of the Cotswolds and North Oxfordshire, although secure evidence is still lacking. However, the wealth may have been produced it is evident that it had created a rich landowning class. It may be that their number was small and their holdings large, but excavations are needed on a selective basis before it is possible to isolate the houses of the owners from those of their tenants or agents.[7] At present it is only possible to guess that the largest of the villas, such as Woodchester, Bignor and North Leigh may have been owner occupied. Size is not the main criterion, however, as has been shown by Winterton, the buildings of which occupy a large area, with no apparent country house; it is essentially a working establishment with enough barns to suggest grain as one of its main products.

Yet when compared with the much larger and more luxurious villas of the Rhineland and Gallia Belgica, Britannia seems a very poor relation. Many survived the depredation of the barbarian incursion of the late third century from which Britain was spared. Ausonius in his remarkable poem *Mosella* presents a glowing picture of a prosperous countryside, although how much of this is poetic licence is difficult to judge.[8] Other sources indicate in Gaul the presence of landowners of the curial class with vast holdings and little interest in trade or contemporary events. Often their estates were not concentrated in a single province, but scattered over a number.[9] Arguing on the basis of income, A.H.M. Jones has estimated that some of the more wealthy land-owners in the western provinces must have held 'several thousand square miles'.[10] Nor must one forget the imperial estates, which could have accounted for as much as fifteen percent of the land,[11] for which there is evidence in Britain.[12] Large well-run estates confiscated by Paulus could well have passed into imperial hands and continued to be managed for profit, but it depends on whether the Emperor needed capital more than income.

It would be reasonable to assume that the considerable changes that took place in Britain were a result of these large-scale confiscations. Some estates may have received new owners with little change, or they could have been divided and redistributed; others may have been enlarged with the addition of adjacent lands or groups of estates under a single owner. The amalgamation of properties would, perhaps, have had the greatest effect since the main purpose would have been economy of management. A new owner, or his agent, may have found too many properties to maintain, at the same time new premises would have been needed for managers in a central or more convenient position relative to the estate, or within reach of an important market. Large estates also allow for specialisation, replacing the general purpose farm with a balanced plant and animal husbandry. Where different soils allowed, some parts of the estate could be given over wholly to sheep, others to crops, all creating a need for different types of farm buildings and yards; those no longer required would then be demolished if building materials were needed elsewhere. If not they would have been abandoned and merely allowed to fall down. The evidence for such changes from past excavations is rarely satisfactory and is almost entirely based on the coins, which, in many cases, is far too slight to offer more than a hint. Many excavators have reported the collapse of buildings with roof tiles lying where they fell, and only rarely is there any evidence of demolition. This desertion and decay could, of course, have occurred at any period. There is, however, another element which has been frequently misunderstood, as indicated in the 1969 paper (p. 232–3): the continued occupation with a serious lowering of living standards. The evidence of hearths over tessellated pavements and trampled black earth accumulated over floors has often been interpreted as 'squatter occupation', as if casual wanderers had found temporary refuge in the ruins of the buildings. A more likely suggestion would be that it is evidence of the estate worker continuing to live on the site and work the land long after the owners, managers or bailiffs had departed. This may be confirmed on a few sites by the presence of a small cemetery over the site of the original house, after it had been thoroughly demolished, since some of the graves have been dug into the wall foundations, showing an ignorance of their existence.[13]

Unfortunately, our present evidence does not permit any refinement in interpretation. The best we can expect is destruction, or a sudden running-down of an establishment or extensive rebuilding on a different plan or scale. The number of establishments which were subjected to a sudden change at this period is considerable, but as can be seen from the map (Fig. 1), there are two main areas, one in parts of Gloucestershire, Somerset and Hampshire and the other in Hertfordshire and north Kent. These, however, include the richest concentration of villas of all periods. If one could select those areas where there appears to be the largest proportion of sites which seem to have been affected, they are in Hampshire, Hertfordshire and north Kent, possibly indicating that

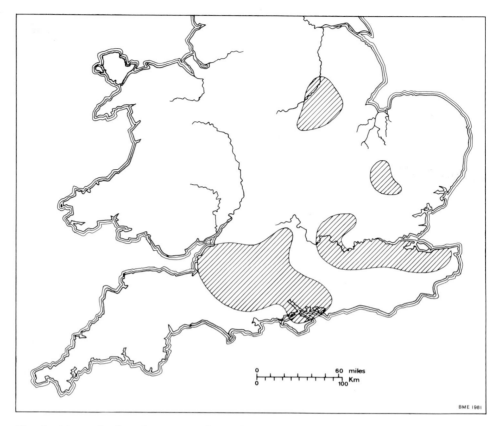

Fig. 1   Map reflecting changes in villa establishments.

they suffered the greatest disturbance. Refinements in the dating evidence could easily change the pattern, and there are examples well outside these areas: in Sussex, for example, at Chilgrove, where there are several sites. At Chilgrove 1, the coin series ends with Magnentius, and Alec Down, the excavator, suggests an amalgamation with Chilgrove 2[14] which could represent the kind of reorganisation to be expected. At Rapsley, near Ewhurst in Surrey, occupation appears to have ceased by *c.* 350,[15] and may be another which underwent a change in ownership. Another site, some distance from the main concentrations, where a major change has been dated to 350–60 is the villa at Great Casterton. Here an aisled barn was converted into a dwelling,[16] involving also the demolition of a large circular corn-dryer and a rectangular building, making a complete transformation of the site.[17]

   In areas which appear to show the greatest change the probable effect of the fall of Magnentius has been recognised by Professor Keith Branigan, who has drawn attention to the evidence from Boxmoor, Latimer and possibly Welwyn, High Wycombe and Harpsden.[18] The possibility has also been accepted by David Neal,[19] as a lowering of standards;[20] Gadebridge, however, deserves special consideration (see below p. 249).

In the south-west, Professor Branigan can detect changes only at the villas at Chew Park, Whateley and Star;[21] a significant change is apparent from recent excavations at Littlecote (Wilts.) with a new building of architectural interest *c.* A.D. 360.[22] But in fact, the best evidence comes from Barnsley Park, Cirencester.[23] On this site there was a small farm with a succession of timber houses and farmyards occupied up to *c.* 360, when they were all demolished for the erection of a stone corridor villa[24] and a large barn. Two coins of Constantius II were found in the foundations of the stone building, which indicates a radical change taking place on the site. The building was not for the new owner, but for a manager, or a bailiff. The site is only four miles from Corinium and this has led to the speculation that the establishment may have had a special function in a large estate. Surrounding the farm area were some eight acres of yards and corrals, suitable for sheep and cattle. The excavation also produced an unusual number of ox-goads and *styli* and all this may indicate the use of the establishment as a place where animals were brought from farms on the estate and prepared for market. Another discovery, was the name FIRMINUS carved on a building stone. Professor Applebaum has drawn attention to the high-ranking officials of the imperial household in Gaul of this name, one of whom was the *comes rerum privatarum* of the West and he has suggested that Barnsley Park was part of an imperial estate.[25] The owner of the estate in the fourth century would thus have been a Firminus, since it is reasonably certain that this building stone belonged to the house built *c.* 360, but any connection with imperial officials is highly conjectural, the more so as Firminus was a very common *cognomen*.

It is thus evident that the fall of Magnentius and the subsequent zeal of Paulus had an effect on the Britons and their estates, but its extent is difficult to quantify, since there is not yet enough large-scale excavation of villas and other rural establishments using modern refined techniques. It is, therefore, worth calling the attention of villa excavators to these possibilities with the hope that they will eventually produce more and better evidence which will help to elucidate changes in this period.

Another consequence of the re-establishment of the authority of Constantius in Britain could well have been an attack on pagan monuments and practices, which had been tolerated under Magnentius. The narrow-minded and mean-spirited Emperor may have been specially severe in Britain and Gaul, and one must consider the evidence from possible destruction of pagan buildings at this time.

There are two aspects of this problem, the monuments themselves and their wealth, lands and estates. It is evident that the larger and more popular temples may have played a considerable part in the economy of any province. They

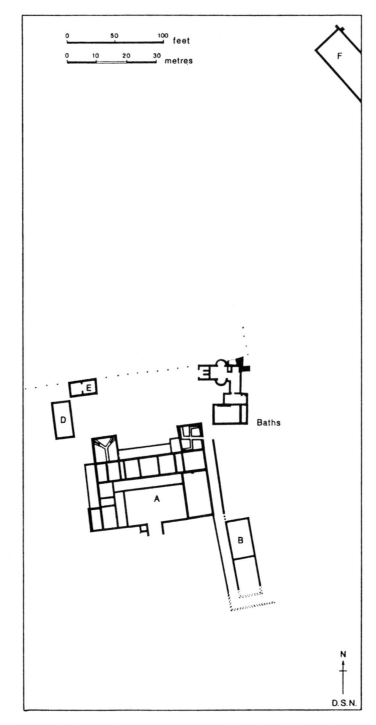

Fig. 2   Plan of villa at Gadebridge Park in Period 5. *(Reproduced by permission of David Neal and the Society of Antiquaries.)*

represented the only equivalent of our modern banking system[26] and those, possessing medicinal springs of great renown, accumulated wealth and acquired lands by dedication and purchase.[27] The great spa-temple at Bath would almost certainly have come into this category. These temples and their priestly organis- ations came under serious threat in times of anarchy and economic recession and they probably suffered from serious depredations in the late third century.[28] Constantine, late in his reign, demolished some temples and confiscated their estates throughout the empire, incorporating them into the *res privata,* but keeping their accounts in a special category as *fundi iuris templorum.*[29] Not all of these lands remained in imperial ownership. Some were given or sold to favoured high-ranking officials and court favourites,[30] a practice developed by Constantius II.[31] Had wealth or estates, belonging to temples in Britain, survived by 350, Paulus would almost certainly have seized them on behalf of his master.

However, not all the healing springs and spas were under priestly ownership. Enterprising landowners may have developed such valuable assets and erected health resorts similar to establishments of recent centuries. The health-giving waters themselves could become commercial products and there is evidence in parts of the Roman world, of their bottling and distribution.[32] Any landowners who had been successful in this kind of enterprise would certainly have been of immediate interest to Paulus in his search for enemies of the State, as exploiters of pagan superstition.

It is possible that the Gadebridge villa (Fig. 2) in Hertfordshire was an estab- lishment of this kind in the middle of the fourth century.[33] The site had a feature which is difficult to identify as part of a normal villa. This is a large pool, 2 m. by 12 m. (6.5 ft. by 39.5 ft.), with a wide flight of steps entering it from one end. The excavator, David Neal, could not explain this as merely for domestic use and concluded[34] that it must have had a public function. Furthermore, he was informed that the water may have had medicinal properties. No less than 173 coins were found at the bottom of the pool together with a large number of rings, bracelets, brooches and other objects: evidence which strongly suggests a votive deposit. He also pointed out in the report[35] that the excavation produced a disproportionate number of cosmetic articles, although the significance of this evidence is not clear; the case for the site having had a religious function is strengthened by a consideration of the other buildings. Connected to the pool is a large anteroom with a sophisticated architectural design[36] and the elaborate bath-house would appear to have been too large for the modest size of 'house'. Two wings of the latter were each divided into small apartments with long, narrow, heated rooms on the east side, the layout of which suggests the existence of internal timber partitions, with the large room on the west side (No. 20) apparently remaining a kitchen. Add to this the large heated dining room at the north-east corner and the whole assemblage resembles a hostelry, rather than a private house. Gadebridge probably began life as a small farm, but from Period 4, during the third century, it began to take on the additional characteristics, even to the extent of a gatehouse, or porter's lodge.[37] Healing spas were based on a local cult figure and the devotees underwent rituals which included bathing and communal eating. Cubicles for accommodation were also needed and Lydney Park provides an excellent example of these provisions. The absence of a temple, or shrine in the near vicinity and of any obvious religious objects or inscriptions, casts serious doubt on this suggestion, but a shrine may be found at a nearby sacred spring. One fact is quite certain, the establishment was totally demolished *c.* A.D. 360, an event which the excavator himself has associated with the fall of Magnentius.

Another temple site where a drastic change took place in the mid-fourth century is Nettleton Scrubb (Wilts.).[38] This remarkable shrine built in a narrow valley was closely associated with a water cult, inscriptions name the deity as Apollo,[39] linked with a Celtic counterpart. The functions of the buildings in their tightly packed site are difficult to determine. The excavator suggests that No. 11 and its successor, No. 12, was a hostel for visitors, that adjacent (No. 10), was a shop for selling votive objects and that No. 26 in a small compound was a workshop, where these objects were probably made. Several of the buildings were destroyed by a fire at a date given as *c.* A.D. 350. Unfortunately, neither the coins nor the pottery are directly related to the chronological horizons in the report, although Group A, associated with the destruction of Building 28, ends with a coin of Magnentius. Clearly the site suffered a sudden change in the middle of the fourth century, although there is evidence of a decline before this. Whether the destruction was accidental or deliberate is impossible to determine, but the pagan shrine was not rebuilt. The later occupation was of a specialist technical nature, the manufacture of pewter vessels with the use of limestone moulds and lead from the local Mendip ores. It could be suggested that the workmen who had made the trinkets and votive objects for visitors continued to use their technical skill for profit, or that a new land-owner was exploiting the commercial potential of the local labour.

There are two other villas with unusual features which could possibly be associated with pagan cults. One at Lufton (Somerset)[40] is distinguished by a remarkable octagonal building with an anteroom, an ambulatory and massive buttresses,[41] which has been identified as a cold plunge; and it is clearly the main focus for whatever activity took place there. It has the appearance of a shrine and an association with a water cult is indicated by the aquatic creatures in its mosaic. There is a small room (No. 15) at the back suitable for housing a cult statue. As at Gadebridge, the Lufton villa is attached to a bath-house and possible heated dining-room (Room 5). Fifteen coins are recorded from the site; some of them are of Valentinian and show that occupation continued to the end of the fourth century. The second site, at Chedworth, has for so long been accepted as the typical Romano-British villa, that one hesitates to question its function. Yet there are serious difficulties in accepting it, either as a working farm or well-appointed house. This is hardly the place to set out any argument to the contrary in detail,[42] but attention should be drawn to the nearby temple, the altars, the cult-figures, the so-called *nymphaeum* and the Christian monogram carved on its stone surround.[43] This last piece of evidence was regarded by Sir Ian Richmond as a necessary attempt by a Christian owner to counteract any remaining pagan influence.[44] The planning of the buildings is very strange if it is merely a dwelling-house, since so much space is taken up with the two baths and the dining-room. The north wing with its range of rooms has more the appearance of a hostelry than a house. Unfortunately, the dating evidence for this building development has not yet been fully established, nor is it known if the pagan shrine was dismantled in the middle or later years of the fourth century, when presumably the site became purely agricultural, maybe as part of a vine-growing estate.

The most famous and important health resort in Britain was undoubtedly Bath, but its late history is still far from certain since the earlier excavations removed most of the evidence in their large-scale clearance. Professor Cunliffe, has, however, been able to examine small areas where remains have survived. The dating evidence is extremely slight; a small group of pottery from the mud sealing the temple precinct has been published by him.[45] It is a late-third to mid-fourth century group and none of the vessels need have belonged to the second half of the fourth century. Professor Cunliffe's conclusions were that it was the rising water-table and neglect of the drainage system which caused serious and periodic flooding, so leading to its abandonment. It may seem strange that such an important and renowned healing centre should have been given up so easily and so early, and this may reflect the despoilation and depredations by members of the House of Constantine. If the temple had been stripped of its wealth and its income from land, then the priestly college would have been unable to maintain such a large establishment, since the rising level of the water-table would have necessitated major engineering works. The excavator noted that domestic rubbish had been tipped inside the precinct because, either it had become a convenient dumping ground, or there had been an attempt at deliberate desecration, as happened at a later date in the orchestra of the Verulamium temple theatre.[46] The sacred spring, however, continued to attract visitors as the latest votive object found to have been cast into it is a pennanular brooch with enamelled terminals of late fourth or early fifth century date.[47]

A temple at Wroxeter, on the west side of the main north-south street, was excavated by Bushe-Fox in 1913.[48] It is evident from his report that the temple was deliberately demolished and the bronze statues and internal fittings broken up, but the only comment on the date comes in a brief account of the discovery of a 'large number of bronze and iron objects including fragments of broken statuary'.[49] Associated with this destruction deposit were coins which ended with Carausius and this could place the desecration under Constantine, rather than in the middle of the fourth century, but better evidence must survive in the unexcavated areas of the site.

The dating evidence of the final period of the temple at Brean Down

(Somerset) presented its excavator A.M. ApSimon with problems,[50] since there was what is described as 'squatter occupation'. A large number of coins was found in 'the mortary destruction layer' of the vestibule and in 'robbing pits' in the cella, and the assumption was that they came from hoards buried in the temple floors or structure and were scattered when demolition took place. But, unless some of the coins had mortar still adhering to them, it would be more correct to assume that they were lost either during the demolition or in the occupation which followed. The matter is obscured by the fact that many of the coins were small barbarous copies of FEL TEMP types. While George Boon rejected the suggestion that the very small coins were votive objects and may thus be found in some quantity on temple sites, he sensibly adds that there could have been a tendency for poor quality coins 'to gravitate to these shrines as easily as to the offertory of a country church'.[51] If the coins were associated with the temple while it was still functioning, it must have survived the effect of any efforts made to destroy pagan sites. The matter is, however, far from conclusive and the presence of the southern building on a different alignment, much nearer to an east-west axis, with the entrance at the west side, raises the possibility that a small Christian shrine[52] was built to sanctify the site; but this, according to the rather tenuous argument over the coins, did not take place until the end of the century.

The evidence presented above does not make a strong case for substantial changes in Britain following the episode of Magnentius, but there is a sufficient number of indicators, at least, to suggest that the proposition cannot be dismissed. The main purpose of this paper, apart from saluting a distinguished colleague, is to alert excavators to the possible existence of evidence which could help to refine and clarify this present vague outline. In excavations of the past ephemeral traces of occupation were rapidly swept away to uncover the more substantial structures. Fortunately, this no longer happens and it is these latest remains on many villas which may help to determine the character of life and the decline from earlier standards. But, above all, more intensive studies need to be carried out on the pottery of the second half of the fourth century to ensure a greater refinement in dating.

NOTES

1. Rivet, A.L.F. (ed.), *The Roman Villa in Britain,* London, 1969.

2. Todd, M., *Roman Britain 55 B.C.–A.D. 40: the Province beyond Ocean,* London, 1981, 233.

3. A thorough examination of areas at Barnsley Park produced over 800 coins.

4. Unfortunately the first surviving book of Ammianus is No. xiv, which starts in 353, after the fall of Magnentius, and deals only with accounts of the aftermath; the earlier events survive only in fragmented form (including Julian, *Orations,* i and ii, and Zosimus I, ii, summarised in *Cambridge Medieval History, I,* Cambridge, 1911, 58–62).

5. An edict closing all temples and prohibiting sacrifices was drafted but never made law (*Codex Theodosianus* I, xvi, tit. x, leg. 4; see Gibbon, E., *The History of the decline and fall of the Roman Empire,* chapter XX, footnote 173). Acts of destruction were probably arbitrary and aimed at supposed enemies of the state, rather than against paganism. Gibbon's comment 'The sons of Constantine trod in the footsteps of their father, with more zeal and with less discretion. The pretences of rapine and oppression were insensibly multiplied . . .' may be a reasonable summary (see also Jones, A.H.M., *The Later Roman Empire,* Oxford, 1964, 113).

6. *ibid.,* 127.

7. The brave attempts by Professor Shimon Applebaum to put statistics into estate management fails to convince through lack of evidence ('Roman Britain', in Finberg, H.P.R. (ed.), *The Agrarian History of England and Wales*, I, 2, London, 1972). One can be more definite in other provinces where more evidence has survived as John Percival has demonstrated (*The Roman Villa,* London, 1976, 123–34).

8. Wightman, E.M., *Roman Trier and the Treveri,* London, 1970, 66–7.

9. Jones, A.H.M., *op. cit.* (see note 5), 781–8; see also Salway, P., *Roman Britain,* Oxford History of England, Oxford, 1981, 599–602.

10. *ibid.,* 784.

11. *ibid.,* 416.

12. *R.I.B.,* 179 from Combe Down, near Bath, suggests the headquarters of an imperial estate.

13. As at Llantwit Major (*Archaeol. Cambrensis,* cii, (1953), 89–163), but A.H.A. Hogg has suggested that these burials could be later (*Britannia,* v, (1974), 237; Norton Disney (*Antiq. Journ.,* xvii, (1937), 138–81); Southwell (*Transactions of the Thoroton Society,* lxx, (1966), 27), although these may have been associated with the Minster.

14. Down, A., *Chichester Excavations IV: The Roman Villas at Chilgrove and Upmarden,* Chichester Excavation Committee, Chichester, 1979.

15. Hanworth, R., 'The Roman Villa at Rapsley, Ewhurst', *Sussex Archaeological Collections,* lxv, (1968), 54.

16. Corder, P. (ed.), *The Roman town and villa at Great Casterton, Rutland: second interim report for the years 1951–1953,* Nottingham, 1954, 27. 'The appropriate date of the erection of this house is attested by the many coins in the hearths and beneath the floors and must be placed in the period A.D. 350–65'.

17. *ibid.,* 25.

18. Branigan, K., *Town and Country: the archaeology of Verulamium and the Roman Chilterns,* Bourne End, 1973, 126–8.

19. *Britannia,* i, (1971), 289.

20. Neal, D.S., *Three Roman Buildings in the Bulbourne Valley,* 1976, 93 (reprinted from *Hertfordshire Archaeology,* iv, (1974–6), 72).

21. Branigan, K., *The Roman Villa in South-West England,* Bradford-on-Avon, 1976, 93.

22. *Britannia,* xii, (1981), 360–1.

23. *Trans. Bristol and Gloucester. Archaeol. Soc.,* lxxxvi, (1967), 74–8 (a brief interim); xcix, (1982), 21–77 (first part of the final report; second part forthcoming).

24. It is worth noting that a building almost

identical in plan was found at Farmington, near Northleach (*Trans. Bristol and Gloucester. Archaeol. Soc.,* lxxxviii, (1969), 34–67). Unfortunately the construction date was not established.

25. Applebaum, S., *op. cit.* (see note 7), 24.
26. Rostovtzeff, M.I., *The Social and Economic History of the Roman Empire,* (second edition revised by P.M. Fraser), Oxford, 1957, 622, footnote 46.
27. See Rostovtzeff's study of the colonate system in his *Studien zur Geschichte des römischen Kolonates,* Leipzig, 1910. *Archiv für Papyrusforschung* Beiheft I, 269, based mainly on evidence from Egypt.
28. There is evidence that Maximinus and Gordian despoiled temples (Rostovtzeff, M.I., *op. cit.* (see note 26), 453 and 457).
29. Jones, A.H.M., *op. cit.* (see note 5), 92.
30. *ibid.,* 415.
31. *ibid.,* 131.
32. Rostovtzeff, M.I., *op. cit.* (see note 26), 212 and pl. XXXV, 2 is a relief on a silver cup depicting the water from such a spring at Flaviobriga in north Spain, being poured into a barrel on a cart for transportation.
33. Neal, D.S., *The Excavation of the Roman Villa in Gadebridge Park, Hemel Hempstead, 1963–8,* Society of Antiquaries of London Research Report 31, London, 1974.
34. *ibid.,* 73.
35. *ibid.,* 75.
36. *ibid.,* fig. 15 and 19–22.
37. *ibid.,* 75.
38. Wedlake, W.J., *The Excavations of the Shrine of Apollo at Nettleton, Wiltshire, 1956–71,* Society of Antiquaries of London Research Report 40, London, 1982.
39. Among the many attributes of this god was healing sickness and disease and an association with springs.
40. *Proc. Somerset. Archaeol. Natur. Hist. Soc.,* xcvii, (1952), 90–112; cxvi, (1972), 59–77.
41. Pagan's Hill, Caerwent 2, and Weycock: Lewis, M.J.T., *Temples in Roman Britain,* London, 1966, 170.
42. It is hoped to do this on another occasion.
43. Goodburn, R., *The Roman Villa at Chedworth,* National Trust Publications, London, 1972.
44. *Trans. Bristol and Gloucester. Archaeol. Soc.,* lxxviii, (1959), 22.
45. Cunliffe, B.W., *Roman Bath Discovered,* London, 1971, fig. 41.
46. *Archaeologia,* lxxxiv, (1934), 239.
47. *Antiq. Journ.,* lx, (1980), 201 and pl. XIX.
48. *Excavations on the site of the Roman town at Wroxeter, Shropshire in 1912–14, Second Report, 1913,* Society of Antiquaries of London, Research Report 2, Oxford, 1914.
49. *ibid.,* 9.
50. 'The Roman Temple on Brean Down, Somerset', *Proc. University of Bristol Speleological Soc.,* x, (1965), 196–258.
51. *ibid.,* 235.
52. The axis of the early church seems to have varied and the altar could have been at the east or west: Thomas, A.C., *Christianity in Roman Britain to A.D. 500,* London, 1981, figs. 34 and 35. See also Frere, S.S., *Archaeologia,* cv, (1975), 277–302.

Romans, Dacians and Sarmatians in the First and Early Second Centuries

by

J.J. WILKES

I

Nothing survives today to recall the role of the Sarmatians in forming the national and ethnic identities of modern Europe. For half a millenium these Iranian horsemen, who spoke an Indo-European language, dominated a vast tract of territory extending from the Hungarian plain to the steppes around the lower Volga. Both the western Sarmatians (Jazyges and Roxolani) and the eastern (Alani) were dispersed by the onslaught of the Huns in the late fourth century and appear occasionally among the peoples driven westwards by the hordes of Attila. Whatever contribution they may have made to the modern Slavonic nations of eastern Europe has been submerged beneath later waves of migrating peoples, Avars, Bulgars and Magyars.[1]

In the fifth century B.C. Herodotus knew of the Sauromatae dwelling in the steppes around the lower Volga, beyond the Scythians with whom the Greek communities on the north coast of the Black Sea had long-standing commercial and cultural contacts.[2] By the fourth century some of the Scythian settlements around the lower Dniepr are known to have been abandoned. Their rulers were driven south-westwards to a refuge in the Dobrudja beyond the Danube delta. The Scythians who remained became subject to the 'Royal Sauromatae', who ruled the area until the second century B.C. Archaeologists have labelled their material remains as 'Scytho-Sarmatian', an appropriate reflection of the amalgam evident in the historical sources, where 'Sarmatian' and 'Scythian' are employed in confusion. What seems clear is that the first wave of these Iranians who took possession of the north Pontic steppes included the Jazyges (Jaxamatae or Ixibatae). There were the 'Royal people' (Basileiai) who dwelt west of the Dniepr in the second century, and may even have been the 'Scythians' who in the fourth century defeated and killed Zopyrion, a general of Alexander the Great, who had laid siege to Olbia with an army of 30,000.[3]

At the end of the third century B.C. the Great Wall of China was devised to prevent the inroads of Hunnic peoples to the north. In the years following there emerged a tribal union of the Huns under a single lord. During the second century they began to move westwards and pressed upon the Iranian peoples in the steppes of Kazakhstan. Using the efficient 'Hunnic' bow, made from laminated wood with a stiffening of bone inlays, and firing long arrows with triple-

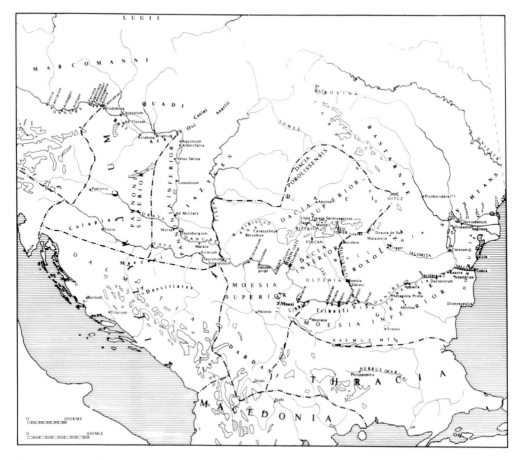

Fig. 1   Map of Danube lands.

edged, tanged iron heads, against the armed cavalry of the Asian steppes they
began a westward movement of several peoples which resulted in the Huns
themselves entering Europe during the fourth century A.D. Around the middle
of the second century B.C. the Aorsi and their eastern neighbours the Alani
('blonds') moved from the Asian steppes into the old Sarmatian homeland (the
old Prokhorovka culture) between the lower Volga and the southern Urals. This
pressed the Roxolani westwards to move into the north Pontic steppes; they in
turn forced the 'Scytho-Sarmatians' to the plains around the lower Dniestr and
up against the Bastarnae, who dwelt along the eastern fringes of the Carpathians
and whose material culture was of Celtic La Tène origin. Checked by the
power of the Dacian Burebista, the Sarmatians moved southwards and appeared

in the area of the Danube delta, where Ovid records them in the last years of Augustus.[4]

Behind these the Roxolani appear first in the second century around the Sea of Azov. Here they came for winter camp but in summer they roamed the steppes to the north. In the coastal marshes they hunted deer and wild boar, and on the steppes wild asses and roe deer.[5] As the Aorsi were moved into the plains of the Don by the Alani, so the former drove the Roxolani westwards into the plains around the Dniepr and the Dniestr. They seem to have moved in the same general direction as the Iazyges and are first recorded somewhere on the lower Danube a little after the middle of the first century A.D. From then large numbers of nomadic herdsmen, who moved back and fore between the coast and inland steppe, between winter camp and summer pasture, travelling with their families in felt-covered wagons, began to impinge upon the limits of the Roman world. From the outset the Romans knew that their movements could be diverted and even restrained, by diplomacy or subsidy; what they were shortly to discover is that in armed attack, on their own open ground, they were unstoppable, by phalanx or legion.

Pl. I Marble relief of a horseman clad in Sarmatian scale armour and holding a lance *(contus)*; from Tanais in south Russia. Set up by Tryphon, son of Andromenos, perhaps in the wall of a temple, in the late second or early third century A.D. See Latyschev, V., *Inscriptiones Antiquae orae Septentrionalis Ponti Euxini Graecae et Latinae. Vol. II.* Petrograd, 1890, 231, no. 424. *(Reproduced by kind permission of Thames and Hudson Ltd.).*

Descriptions of the Sarmatian mode of life over eight hundred years
(Herodotus, Strabo and Ammianus Marcellinus) differ little in essentials. They
were nomads who had few possessions.[6] Their diet was said to be milk and meat
from their herds and they hunted anything else. Instead of houses they had ox-
drawn wagons to which their felt tents were attached. No settlements of the
Sarmatians have been identified: what is known of them has been almost without exception recovered from their graves, scattered over more than three
thousand miles from the Altai mountains in Siberia to the plains of the middle
Danube west of the Carpathians. When first observed by ancient writers they
were portrayed as little different from the better known Scythians. They wore
long trousers, soft leather boots and round or pointed caps. They fought on
horseback but also on foot, and were armed with a short bow, a long iron
sword, and sometimes a light spear with an iron head and, occasionally, a battle-
axe. In the second century B.C. a different panoply appears, long heavy lances
with iron heads *(contus)* (Pl. I) and large two-handed swords with a wooden grip
and large pommel. Bows and arrows were for the most part discarded. They
were clad in armour made of small iron plates sewn on to a leather tunic, or of
thick hide. Their horses were similarly protected. Later there appears a wide
battle-belt made from bronze or iron plates.[7] This was the panoply of the
Roxolani, who had perhaps adopted the battle tactic of armoured *(cataphracti)*
cavalry in close formation from the Chorasmians and Massegetae of Central
Asia. The Jazyges did not at first fight in this fashion; the famous depictions of
mailed cavalry on the Column of Trajan (in flight from the Romans) and the
Arch of Galerius (in the service of the Romans) portray the armament of
Roxolani (Pls. II and III).

II

Until the last year of Nero Roman contact with the Sarmatians, first with the
Jazyges and later with the Roxolani, nowhere amounted to armed collision. First
contact may have been made in the seventies B.C. when the campaigns of
proconsuls advancing from Macedonia brought at least one Roman army to the
lower Danube.[8] It was feared that the growth of Dacian power under Burebista
a decade later would threaten not only Roman power in the Balkans but even
Italy itself, in the context of civil war.[9] The Dacian peril was subsequently
magnified for political advantage in Rome. In the years before Actium Caesar
Octavianus made it known that a modest advance beyond the north-east Alps
was preliminary to an expedition against the Dacians.[10] When the proconsul
Crassus achieved a victory in 29 B.C. over the Bastarnae, long-standing allies of
the Dacians, there was no sign of Dacian hegemony in the area; unless, that is,
the official record of a victory over 'Thracians and Getae' was devised by Caesar
Octavianus to suppress a prestigious victory over the Dacians.[11] The efforts of
Augustus and his generals in the Danube lands were directed principally to the

conquest of Illyrians and Thracians. By A.D. 9 this task had been barely completed, and at great cost — though this was partly offset by the acquisition of major sources for army recruitment.[12] Beyond the mountains of Thrace and Illyricum Roman commanders had made expeditions into the plains east and west of the Carpathians, reporting diplomatic courtesies with distant peoples; the most that can be said is that none of these commanders led his force into disaster.[13] A significant incident, perhaps the first direct Roman contact with the movements of peoples across the steppes beyond the lower Danube, is reported by Strabo for the middle years of Augustus: 'for at any rate, even in our own times, Aelius Catus transplanted from the country on the far side of the Ister into Thrace fifty thousand persons from among the Getae, a tribe with the same speech as the Thracians. And they live there in Thrace now and are called Moesi.'[14] Whatever the particular location or circumstances of this 'reception' into the Empire the backround to it is likely to be the pressure on peoples around the lower Danube caused by a south-westward movement of the nomads.

Sometime between the last years of Augustus and early in the reign of Claudius the Jazyges moved from the vicinity of the Danube delta to the Hungarian plain between the Danube and the Tisza. When, and under what circumstances, they passed from east to west of the Carpathians is not reported, nor is it certain by what route they travelled. It is possible, as some have argued, they passed around the north of Transylvania via Bukovina but since they appeared to have occupied Oltenia west of the river Alutus (Olt) around this time, a southern route is more likely, possible even via Roman territory south of the Danube. If the migration was contrived by the Romans it may have taken place late under Augustus or, perhaps, in the years 17–20 when Drusus was ordering the affairs of Illyricum. The advantage of the settlement to the Romans is clear: in the plain between the Danube bend and Transylvania they drove back the Dacians into their mountains and formed a protective barrier for the Celtic peoples of Pannonia against the Dacian raids they had suffered for more than a century. No longer did the Suebic Germans (Marcomanni and Quadi) have a common boundary with the Dacians: 'Sarmatia' was now interposed.[15] Around the year 50 the horsemen of the Jazyges are recorded in the service of the Roman client rulers of the Quadi, their immediate neighbours to the west. Whatever the short-term benefits, the transplanted Sarmatians remained uncomfortable neighbours of Roman Pannonia.[16] In A.D. 69 the Flavian commanders dared not include all the Jazyges in their expedition to Italy against Vitellius, because it was feared they would have simply changed sides had they received a better offer, although their rulers were taken.[17]

The earliest record of contact, though almost certainly not the first, between Romans and the Roxolani occurs on the career inscription of Ti. Plautius Silvanus Aelianus (cos. 45), governor of Moesia in the middle years of Nero. The unusually full account of his actions in this post recalls an elogium from the time of Augustus. In the case of Plautius it has been suspected, on good grounds, that the reality of his achievement has less substance than the high-flown language seeks to convey:

> 'legate of Moesia, with the rank of praetor, into which he brought across, with the object of ensuring the payment of tribute, more than 100,000 from the mass of Transdanubian peoples, along with their wives and families, and with their chiefs or kings. He "nipped in the bud" a threat that was developing from the Sarmatians, even though the greater part of his army he had sent away for the expedition into Armenia. Kings hitherto unknown or hostile to the Roman people he conducted to the river bank which was under his protection in order to pay solemn respect to Roman standards. To the kings of the Bastarnae and the Roxolani he restored their sons and to the king of the Dacians his brothers whom he had captured or rescued from enemies; from other rulers he received hostages. By these measures he strengthened and extended the security of the province. He also pushed back the king of the Scythians from a blockade of Chersonesus which lies beyond the river Borysthenes (Dniepr). He was the first to obtain from that province a great quantity of wheat for the grain supply to the Roman people.'[18]

The reality behind this succession of missions, negotiations, conferences and the occasional show of force, was the *receptio* of peoples who were probably being pressed against the lower Danube by nomads in the Pontic steppes, a settlement in the province that was evidently blessed by an abundant first harvest. It may have been made in circumstances similar to that by Aelius Catus around half a century before; at the same time it is likely that governors of Moesia under Claudius and Nero had become more directly concerned with the affairs of peoples beyond the lower Danube, following the annexation of Thrace in 46 and the incorporation of the Thracian bank (*ripa Thracia*) into Moesia. Roman forces had been active in the Crimea around the same period and a detachment of troops placed there to watch for signs of trouble.[19] This and the expedition deep into Armenia under Nero will have given the Romans a clear appreciation of the dangers which threatened from the nomads beyond the Caucasus. Beyond the Roxolani and other Sarmatians were the 'eastern' Sarmatians, of whom the fearsome Alani were already roaming the steppes around the lower Volga. The annexation of Pontus on the south shore of the Black Sea may have been the first step in an ambitious scheme of military advance directed towards the 'Gate of the Alans' through the Caucasus.[20] The Romans may have contemplated concerted operations on the west and the east shores of the Pontus, a grand strategy on Augustan lines which, as happened in A.D. 6, was brought to nothing by rebellion within the empire, in this instance the Jewish uprising in A.D. 66. When the Sarmatians did come the Roman world was engulfed in civil war.

III

The danger to Pannonia and Moesia was particularly acute not only when the Danube itself froze over in winter but when ice fields formed over the marshes which made the north bank difficult to approach at other times. In these conditions there would be little point in deploying cavalry to watch only the normal crossing places, when these could be so easily by-passed.

The early months of A.D. 69 were crowded with events. On the 15th January Galba was murdered by the praetorians amid scenes of shameful disorder. His successor Salvius Otho was energetic and resourceful but for ever tainted by earlier profligacy. Before his suicide at Brixellum on the 16th April, after the battle of Bedriacum, the Arval Brethren made sacrifice on the 1st March for a laurel of victory placed in the temple of Jupiter on the Capitol.[21] We learn from Tacitus what had taken place: 'Preoccupation with civil war had led to some slackness in the face of danger from abroad. The Rhoxolani, a Sarmatian tribe, had cut to pieces two auxiliary cohorts in the previous winter, and they were now encouraged to stage an ambitious invasion of Moesia. Their forces numbered some 9,000 wild and exulting horsemen, keener on booty than battle. These unwary rovers were suddenly set upon by the third legion, with its auxiliaries. On the Roman side all was set for the encounter. Not so the Sarmatians. Dispersed for plunder, laden with heavy spoils, and unable to profit by their horses' pace because the tracks were slippery, they were delivered as sheep to the slaughter. It is indeed curious to observe how completely the formidable Sarmatians depend on extraneous aids. An engagement on foot finds them ineffective, but when they appear on horseback, there is scarcely a line of battle that can stand up to them. But this particular day was wet, and a thaw had set in. Neither their lances nor their enormous two-handed swords were of any use, because the horses lost their footing and the dismounted warriors were weighed down by their body-armour. This protective clothing is worn by the chiefs and notables and consists of iron plating or toughened leather. Proof against blows, it is cumbersome when a man tries to get up after being unhorsed by an enemy charge. Moreover the Sarmatians were time and time again swallowed up in the deep, soft snow. The Roman troops on the other hand wore breastplates allowing easy movement. They moved up, throwing their javelins or using their lances and, as occasion required, their light-weight swords to close in and wound the unprotected Sarmatians, who do not normally carry shields. Finally, the few survivors took refuge in swampy country, where they succumbed to the severity of the weather or their wounds.

When news of this reached Rome, Marcus Aponius, the governor of Moesia, was granted a triumphal statue, and the legionary commanders Aurelius Fulvus, Tettius Julianus and Numisius Lupus received consular decorations. Otho was delighted, and plumed himself on the victory as if he had won it himself and exalted his country by means of commanders and armies that were his.'[22]

It is possible that the invaders who will have entered Moesia from Wallachia, were intercepted in the northern foothills of the Haemus (Balkan) or possibly further west in the Timok valley. There was worse to come, and that within a year.

In the civil war the legions of Pannonia and Moesia, who had been strongly for Otho, moved too late to fight in April but won victory for the Flavians at Cremona in October. Moesia was again exposed to attack, on this occasion, records Tacitus, from the Dacians: 'It was at this same time (the Flavian victory at Cremona) that there was trouble in Germany, and the slackness of our commanders, the mutiny of our legions, foreign invasion and allied treachery nearly caused the downfall of Rome. . . . There was also a movement among the Dacians. Never a trustworthy people, they had now nothing to fear as the Roman army had been withdrawn from Moesia. They studied the initial phases of the civil war but took no action for the moment. When, however, they heard that fighting had flared up in Italy and that the whole world was at loggerheads, they stormed the winter quarters of the cohorts and cavalry, and proceeded to make themselves masters of both banks of the Danube. They were on the point of moving in on the legionary bases when Mucianus barred their way with the sixth legion. He had not yet heard of the victory at Cremona and was anxious to forestall the overwhelming and double threat which would have been prevented by a Dacian and German invasion at two different points. As so often it was the luck of Rome that saved the day by bringing Mucianus and the forces of the East upon the scene, and because we meantime settled the issue at Cremona. Fonteius Agrippa, who had governed Asia as a proconsul for the normal period of one year, was appointed to administer Moesia, and was given additional forces from the army of Vitellius. To distribute this army among the provinces and to tie it down in a foreign war was an act at once of statesmanship and peace.'[23]

What point Mucianus and his forces had reached in their long overland march when *Legio VI Ferrata* was detached to block the invasion cannot be determined. Rather than the Hebrus (Marica) in the southeast, the area of Naissus, whence the Timok valley led to the lower Danube is to be preferred. The Dacians may have made mischief in the absence of the legion from Viminacium but there is a clear indication that the danger was from the Sarmatians.[24] When, later in the same year, Mucianus was awarded triumphal honours from the Senate this action, employed to conceal the shame of success in civil war, was designated a 'campaign against the Sarmatians'.[25] In the following winter the Roman army in Moesia, still disorganized after the turmoil of the civil war, was unprepared to face another attack from the Sarmatians, described by Josephus:

'The German revolt which I have described coincided with a bold Scythian attack on the Romans. A very large Scythian tribe called the Sarmatians crossed unnoticed to the right bank of the Danube, and launched a very violent attack so completely unexpected that resistance was swept aside. Many of the Roman guards were killed, and when the consular legate Fonteius Agrippa advanced to meet them and put up a strenuous fight he too fell. The whole of the province was overrun and stripped bare. When news of these events and of the devastation of Moesia reached Vespasian, he sent out Rubrius Gallus to punish the Sarmatians. Rubrius slaughtered vast numbers of them in a series of battles, the panic-stricken survivors scurrying back to their own country. Having brought the war to this conclusion the general provided for security in the future by stationing garrisons in greater number and strength about the area, so that the natives were denied the least chance of getting cross again. Thus the Moesian war was very quickly settled.'[26]

This is not the first record of Roman troops being positioned along the bank of the Danube to forestall raids. Yet Dacian incursions from their mountains never, it appears, amounted to more than a local nuisance, and were certainly nothing to be compared with sudden attack by 9,000 Iranian cataphracts intent on plunder. That was the threat from the Roxolani across the lower Danube and, to a lesser degree, from the Jazyges in the Hungarian plain. The Roman army was facing on two broad fronts an enemy which it dared not meet in open battle until dispersed for plunder. Since no offensive deployment of legions and *auxilia* could be contemplated in the vast plains where the nomads had no regular seasonal pattern of movement the river Danube had now to become a fortified line of defence for the Empire. Half a century later, with Dacia a Roman province, there were nine legionary bases on the right bank of the river between Vienna and the delta, along with chains of forts containing the *auxilia*, the whole system sustained by two powerful Roman fleets in Pannonia and Moesia.

In the matter of diplomacy the uncomfortable presence of the Sarmatians will have made the Romans pay close attention to relations with their longer-standing neighbours beyond the river, the Suebic German Marcomanni and Quadi north of Pannonia and the Dacians in the southern mountains of Transylvania. The Romans could realistically strive for stable relations towards both through client rulers sustained with generous subsidies. The alternative was the likely prospect that another Maroboduus or Burebista might appear to threaten Roman territory not only with their own forces but with the Sarmatian horsemen as allies. Annexation, with all the attendant hazards, was the least satisfactory option. In the case of Dacia the aim may have been to hope for a ruling dynasty that could be trusted and sustained by Rome against internal enemies.[27] If that could not be achieved (as it was with the Marcomanni and Quadi for more than half a century between Domitian and Marcus Aurelius) then incorporation as a province must have seemed the only alternative. Such a course of action would necessitate in consequence the permanent deployment of large numbers of Roman troops not only to secure the new province but also, and in the light of recent experience considerably more important, to complete the encirclement of the Jazyges on the west and the Roxolani on the east.

An excessive, and inevitable concentration on the high drama of Domitian's wars in 85–92, and on Trajan's great expeditions into Transylvania in 101–2 and 105, has accorded to Dacia a prominence in the historical record it does not merit. Rich in minerals, enjoying long-standing contacts with the Greek world, a clearly defined social structure and an acknowledged sophistication in such matters as religion and astronomy, Dacia has something of the character of a Hellenistic state, comparable to a Macedon or a Pontus.[28] For a period the Romans treated with Decebalus as they once did with Philip or Mithridates, and Domitian's peace with Dacia brought a coronation staged in Rome (below p. 269) to compare with that of Tiridates of Armenia under Nero.[29]

IV

Before Flavian times there was no such thing as a 'Roman frontier', at least in the sense of a line of demarcation maintained through a concerted deployment of legionary bases and auxiliary forts. Of seven legions in the Danube lands at the death of Augustus two stood on the Danube, pointing the direction for the next advance. Like the eight legions of 'Germania' set along the Gallic bank of the Rhine, the legions at Carnuntum and Oescus were placed for an advance against the Marcomanni and the Dacians.[30] That they, like the Rhine legions, were for ever to remain in those bases stemmed from Augustus' famous advice to his successor not to enlarge the Empire.[31] A contemporary vision of the Roman Empire 'closed off by the Ocean or by distant rivers, the legions, provinces and fleets all bound together, one with another' reflects not protected frontiers but security against rebellion.[32] Of the remaining five Danubian legions, two in southern Pannonia (at Poetovio and probably at Siscia) and two in the Adriatic hinterland of Dalmatia (at Tilurium and Burnum) were strategically placed to watch for trouble from the Pannonians along the Drave and Save, and in the Bosnian valleys to the south. In Moesia the other legion was somewhere in the south, watching the Dardanians and Thracians.[33]

Local supervision of native peoples was exercised by senior centurions of the legions or by commanders of auxiliary units deployed conveniently for the purpose. In some areas these commissions would include specific responsibility for local security along the Danube. Thus the prefect of an auxiliary unit based at Arrabona (Győr) east of Carnuntum was charged with supervision of the Boii and Azali and the Danube bank, which formed the northern boundary of these peoples as far as the Danube bend.[34] In the interior the chief centurion of the legion at Poetovio administered the neighbouring Colapiani.[35] In Dalmatia the powerful Maezaei and Daesitiates were similarly controlled, and here the system lasted into the Flavian period when native *principes* were permitted to recover their titular authority.[36] In Moesia below the Danube gorge the chief centurion of the legion at Oescus administered the peoples of Moesia and Treballia who dwelt along the river from the gorge to the Thracian bank.[37] Around the same time a cavalry commander from the Moesian army may have had responsibility for the area of the Danube gorge, through which the two legions are recorded constructing a towpath in the later years of Tiberius, but without, it seems, any specified responsibility for native affairs.[38] In the last years of Augustus the poet Ovid in exile at Tomis tells of the achievement, in A.D. 12, of the senior centurion Julius Vestalis in recapturing Aegyssus (Tulcea) on the delta from the troublesome Getae. He may have been prefect of the shore operating with a flotilla from the west coast of Pontus but perhaps 'prefect of the Danube bank' is more likely since his action was concerted with the movement of Roman troops along the river.[39]

Pannonia lost one of its legions to Claudius' invasion of Britain. In Moesia the annexation of Thrace three years later brought a legion to the Thracian bank, in a new base at Novae, a crossing-place of the Danube fifty miles east of Oescus.[40] A legion was moved from Dalmatia to Moesia above the Danube gorge, probably under Nero when the latter province saw two of its legions moved to the eastern front. Late under Nero a legion was transferred from the east to bring up the garrison of Moesia to three legions.[41] In 68 the following deployment prevailed: two legions in Pannonia (*XV Apollinaris* at Carnuntum and *XIII Gemina* at Poetovio), one in Dalmatia (*XI Claudia pia fidelis* at Burnum) and three in Moesia (*VII Claudia pia fidelis* at Viminacium, *III Gallica* at Oescus (?) and *VIII Augusta* at Novae).

In A.D. 85 the same six bases still held the legions of the three provinces, though overall the total of legions may have risen to seven if one of the defeated Vitellian legions survived in Moesia until its extinction in the war of Domitian.[42] It must be observed that this unaltered deployment does not suggest major changes in the face of danger from the Sarmatians. But legionary bases are not the whole story, especially in the Danube provinces. Distances are great and movement is difficult: a whole army could be cut off and destroyed so suddenly that news of a disaster could be the first intimation that the enemy was on the move. The attack by the Roxolani early in 69 did not, it seems, overwhelm any of the legionary bases but it is hard to imagine that this was also the case with the disaster of Fonteius Agrippa in the following year. Yet it is in the increase and redeployment of the *auxilia,* both cavalry and infantry, along with measures to secure passage along the Danube and some of its principal tributaries, that the scale and nature of the Flavian reorganization in defence of the Danube provinces in the aftermath of the disaster of Fonteius is indicated.

In Pannonia diplomas issued for *auxilia* seem to indicate the steady arrival of new units: in A.D. 80 four *alae* and thirteen cohorts are listed, in 84 five *alae* and thirteen cohorts and in 85 six and fifteen respectively.[43] Important recent discoveries and new analyses of finds already published (notably imported pottery and bricks made and stamped by individual units) are contributing to a better understanding of measures taken between 70 and 85 and thus putting the wars of Domitian and their aftermath into a healthier perspective — an emergency which interrupted rather than originated the provision of defence for Pannonia and Moesia. South of the Danube bend an imposing building slab records the construction, probably by a cavalry regiment, of a new military base at Aquincum, at a crossing of the Danube directly opposite the heartlands of the Jazyges. The date is 73 or 74.[44] In that year also new construction is recorded in the legionary base at Carnuntum.[45] Elsewhere it now appears that a number of bases for *auxilia* were first constructed on the river during the seventies and early eighties. The import of arretine pottery into Pannonia appears to cease quite abruptly during the early eighties and was replaced by the products of south Gaulish factories. The key site for the dating of forts on the Danube in Pannonia is Vetus Salina (Adony), where a succession of earth and timber forts was identified more than thirty years ago. It seems now clear that the first fort dates not from the time of Domitian's German and Sarmatian wars in 89–92 but to the middle or later years of Vespasian. It now emerges, thanks to the study of Gabler and Lorincz, that the chain of auxiliary forts along the Danube, once believed to have been created in the later years of Domitian, has its origins in the reign of Vespasian.[46]

For undivided Moesia, that is before its division into Superior and Inferior in 85/6, two diplomas afford lists of *auxilia*, but only for cohorts: that of 75 registers ten, the second of 78 names eight, though only two units are common to both lists. The findspot of the earlier suggests that a cohort was in garrison at Taliata (Donji Milanovac), the only place where the Danube gorge between Golubac and Orşova is approachable from the south, by the Porečka valley. The findspot of the second similarly suggests a unit in garrison at Montana (Mihailovgrad) southwest of Oescus, where the principal east to west road of Moesia crossed the river Augusta (Ogosta).[47] The transfer of an *ala* and two cohorts from Germany to Moesia recorded on a diploma of A.D. 82 indicates not 'disturbance' but more the steady reinforcement of the armies of the Danube, a river which had so many crossings and inland routes to make safe against sudden invasion.[48]

Along the river early forts appear to have been established at Augustae (Hurlec) for a cavalry unit and at Variana (Leskovec). A cavalry unit was once in the vicinity of the legionary base at Oescus and another may have been placed at Nikopol, roughly halfway towards Novae.[49] The appearance of a building inscription dated to A.D. 76 at Appiaria (near Orehovo) fifty miles east of Novae is precious evidence for deployment under Vespasian: in this instance two cohorts appear to have been involved.[50] Other places along the lower Danube, where *auxilia* are known to have been stationed in the second century, may well have been first occupied during this time.[51] This appears not to have been the case with the lowest stretch of the river, from Appiaria to the delta. No inscription or excavated material has been produced to indicate occupation before the reign of Trajan. This is certainly the case for Durostorum, where a legion was established after the completion of the conquest of Dacia; yet some have suggested a much earlier origin as a legionary base, for example for the victorious *III Gallica* which caught the Roxolani off guard in 69.[52] Several forts in the

Dobrudja have been extensively excavated and nothing has been reported from any of these sites, with the exception of the naval base Noviodunum (Isaccea), to indicate occupation beginning before the second century, though it must be stressed that diligent search has rarely if ever been made for the earliest levels of stratified occupation.[53]

From the first Roman campaigns in the area the movement of ships along the Danube and its principal tributaries is likely to have played an important role in sustaining military operations and securing the resulting acquisitions of territory.[54] Two Roman fleets were created for the Danube, that of Pannonia with its base at Taurunum (Zemun) at the Save confluence directly opposite Singidunum (Belgrade), where a legion of Moesia was later to be established on the dominating plateau of the Kalmegdan; and that of Moesia whose base was located in similar fashion far downstream at Noviodunum, on an eminence overlooking the beginnings of the delta marshes.[55] In Flavian times at least one commander of the Moesian fleet had specific responsibility for 'the bank of the Danube', possibly the stretch of the river below Appiaria not yet controlled by auxiliary forts.[56] The name Sexaginta Prista (Ruse) some thirty miles east of Novae, which means 'sixty ships' may indicate the location of another base for the Moesian fleet which, since it lies west of Appiaria, was in that part of the Thracian bank known to have been brought under direct control by Vespasian.[57] Further upstream there are also grounds for supposing that Ratiaria (whose name means 'ferry-boats') had in its earliest days been a naval base.[58] Both Pannonian and Moesian fleets later bore the title Flavia, though for neither formation is there any indication as to whether it was conferred by Vespasian, Titus or Domitian. A great programme of fort construction in both provinces, commencing early under Vespasian, will have placed a great additional burden upon Roman fleets sailing on the Danube. If the titles had not been conferred for distinguished conduct in the emergencies during and after the civil wars, then his reign is the most likely period for a reorganization of the existing fleets and a grant of the new titles.[59]

The river Save offers the shortest route between Italy and the lower Danube. Flavian colonies were established at Siscia and Sirmium, strategic positions at either end of its course. Neither has produced evidence for original legionary settlers but there is sufficient to indicate that both were in fact settlements of discharged sailors, made probably under Vespasian from those who had served in the Italian fleets (which drew many recruits from Pannonia and Dalmatia) and to whom generous privileges were granted in respect of traffic along the river. Such settlements would accord well with a reorganisation of the Danube fleets under Vespasian. With regular maintenance of the towpath necessary to conduct river traffic through the Danube gorge the Roman response to the disasters of 69 and 70 can be recognized: nothing less than the creation of a Roman defensive frontier along the river Danube.[60]

In those years when the Roman army was tightening its grip on the Danube nothing is reported of relations with the peoples dwelling beyond the river. The

German Marcomanni and Quadi may still have held to their custom of obeying Roman clients, as they did in A.D. 69: as a people, comments Tacitus, 'they were more disposed to keep faith than break it.'[61] Towards the Dacians, perhaps, overtures were made: as more and more units of the Roman army took up station along the river and Roman fleets became a more frequent sight on it embassies of reassurance may have been dispatched. With the Sarmatians there will have been little prospect of lasting peace with the people as a whole but individual leaders may have responded to offers of Roman friendship.

In A.D. 73 Vespasian summoned to Rome the governor of Spain (Hispania Citerior) and appointed him prefect of the city, a distinction that was marked, in the normal fashion, by the honour of a second consulship early in the following year.[62] The recall of Plautius Silvanus Aelianus to Rome may not have been unconnected with the fact that he had gained much experience treating with peoples beyond the lower Danube from his governorship of Moesia ten years earlier. This seems to be confirmed by the belated acknowledgement of his achievement in that post which appears in the record of his career: 'during his prefecture the Senate honoured him with triumphal decorations on the motion of the emperor Caesar Augustus Vespasianus, whose address contained the words recorded below: "He governed Moesia so ably that the bestowing of triumphal decorations on him should not have been delayed to my time, save only that in the course of the delay he obtained a more distinguished honour, namely the prefecture of the city".'[63] This imperial tribute may have served to remind the Senate that there were ways of warding off the Sarmatians, without hazarding the army of the province.

V

The year 84 opened at Rome with Domitian, for the tenth time, and C. Oppius Sabinus the consuls. Within two years Domitian's colleague was dead, following a Dacian attack on his province of Moesia.[64] The victory achieved later by Tettius Julianus at Tapae (see below) permits the assumption that the disaster of Sabinus took place somewhere in the western part of the Dacian front, that is between the mouth of the Tisza and the Danube gorge. This event, which brought the emperor to Moesia to take charge of measures against the Dacians, marks the first appearance on the scene of Decebalus though he, it appears, was not responsible for the attack on Moesia.[65] Domitian perceived how the province had now become an unwieldy military command, a consequence of the build-up of its forces since the defeat of Fonteius fifteen years before. He divided Moesia into two consular commands, Superior in the west and Inferior in the east. The limits of the former were at first not the same as the later province (river Save on the west and Ciabrus (Cibrica) on the east) and on the west comprised the tongue of land between the Save and the Drave, including Sirmium and Mursa (Osijek).[66] The speedy transfer of at least one legion into this area facing the Banat across the river suggests that it was the sector most exposed to Dacian attack.[67]

The emperor had left Moesia before his praetorian prefect Cornelius Fuscus met shattering defeat on expedition into Dacia, either in 86 or 87.[68] Moesia Superior had, it seems, already been placed in the charge of Funisulanus Vettonianus governor of Pannonia who received military honours in a Dacian war, when the emperor returned to the Danube.[69] It was for opinion at Rome a particularly spectacular and unnerving defeat: the spectre of a Dacian battlefield covered with Roman corpses, including praetorians and their prefect, soon became as famous as that of Varus and his slaughtered legions in Germany.[70] Domitian rejected any overtures of peace which may have come from Decebalus. In 88 another Roman army advanced into Dacia under Tettius Julianus who had commanded the seventh legion when the Roxolani attacked in 69.[71] Starting probably from Viminacium the army marched across the Banat to win a victory at Tapae in the Bistrica valley at the Iron Gates of Transylvania, through which pass ran the route to the Dacian capital Sarmizegetusa. Dacian losses were heavy but Decebalus was able to prevent the invaders from entering the heartland of his kingdom. Perhaps the Roman army spent the winter in camp near the scene, poised to strike at the Dacian capital as soon as the pass could be forced.

Like Maroboduus in A.D. 6, Decebalus may have been saved by rebellion in the empire; in January 89 the legate of Germania Superior who commanded an army of four legions rose in revolt. It was supressed by the legate of the lower province before Domitian arrived on the scene.[72] The emperor was still in the north-west when disturbing news came of sudden and hostile movements among the Germans north of Pannonia and, no less serious, among the Jazyges to the east. Diplomacy may have been employed to hold off the Germans until a victory, or at least a satisfactory accommodation, had been achieved with Dacia.[73] News of a Roman defeat brought Domitian again to the Danube, on this occasion with reinforcements for Pannonia.[74] The conclusion of negotiations with Dacia was announced: in return for subsidies and the services of Roman engineers Diegis the brother of Decebalus travelled to Rome to accept the diadem on behalf of the king. A hostile tradition has suppressed the real merits of this timely peace, made at a time when war was imminent with an alliance of Germans and Sarmatians.[75] Negotiations with the Germans were broken off, perhaps as soon as the success at Tapae had been reported. An embassy from the Marcomanni and Quadi, not the first, was summarily put to death 'because they had not assisted him with help against the Dacians'.[76] Decebalus kept the bargain and the army which had been concentrated against him in Moesia Superior could be moved to watch the Germans and Sarmatians. At the end of the year Domitian was back in Rome and celebrated a double triumph, over the Chatti in Germany and the Dacians.[77]

Nothing is recorded of the course of events in Pannonia until the Jazyges crossed the river and wiped out a legion, a disaster which brought Domitian back to the Danube, this time for a stay of eight months in A.D. 92.[78] Two isolated incidents serve to indicate Roman methods in diplomacy and military strategy. We learn that Domitian brought into the war the Lugii, a German people who dwelt beyond the Marcomanni and Quadi, by sending them 100 cavalry when they asked for help. This was the action which caused the Germans to bring into the war the horsemen of the Jazyges, with devastating results.[79] On the Roman side C. Velius Rufus, chief centurion of a legion, who in the course of a long career conducted a number of delicate missions, and served with distinction in the Dacian war, led an *expeditio* against the Marcomanni, Quadi and Sarmatians through the realm of Decebalus 'king of the Dacians'; this facility was evidently permitted to the Romans under the terms of the recent treaty.[80] The war with the Germans was evidently not concluded since on his return to Rome the emperor celebrated an *ovatio* in respect of a victory over the Sarmatians alone, though military decorations were awarded for the war against both peoples.[81] In A.D. 97 the adoption of Trajan by Nerva was accorded a favourable omen by report of a victory over the Germans in Pannonia, a success for which both adopted the epithet Germanicus.[82]

Two new legionary bases on the German frontier of Pannonia (Vindobona and Brigetio) and another on the 'Sarmatian bank' (Aquincum) brought the total of legions on the Pannonian Danube to four before the end of the first century, a deployment that was to persist until the chaos of the third century.[83] The construction of new auxiliary forts, along with the repair of existing ones, continued during the years following the war.[84] In Moesia Superior, which still included the area of Sirmium, two legions were on or close to the river, one perhaps at Mursa near the Drave confluence and the other in the long-established base Viminacium. In the lower province legions remained at Oescus and Novae, and there may have been a third.[85] As in Pannonia new forts for the *auxilia* were created on the Danube, though in Moesia the move to concentrate forces on the river is less marked than in Pannonia.[86]

VI

Trajan spurned the alliance with Decebalus, it seems on no reasonable grounds. The growing prosperity and prestige of the Roman client made the annual subsidy all the harder to stomach.[87] The new emperor opted for conquest, an aspersion on the achievement of Domitian certain to please sentiment at Rome but at what cost in men and resources can only be imagined. Recruits were sought for the *auxilia,* reflected by the grants of citizenship to those on the point of discharge, documents which reveal the concentration of units for the coming war. A diploma for Moesia Superior of A.D. 96 lists one *ala* and ten cohorts but on another issued four years later there appear no less than twenty-one cohorts. Many of these had evidently been recently moved into the area; the absence of cavalry units reflects perhaps that new troopers were harder to recruit and train.[88] A similar 'shake-out' may have taken place with the army of Moesia

Inferior during the previous year. Two grants issued on the same day contain separate lists of units, three *alae* and six cohorts, the other three and seven, which may together represent the entire auxiliary garrison of the province, complementary to its two legions.[89] There was much for the fleets to do. The old towpath through the Danube gorge had evidently required repair on several occasions since its first construction under Tiberius. On the eve of the Dacian expedition it received a major overhaul: in the lower gorge (Kazan) a road was hacked out of the sheer rockface in A.D. 100 and in the following year was completed the excavation of a new canal to by-pass the Iron Gate, a wall of rock across the bed of the river below Orşova, to open for the first time continuous passage along the Danube.[90]

From the fascinating but enigmatic reliefs on the Column of Trajan it has been deduced that the first expedition passed across the Banat, a route indicated by a fragment of the emperor's commentaries, but the attack was forestalled by a Dacian attack across the lower Danube, in which Sarmatians are represented as having played a significant role. In the following year A.D. 102 it is inferred that the Romans invaded from below the Danube gorge, following the river Alutus northwards to enter Dacia by the Red Tower pass; or perhaps by a more westerly route, from Drobetae (Turnu Severin) across to the river Jiu and into Dacia by the Vulkan pass.[91] If the reliefs provide guidance to the course of the war, as well as the details of well-remembered incidents, they convey little or nothing of the political reality. A peace in 102 left the power of Decebalus intact, confirmed by the Senate in Rome. The Romans had been alarmed by the number of persons who had come to him from Roman territory: 'for he had been acquiring the largest and best part of his force by persuading men to come to him from Roman territory.' Now he was forbidden to receive deserters or employ any soldier from the Roman empire.[92] The background to this will have had much to do with the heavy burdens laid upon the frontier lands of the Danube by the steadily growing Roman army.

Within a few years of the first Dacian war come the first records for the Roman army on the lowest stretch of the river. Under the legate Q. Fabius Postuminus (cos. 96) a building record (now lost) attests construction by a cavalry unit in the fort at Carsium (Hîrsova) on the Dobrudja bank facing the river Jalomiţa. The same governor is recorded at Tomis, on an imposing marble inscription, fragmentary but dated firmly to 103; he appears also on a recently discovered milestone (evidently of 103–5) which suggests that the cohort involved in the road construction was already in garrison at Sacidava (Muzait-Dunareni), not far east of the later legionary base at Durostorum.[93] If the first Dacian war brought Roman units to secure the principal crossings of this lowest stretch of the river it would be surprising if it did not also bring at least one legion into the area. Neither of the two later permanent bases, Durostorum (Silistra) and Troesmis (Igliţa), has so far produced any evidence for the presence of a legion before the end of Trajan's reign. It can be assumed, however, that both were occupied after the second Dacian war when the province of Moesia

Pl. II and III Scenes from Trajan's column showing armoured Sarmatians; see p. 258.
(Photograph: Deutsches Archäologisches Institut in Rome, reproduced by kind permission of Thames and Hudson).

Inferior was greatly enlarged by the occupation of the Wallachian plain as far east as the river Siret.

On the west the Jazyges appear to have fought for the Romans in both Dacian wars. On the eve of the second it is recorded that Decebalus had made attacks on those with whom he was at odds 'and even went so far as to annex a portion of the territory of the Jazyges, which Trajan later would not return to them when they asked for it, and therefore the Senate again declared him an enemy.'[94] The territory in question could be either the Banat or Oltenia. After the organization of the province Dacia in 106 the Jazyges were corralled by a defensive deployment of Roman troops on three sides. To their west the Sarmatian front of Pannonia, with its legion at Aquincum, was hived off as the separate command of Pannonia Inferior.[95] To their east the Tisza had for long been the boundary between Sarmatians and Dacians and was evidently still so in the time of Decebalus. Trajan kept the army of Dacia within the mountains of Transylvania and acquiesced in their expansion east of the Tisza. This adjustment to their situation may lie behind the report that trouble with the Sarmatians was dealt with by the first governor of Pannonia Inferior, P. Aelius Hadrianus.[96] We can infer from the brief record of later disturbances that the Romans took great pains to maintain good relations with Sarmatians in the plains on either side of Dacia. On the east the Roxolani, who fought against the Romans at least once during the Dacian wars, saw their lands crossed regularly by Roman formations from bases on the Alutus (Slaveni, Romula and Buridava) and further east near the southern foothills of the Carpathians (Jidava, Tirgşor, Drajna de sus, Malaieşti and Piroboridava = ?Poiana).[97] This deployment was the closest the Romans ever came to a conquest of Sarmatian territory. Subsidies were paid to both Jazyges and Roxolani but there is no indication that the Romans ever succeeded in making a long-standing accommodation with them, such as they had with the Germans for most of the first and second centuries or had had with the Dacian state.

In A.D. 105 'Trajan, having crossed the river by means of the bridge, conducted the war with safe prudence rather than with haste, and eventually, after a hard struggle, vanquished the Dacians.'[98] Two items of evidence indicate that long-ranging and costly operations, involving Dacians and Sarmatians, were taking place at the same time on the lower Danube. These are a register of manpower *(pridianum)*, preserved on papyrus, for the *coh. I Hispanorum veterana*, stationed at Stobi in Macedonia, and the three monuments at Adamklissi in the southern Dobrudja. The papyrus names Fabius Justus as governor and its date can now be firmly fixed to the time of the second war or its immediate aftermath by a monumental building inscription from Rasova, on the river a dozen miles east of Sacidava, erected in the second half of A.D. 106 and which names L. Fabius Justus as the governor of Moesia Inferior.[99] Since the register was drawn up on the 16th September it will date to 105 or later since Justus' predecessor is recorded by a diploma to be still in charge of the province in May of that year. Its contents reveal an astonishingly widespread dispersion of the unit's manpower, which makes uncertain the deductions of Roman strategy from over-schematic reconstructions of auxiliary deployment based on diplomas, inscriptions and brick stamps. Some are listed far beyond the lower Danube 'in garrison at Piroboridava' (which may be Poiana on the Siret east of the Oituz pass, the route between east Transylvania and Dobrudja);[100] another detachment is 'in garrison at Buridava' (Stolniceni, on the Alutus south of the Red Tower pass, the route from Oescus into Transylvania). Some are 'on expedition beyond the Danube' and others, likewise beyond the river, 'scouting with the centurion . . .' It is hard to believe that, given the range and nature of such operations, there were not by now legions established at Durostorum and Troesmis — if indeed they were not already there before the second Dacian war.

The great trophy dedicated to Mars the Avenger in 109 portrays in its relief sculpture scenes of Roman soldiers in fierce hand-to-hand combat with, it seems, Sarmatians, Dacians and Germans. Whatever may be indicated by its location (and the distant prospect of the modern reconstruction *in situ* leaves no doubt that it must have been so positioned for dramatic effect), it stands not far from the river between the two legionary bases on the lowest stretch of the Danube. Everything indicates that it was a monument specific to the army which had fought a war in Lower Moesia, and that it is their local adversaries who are portrayed, prominent among whom were the Sarmatian Roxolani.[101] Not far away from the trophy, but off the crest of the hill, are the remains of an altar, whose four sides were inscribed with the names of up to 3,800 Roman casualties, inscribed in columns according to unit. Conjecture that a name at the head of the fallen with the title *praefectus* may have been that of Domitian's praetorian prefect Cornelius Fuscus has been challenged on good grounds.[102] Once this is removed nothing links the altar with any event before the arrival of the Roman army into the area, which at the earliest was the first Dacian war of Trajan. The matter is further complicated by the existence of a third monument (what is now termed mausoleum) in the vicinity of the trophy and also by the fact that the stones employed in the trophy, on the one hand, and in the altar and the mausoleum (?), on the other, were obtained from different quarries; and, no less significant, there is no similarity in the style and execution of their architectural ornament.[103]

VII

In the years following the Dacian wars movements of the Jazyges were watched by three legions, one in Pannonia Inferior (Aquincum), one in the Banat (Berzobis) and a third in Transylvania.[104] On the east the plain of the Roxolani east of the Alutus was confronted by three legions on the lower Danube (Novae, Durostorum and Troesmis). On the old 'Dacian bank' a legion remained at Viminacium but, below the gorge, veteran colonies were established under Trajan in the old bases at Ratiaria and Oescus.[105]

The Sarmatians moved to attack again at the beginning of the next reign, probably in the winter 117/8.[106] By the time Hadrian had reached Moesia in the spring of 118, on his journey to Rome from the east, he had news of the all too familiar outcome of a sudden attack — a Roman governor caught and killed. On this occasion it was C. Julius Quadratus Bassus (cos. 105), a noble of Pergamum and a general of Trajan in the conquest of Dacia, and now the last consular legate of undivided Dacia. His body was born back to Asia by his own troops and a magnificent funeral was provided by the emperor.[107] The attack came from Jazyges and Roxolani, probably in concert. The king of the latter (who may later have sought asylum in the Empire) had complained that the subsidies paid to them by Trajan had been reduced: Hadrian looked into the matter personally and a peace was made. The demands of the Jazyges could not be so easily settled and extraordinary measures were taken. Hadrian created a single command with three legions against the Jazyges by uniting Pannonia Inferior and Dacia under the command of his trusted equestrian officer Q. Marcius Turbo, with a status equivalent to the Prefect of Egypt.[108] When he departed in 119 most of a major reorganization had been completed: Dacia was to become three separate commands, Superior comprising the heartland of Decebalus' old kingdom with the legion at Apulum (Alba Julia); in the north-west Porolissensis (which may have been established in 120 after the conclusion of hostilities with the Jazyges) with a screen of forts watching the north-east of the Hungarian plain around the upper Tisza and the Someş; and Inferior comprising eastern Transylvania and Oltenia west of the Alutus hitherto parts of Moesia Inferior, following the withdrawal of the Roman troops from the plain of Wallachia.[109] Superior was placed in the charge of a praetorian legate but Inferior and Porolissensis were assigned to equestrian officers with the title of *procurator*, recalling the *praefecturae* which were widespread in the Danube provinces during the first century. In the west the occupied area of the Banat was let go and the second legion of Dacia returned across the river to a base in Moesia, at Singidunum overlooking the mouth of the Save. The dismemberment, not abandonment, of Trajan's Dacia can be understood as necessary measures against the Sarmatians: Pannonia Inferior with Porolissensis and Dacia Superior would concert against the Jazyges, while Dacia Inferior and Moesia Inferior encircled the Roxolani. The concerted watch on the Sarmatians gave the Romans peace for half a century. In the event it was only broken by the collapse of long-standing treaties with the Germans, leading to the terrible wars under Marcus Aurelius. Then the Sarmatians were once again to prove the most dangerous and intractable of Roman enemies.

NOTES

1. On the history and material culture of the Sarmatians, see Sulimirski, T., *The Sarmatians,* Ancient Peoples and Places series, London, 1970.

2. Herodotus, iv, 21; 110–17. The identification of Sauromatae and Sarmatae has been accepted by most scholars, with the notable exception of M. Rostovtzeff, though he modified his view in later publications; see *Cambridge Ancient History,* xi, 91. On the many difficult problems which arise in the interpretation of the ancient sources for the Sarmatians, see Harmatta, J., *Studies in the History and Language of the Sarmatians,* Acta Universitatis de Attila Joszef nominatae, Acta Antiqua et Archaeologica, tomus xiii, Opera Minora xiii, Szeged, 1970.

3. Strabo, vii, 3, 17; cf. Harmatta, J., *op. cit.* (see note 2), 12–15. For the episode of Zopyrion, see Justinus, xii, 2, 16; Quintus Curtius, x, 1, 44; Macrobius, *Saturnalia,* i, 11, 33, and *Cambridge Ancient History,* vi, 394.

4. Sulimirski, T., *op. cit.* (see note 1), 112.

5. Strabo, vii, 4, 8.

6. Herodotus, iv, 21; 110–17; Strabo, vii, 3, 17; Ammianus Marcellinus, xvii, 12.

7. Sulimirski, T., *op. cit.* (see note 1), 28.

8. Ancient sources in Broughton, T.R.S., *The Magistrates of the Roman Republic,* Vol. II, New York, 1952: L. Cornelius Scipio Asiagenus (Asiaticus), 85–4 B.C., 58; Ap. Claudius Pulcher, 77–6 B.C., 89; C. Scribonius Curio, 75–3 B.C., 99, 104, 112; M. Terentius Varro Lucullus, 72–1 B.C., 118 and 124. Of these Ap. Claudius is said to have penetrated as far as the Sarmatians, Florus, *Epitome,* i, 39, 6.

9. Early in the civil war it was feared that Pompey might stir up fierce peoples from the Danube area to invade Italy, Cicero, *Letters to Atticus,* ix, 10, 2 (referring to Getae = Dacians) in March 49 B.C. During the following year negotiations between Pompey and Burebista were being conducted by Acornion, a citizen of Dionysopolis

(Balcik) on the Thracian coast of the Black Sea: Mihailov, G., *Inscriptiones Graecae in Bulgaria repertae* i², (1970), 51, no. 13.

10. Appian, *Illyrike* 23. On Roman aspirations towards the Dacians at this time, see Mócsy, A., *Pannonia and Upper Moesia,* Budapest, 1974, 21.

11. Deduced from Cassius Dio, li, 23–7 and Horace, *Odes,* iii, 8, 18, by Mócsy, A., *Historia,* xv, (1966), 511.

12. See Syme, R., *Cambridge Ancient History,* x, 351, and the same scholar's papers reprinted in *Danubian Papers,* Association Internationale d'Études du Sud-Est Européen, Bucharest, 1971, each with an addendum compiled in 1968. On early recruitment from Illyricum see Mócsy, A., *op. cit.* (see note 10), 39.

13. Notably by M. Vinicius (cos. 19 B.C.), whose achievements may be recorded on the fragmentary *elogium* at Tusculum (*I.L.S.* 8965), which names Bastarnae, Cotini and Anartii in a record of military operations across the Danube; see Syme, R., *Danubian Papers* (see note 12), 26. More significant were perhaps those ill-recorded operations of Cn. Cornelius Lentulus (cos. 14 B.C.) on the lower Danube. He is said to have denied the Sarmatians access to the Danube, Florus, *Epitome,* ii, 28, perhaps the first attempt to make them acknowledge the Danube as the boundary of Roman territory; see Syme, R., *Danubian Papers* (see note 12), 40. In his *Res Gestae, c.* 31, Augustus lists embassies of friendship which came to him from peoples to the north and east of the Black Sea: 'The Bastarnae, Scythians and the kings of the Sarmatians on either side of the river Don, and the kings of the Albanians and the Iberians and the Medes sent embassies to seek our friendship.'

14. Strabo, vii, 3, 10, referring probably to Sex. Aelius Catus (cos. A.D. 4). There is some doubt whether an inscription from Athens, *L'Année épigraphique,* (1966), 379, relates to this command; see

Syme, R., *Danubian Papers* (see note 12), 69.

15. A. Alföldi believed that the migration was likely to have been contrived, or at least controlled, by the Romans, probably in the reign of Tiberius, *Cambridge Ancient History*, xi, 85, note 2: 'no one who reflects how the legates dealt with the frontier peoples at this time will imagine that they came without the permission from the governor of Pannonia'. Others have linked the migration with the operations of Cn. Lentulus under Augustus, which certainly involved Sarmatians (see note 13), Mócsy, A., *op. cit.* (see note 10), 37. More recently the latter scholar, developing a suggestion of Harmatta, has invoked the raid by Dacians and Sarmatians on Moesia in A.D. 6/7, Cassius Dio, lv, 30, 4, which gave Tiberius a success over Sarmatians in A.D. 7, Eusebius, *Chronicle*, (Helm, R. (ed.), Leipzig, 1913 and 1926, second edition Berlin, 1956, 170); see *Acta Antiqua Hungarica*, xxv, (1977), 439.

16. Tacitus, *Annals*, xii, 29.

17. Tacitus, *Histories*, iii, 5.

18. *I.L.S.* 986 (Tibur). For a commentary see Pippidi, D.M., *Epigraphische Beiträge zur Geschichte Histrias in hellenistischer und römischer Zeit*, Berlin, 1962, 106. The first accurate description of Sarmatian battle tactics and arms, the heavy lance *(contus)* and mail coat, in a Roman author occurs in the *Argonautica* of Valerius Flaccus, vi, 162, 231, and would appear to have been compiled from knowledge of the Danubian wars of Domitian: Syme, R., *Classical Quarterly*, xxiii, (1929), 129.

19. Tacitus, *Annals*, xii, 15, making reference to the installation of a client ruler of the Bosporani by A. Didius Gallus, evidently in 45–6. On his career, see Birley, A.R., *The* Fasti *of Roman Britain*, Oxford, 1981, 47.

20. Anderson, J.G.C., *Cambridge Ancient History*, x, 773.

21. McCrum, M. and Woodhead, A.G., *Select Documents of the Principates of the Flavian Emperors A.D. 68–96*, Cam-

bridge, 1961, 13.

22. *Histories*, i, 79, translated by Wellesley, K., Harmondsworth, 1972.

23. *Histories*, iii, 46.

24. The attempt by Kenneth Wellesley: *Commentary on the Histories of Tacitus Book iii*, Sydney, 1972, 208–15, to reconstruct a chronology for events in Moesia during 69–70 may take too little account of uncertainties in travel and the transmission of news; see Syme, R., *Antichthon*, xi, (1977), 78, who objects to reading *ignarus* in place of *gnarus* at *Histories*, iii, 46, 2, making Mucianus unaware of the Flavian victory when he took measures against the invaders.

25. Tacitus, *Histories*, iv, 4.

26. *Jewish War*, vii, 4, 3. On the career of Fonteius see Groag, E., Stein, A. and Petersen, L., *P.I.R.* 1933–, F 466. The report of rumours current in Germany during the war against Civilis that legionary bases in Pannonia and Moesia were under threat from Dacians and Sarmatians appears to be dismissed by Tacitus: *Histories*, iv, 54, *fingebantur*, along with similar stories concerning the Britons.

27. The idea of a marriage alliance between Roman and Dacian leaders was evidently not inconceivable in the thirties B.C., even if the actual rumour may have been Antonian propaganda circulated against Octavianus: Suetonius, *Divus Augustus*, 63; cf. Charlesworth, M.P., *Classical Quarterly*, xxvii, (1933), 173.

28. Alföldi, A., *Cambridge Ancient History*, xi, 86–9; Glodariu, I., *Dacian Trade with the Hellenistic and Roman World*, British Archaeological Reports Supplementary Series 8, Oxford, 1976. Slave trading may be the background to the large quantities of Roman Republican *denarii* circulating in Dacia from around the middle of the first century B.C.; see Crawford, M.H., *Journal of Roman Studies*, lxvii, (1977), 117–24. For a brief survey of the impressive Dacian citadels in the Orastie mountains, including the Dacian capital Gradistea Muncel (Sarmizegetusa), see Condurachi, E.

and Daicoviciu, C., *The Ancient Civilisation of Romania,* London, 1971, 101–111; see also *Die Daker,* Mainz, 1980, prepared for an exhibition in Cologne in 1980. On the material culture of the Dacians in the wider European context, see Nandris, J., *Festschrift für Richard Pittioni,* Vienna, 1976, 723.

29. Described by Cassius Dio, lxiii, 1.

30. Excavations by M. Kandler within the fortress at Carnuntum yielded no evidence for occupation before the reign of Claudius, yet there is no doubt that a legion was based there, or somewhere in the near vicinity, from the later years of Augustus; Mócsy, A., in Hanson, W.S. and Keppie, L.J.F. (eds.), *Roman Frontier Studies,* Limeskongresses XII, British Archaeological Reports International Series 71, Oxford, 1980, 629. For Oescus, the earliest evidence is a building inscription set up early under Claudius; *L'Année épigraphique,* (1957), 286; though legionary tombstones attest the presence of the legion long before that date: Gerov, B., *Acta Antiqua Hungarica,* xv, (1967), 87.

31. Tacitus, *Annals,* i, 11: 'he had further advised against extending the Empire beyond its present boundaries — whether from motives of fear or jealousy'.

32. Tacitus, *Annals,* i, 9.

33. For the legions in Pannonia, see Mócsy, A., *op. cit.* (see note 10), 42; in Dalmatia; Wilkes, J.J., *Dalmatia,* London, 1969, 95. The second base in Moesia is believed to have been Naissus or Scupi, both places of strategic importance. In the case of Naissus, where units of *auxilia* were stationed in the first century, doubt has been expressed by Petar Petrović: *Inscriptions de la Mésie Supérieure,* Vol. IV, Belgrade, 1979, 30. The finds do not suggest military occupation from the time of Augustus, while traces of a legionary camp in the valley around Niš, the only possible location, are hardly likely to have remained unobserved.

34. *I.L.S.* 2737 (Firmum Picenum): *praef. coh. Noricor. in Pann., praef. ripae Danuvi et civitatium duar. Boior. et Azalior.*

35. *I.L.S.* 9199 (Heliopolis/Baalbek): [*praefecto*] *civitatis Colaphianorum.* Later he was dismissed by Galba from a tribunate in the praetorian guard: Tacitus, *Histories,* i, 20, but was restored to favour under Otho.

36. *C.I.L.* IX 2565 (Bovianum Vetus): *(centurio) leg. XL Cl.* [*p. f. pr*]*aef. civitatis Maeze*[*iorum item Daesit*]*iatium.*

37. *I.L.S.* 1349 (Iulium Carnicum): *praef. civitatium Moesiae et Treballia*[*e.*

38. *Journal of Roman Studies,* xiv, (1924), 188, no. 12 (of the early first century, judged W.M. Ramsay) = *L'Année épigraphique,* (1926), 80: *. . . prae*]*fec. coh. I Tyr., tribun. mil. leg. IV Scythic., praef. equit., praef. rip(ae) Danuvi.* A Claudian date is favoured by Holder, P.A., *The Auxilia from Augustus to Trajan,* British Archaeological Reports Supplementary Volume 70, Oxford, 1980, 76. Dr. David Kennedy (University of Sheffield) writes that, in his view, 'an earlier date cannot be ruled out'.

39. Ovid, *Ex Ponto,* iv, 7. He was a native prince, son of Cottius of the 'Cottian' Alps. *P.I.R.* , J 621. Most have preferred *praefectus orae maritimae,* as Syme, R., *History in Ovid,* Oxford, 1978, 82.

40. *IX Hispana* left Pannonia in 43, probably with A. Plautius, who was appointed to command when legate in Pannonia; see Birley, A.R., *op. cit.* (see note 19), 39. The earliest record of a legion at Novae (*VIII Augusta*) is a tombstone from the time of Claudius or Nero, *L'Année épigraphique,* (1914), 93. Traces of its fortress (a ditch about 70 m. (76.5 yards) west of the later fortress of *I Italica*) may have been identified: see Sarnowski, T., in Fitz, J. (ed.), *Limes. Akten des XI internationalen Limeskongresses,* Budapest, 1977, 411.

41. *Legio VII* remained at Tilurium long enough after A.D. 42 to manufacture bricks stamped with its honorific titles (*Claudia pia fidelis*) conferred in that year; see Wilkes, J.J., *op. cit.* (see note 33), 96. The suggestion that *IV Scythica* had been moved out of Moesia to somewhere in the upper district of Germania,

whence it was transferred to Syria (as in Tacitus, *Annals*, xiii, 35), once propounded by Nesselhauf, H., *Laureae Aquincenses*, ii, (1941), 44, has recently been revised by Dušanić, S., *Germania*, lvi, (1978), 461 and *Zeitschrift für Papyrologie und Epigraphik*, xlvii, (1982), 155. *III Gallica* came to Moesia in 67 or 68. Its likely destination was Oescus, vacated by *V Macedonica* by 62, though Syme, R., *op. cit.* (see note 24), 85, prefers Novae since that was the position most exposed to Sarmatian attack: hence its prominent role in the victory of early 69 (above p. 261).

42. Tacitus, *Histories*, iii, 46 (above p. 262), does not specify the Vitellian units sent to Moesia under Fonteius. *V Alaudae* was at Cremona with its eagle. The only record of it to suggest survival after 70 is the epitaph of a veteran at Scupi in Moesia: Vulić, N., *Spomenik Srpska Academija Nauke*, xcviii, (1941–8), 224, no. 441 (with photograph): *C. Iulius C. f. Volt. Velox domo Luc. Vocon[ti.] vet. leg. V Alaud. mil. ann. XXXV vix. ann. LX, Iulius Valens heres f. c. h. s. e.* The high *stipendia* and absence of household suggest a date in the first half of the first century. Moreover, in the matter of survival, the same argument could be advanced for *IIII Macedonica*, disbanded by Vespasian after disgrace in 70 or more probably, as Birley, E., *Journal of Roman Studies*, xviii, (1928), 56, reformed as *IIII Flavia felix* after a return to allegiance. The legion also had a veteran settled at Scupi, *Živa Antika*, iv, (1954), 196, no. 2 (with photograph): *L. Valeri(u)s L. f. Gal. Galenus, Luc., veteranus leg. IIII Mac. vixit ann. LV militavit ann. XXVIII h.s.e., h.f.c.* See Mócsy, A., *Gesellschaft und Romanisation in der römischen Provinz Moesia Superior*, Budapest, 1970, 68, arguing for *viritim* settlement in the Julio-Claudian period. The notion that *V Alaudae* survived in Moesia after 70 originated as an explanation for the legionaries of Rhineland origin in the casualty lists of the Adamklissi altar (see note 102), where C. Cichorius had

restored the name of Domitian's praetorian prefect Cornelius Fuscus who perished in 86 or 87: see Ritterling, E., *Germania*, ix, (1925), 141. The *semeion* captured then by the Dacians and later retrieved by Trajan, Cassius Dio, lxviii, 9, 3, is perhaps less likely to be a legionary eagle than a praetorian standard *(signum)*; cf. Syme, R., *Cambridge Ancient History*, xi, 171, note 1. But if, as seems very probable, Adamklissi has nothing to do with the wars of Domitian (p. 274), then there are no grounds whatsoever to postulate the survival of *V Alaudae*, in Moesia or anywhere else. There is not a trace of a brick-stamp or any comparable evidence: for the Flavian era *c.* 70–86 that seems hard to credit, but is obviously not decisive against survival.

43. *C.I.L.* XVI 26; 30; 31. As my colleague Dr. Margaret Roxan points out, these diplomas do not, inevitably, reveal the full state of military deployment in Pannonia. Some units appear on an early grant, are missing on a later one, but reappear in a subsequent list. Thus, by way of example, cohorts *II Alpinorum* and *V Lucensium et Callaecorum*, listed in Pannonia in A.D. 60 (*C.I.L.* XVI 4) are missing in A.D. 80 (*C.I.L.* XVI 30). Similarly two cohorts in the list of 84, *I Lepidiana* and *I Lucensium* are missing in A.D. 85 (*C.I.L.* XVI 31) and appear respectively in Moesia Inferior by 99 (*C.I.L.* XVI 45) and Syria by 88 (*C.I.L.* XVI 35). While the specific totals of units may be misleading, an overall increase of the auxiliary garrison of the province in these years is still a valid inference.

44. Once dated to the reign of Tiberius, a new reading has placed it in the governorship of G. Calpetanus Rantius Quirinalis *c.* A.D. 73. The unit is probably *ala I Hispanorum*. See Tóth, E. and Vékony, G., *Acta Archaeologica Hungarica*, xxii, (1970), 133 and Mócsy, A., *op. cit.* (see note 10), 80.

45. *C.I.L.* III 111 94–7 (three records of building by *XV Apollinaris*).

46. Gabler, D. and Lőrincz, B., 'Some

remarks on the history of the Danubian Limes of the first and second centuries A.D.'. *Archaeologiai Értesitö*, civ, (1977), 105 (in Hungarian with English summary).

47. *Starinar*, xviii, (1967), 22 = Roxan, M.M., *Roman Military Diplomas 1954–77*, London, 1978, no. 2, issued in A.D. 75 to a *pedes* from Antioch serving in *coh. I Raetorum,* found at Taliata; *C.I.L.* XVI 22 (A.D. 78) issued to a Cilician from Aeg(is) in *coh. I Cilicum* (on which see now Scorpan, C., *Journal of Roman Studies,* lxxi, (1981), 98) from Mihailovgrad. For an analysis of the two lists see Mirković, M., *Epigraphische Studien,* v, (1968), 177. At the moment it seems that up to eight *alae* and twenty cohorts may have been deployed in Moesia at different times before A.D. 85.

48. *C.I.L.* XVI 28 (20 Sept. 82) from Debelec south of Trnovo. R. Syme observes: 'Signs of unrest can, however, be detected', *Cambridge Ancient History,* xi, 169.

49. *C.I.L.* III 12347 (Hurlec), an early tombstone naming *eq. alae Au*[. . ., presumably the original garrison which gave the fort its name. *L'Année épigraphique*, (1967), 425 (Leskovec) records a serving member of *ala (I Claudia Gallorum) Capitoniana,* though a veteran of the same unit is recorded at Hurlec, *L'Année épigraphique,* (1912), 187. The tombstone of a *duplicarius* of an *ala Pansiana,* who may have served thirty-six years, at Oescus, *L'Année épigraphique,* (1960), 127, is early first-century and does not indicate an auxiliary presence under the Flavians. At Nikopol there is a serving *decurio* of the *ala Scubulorum,* Gerov, B., *op. cit.* (see note 30), 94, fig. 4, and an *eques* of the *ala Bosporanorum, L'Année épigraphique,* (1925), 70. Both are of Julio-Claudian date.

50. *L'Année épigraphique,* (1957), 307 (Orehovo), damaged and in two fragments. The second may be read: [*le*]*g. Aug.* p[*r.*] *pr. coh.* [*Mattiacorum ? et*

Gall]*orum qu(i)bus pra*[*esunt* . . .] *e*[*t*] *Q. Varius Secundus.*

51. For example Ratiaria (Arćar) and Sexaginta Prista (Ruse), both of which may have been bases for the fleet in the first century (see note 57 and 58).

52. Thus Patsch, C., *Der Kampf um den Donauraum unter Domitian und Trajan,* Beiträge zur Volkerkunde von Sudosteuropa V/2, Sitzungs-berichte der Akademie Wien, 217, 1, Vienna, 1937, 3, and note 3. Andrew Poulter, who has inspected the site and its finds, confirms that no evidence for an occupation in the first century has come to light.

53. Some scholars appear still to assume a deployment of *auxilia* along the Danube in the Dobrudja but no evidence is produced. I am grateful to Andrew Poulter for information that, except for Noviodunum, no site on the Danube bank has yielded material evidence to suggest a military occupation before the reign of Trajan. The suggestion once current (e.g. *Cambridge Ancient History,* ix, 169) that the larger of the two earth ramparts across the southern Dobrudja was a Domitianic defence constructed *c.* 85–6 must now be discarded. Though the relative chronology of the three ramparts (two of earth, one of stone) worked out by Tocilescu, G.G., *Fouilles et Recherches Archéologiques en Roumanie,* Bucharest, 1900, 143, still holds good, recent investigations have revealed that they belong to a much later period, though they do have an undoubted Roman character. The large earth rampart with *castella* appears to be ninth-century, as the later stone barrier, also with *castella,* belongs to the tenth. Most significant is that both face north, as also does the earliest of the three, the small earth rampart which has a ditch on the north side. Thus a Roman date is ruled out for all three. For recent research see Diaconu, P., *Peuce,* v, (1972), 375; Panaitescu, A., *Pontica,* xi, (1978), 241. The notion that Domitian in any sense 'abandoned' the Dobrudja was refuted by Pippidi, D.M.,

Hommages Grenier, Brussels, 1962, 1265, publishing the base of a statue to Domitian from Istros, *L'Année épigraphique,* (1964), 199a–b. Finally some suspicion must attach to the manuscript record (1868) of a dedicaton to Titus from Aegyssus (Tulcea): *imp. T. Caes. / pontif. Max. trib. pot. / p. p.,* (*C.I.L.* III 6221). The copyist read line 3 as *PF* but the latest publication in Doruţiu — Boila, Em. (ed.), *Inscriptiones Scythiae Minoris,* Bucharest, 1980, V, no. 286 retains *p(atri) p(atriae),* a title never borne by Titus, though it was taken by Vespasian.

54. Ships on the river Save played a major role in Octavianus' operations in 35 B.C., Appian, *Illyrike,* 23 and Cassius Dio, xlix, 36, 1. On the Danube in A.D. 50, Tacitus, *Annals,* xii, 30.

55. On the two fleets in general see Starr, C.G., *Roman Imperial Navy,* New York, 1941 (reprinted 1960), 129 and 138. Cuntz, O., (ed.), *Itineraria Antonini Augusti et Burdigalense,* Leipzig, 1929, 131.6: *Tauruno classis iii Singiduno castra.* Bricks manufactured at Taurunum by *cl(assis) Fl(avia) P(annonia),* Szilagyi, J., *Inscriptiones Tegularum Pannonicarum,* Dissertationes Pannonicae, 2 series, 1, Budapest, 1933, plate XXII, no. 1. Similarly bricks from Noviodunum stamped *cl(assis) F(lavia) M(oesica),* *Inscriptiones Scythiae Minoris,* (see note 53), V, no. 283.

56. The bilingual *cursus* at Ephesus of M. Arruntius M. f. Ter. Claudianus, an equestrian officer active under Domitian, registers: *praefectus classis Moesiacae et ripae Danuvi,* Knibbe, D., *Jahrbuch des Österreichischen Archäologischen Instituts,* xlix, (1968–71), Bb. 6, no. 1, with fig. 4 = *L'Année épigraphique,* (1972), 572. Discussed by Doruţiu-Boila, Em., *Studien zu den Militärgrenzen Roms,* ii, Cologne/Bonn, 1977, 289.

57. The name is first recorded on a fragmentary building record by *cives Roman[i consistentes] Sexaginta Pri[st(is),* under the legate M. Laberius Maximus

c. A.D. 101–2, Velkov, V., *Epigraphica,* xxvii, (1965), 90 = *L'Année épigraphique,* (1966), 356. *Pristis* was a light, oared vessel, from the name of a swordfish; see *Oxford Latin Dictionary,* 1460. Immediately south-west of the fort, at the mouth of the river Lom, the footings of long rectangular buildings were interpreted as the remains of dry-docks by Škorpil, K., *Opis na starinite po techenieto na reka Rousenski Lom,* Sofia, 1914 (I owe this reference to Andrew Poulter).

58. Ratiarius (from *ratis*) means ferryman, or a boatman connected with rafts or flat bottomed boats, *C.I.L.* XII 2331; VIII 24512; also *C.I.L.* XIII 2035: *negotiator artis ratiariae,* and there seems no grounds for rejecting this origin in favour of a Celtic or Thracian root, Velkov, V., *Eirene,* v, (1966), 157. An auxiliary cavalry regiment may have been based there at some period; Hošek, R. and Velkov, V., *Listy Filologické,* vi, (*Eunomia,* ii, 1, 1958), 32; an *eques* in an *ala Gal(l)ica,* perhaps of the Julio-Claudian period.

59. *Flavia* is first recorded for the Moesian fleet on a diploma of 92 (*C.I.L.* XVI 37). Neither that, nor the Pannonian fleet is officially recorded before the Flavian era. Starr, C.G., *op. cit.* (see note 55), 132, suggests that the titles were conferred during the reorganization under Rubrius Gallus, matching *praetoria* for the Italian fleets and *Augusta* for the German and Egyptian fleets, which, in none of these cases, denoted foundation or even reorganization.

60. The cataracts and whirlpools of the Danube gorge were already notorious in Augustan and Tiberian times, Strabo, vii, 3, 13. The inscriptions on the rock face relating to the towpath through the upper and lower gorges are assembled and edited in Sašel, A., and Sašel, J., (eds.), *Inscriptiones Latinae quae in Iugoslavia inter annos MCMXL et MCMLX repertae et editae sunt,* Situla 5, Ljubljana, 1963, 31. In the upper gorge the first record of construction is two

similar texts dated A.D. 33/4, *ibid.,* nos. 57 and 60. A repair in the same sector is attested early under Claudius, *ibid.,* no. 56. The second record of repair is two similar texts of A.D. 93, *ibid.,* 55 and 58. The towpath through the lower gorge may not have been completed until the reign of Trajan (see note 90).

61. Tacitus, *Histories,* iii, 5.

62. On the date see Alföldi, G., *Fasti Hispanienses,* Wiesbaden, 1969, 17.

63. *I.L.S.* 986 (see above p. 260).

64. The Danubian wars of Domitian, the order of events, military dispositions, strategy and topography, have attracted the industry and tempted the ingenuity of many scholars, though it is surprising that the two modern reconstructions still in general use were written nearly half a century ago: Syme, R., *Cambridge Ancient History,* xi, (1936), 168–78 and the longer study by Patsch, C., *op. cit.* (see note 52), 3–52. Both were written independently. Among more recent works there is a great deal of value in Mócsy, A., *op. cit.* (see note 15), 82. The principal ancient sources are the *Epitomes* of Cassius Dio, lxvii, 5–7; cf. lxviii, 9, 3, reconstructed in the edition of U.P. Boissevain, Berlin, 1898–1931, currently available in vol. viii of the Loeb edition. Otherwise brief but valuable summaries are to be found in Jordanes, *Getica,* 76; Suetonius, *Domitian,* 6; Tacitus, *Agricola,* 41; Orosius, vii, 10, 3–4 (following Tacitus); Eutropius, vii, 23, 4. Several allusions to the wars are to be found in the contemporary poets, Martial and Statius; for interpretations of these Gsell, S., *Essai sur le règne de l'empereur Domitien,* Paris, 1894, remains indispensable. The record of the emperor's salutation as *imperator* from the coins issued during this period is important for reconstruction of chronology; see now Buttrey, T.V., *Documentary evidence for the evidence of the Flavian titulature,* Beiträge zur klassischen Philologie 112, Meisenheim am Glan, 1980, 30–1 and 38. An order of events was set out

by Stein, E., *Die Legaten von Moesien,* Dissertationes Pannonicae, 1 ser., fasc. 11, Budapest, 1940, 38; discussed by Syme, R., *Journal of Roman Studies,* xxxv, (1945), 110, who places the disaster of Oppius in 85, taking account of Domitian imp. ix, x and xi in the autumn and winter of 85–6, rather than in 86 as Stein. These events and their date have more recently come under scrutiny by Alföldy, G. and Halfmann, H., *Chiron,* iii, (1973), 356 in a study of the career of M. Cornelius Nigrinus Curiatius Maternus. It is suggested that he, and not Oppius Sabinus may have been the last legate of undivided Moesia, and that the defeat of the latter must be placed early in 85. The matter also relates to the chronology of Agricola in Britain, on which see now Birley, A.R., *op. cit.* (see note 19), 79.

65. A certain Diurpaneus (or Dorpaneus) is credited with the victory over Oppius, Jordanes, *Getica,* 76, and also with that over Fuscus, *idem,* 78; cf. Orosius vii, 10, 4 and *P.I.R.,* D 110, though Decebalus is generally given the credit, *P.I.R.,* D 19. It is not certain that the Duras who abdicated in favour of Decebalus, because the latter was more skilled in warfare, (Cassius Dio, lxvii, 6, 1), is to be identified with Diurpaneus, as suggested by Patsch, *op. cit.* (see note 52), 5 with note 3, though Stein, *P.I.R.,* D 110, suggested that Diurpaneus may have been the ruler of only part of Dacia, but Duras and Decebalus of the whole state.

66. Suggested by Ritterling, E., in *Realencyclopädie,* s.v. Legio 1444 and seemingly confirmed by auxiliary units recorded in Pannonia in 85 and 93 and 100 in Moesia Superior; see Syme, R., *Danubian Papers,* (see note 12), 206.

67. Legionary movements have been examined in detail by Syme, R., *Laureae Aquincenses,* i, (1938), 267 = *Danubian Papers,* (see note 12), 84 with addendum 104, considering, among other matters, the modifications suggested in a similar study by Alföldy, G., *Acta Archaeologica*

Hungarica, xi, (1959), 113. The first arrivals were probably *IIII Flavia felix* from Dalmatia (Burnum) and, though this is less certain, *II Adiutrix* from Britain. The latter was stationed in the Sirmium area before moving to Aquincum, perhaps *c.* 89 (see note 83). It now emerges that *IIII Flavia* was not at Aquincum during this period: the evidence from there relates to its various sojourns in the second and third centuries, Lörincz, B., *Acta Archaeologica Hungarica,* xxx, (1978), 299.

68.   For his earlier career and the sources for the disaster see *P.I.R.,* C 1365 and Syme, R., *American Journal of Philology,* lviii, (1937), 7 = *Danubian Papers,* (see note 12), 73 and 82. That scholar still accepts the suggestion that the casualties on the altar at Adamklissi may have been members of *V Alaudae* who perished with Fuscus: that is unlikley (see note 42). It is worth noting that remains of ancient timber piles in the bed of the Danube linking stone abutments between Vadin and Orlea, a little to the west of Oescus, have been suggested as the supports for the bridge of boats by which Fuscus' expedition is said to have crossed the river. See Tudor, D., *Collections Latomus,* xx, (1961), 501–9 and *Les ponts romaines du Bas-Danube,* Biblioteca Historica Romaniae, 51, Bucharest, 1974, 19–29, citing the testimony of Jordanes, *Getica,* 77. Leaving aside the improbability of so massive a construction for such an occasion, the association rests on the believe that Fuscus crossed the Danube somewhere near Oescus to advance up the Alutus (Olt) and meet his end in the Red Tower Pass. That is far from certain; an approach from the west across the Banat is to be preferred.

69.   *I.L.S.* 1005 (Audautonia, Pannonia) with *L'Année épigraphique,* (1946), 205 (= *C.I.L.* XI 571). He was still legate of Pannonia on 5 September 85 (*C.I.L.* XVI 31). The statue-base from Andautonia, *leg. pro pr. provinc. Delmatiae item provinc. Pannoniae item Moesiae superioris*

donato [*ab imp. Domitiano Aug. Germanico*] *bello Dacico coronis iiii,* etc. implies that the awards were made for his tenure of Moesia, an appropriate occasion for the statue in a Pannonian city of which he had become *patronus.*

70.   Juvenal, *Satires,* iv, 111–2. Among those attending the imperial council summoned to consider the turbot came Fuscus 'who dreamed of battle in his marbled villa, but whose intestines were destined a feast for Dacian vultures'; see also Martial, *Epigrams,* vi, 76.

71.   Cassius Dio, lxvii, 10, 1–3. Tapae was also the site of an indecisive battle during Trajan's first Dacian war, lxviii, 8, 1–12. It is specified as the western gateway to inner Dacia by Jordanes, *Getica,* 74; and there is little doubt that it can be identified with the pass which leads from the valley of the Bistrica, a tributary of the Tibiscus (Timiş), into south-west Transylvania. It has been known as the Transylvanian Iron Gates since the time of the Turkish wars. To reach Tapae the route of Julianus must have been similar to that of Trajan in 101, a crossing of the river in the area of Viminacium and then across the Banat to follow the Timiş as far as Caranşebeş: Patsch, C., *op. cit.* (see note 52), 29.

72.   Its suppression, by A. Bucius Lappius Maximus (*P.I.R.,* L 84), was already being celebrated at Rome by the Arval brethren on 25 January. Domitian had left the city by the 12th. See Syme, R., *Cambridge Ancient History,* xi, 172–2, citing the reconstruction of events by Ritterling, E., *Westdeutsche Zeitschrift,* xii, (1893), 218.

73.   Mócsy, A., *op. cit.* (see note 10), 83.

74.   Almost certainly the rebellious *XXI Rapax* from Mogontiacum, which disappears from the record around this time. Also perhaps *I Adiutrix,* first attested in the Danube lands in the Suebic war of Nerva in 97 (*I.L.S.* 2720), that is if it had not already been moved across from Germany after the defeat of Oppius Sabinus or Cornelius Fuscus. Before it occupied the new base at

Brigetio, in 97 it now appears (see note 83) *I Adiutrix* was based somewhere in the area of Sirmium, whence comes a brick-stamp of early date, Milošević, A., *Sirmium*, vol. i, Belgrade, 1971, 96 no. 2, and a dedication by a serving soldier which may date to this period, Mirković, M., *Sirmium*, vol. i, 62, no. 12.

75. Cassius Dio, lxvii, 7, 2–4; cf. Martial, *Epigrams*, v, 3. Syme, R., *Cambridge Ancient History*, xi, 176: 'On both sides expediency prevailed and honour was saved.'

76. Cassius Dio, lxvii, 7, 1.

77. Suetonius, *Domitian*, 6: *duplex triumphus* over Chatti and Dacians. The date is furnished by Eusebius, *Chronicle* (see note 15), 191, between 1 October 89 and 30 September 90. For the occasion were issued coins of Domitian GERMANICVS COS XIIII with the emperor in a quadriga holding laurel and sceptre, with defeated barbarians, etc., *B.M.C.*, ii, (1930), p. 329 no. 144. The record in Cassius Dio, lxvii, 7, 3–8, 4, is hostile, engrossed with excesses in Rome.

78. Suetonius, *Domitian*, 6: 'Some expeditions he made by design, others through force of circumstance . . . in one of the latter against the Sarmatians a legion along with its legate was wiped out;' cf. Eutropius, vii, 23. That the disaster took place in Pannonia rather than in 'Sarmatia' may be inferred from Tacitus, *Agricola*, 41: 'So many armies lost in Moesia, Dacia, Germania and Pannonia . . .'. The sojourn of eight months in Pannonia is indicated by Martial, *Epigrams*, ix, 31; cf. viii, 2; 8. Since the time of Borghesi, *Oeuvres*, iv, 217, most scholars have accepted that the legion involved was *XXI Rapax*.

79. Cassius Dio, lxvii, 5, 2. The warm reception at Rome accorded around this time to Masyas king of the Semnones and the priestess Ganna is hardly likely to be unconnected with affairs in Pannonia. After receiving honours from Domitian they returned home, lxvii, 5, 3.

80. *I.L.S.* 9200 (Heliopolis/Baalbek): 'In the war with Marcomanni, Quadi and Sarmatians, against whom he made an expedition through the realm of Decebalus, king of the Dacians, he was awarded the mural crown, two spears and two standards.' In Pannonia he was appointed provincial procurator of Pannonia and Dalmatia. For his remarkable career see Dobson, B., *Die Primipilares*, Bonn, 1978, 216.

81. Suetonius, *Domitian*, 6; Eutropius, vii, 23. His return to Rome was marked by a temple to Fortuna Redux and the erection of a triumphal arch, Martial, *Epigrams*, viii, 65. Domitian had been saluted *imp(erator) xxii* at the beginning of his visit. Neither the earlier *Dacicus* nor the new *Sarmaticus* employed by the poets was officially proclaimed, *Realencyclopädie*,, VI A 2572; 2576. In the records of military decorations awarded the war is titled *Bellum Germanicum* (or *Suebicum) et Sarmaticum* with, in addition to that of Velius Rufus (see note 80), an instance of *Bellum Marcomannicum*, *L'Année épigraphique*, (1952), 99 (Carthage). The relevant inscriptions are reproduced in full by Dobó, A., *Inscriptiones extra fines Pannoniae Daciaeque repertae ad res earundem provinciarum pertinentes*, fourth edition, Budapest, 1975, 94.

82. In October 97. Pliny, *Panegyricus*, 8, 2: 'the laurel was borne from Pannonia, an action of the gods to adorn the emergence of the unconquered emperor with the sign of victory' and 16, 1: 'The laurel dedicated in the Capitol on the day of your adoption.' One legion certainly involved was *I Adiutrix* from the evidence of decorations then conferred, *I.L.S.* 2720, *L'Année épigraphique*, (1923), 28, when it may have occupied the new base at Brigetio, if indeed it had not already been there since *c.* 92. Lörincz, B., *op. cit.* (see note 67).

83. For some period under Domitian Vindobona was the base of a cavalry unit, the *ala I F(lavia) D(omitiana) Britannica*. It is not certain when *XIII*

Gemina left Poetovio (which became a Trajanic colony) before *c*. 103, *C.I.L.* III 4566 with 14359/32 cf. Bechert, T., *Epigraphische Studien*, viii, (1969), 47, an imposing inscription with letters 20 cm. (8 in.) high, which from its findspot may have been set in the *principia*. No legion appears on the surviving fragments: A. Neumann held that *XIII* remained at Vindobona until *c*. 17, *Realencyclopädie*, IX A (1961) 67; but that is contradicted by *L'Année épigraphique*, (1934), 2. It was replaced there by *XIIII Gemina Martia victrix* from Ad Flexum, probably in 101. The origin and construction of Brigetio is complicated by bricks stamped by vexillations from three Pannonian Legions. The most recent study, by Lörincz, B., *op. cit.* (see note 67), places *I Adiutrix* in garrison 97–101, with a construction party from *XIII Gemina*, *XV Apollinaris* and *XIIII Gemina*, which was replaced by *XI Claudia* for the period 101–5, with a construction party from *XIIII Gemina* and *XV Apollinaris*, then *XXX Ulpia victrix*. As with Vindobona, it is possible that Brigetio was first occupied in the aftermath of Domitian's war with the Suebic Germans. As already noted above, it is now suggested that *II Adiutrix* was at Aquincum from *c*. 89 and that the records of *IIII Flavia* there do not relate to this period but the later second century (see note 67). *Leg. XIIII Gemina* is believed to have been brought to Pannonia following the destruction of *XXI Rapax c*. 92 by the Sarmatian Jazyges (see note 74). Its whereabouts before *c*. 97 when it may have moved to Ad Flexum (Magyaróvár) east of Carnuntum on the 'German front', whence it contributed a party for the construction of Brigetio (see above): Barkócsi, L. and Mócsy, A. (eds.), *Römische Inschriften Ungarns*, Budapest/ Amsterdam, 1972, nos. 235–6; later it moved to Vindobona. From *c*. 92–7 it may have been based somewhere on the 'Sarmatian front', perhaps in what was then Moesia Superior between the Save

and Drave. Possible in the vicinity of Mursa: there is a stamped brick at Petrievci, *C.I.L.* III 3755; cf. Syme, R., *Danubian Papers* (see note 12), 88.

84. Flavian forts against the Germans include a) in Noricum, cf. Alföldy, G., *Noricum,* London, 1974, 146: Boiodurum (Passau-Innstadt), Lentia (Linz), Lauriacum (Enns-Lorch), Ardagger Markt (?), Arelape (Pöchlarn); then a concentration of forts in the north-east opposite the plain of Krems where Noricum was most exposed to attack from the north, Faviana (Mautern), Augustiana (Traismauer), Zwentendorf, Commagena (Tulln) and Astura (Zeiselmauer); b) in Pannonia, cf. Mócsy, A., *op. cit.* (see note 10), 88 and Gabler, D. and Lörincz, B., *op. cit.* (see note 46): Cannabiaca (Klosterneuburg, Ad Flexum (Magyaróvár), Arrabona (Györ) and Brigetio. On the 'Sarmatian front' in Pannonia were Aquincum, Albertfalva, Vetus Salina (Adony), Lussonium (Dunakömlöd), Ad Militare (Kisköszeg-Batina), Teutoburgium (Dalj) and Malata (Banoštor).

85. There is not sufficient evidence to permit reasonable conjecture. If *II Adiutrix* moved from the Sirmium area to Aquincum in *c*. 89 (see note 83), then legions in Moesia Superior may have been *XIIII Gemina* (?Mursa), *VII Claudia* (Viminacium) and *IIII Flavia* (whose brick-stamps with the early form LEG IIII F F are known from Viminacium, *Jahreshefte des Österreichischen Archäologischen Instituts*, xv, (1913) Bb. 213). The record of *lapidarii* from *IIII Flavia* and *VII Claudia* (see note 90) working on the towpath through the Danube lower gorge, perhaps early under Trajan, seems to indicate that the former was in Moesia Superior at the end of the first century. There remains the problem of *I Adiutrix*, which may have been for some time in the Sirmium area (see note 74). As regards the lower province *V Macedonica* was at Oescus and *I Italica* at Novae but there may have been more. We simply cannot

deduce the extent to which Domitian felt able to move legions away from the 'Dacian front' from a confidence in the settlement made with Decebalus in 89; see Syme, R., *Danubian Papers* (see note 12), 89, note 22.

86. No evidence has yet been forthcoming to suggest the construction of auxiliary bases along the river between Vespasian (see notes 47 ff.) and the reign of Trajan (see note 93).

87. Cassius Dio, lxviii, 6, 1–2.

88. Roxan, M., *op. cit.* (see note 47), no. 6 (from Viminacium) issued 12 July 96 to a Bessus in the *coh. VI Thracum; C.I.L.* XVI 46 (from Siscia) issued 8 May 100 to a Cilician in *coh. I Antiochensium.*

89. *C.I.L.* XVI 44 (from near Durostorum) issued to M. Antonius M. f. Rufus from Abrittus in Moesia Inferior, serving in *coh. II Gallorum; C.I.L.* XVI 45 (near Philippopolis/Plovdiv) issued to Meticus son of Sola, a Thracian (Bessus) in *ala I Asturum.* Both dated 14 Aug. 99. In addition to *auxilia* the latter lists also sailors *(classici)*, presumably from the Moesian fleet.

90. The famous *Tabula Traiana* on the south face of the lower gorge near Tekija: Šašel, A. and Šašel, J. (eds.), *op. cit.* (see note 60), no. 63. It remains uncertain whether or not this was the original construction or a repair of the towpath through the gorge. The reading by E. Swoboda of *r]ę[fecit*, that is 'restored', in the last line would, if correct, prove that it was not. The record of the canal; Šašel, J., *Journal of Roman Studies,* lxiii, (1973), 80, leaves no doubt that this was a new construction: . . . *ob periculum cataractarum derivato flumine tutam Danuvi navigationem decit.* It must remain doubtful if the towpath through the lower gorge, depicted with the *Tabula* on the Column of Trajan, Rossi, L., *Antiq. Journ.,* xlviii, (1968) 41, existed in any form before *c.* A.D. 100. While there are no fewer than five records of its construction in the upper gorge (see note 60), only the *Tabula* is known from the lower. Connected with the latter may

be the dedication by stonecutters *(lapidarii)* from *IIII Flavia* and *VII Claudia* to their patron god Hercules when they were occupied 'in the construction of the brackets' — *at ancones fac[ien]dos,* Gabričević, M., *Arheološki Vestnik,* xxiii, (1972), 408 with the reading of J. Šašel = *L'Année épigraphique,* (1973), 473, which also has implications for the whereabouts of *IIII Flavia* (see note 85).

91. For reconstructions of Trajan's Dacian wars, Patsch, C., *op. cit.* (see note 52), 52 and Longden, R.P., *Cambridge Ancient History,* xi, 223. The reliefs of Trajan's column are conveniently, though in most cases far from clearly, illustrated by Rossi, L., *Trajan's Column and the Dacian Wars,* London, 1971; see now Gauer, W., *Untersuchungen zur Trajanssäule,* Monumenta Artis Romanae, xiii, Berlin 1977. Trajan's own comment *Inde Berzobim, deinde Aizi processimus* is preserved in the *Institutiones Gramaticae,* vi, 13, of the sixth-century grammarian Priscianus, from Caesarea (Cherchel) in Mauretania. Scene XXXI (Cichorius) cf. Rossi, *op. cit.,* 147 nos. 26–7, has been interpreted to represent Sarmatian mailed cavalry attacking a Roman fort on the bank of the Danube(see Pl. II). The reasoned protest of Richmond, I.A., *Papers of the British School at Rome,* xiii, (1935), 1, against attempts to construct an historical narrative from the reliefs has attracted few adherents. Theme and composition dictated the selection and juxtaposition of the scenes. It remains a startling incongruity that the monumental inscription on the base of the Column, *I.L.S.* 294, relates not to the Dacian wars but to the scale of excavation undertaken to prepare the site of the imperial forum.

92. Cassius Dio, lxviii, 9, 5–7.

93. *Inscriptiones Scythiae Minoris,* (see note 53), v, (1980), no. 94 (Hîrsova); Tocilescu, Gr. *Fouilles et Recherches* (see note 53), 215, no. 45, *C.I.L.* III 14451; cf. Stoian, I., *Tomitana,* Bucharest,

1962, 123, no. 23 (Tomis), Radulescu, A. and Barbulescu, M., *Dacia,* xxv, (1981), 353. The milestone, erected by *coh. IIII Gallorum* is by far the earliest from the Dobrudja. I owe to Andrew Poulter the suggestion (in a forthcoming paper) that the first stationing of legions at Durostorum and Troesmis, and of *auxilia* at river crossings such as Capidava, was a necessary accompaniment to the occupation of northern Walachia in the years 101–3.

94. Cassius Dio, lxviii, 10, 3–4.

95. Now that L. Neratius Priscus (cos. 97) appears to have succeeded Glitius Agricola, attested in November 102, as governor of undivided Pannonia, *L'Année épigraphique,* (1978), 287, the division can be linked with the organization of Dacia in 106, as Syme, R., *Danubian Papers* (see note 12), 106, with Hadrian the first governor of Inferior in 106–7.

96. S.H.A. *vita Hadriani,* iii, 9; Cassius Dio, lxviii, 10, 3; Eusebius, *Chronicle* (see note 15), 194; Eutropius, viii, 3, 1. Mócsy, A., *op. cit.* (see note 10), 95, suggests that Oltenia was the territory demanded back by the Jazyges after the Dacian war (see note 94), and that in place of this they were permitted to occupy the lands east of the Tisza towards Dacia. A Sarmatian expansion in this area appears to be indicated in the archaeological finds, *Acta Archaeologia Hungarica,* iv, (1954), 124.

97. It has been argued that the Roman occupation of Wallachia indicated by the forts along the south fringes of the Carpathians was a consequence of the army in Moesia Inferior defeating the Dacian and Sarmatian counter attack in the first Dacian war, deduced from the reliefs of Trajan's column (see note 91). On these forts, which have earth and timber ramparts only and which were given up at the end of Trajan's reign, see now the useful survey of Cătăniciu, I.B., *Evolution of the Defensive Works in Roman Dacia,* British Archaeological Reports Supplementary Series 116,

Oxford, 1981, 9.

98. Cassius Dio, lxviii, 14, 1. The famous bridge, constructed evidently in *c.* 103–4; cf. Tudor, D., *op. cit.* (see note 68), has recently been examined on the south (Serbian) bank of the river; Garašanin, M. and Vasić, M., 'Le pont de Trajan et le castellum pontes', in Kondić, V. (ed.), *Cahiers des Portes de Fer,* i, Belgrade, 1980, 25.

99. Now published in Fink, R.O., *Roman Military Records on Papyrus,* American Philological Society, Monograph 26, Case Western Reserve University, 1971, 217, no. 63. See the observations of Syme, R., *Danubian Papers* (see note 12), 122, arguing for a date *c.* 105, which now appears to have been confirmed by the record of L. Fabius Justus published by Radulescu A. and Barbulescu, M., *op. cit.* (see note 93), 356 with photograph.

100. Piroboridava is located by Ptolemy, iii, 10, 8, somewhere north of the Danube in the vicinity of the Siret (Hierasus). The identification with Poiana on the left (east) bank of that river, made by Pârvan after excavation of the site, remains uncertain: Polaschek, E., *Realencyclopädie,* XX, 1723. Objects of Roman origin are reported from there, including coins, but they date before the end of the first century; see Babeş, M., *Dacia,* xix, (1975), 136. There is no trace of a fort.

101. This famous monument, first described by the Prussian von Moltke in 1837, and accorded detailed study from the end of the last century, has generated furious controversy. The principal modern study is Florescu, F.B., *Monumentul de la Adamklissi,* second edition, Bucharest, 1961. A fragment, evidently from a duplicate version of the dedication on the six-sided base of the trophy, has been published by Doruţiu-Boila, Em., *Studi Clasice,* vii, (1965), 209; cf. Gostar, N., *Collections Latomus,* xxviii, (1969) 120. This seems to dispose once and for all of the notion that the Trajanic inscription had been added to the

monument some considerable time after its original construction. On the sculptures, metopes and their import see Richmond, I.A., *Papers of the British School at Rome*, xxii, (1967), 29.

102. Explored and described by Tocilescu, Gr., *op. cit.* (see note 53), 63 who bestowed on it the label 'mausoleum'. The inscriptions, *I.L.S.* 9107, along with some recently identified additional fragments, have been published by Doruţiu-Boila, Em., *Dacia*, v, (1961), 345 (in English). For the arguments against the suggestion that Cornelius Fuscus may be named at the head of the list, see Syme, R., *Danubian Papers* (see note 12), 73, and note 42 above against the connection with *V Alaudae*.

103. The architectural ornament of *tropaeum* and altar was first accorded detailed study by Furtwängler, A., *Sitzungsberichte der bayerischen historischen Akademie der Wissenschaften*, 1897, 2, 247 and *Abhandlungen der Klassischen bayerischen Akademie der Wissenschaften*, xxii, 3, (1903), 455, who indicated the differences and inferred that the *tropaeum* was the earlier of the two, in fact a commemoration of M. Licinius Crassus Frugi in 29–8 B.C. (see above p. 258). The circular monument was explored by Tocilescu, Gr., *op. cit.* (see note 53), 89 with plan p. 88, fig. 53. Only systematic investigation in the area of all three monuments is likely to show how they were interrelated, if they ever were.

104. The turf and timber legionary base identified at Reşiţa has produced stamped bricks of LEG. III F. F., see Protase, D., *Acta Musei Napocensis*, iv, (1967), 47 and *Acta of the Fifth international Congress of Greek and Latin Epigraphy, Cambridge 1967*, Oxford, 1971, 337. The site is the Berzobis named in the fragment of Trajan's Commentaries (see note 91), also on the Peutinger Map and by the Anonymous of Ravenna, *Geography*, iv, 14. The dates of its occupation by *IIII Flavia*, hitherto assumed to have been *c.*

101–106, has now been complicated by the discovery of remains which suggest that the same legion may also have occupied a base on the site of the later *colonia Ulpia Traiana Sarmizegetusa* (Haţeg) founded *c.* 108; see Alicu, D., *Potaissa*, (1980), 23. This has led to the suggestion that *IIII Flavia* was the garrison left in Dacia after the first war, Cassius Dio, lxviii, 9, 7. The name of the legion is inscribed on blocks of dressed masonry recovered from the slopes of Dacian Sarmizegetusa (Gradistea Muncel), Glodariu, I., *Acta Musei Napocensis*, ii, (1965), 128, *Die Daker* (see note 28), 209 no. 417. Thus *IIII Flavia* was on the site of the later *colonia c.* 101–108, then south to Berzobis until to *c.* 117/8. *Leg. XIII Gemina* was presumably at Apulum from *c.* 106.

105. *XI Claudia* is first attested at Durostorum under the legate Pompeius Falco, *L'Année épigraphique*, (1936), 14, in 116/7, *C.I.L.* 7537 (Tomis); 12740 (Tropaeum Traiani). On his career see now Birley, A.R., *op. cit.* (see note 19) 95. The appearance of its stamp on bricks from forts occupied until the end of the reign of Trajan north of the lower Danube would indicate that the legion was in Moesia Inferior by *c.* 105 at the latest, though not necessarily at Durostorum. For a detailed catalogue of its stamped products see Culica, V., *Dacia*, xxii, (1978), 225. A few with the early form LEG XI C P F match those produced in Pannonia and are found in Oescus and in some of the forts north of the Danube, Drajna de sus, Tîrgşor. Since they appear not to have been produced by the *figlina* at Durostorum perhaps the legion was for a time at Oescus, between the departure of *V Macedonica* and the settlement of the *colonia* under Trajan. The first record of *V Macedonica* at Troesmis is a list of legionaries recruited in 108 and 109 and discharged in 134, *C.I.L.* III 6178 = *Inscriptiones Scythiae Minoris* (see note 53), V no. 137, among whom two have

names (Aponius, Fonteius) which recall those of earlier governors; see Syme, R., *Danubian Papers,* (see note 12), 211.

106. S.H.A., *vita Hadriani, vi, 6.*

107. His death and funeral are described in the lengthy record of his career at Pergamum, Habicht, Chr., *Altertümer v. Pergamon,* viii, 3 (1969), 21; cf. *P.I.R.,* J. 508.

108. Syme, R., *Journal of Roman Studies,* lii, (1962), 87 = *Roman Papers* ii, Oxford, 1979, 543. Two inscriptions record P. Aelius Rasparaganus, king of the Roxolani, along with his son P. Aelius Peregrinus, his wife and household, dwelling on a small island (degli Olivi) in the harbour of Pola (Pula) in Istria, *C.I.L.* V 32–3 = *Inscriptiones Italiae,* Rome, 1936, X, 1 nos. 153–4 cf. *Jahreshefte des Österreichischen Archäologischen Instituts,* iv, (1901), Bb. 203. The Hadrianic citizenship invites identification with the unnamed ruler of the Roxolani who made peace with Hadrian. The location suggests a not uncomfortable exile, perhaps following an expulsion by his aggrieved subjects.

109. The evidence for the tripartite division of Dacia has only recently accrued: Roxan, M.M. *op. cit.* (see note 47), no. 17, a diploma issued for Dacia Superior on 29 June 120; no. 21, issued on 10 August 123 for Dacia Porolissensis to auxiliaries who had been discharged under Turbo, and for one unit which at the time was in Pannonia Inferior. Though there is some difficulty in the identification of the units involved, the document seems to provide evidence for a continuing tactical collaboration between the two provinces after the period of unified command under Turbo.

The Lower Enclosure at Carisbrooke Castle, Isle of Wight

by

C.J. YOUNG

Among Sheppard Frere's many interests is the late Roman military history of Britain. Since its discovery in 1923 the so-called Lower Enclosure at Carisbrooke Castle in the centre of the Isle of Wight has been widely assumed to be in some way a part of the Saxon Shore defences of later Roman Britain. Most recently this was the conclusion of Stuart Rigold, whose discussion of the problem was published in 1969, although originally written in 1966.[1] Recent work at Carisbrooke has, however, reinforced the doubts that have always existed in the minds of those who have studied this problem, which is now re-examined in this paper in the light, not only of these new discoveries, but also of advances made in the past few years in the study of late Saxon defended sites in southern England.

Carisbrooke Castle lies on a small hill in the centre of the Isle of Wight, blocking one of the north-south gaps that pass through the central east-west ridge of chalk which bisects the island (Fig. 1). The existence of the Castle is attested in Domesday Book, but there is no documentary evidence for any earlier occupation of the site.

The recent series of excavations has proved archaeologically that the hilltop was occupied before the Norman Conquest, and a brief summary of the sequence of occupation must be one of the starting points for this discussion. Between 1976 and 1981 eleven different parts of the Castle were examined. Many of these trenches were quite small and were concerned primarily with specific aspects of the Castle's medieval and post-medieval use. One site, however, (Fig. 2, Site 5) was intended to examine a large area of the centre of the Castle to establish the general sequence of occupation before and after the Norman Conquest. An area of 365 sq. m. (435 sq. yds.) was excavated to natural. Although large parts of it had been removed by two defensive ditches of the later eleventh century, a sufficient area remained to establish the pre-Norman sequence.

A Saxon cemetery, probably of the sixth century, first used the site; two cremation urns and three inhumations were found. The next occupation was of early or mid-eleventh century date, when at least two timber buildings with massive postholes were erected, but neither lay wholly within the excavated

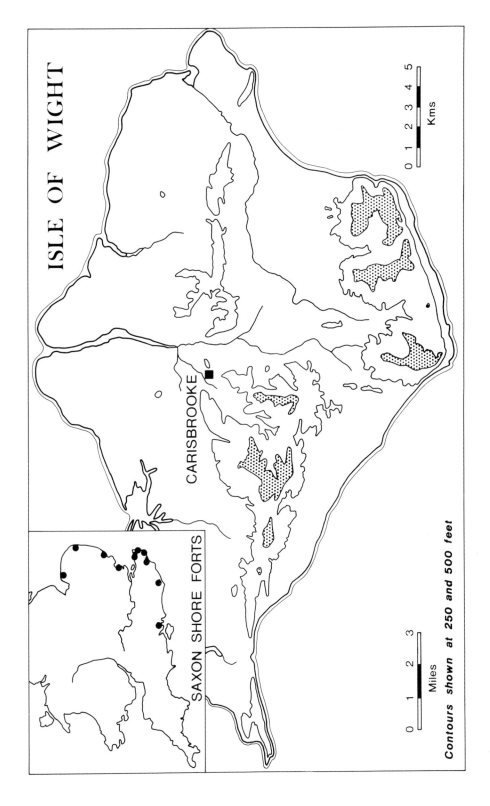

ISLE OF WIGHT

CARISBROOKE

SAXON SHORE FORTS

Contours shown at 250 and 500 feet

0   1   2   3   4   5
Kms

0   1   2   3
Miles

Fig. 1   The Isle of Wight, showing Carisbrooke; inset locating the Isle of Wight and Saxon Shore Forts in southern Britain.

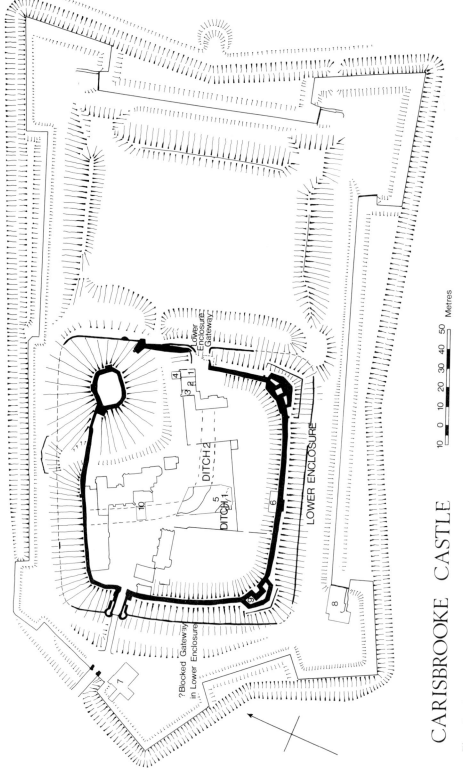

CARISBROOKE CASTLE

Fig. 2 Carisbrooke Castle showing the Lower Enclosure, the present Castle, excavated sites, possible ringworks and seventeenth-century defences.

10 0 10 20 30 40 50
Metres

LOWER ENCLOSURE

Lower Enclosure Gateway

?Blocked Gateway in Lower Enclosure

DITCH 2

DITCH 1

Pl. I   Air photograph of Carisbrooke, from the south-west, showing Lower Enclosure wall at base of castle bailey bank. *(Crown Copyright)*.

area. Both were demolished to make way for a large defensive ditch which, in its turn, was soon filled and replaced by another, *c.* 8 m. (26 ft.) wide and 4 m. (13 ft.) deep. Both ditches dated to the late eleventh century and appeared to relate to successive phases of a small Norman ringwork castle established in one quadrant of the pre-existing Lower Enclosure, which was, in its turn, super-ceded in *c.* 1100 by the present massive motte and bailey under which the walls of the Lower Enclosure were hidden until 1923.

No evidence whatsoever was found of Roman features or structures in Site 5 or in the other sites in which natural was reached (Fig. 2, Sites 1, 2, 3, 7, 10), apart from the possibly Roman masonry building discussed below in relation to the gate of the Lower Enclosure. In one or two places, this absence could be accounted for by the intensive medieval and later disturbance which had removed all pre-medieval features. This was not the case, however, on Site 5 where, as we have seen, pre-Norman levels survived, and it seems quite acceptable to suggest that no Roman features were ever there. This is supported by the scarcity of Roman artefacts which might have been expected to survive in post-Roman levels, even if their original contexts had been destroyed. Only one Roman coin was found (in a sixteenth-century make-up layer outside the Castle) and less than twenty sherds of Roman pottery. These ranged in date from the second to the fourth century and included samian, black-burnished ware and Oxfordshire colour-coated ware. The quantity is less than one might expect to find in fields used by the nearby Carisbrooke villa.

The only Roman artefacts which occurred in quantity were fragments of building material, a feature of the site noted by Rigold in his excavations in the early nineteen-sixties.[2] It is difficult to postulate an extensive Roman occupation on broken tiles alone; they could have been brought to the site in Saxon or Medieval times from the nearby villa. Rigold also noted the general absence of Roman finds, other than building material, although he had not been able to examine large areas of stratified, pre-Norman levels. The fact that Roman features and artefacts are still just as few after much more extensive examination of these pre-Norman levels must cast considerable doubt on whether any extensive Roman use of the site ever occurred, although there are always obvious dangers in arguing from negative evidence.

The second starting-point for this discussion of the lower Enclosure must be the nature of the defences themselves. They were discovered in 1923 when the banks of the Norman motte and bailey were cleaned back (Pl. I; Fig. 2). The remains of a wall were found buried at the base of the Norman banks. It was possible to trace this along the whole of the west and south sides and for about three-quarters of the east side of the Enclosure. On the north side the wall was located at only one point, but it is generally assumed that the line of the present bailey bank followed it. In shape the Enclosure appears at first sight to be a rough quadrilateral, widening towards its eastern end. In fact, as Rigold was the first to point out,[3] a very oblique angle in the line of the western face makes the Enclosure an irregular pentagon.

The external face of the wall survives best on the east side. On the west no more than the lowest course of the face is intact while, elsewhere, only wall-core is visible. Where the face survives, the lowest course is of well-shaped rect-angular blocks of some size. Above this course the wall is slightly offset and faced with smaller but still well-shaped stones (Pl. II). The core of the wall varies and is difficult to examine now because of the protective capping which covers it. Rigold observed that large boulders laid in a herringbone pattern predominated in the lower courses and that, at least in one place, tiers of flat stones penetrated the thickness of the wall at footing level.[4] Little is known of the inner face of the wall because it is buried so deeply below the massive banks of the Norman defences. Rigold managed to examine the inner face in one section and con-sidered that the wall was cut into and built against a pre-existing bank. The width and height of the bank are uncertain.[5] There was presumably a ditch in front of the wall originally, but this must have been entirely removed by later defensive works.

Pl. II View of the east gateway of the Lower Enclosure: scale 2m. *(Crown Copyright)*.

Pl. III Masonry structure possibly associated with the gateway: scale 50 cm. *(Crown Copyright)*.

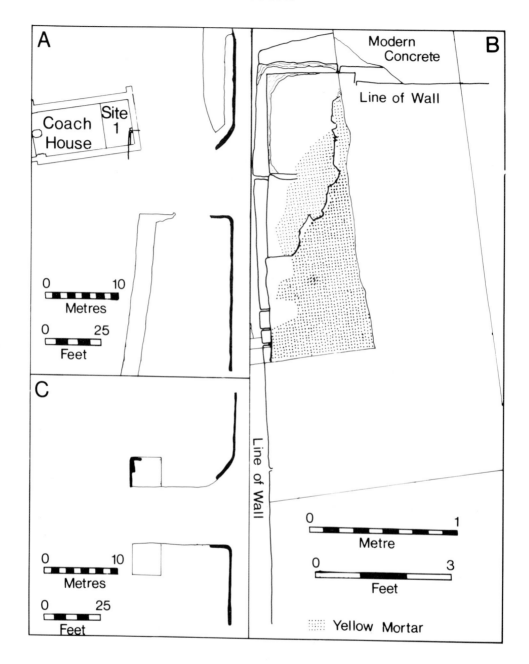

Fig. 3 A. Plan showing Coach House, excavation Site 1, and curtain walls of the Lower Enclosure and medieval castle;
B. South-east corner of Site 1 showing large stone footing as excavated and as traced under east and south walls of the Coach House;
C. possible reconstruction of Lower Enclosure gateway.

Only one definite entrance is known. It lies in the middle of the east face of the circuit, but again cannot be examined fully because of the superimposed Norman defences. On each side of the entrance the wall curves inward. To the south the turn is tight and right-angular, whereas on the north side it is much shallower, producing a very uneven effect (Pl. II). The width of the passage proper thus remains uncertain, as does its length. If the footings described below are part of the gate structure, it could be about 14 m. (45 ft.) long. These structures were discovered about twenty-five years ago and it is not now possible to establish their stratigraphic relationships with surrounding features. They are therefore dated only to the extent that they lie under one corner of a fourteenth-century building. They have been thought to be Roman because of the character of their masonry, but this can only be supposition. The visible portion consists of a right-angled corner built of massive well-dressed ashlars (Pl. III; Fig. 3). Only two courses survive, the upper offset slightly from the lower. The structure can be traced outside the excavated area, under the walls of the later building, for a further 2 m. (7 ft.) to the south, and for about 1 m. (3 ft.) to the east.

It is far from certain whether these footings are part of the entrance into the Lower Enclosure, and it is equally possible that they might relate to other foundations, of unknown date and character, which were noted in the area half a century ago. It is uncertain how this structure, if part of the entrance, relates to the visible fragments of the gateway, owing to the asymmetry of the latter. It is almost certain that the corner which was found must have stood back from the line of the gate passage, and the building of which it was part could have been one of a pair, either of guard-rooms or of guard-towers, flanking the sides of the gateway, or part of a building in which the gate was included. In each case this would presuppose an entrance passage some 14 m. (45 ft.) long and perhaps about 5 m. (17 ft.) wide. But if this masonry corner is not part of the gate structure, then the gateway would have had a much shallower courtyard between the inturns in front of it. It is difficult to find parallels for either hypothesis. While the concept of an open courtyard flanked on three sides is obviously similar to that illustrated by the main gates at the Roman forts at both Portchester and Pevensey,[6] the execution and details of the plan appear to be very different.

It is possible that a second gate lay opposite this one, on the west face of the defences, since there is an apparent blocking visible in the core of the wall at this point. No evidence for a gate, however, survives on the south side, and on the north side too little is left for any inferences to be made.

The other noteworthy feature of the Lower Enclosure is the small bastion midway between the east gate and the north-east corner. It survives to a height of 1.6 m. (5 ft.), is segmental in plan, measures about 4 m. (13 ft.) across its base and projects about 1 m. (3 ft.) from the wall. It is built of solid masonry. Rigold considered that a visible irregularity in a similar position in the wall on the west side of the Enclosure was slight evidence for a second bastion and that both could be part of a regularly disposed series around the fortification, although no evidence for the others now survives.[7] Solid bastions of this type have obvious links with late Roman defensive works, but they would have been shallow for the size of the Enclosure (see below p. 299).

Rigold considered that the Lower Enclosure was Roman on the grounds of its plan, in particular the rounded corners, the nature of the masonry and the use of 'dead men' to level up the coursing, the use of a stone revetment to an earth bank, and the presence of a possible gateway at an obtuse angle on the western face, which he compared to Caistor-by-Norwich and to Lympne Castle, although in the latter case the parallel no longer applies since the most recent excavation suggests that the fort was originally rectangular.[8] He was concerned about the plan of the gateway and the slightness of the bastion but felt that they were even more out of place in a Medieval context. He was concerned also about the lack of Roman material from within the Enclosure, but thought that this could be explained if the fort was built early in the Saxon Shore sequence, at a time when the discipline of the Roman army was still sufficient to enforce disposal of rubbish outside the fort. He did not consider other possible uses of a defended Roman site in the centre of the Isle of Wight, of which there are three.

It is worth discussing these possibilities as well as that of a Saxon Shore fort. The earliest possible use of the site could have been as a fort in the conquest period, as no first-century military post is yet known on the Isle of Wight and it is reasonable to assume that one existed somewhere, for at least a short period, after the Roman invasion. However, this possibility must be ruled out because of the secondary stone defences, implying a period of use which is not compatible with the absence of Roman features or artefacts within the fort, and because of the irregularity of the plan and the oddity of the gates and bastion. The absence of structures or pottery must also rule out the possibility of the site having been a small town or market (unaccountably lacking on the island) or a defended rural centre of the type suggested by Gatcombe (Avon) and similar places on the continent.

Thus the only possible Roman context left is that put forward by Rigold. As noted above, he argued that the combination of stone defences and the lack of evidence for a prolonged occupation could only be reconciled in the short-term occupation of an early third-century fort. In order to accept this it would still be necessary to discount the negative evidence of the recent excavations on the grounds that the area investigated was too small to be representative of the whole site. There are, however, other substantial difficulties to overcome in accepting this hypothesis.

Firstly there is the position of the site. The British Saxon Shore forts were designed to be used in conjunction with the fleet and all are sited close to harbours;[9] Carisbrooke is not. While the River Medina is navigable in part, and one tributary flows past the Castle, the head of navigation can never have been much nearer than Newport, about 2 km. (1.3 miles) from Carisbrooke. The

Castle, on its hilltop, is also too high above the river to have any direct control over it. Thus a fort sited at Carisbrooke could not have provided protection for an adjacent naval base.

Secondly there are the problems of the detailed planning of the defences of the fort. As already noted, the Lower Enclosure is encircled by a bank, subsequently faced by a stone wall. This use of a stone-faced rampart is found only at the two Saxon Shore forts normally thought to be the earliest, Brancaster and Reculver. Both had regular, rectangular plans, simple gates of types normally found in second and early third-century forts, and no external bastions. Saxon Shore forts with irregular circuits do not seem to have had ramparts backing their walls.

Nor, for that matter, is the very oblique bend in Carisbrooke's western face easily paralleled in any late Roman fort. The irregularity of Lympne is now in doubt as the result of the most recent excavation.[10] At Pevensey the plan of the circuit is quite unlike that of any other late fort or of Carisbrooke. At Dover the changes of direction are marked. At Carisbrooke the change is so slight as to suggest that the original intention was to produce a straight wall, and that the slight change of direction was the result of an error in laying out or in building. It is difficult to reconcile this with the normal professionalism of Roman military planning.

The use of bastions at Carisbrooke is also unusual in the context of the Saxon Shore. Although the architects of the forts were not wholly conversant with the purposes of bastions,[11] such shallow bastions were elsewhere only used in very small fortifications such as East Yorkshire signal stations. The proper forts of the Saxon Shore possessed much more substantial bastions. At Burgh Castle they project about 4 m. (13 ft.), at Bradwell slightly less, at Lympne 4.5 m. (15 ft.) and at Pevensey 6 m. (20 ft.); all well in excess of the metre (3 ft.) at Carisbrooke.

The problems of finding parallels for the gate-plan have also been mentioned above. Gates set back from the wall-face behind an open courtyard and flanked by guard-towers are known at Portchester[12] and at Pevensey.[13] The Carisbrooke gate is possibly similar in concept, but very different in execution. The irregularity and asymmetry of the visible part have already been mentioned. In the masonry structure described above (p. 000), the space contained between the walls is not so much a courtyard as a long narrowing passage, with its guard-towers or guard-chambers apparently set back behind the inturned walls of the gate passage. As with the bastion and, to a certain extent, the plan, the gate at Carisbrooke seems not so much the work of late Roman military engineers as that of later builders influenced by, and not fully understanding, surviving late Roman fortifications.

These problems of siting, planning and defensive detailing are alone sufficient to cast doubt on the attribution of Carisbrooke to the Saxon Shore or, indeed, to any other type of late Roman fortification. Combined with the negative evidence of the lack of Roman features and structures, and the scarcity of Roman artefacts, it must surely be evident that the Lower Enclosure at Carisbrooke is not of Roman date. It is therefore necessary to look for a later context in which to place it.

A *terminus ante quem* is effectively provided by the Norman conquest of 1066, since the recent excavations have shown that the first two phases of the Norman castle defended one quadrant of the pre-existing Lower Enclosure, in the same way that castles were constructed in the Saxon Shore forts at Portchester and Pevensey, and within the late Saxon burh at Wallingford. The closest parallels to Carisbrooke are the late Saxon burhs of Wessex and such an equation is rein- forced by the discovery of late Saxon occupation within the Castle. As with Kent and Cornwall, the Isle of Wight does not appear in the Burghal Hidage, which lists burhs for most of Wessex,[14] so that there is no documentary evidence for a burh on the island. On the other hand one must undoubtedly have been needed since the island is very exposed to sea-borne raiders, and was indeed raided on a number of occasions by the Danes.

Seen as a refuge for the Isle of Wight, Carisbrooke is well sited away from the vulnerable coasts but accessible to the bulk of the population because of its central position. The Lower Enclosure also matches known burhs elsewhere both in plan and in its defensive works. A number of burhs, of course, were reused hillforts or Roman fortifications. Elsewhere they tended, if topographical conditions permitted, to be roughly rectangular in form.[15] The defences of a number of burhs founded *de novo* have now been examined archaeologically. The sequence discovered in all instances so far investigated has been an initial defence-work of an earth or turf rampart followed, in Wessex at Cricklade, Lydford, Wallingford and Wareham, by a facing of masonry in a second phase, as is the case at Carisbrooke.[16]

Little work has been done on details such as gates. At South Cadbury, the west gate of the late Saxon burh had an inturned passage 9 m. (30 ft.) long and 3 m. (10 ft.) wide, with gates at its outer end, unlike Carisbrooke, although the concept of the inturned passage is the same. As yet, bastions are unparalleled in Saxon burhs. However, stone fortifications in the late tenth and early eleventh centuries were presumably in an innovatory and developing phase, and it is perhaps not surprising that clumsy attempts should be made to adopt details of design of fortification, which were still clearly visible, and indeed were integral parts of some fortifications reused for the defence of Wessex, for example at Portchester.

It does not, therefore, seem unreasonable to argue that the Lower Enclosure at Carisbrooke is most probably the remains of a late Saxon burh-type fortifi- cation, constructed as a central refuge for the Isle of Wight. This suggestion has in fact been put forward before in passing,[17] but it is felt that the results of the recently-concluded excavations at Carisbrooke and of the reconsideration of the Lower Enclosure in the light of those results and of discoveries elsewhere, justifies offering this rather longer discussion of the problem to Sheppard Frere as the possible solution to the date and purpose of the Lower Enclosure, so often claimed as a late Roman fortification.

NOTES

1. Rigold, S.E., *Château Gaillard*, iii, (1969), 128–138.
2. *ibid.*, 134.
3. *ibid.*, 132.
4. *ibid.*, 134.
5. *ibid.*, 134.
6. Johnson, J.S., *The Roman Forts of the Saxon Shore*, London, 1976, Fig. 66.
7. Rigold, S.E., *op. cit.* (see note 1), 133.
8. Cunliffe, B.W., *Britannia*, xi, (1980), 254–5.
9. Johnson, J.S., *op. cit.* (see note 6), 123–4.
10. Cunliffe, B.W., *op. cit.* (see note 8), 254–5.
11. Johnson, J.S., *op. cit.* (see note 6), 115.
12. Cunliffe, B.W., *Excavations at Portchester Castle: Vol. I, Roman*, London, 1975, 29–36.
13. Johnson, J.S., *op. cit.* (see note 6), 121.
14. Hill, D., *Medieval Archaeology*, xiii, (1969), 84–92.
15. Radford, C.A.R., *Proceedings of the British Academy*, lxiv, (1978), 131–153.
16. Radford, C.A.R., *Medieval Archaeology*, xiv, (1970), 83–103 and Radford C.A.R., *op. cit.* (see note 15), (1978), 131–153.
17. For example, Johnson, J.S., *op. cit.* (see note 6), 1976, 141.

BIBLIOGRAPHY

Cunliffe, B.W., 1975, *Excavations at Portchester Castle. Vol. I: Roman*, Society of Antiquaries of London Research Committee Reports 32, London.

Cunliffe, B.W., 1980, 'Excavations at the Roman Fort at Lympne, Kent, 1976–78', *Britannia*, xi, 227–88.

Hill, D., 1971, 'The Burghal Hidage: The Establishment of a Text', *Medieval Archaeology*, xiii, (1969), 84–92.

Johnson, J.S., 1976, *The Roman Forts of the Saxon Shore*, London.

Radford, C.A.R., 1971, 'The later pre-conquest boroughs and their defences', *Medieval Archaeology*, xiv, (1970), 83–103.

Radford, C.A.R., 1980, 'The pre-conquest Boroughs of England, ninth to eleventh centuries', *Proceedings of the British Academy*, lxiv, (1978), 131–153.

Rigold, S.E., 1969, 'The earliest defences of Carisbrooke Castle', *Château Gaillard*, iii, 128–138.

Index

Adamklissi, monuments at, 273
Aegyssus (Tulcea), 265
Aelius Catus, 259, 260
Aelius Hadrianus, P., 273
Ager Veientanus, villas in, 64
agriculture:
    agricultural buildings, 56, 59–62, 244–247, 249–250
    at villa sites, 63, 64, 244–251
Ain Sinu (Zagurae), fort at, 112, 121–122
Alani, 255–257, 260
Alba Fucens, 215
Albano, fortress at, 112, 121–123
Alcester, defences at, 88
Aldborough, defences at, 85
Alexander, M., 77
Alexander the Great, 255
Alföldi, A., 170, 171
Alföldy, G., 214
Alise-Ste-Reine, *sacella* at, 41
Allen, D.F., 203, 206
Amberloup, *curia* at, 210
Amiens, 156
Ammianus Marcellinus, 192, 240, 241, 242, 243, 258
Antonine Wall, 25
Antoninus Pius, 24, 25, 26
Aorsi, 256, 257
Apollonius of Tyana, 190–191
Appian, 171
Appiaria, 266, 267
Applebaum, Prof. S., 247
Appleford, cauldron chain from, 142, 149, 150
ApSimon, A.M., 252
Apulia, villas in, 59
Apulum (Alba Julia), 275
Aquileia, 170, 171
Aquincum, 171, 189, 266, 270, 273, 274
Arisenius Marius, P., 16, 17
Armenia, 260, 264
Arminius, 171–172

army, Roman:
    Ala Augusta ob virtutem appellata, 101, 103
    Ala I Hispanorum, 105
    Ala I Thracum, 20
    Ala Petriana, 105
    ala milliaria, 97, 105, 119
    ala quingeneria, 97, 98, 101, 105, 119
    alae Breucorum, 175
    alae Latabicorum, 175
    alae Pannoniorum, 175
    alae Varicianorum, 175
    auxiliary units, composition of, 96–101, 119–120
    Cohors I Augusta Praetoria Lusitanorum equitata, 100–101
    Cohors I Hispanorum Veterana, 100, 101, 273
    Cohors I Nervana Germanorum milliaria equitata, 110
    Cohors I Tungrorum milliaria, 113
    Cohors III Campestris C(ivium) R(omanorum), 102, 103
    Cohors III Gallorum equitata, 108, 109
    Cohors III Thracum (Civium) R(omanorum) quingenaria equitata, 105
    Cohors V Bracaraugustanorum, 105
    Cohors XX Palmyrenorum, 97–98, 99, 100, 110
    Cohors Usiporum, 173
    cohors milliaria equitata, 96, 97, 98, 99, 101, 111, 116, 119–120
    cohors peditata milliaria, 96–97, 103, 114, 117, 119
    cohors peditata quingenaria, 96, 112, 119
    cohors quingenaria equitata, 96, 97–98, 99–100, 101, 107, 109, 112, 116, 119–120
    cohortes Breucorum, 175
    cohortes Latobicorum, 175
    cohortes Pannoniorum, 175
    cohortes Varcianorum, 175
    Constantius II, under, 243–244
    Dacian and Sarmatian campaigns, 258–275

Gaulish settlements, role in development of, 155, 162–164
Herculiani corps, 241
Icenian revolt, role in, 202–203
Ioviani corps, 241
Legio I Minervia, 17, 214, 215
Legio II Augusta, 24–27, 238
Legio II Parthica, 112, 121
Legio II Traiana, 189
Legio III, 261
Legio III Gallica, 265, 266
Legio III Italica, 235, 238
Legio V Alaudae, 119
Legio V Macedonica, 189
Legio VI Ferrata, 262
Legio VI Victrix, 24–27, 238
Legio VII Claudia pia fidelis, 265, 269
Legio VIII Augusta, 185, 265
Legio IX Hispana, 185, 238
Legio XI Claudia pia fidelis, 265
Legio XIII Gemina, 265
Legio XV Apollinaris, 265
Legio XV Primigenia, 119
Legio XX Valeria Victrix, 24–27, 205, 238
Magnentius, under, 241–242
military papyri, 97–101, 108, 120, 273
military standards, 179–192, 195–196, 198
Pannonian/Dalmatian auxiliaries, 171–175
sacramentum, 179, 190–198
veterans, 92, 203, 206, 274
Arrabona (Györ), 264
Arval Bethren, 261
Asia, 262
Asse, 161–162, 164
Atrebates, 206
Attersee, cauldron chain from, 133–134
Attila the Hun, 255
Augustae (Hurlec), fort at, 266
Augustus, 46, 162, 170–171, 173, 175, 210, 214, 257, 258–259, 264, 265
Aurelius Fulvus, 261
Aurelius Verus, C., 18, 19–21
Aurelius Victor, 169
Ausonius, 244
Avars, 255
Azali, 264

Bagendon, 203, 206
Banat, 269, 271, 273, 275
Bannaventa, defences at, 88
Barbarian Conspiracy, The Great, 240–241

Barburgh Mill, fortlet at, 228
Barnsley Park, villa at, 247
Barrett, A.A., 206
Bartlow, cauldron chain from, 145–146, 150
Basilicata, villas in, 59
Bastarnae, 256, 258, 260
Batavian revolt, 173, 210
Bath (Aquae Sulis):
    baths at, 67–74, 77–80, 251
    defences at, 88
    forum at, 68
    Saxon period at, 67, 72–79
    temple at, 68, 70, 72, 80, 249, 251
    theatre at, 68
bath-houses:
    Bath, 67–74, 77–80, 251
    villas, 56, 58, 63, 249–251
Bato, 172
Bavay (Bagacum), 155, 158, 159, 160, 161, 163, 164
Beckford, 206
Bede, 79
Bedriacum, 261
Belgae, *civitas* of, 206, 207
Bigbury, cauldron chain from, 136, 138–140, 142, 143, 150
Bignor, villa at, 2, 56, 244
Birley, Prof. A.R., 22, 26
Birley, Prof. E., 20–21, 38, 215
Birrens (Blatobulgium), fort at, 110–112, 119, 120, 121, 122
Bitterne (Clausentum), defences at, 88
Bituriges Cubi, 20
Blackburn Mill, cauldron chain from, 143–144, 145, 150
von Blanckenhagen, Prof. P., 56
Bledlow, cauldron chain from, 136, 140, 150
Bodvoc, 203, 206–207
Boii, 170, 264
Bonn (Bonna), *matronae Aufaniae* cult at, 213–218
Boon, G.C., 112, 252
Boresti, 204
Boudican Revolt, 204
Boulogne, 155, 159–160
Bowes, 2
Boxmoor, villa at, 247
Boyce, G.K., 33
Brading, villa at, 36
Bradley, K.R., 203
Bradwell, Saxon shore fort at, 299

Braives, 155, 156, 158
Brancaster, Saxon shore fort at, 299
Brandon:
   cauldron chain from, 142, 147, 149, 151
   Brandon Camp, 2
Branigan, Prof. K., 246–247
Braund, J., 91
Brean Down, temple at, 251–252
Breeze, D., 101, 110, 117
Breuci, 172, 174
Brigantes, 203, 204, 205
Brigantian Revolt, 25, 84, 92
Brigetio, 196–197, 270
Brixellum, 261
Brough-on-Humber (Petuaria), defences at, 85
Buck, R.J., 62
Bulgars, 255
Bu Ngem, fort at, 99
Burebista, 256, 258, 263
Burgh Castle, Saxon shore fort at, 299
Burivada, 273, 274
Burnum, 264, 265
Bury, J.B., 204
Bushe-Fox, J.P., 251
Butley, cauldron chain from, 136, 137, 140,
   143, 147, 151

Caburn, cauldron chain from, 136
Caerhun (Kanovium), fort at, 103, 116–118,
   119, 120
Caerleon, fortress at, 43, 47, 48
Caerwent (Venta Silurum):
   defences at, 85, 92
   shrine at, 38, 43–45
Caistor-by-Norwich (Venta Icenorum):
   defences at, 85, 298
Caistor-by-Yarmouth, defences at, 88
Calabria, villas in, 59
Calgacus, 205
Campania, villas in, 56, 59
Cannstatt, cauldron chain from, 134, 135
Canterbury:
   defences at, 85
   excavations at, 1–2
Cantia, 13, 14, 15
Caracalla, 23, 24
Carandini, Prof. A., 63
Caratacus, 207
Carisbrooke Castle, 290–300
Carisbrooke villa, 294
Carlingwark Loch, cauldron chain

from, 143, 151
Carmarthen, defences at, 85
Carnuntum, fortress at, 264, 265, 266
Carpow, fort at, 237, 238
Carrawburgh, shrine at, 47
Carrington, R.C., 59
Carsium (Hîrsova), fort at, 271
Carzield, fort at, 222
Cassel (Castellum), 155, 164
Cassius Dio, 172, 173, 174, 204, 205
Catterick, shrine at, 36–38
Catti, 206
Catuvellauni, 207
celtic:
   art, 218
   chieftains, 171
   coinage in Pannonia, 170–171
   etymology, 17, 20, 23
   religion, 34, 47–48, 49, 250
Chariovalda, 172
Charlton, J., 38
Chastagnol, A., 24
Chatti, 269
Chauci, 93
Chedworth, villa at, 36, 250–251
Chelmsford, defences at, 89
Chersonesus, 260
Chester, 67
Chesters (Cilurnum), fort at, 101, 103–104,
   105, 119
Chew Green, fort at, 226
Chew Park, villa at, 247
Chichester, defences at, 86
Chilgrove, villa at, 246
Christlein, R., 237–238
Ciabrus (Cibrica), 268
Cirencester (Corinium), 247
   cauldron chain from, 142, 145, 147–148, 151
   defences at, 86, 92
citizenship, 23
civitates, 155, 159, 163, 213
Classis Britannica, 237, 298–299
Classis Germanica, 237
Claudius, 175, 182, 184, 207, 259, 260, 265
Claudius Stratonicus, 214–215
Clodius Albinus, D., 84
Cogidubnus, 92, 205, 206, 207
coins:
   Brean Down, from, 252
   celtic, in Pannonia, 170–171
   Dobunnic, 43–44, 203, 205–206

Gaulish, 158, 160, 161, 162, 164
Genio Augusti, inscribed, 47
Nervian, 159
representations of raised hands on, 179–182,
    191, 198
Colapiani, 264
Colchester (Camulodunum), 38, 203, 205
Colijnsplaat, altars from, 13–20, 22–24
Collingwood, Prof. R.G., 3, 210
Cologne, 15, 19–21, 155, 158, 160, 213
Commodus, 93
Comux, 206
Constans, 241, 242
Constantine, 242, 243, 249, 251
    arch of, 186, 189, 190
Constantius II, 241–244, 247, 249
Constitutio Antoniniana, 23
Corder, P., 84, 92
Corio, 206–207
Coritani, 206
Cornelius Fuscus, 269, 274
Costa, D., 40
Cotton, M.A., 87
Courtai, 164
Crassus, 258
Cremona, battle at, 262
Cricklade, Saxon burh at, 300
Crocicchie, villa at, 60
Cunliffe, Prof. B., 251
curiae:
    curia Arduennae, 210
    curia Etratium, 213
    curia Textoverdorum, 210
Cyprian, 198

D'Arms, Prof. J., 59
Dacia, 105, 258–260, 262–264, 269–271, 273–
    275
Daesidiates, 172, 174, 264
Dalmatia, 264–265, 267
    auxiliary troops from, 172, 174–175
    Pannonian/Dalmatian revolt, 169–175
Dalswinton, fort at, 222, 232–233
Dannell, G., 88
Danube:
    Danubian fleets, 237, 263, 267–268, 271
    Danubian frontier, 102–103, 105, 115, 235–
        238, 255–275
Dardanians, 264
Davies, R., 99–100
Davis, Major, 68

Decangi, 202–203, 204, 207
Decebalus, 264, 268, 269, 270, 271, 273, 275
defences:
    Alcester, 88
    Aldborough, 85
    Bannaventa, 88
    Bath, 88
    Bitterne, 88
    Bradwell, 299
    Brancaster, 299
    Brough-on-Humber, 85
    Burgh Castle, 299
    Caerwent, 85, 92
    Caistor-by-Norwich, 85, 298
    Caistor-by-Yarmouth, 88
    Canterbury, 85
    Carisbrooke Castle, 290, 292–299
    Carmarthen, 85
    Chelmsford, 89
    Chichester, 86
    Cirencester, 86, 92
    Dorchester, 86, 92
    Dorchester (Oxon), 89, 91
    Dover, 299
    Eining-Unterfeld, 235
    Exeter, 86, 92
    Gatehouse of Fleet, 225–227
    Gaulish towns, 93, 158–160
    Godmanchester, 89
    Great Casterton, 84, 89
    Icenian, 202, 205
    Ilchester, 86–87
    Irchester, 89
    Kenchester, 89–90
    late Roman, 298
    late Saxon, 300
    Leicester, 87
    Lympne, 298, 299
    Margidunum, 90
    Mildenhall, 90
    Pevensey, 299
    Porchester, 299
    Reculver, 299
    Rocester, 90
    Rochester, 90
    Romano-British towns, 84–85, 91–93
    Silchester, 87, 92
    Thorpe, 90
    Verulamium, 87, 91–93
    Wanborough, 90
    Winchester, 87, 92

Worcester, 90
Wroxeter, 88
York, 91
Devizes, figurines from, 45, 47–49
Diegis, 269
Diocletian, 241, 243
Dobbie, E.V.K., 67, 74
Dobson, B., 101, 117
Dobunni, 203, 205–207
Dobunnic coins, 43, 44, 203, 205, 206
Domitian, 263–270
Dorchester:
  defences at, 86, 99
  shrine at, 38, 39
Dorchester (Oxon):
  defences at, 89, 91
  excavations at, 2
Dorn, cauldron chain from, 142, 146, 147, 151
Dover, Saxon shore fort at, 299
Down, A., 246
Drajna de sus, 273
Drew, C.D., 38
Drobeta (Turnu Severin), fort at, 102–103, 109, 119, 120, 121, 271
Drusus, 259
Dühren, cauldron chain from, 136
Dumnonii, 84
Dura, fort at, 99, 108, 120, 198
Durisdeer, camps at, 222
Durostorum, fortress at, 266, 271, 274
Durotriges, 206

Earle, J., 78
Eckford, cauldron chain from, 143, 151
Edgar, King of England, 74
Eining-Abusina, fort at, 235
Eining-Unterfeld, fortress at, 235–238
Elagabalus, 22
Elewijt, 161, 164
Eliade, M., 218
Emmendingen, cauldron chain from, 140
Eravisci, 170–171
Etruria, villas in, 61, 64
Exeter, defences at, 86, 92
Exeter Book, The, 67–68, 74–79

Fabius Justus, 100, 273
Fabius Postuminus, Q., 271
Felmingham Hall, figurines from, 45, 48–49
Fendoch, fort at, 113–114, 119, 228
Fischer, H.T., 237, 238

Flavia Tiberina, 214–215, 216
Flavius Philostratus, 190
Florescu, R., 103
Florus, 173
Fonteius Agrippa, 263, 265, 268
forts, fortresses and fortlets – see also individual
    sites
  internal plans of forts, 96–98, 101–123, 227–
    232
  possible military sites in N. Gaul, 157–164
  Saxon shore forts, 290, 297–300
Forum Claudii, 195
Forum Livi, 184
Fox, G.E., 33, 43
de Franciscis, Prof. A., 56
Franks, 241
Frere, Prof. S.S., 1–3, 33, 36, 56, 80, 84, 85,
    93, 96, 155, 207, 210, 240, 290, 300
  and Frere, J., 223
Fulford, M., 47
Funisulanus Vettonianus, 269

Gabler, D., 266
Gadebridge Park, villa at, 247, 248, 249–250
Gaiso, 241
Gaius (Caligula), 191
Galba, 261
Galerius, Arch of, 258
Ganuenta (um?), altars from, 13–20, 22–24
Gatcombe, 298
Gatehouse of Fleet, fortlet at, 222–233
Gaul, 241, 247
  cauldron chains from, 134–136
  coins from, 158, 159, 160, 161, 162, 164
  defences in, 93
  nomenclature, practice of, 23, 24
  oppida in, 162
  road system in, 155–156, 158–164
  terracotta industry in, 43
  towns, development of in N. Gaul, 155–164
  villas in, 163, 244
  worship of Mars in, 198
Gelligaer II, fort at, 112–113, 119
Germany, 155, 171, 241, 273, 274, 275
  army in, 25–27, 264, 266, 269
  cauldron chains from, 134–136
  German campaign, 172, 174
  German revolts, 262, 266, 269, 270, 274
  Germanic kings, 62
  nomenclature, practice of, 23, 24
  Roman domestic religion in, 45

Gesoriacum, 13, 14, 15
Gestingthorpe, cauldron chain from, 143, 151
Getae, 258, 259, 265
Glasbergen, Prof. W., 109
Glenlochar, forts at, 222, 225, 233
Gloucester, 205
Godmanchester, defences at, 89
von Gonzenbach, V., 190
Gorni Voden, oath hand from, 196
Gothic war, 62
Graff, T., 158
Gratus, 22
Great Casterton:
   defences at, 84, 89
   villa at, 246
Great Chesterford, cauldron chains from, 132,
   138, 142, 143, 145, 147, 148, 151
Grignon, J. Cl., 41–42
Grivaud, C., 42
Groenman-van Waateringe, W., 109
Gross-Krotzenburg, cauldron chain from, 134

Hadrian, 27, 275
Hadrian's Wall, 47, 67, 101, 103, 105, 110
Haltern, fort at, 164
Ham Hill, cauldron chain from, 136, 140, 151
Harpsden, villa at, 247
Hartley, B.R., 232
Hassall, M., 22, 23
Haverfield, Prof. F.J., 3, 210
Hawkes, Prof. C.F.C., 203, 206
Heraeus, W., 203
Herculaneum, shrine at, 34–36
Herculius Augustus, 169
Herodian, 197
Herodotus, 255, 258
High Wycombe, villa at, 247
Holder, P., 96, 101
Holmes, J., 86
Hope, W.H. St. J., 33, 43
Hotchner, C.A., 67
Housesteads:
   fort at, 114
   shrine at, 38
Huns, 255, 256
Hunsbury, cauldron chain from, 136, 139, 141,
   143, 147, 151
Hyginus, 96, 97, 98, 99

Iceni, first revolt of, 202–207
Ilchester, defences at, 86–87

Illyricum, 172, 173, 174, 259
Inchtuthil, fort at, 227
industry, 63
   carpentry, 228
   metalworking – see METALWORK
   oil processing, 58, 61
   terracotta, 43
   tile-making, 58, 61
inscriptions, 26, 62, 247, 271, 273, 274
   altars, 13–20, 22–24, 27, 192–193, 211–218,
      250, 274
   coffins, 20
   dedications, 19–27, 210, 213, 215
   genius augusti, 47–48
   honorific, 163, 237
   milestones, 271
   military, 99, 101, 120, 192–193, 257, 259–
      260, 266, 270, 273–274
   oath hands, 193–197
   stamps, 235, 238, 274
   tombstones, 17, 20
Intercisa (Dunaújváros), fort at, 189, 192
Irchester, defences at, 89
Iron Age:
   cauldron chains and cauldrons, 132–143,
      147, 150, 151, 152
   metalworking, 142
   militia, 213
Ivinghoe Beacon, 2

Járdányi-Paulovics, S., 192–193
Jarrett, M.G., 101
Jazyges, 255, 257–259, 263, 266, 269, 270, 273–
   275
Jewish uprising, 260
Jidava, 273
Johannowsky, Prof. W., 56
John of Tours, 79
Jones, Prof. A.H.M., 244
Jones, Prof. G.D.B., 60
Josephus, 262–263
Julius Agricola, Cn., 13, 204–5
Julius Caesar, 162, 191
Julius Quadratus Bassus, C., 275
Julius Verus, 24–25
Julius Vestalis, 265
Juvenal, 47

Kenchester, defences at, 89–90
Kingsdown Camp, cauldron chains from, 136,
   151

Köln-Alteburg, fort at, 237
Krapp, G.P., 67, 74
Kunckel, H., 47
Künzing (Quintana), fort at, 103, 105–108, 109, 116, 119, 120, 121

La Tène, cauldron chain from, 132, 133, 134
Labienus, 191
Lamyatt Beacon, figurines from, 45, 47–48
Latimer, villa at, 247
Laubscher, H.P., 182
Le Châtelet, *sacella* at, 41
Lehner, H., 213, 214
Leicester, defences at, 87
Leofric, Bishop of Exeter, 67
Leslie, R.F., 67, 77
Lezoux:
    excavations at, 2
    potters from, 85–88, 90–91
Liberchies, 155, 158
Littlecote, villa at, 247
Livy, 191, 192, 197
Llanwit Major, villa at, 38
Longthorpe, fortress at, 2, 96, 238
Lörincz, B., 266
Lufton, villa at, 250
Lugdunum, 22
Lugii, 270
Luttrell, A., 62
Lydford, Saxon burh at, 300
Lydney Park, villa at, 250
Lympne, Saxon shore fort at, 237, 298, 299
Lyon, 155, 242
Lyttleton, M., 62

Mackie, W.S., 74, 77
Maezaei, 264
Magnentius, 241–243, 246–247, 250, 252
Magyurs, 255
Mainz-Kastel, shrine from, 40
Malaiesti, 273
Mamertinus, 169
Mancini, G., 182
Mann, Prof. J.C., 20
Marcellinus, 241
Marcius Turbo, Q., 275
Marcomanni, 237, 259, 263, 264, 268, 269, 270
Marcus Aponius, 261
Marcus Aurelius, 93, 186, 187, 263, 275
Marcus Fabius, 191
Margidunum, defences at, 90

Maroboduus, 171, 173–174, 263, 269
Martinhoe, fortlet at, 226, 228
Martinus, 243
Masseria Nocelli, villa at, 60
Mauer an der Url, oath hands from, 195–196, 198
Maximianus, 169
Mazzarino, S., 99, 100
Menappi, *civitas* of, 155
metalwork:
    cauldron chains and cauldrons, 132–152
    hoards, 47–49, 132, 136, 138, 142, 143, 145, 147, 206, 252
    showing open hands, 182–185
    metalworking, 47, 48, 142, 228, 250
Metz, 155, 156
Mildenhall, defences at, 90
Milseburg/Rhön, cauldron chain from, 134
Modena, sarcophagus from, 186, 188
Moesi, 259
Moesia, 100, 259–271, 273–275
Montana (Mihailovgrad), 266
Monte Irsi, villa at, 59, 62
Morini, 15, 20
    civitas of, 155
Mucianus, 262
Mura di San Stefano, villa at, 62–63, 64
Mursa (Osijek), 242, 268, 270
Musgrave, W., 45, 48, 49

Nagydém, figurines from, 45–46
Naix, Lady of, 43
Namur, 164
Nash-Williams, V.E., 85, 101
Naskovo, oath hand from, 196
Neal, D., 247, 249
Nennius, 79
Nero, 259, 260, 264, 265
Nerva, 270
Nervii, 158, 159
    civitas of, 155
Nettleton Scrubb, temple at, 250
Neuss, fort at, 164
Neuvy-Pailloux, cauldron chain from, 136
Newcastle-upon-Tyne (Pons Aelius), inscription from, 24–27
Newstead:
    cauldron chain from, 143, 144, 151
    fort at, 119, 120
Nida, oath hand from, 194, 195
Niha, oath hand from, 193, 196, 197

Nijmegen, fort at, 164
Nikopol, fort at, 266
Noricum, 171
North Leigh, villa at, 244
Novae, fortress at, 265, 266, 270, 274
Novidunum (Isaccea), 267
Numisius Lupus, 261
Nunney, hoard from, 206

Oates, D. & J., 121
oath hands, 193–198
Oberaden, fort at, 164
Oberstimm, fort at, 109, 115–116, 119, 120, 121
Odoacer, 62
Oescus, fortress at, 264, 265, 266, 270, 274
Olbia, 255
Oliver-Smith, Prof. P., 61
Oltenia, 259, 273
Oppius Satinus, C., 268
Ordovices, 204
Osthoff, H., 20, 21
Ostorius Marcus, 202, 203
Ostorius Publius, 202, 203, 204, 205, 207
Ostorius Scapula, M., 206
Otho, 261–262
Over Fen, cauldron chain from, 136, 137, 138, 140, 143, 151
Ovid, 257, 265

Pannonia, 237, 259–275
    auxiliary troops from, 171–175
    inscription from, 192
    oath hand from, 197
    Pannonian/Dalmatian revolt, 169–175
    Pannonii, 170, 174, 259
    Roman domestic religion in, 45–46
    Romanisation of, 169–175
    trade in, 170–171
papyri, 97–101, 108, 120, 273
Parenteau, F., 40–41, 43
Pârvan, V., 170, 173
Paulus, 243–244, 247, 249
Pen Llystyn, fort at, 118–119, 120, 121
Pentyrch, cauldron chain from, 136, 139, 140, 143, 151
von Petrikovits, Prof. H., 213
Pevensey, Saxon shore fort at, 297, 299, 300
Philip the Arab, 190
Piazza Armerina, villa at, 56, 64
Piggott, Prof. S., 132, 142
Pinnes, 172

Plautius, Aulus, 206–207
Plautius Silvanus Aelianus, Ti., 259, 268
Plautus, 46
Poetovio, fortress at, 264, 265
Poiana (Piroboridava), 273, 274
Polybios, 191
Pompeii:
    gladiators helmet from, 184
    Roman domestic religion at, 33–34, 36, 38, 40, 45, 46
Pompey, 191
Pontus, 260, 265
Porchester, Saxon shore fort at, 297, 299, 300
Porolissensis, 275
Posto, villa at, 56, 59, 60
Postumius Albinus, Sp., 197
Potter, T.W., 61
Prasutagus, 204, 205, 206, 207
Punic Wars, 170

Quadi, 259, 263, 268, 269, 270
quernstones, 228, 230, 233
Quintilian, 198

Raeti, 173
Raetia, 17, 105, 115, 121
Rapsley, villa at, 246
Rasova, inscription from, 273
Ratiaria, 267, 274
Ratiatum, 41
Ravazd, oath hand from, 196
Reculver, Saxon shore fort at, 299
Regensburg, fortress at, 235
Reims, 155, 156
religion:
    aediculae, 34, 36, 40, 41
    Aesculapius, 45, 47
    altars, 13–20, 22–24, 27, 38, 68, 192–193, 211–218, 250–251, 274
    Apollo, 18, 19, 20, 45, 250
    Ba'al, 193, 198
    Bacchanalian scandal, 197
    Bacchus, 48, 197
    celtic, 34, 47–48, 49, 213, 250
    Christianity, 191, 198, 243, 251, 252
    Epona, 40
    female deities, 42–43
    Fortuna, 38
    genii, 21–22, 38, 45–48, 193
    Genii Augusti, 46–48
    Genii Cucullati, 38

Genii Togati, 45–46, 47, 48
Genius Centuriae, 47
Heliosarapis, 49
Hercules, 34, 45, 47
imagines majorum, 45
Juno, 46, 195, 196
Jupiter, 48, 191
Jupiter Dolichenus, 22, 193, 195, 196, 197
Jupiter Hadaranēs, 196
Jupiter Heliopolitanus, 193
lararia, 33–48
Lares, 36, 45–47, 48–49
Lares Compitales, 46
Mars, 47–48, 190, 191, 198, 274
Matronae Aufaniae, 210–216, 218, 219
Mercurius Gebrinius, 215
Mercury, 36, 45, 47–48, 210, 213
Minerva, 47–48, 49
Mithras, 193, 197
mother goddesses, 43, 44, 45, 213, 214
mystery cults, 197–198
Nantosuelta, 34
Nehalennia, 13–20, 22–23
Neptune, 22, 27
Nurse, 43, 45
Oceanus, 27
Penates, 46, 48
Roman domestic religion, 45–47
rural pagan cults, 38
sacella, 41–42
sacramentum, 179, 190–193, 197–198
shrines, 22, 27, 34, 47, 243, 250, 251
Sucellus, 34
Sulis Minerva, 68
temples, 43, 47–48, 68, 70, 72, 198, 213, 215, 247, 249–252, 261
Venus, 36, 43, 45, 48
Virgo Vestalis, 48
Vulcan, 48
Reynolds, J., 62
Rezé, shrine at, 40–43
Rhineland, 40, 163, 210, 213, 244
Rhoemetalces, 172–173
Richmond, Prof. Sir I., 2–3, 96, 101, 103–104, 112, 116, 120–121, 251
Rigold, S., 290, 294, 297–298
roads – see also individual roads, 271
  road system in Gaul, 155–164
Robertson, Prof. A.S., 110
Rocester, defences at, 90
Rochester, defences at, 90

Rödgen, fort at, 164, 237, 238
Rogge, M., 160
Rome, oath hands from, 193, 194, 198
Romula, 273
Rossiter, J., 60
Rouen (Ratomagus), 22
Roxalani, 255–261, 263, 265, 266, 269, 273–275
Rubrius Gallus, 263

Sacidava (Muzait-Dunareni), 271
St. Aubin, cauldron chain from, 134, 135
St. Dunstan, 79
St. Jerome, 46
St. Joseph, J.K., 2
Salins, cauldron chain from, 132
Sambuco, villa at, 59
Samnites, 192
San Giovanni di Ruoti, villa at, 62, 64
San Rocco, villa at, 56–59, 60, 61
Sarmatians, 255–263, 265–266, 268–275
Sarmizegetusa, 269
Saxon Shore Forts, 290, 297–300
Saxons, 241
  Bath, period at, 67, 72–79
  burhs, 300
  cauldron chains, 147, 149–150, 152
  cemeteries, 73, 290
  late defended sites, 290, 300
  poetry, 67, 68, 74–79
Schele, R.H., 98
Schönberger, H., 105, 107, 108, 109, 116, 121
Scythians, 255, 256, 258, 260, 262
Sear, F., 62
Segontium, shrine at, 36, 38
Seianus, 215
Selby, K.C. Collingwood, 38
Seleucus, 22
Seneca, 192
Senlis, 156
Servius, 46
Sette Finistre, villa at, 63–64
Severus Alexander, 22
Severus, Septimius, 84, 105, 112, 238
Sexaginta Prista (Ruse), 267
Sherborne, hoard from, 206
Sidon, oath hand from, 197
Silchester (Calleva Atrebatum):
  basilica at, 47
  cauldron chain from, 143, 144, 145, 146, 147, 151, 152
  defences at, 87–88, 92

domestic shrine at, 33, 36, 37, 40, 43, 45
figurines from, 43, 46, 47
forum at, 47
niche head from, 38
Silures, 203, 204, 207
Simpson, G., 85, 86
Singidunum (Belgrade), 267, 275
Sirmium, 267, 268, 270
Siscia, 171, 264, 267
Sittl, C., 179
Skydsgaard, J.E., 59
Slăveni, fort at, 105, 106, 119, 121, 273
Small, Prof. A., 59, 62
South Cadbury, Saxon burh at, 300
South Shields, fort at, 238
Spain, 45, 268
Springhead, shrine at, 38
Stanfield, J.A., 86
Stanfordbury, cauldron chain from, 132, 136, 140, 141, 142, 152
Stanwix, fort at, 105
Star, villa at, 247
Statilius Proculus, 212, 214, 217
Stevens, C.E., 210, 213
Stobi, 273
Strabo, 170, 171, 258, 259
Strageath, fort at, 1–2, 96
Stuart, P., 19
Sucidava, gravestone from, 189
Suetonius, 170, 191
Sutoria Pia, 212, 214–215, 217
Sutorius Marco, Q. Naevius Cordus, 215
Sutton Hoo, cauldron chain from, 147, 149, 150, 152
Swobeda, E., 171
Syria, 193, 197, 198

Tacitus, 46, 172, 192, 202, 203, 204, 205, 206, 207, 261, 262, 268
Taliata (Donji Milanovac), fort at, 266
Tapae, 268, 269
Tatton-Brown, T., 63
Taurunum (Zemun), 267
Tertullian, 48, 192, 198
Tettius Julianus, 261, 268, 269
theatres, 68
Theodoric, 62
Theodosius I, 240
Thérouanne (Tervanna), 20, 155, 156, 163
Thetford, 205
Thevenot, E., 47

Thorpe, defences at, 90
Thrace, 172, 173, 258–259, 260, 264, 265, 267
Tiberius, 163, 169, 170, 171, 172, 173–174, 265
Tienen, 164
Tilurium, fortress at, 264
Tirgsor, 273
Tiridates, 264
Titelberg, shrine from, 40
Titus, 267
Todd, Prof. M., 240
tombstones/funery monuments, 17, 20, 38, 184, 185, 186, 188, 189, 214
Tomis, 265, 271
Tomlin, R.S.O., 21, 22
Tongres (Atuatuca), 155, 157–158, 163, 164
Torelli, M., 182
Tournai (Turnacum), 159, 160
trade, 163–164, 170–171, 266
merchants, 15, 17, 19, 20, 22, 163, 170, 171
Trajan, 112, 264, 266, 270, 271, 273, 274, 275
Trajan's column, 184, 185, 186, 258, 271
Trawscoed, 2
Treballia, 264
Treveri, 173
Trier, 155, 156, 213
Trimalchio, 36
Trinobantes, 204
Troesmis (Iglita), fortress at, 271, 274
Tudor, D., 105
Tungri, *civitas* of, 155
Turum, 17

Valerius Mar(......), 13, 14, 15
Valerius Maximianus, M., 237
Valerius Messalinus, 172, 174
Valkenburg, fort at, 108–110, 119, 120, 121
Variana (Leskovec), fort at, 266
Varus, 269
Vegetius, 191
Velius Rufus, C., 270
Velleius Paterculus, 169–174
Velzeke, 160, 161, 164
Verecundius Diogenes M., 20
Vertault, cauldron chain from, 134
Verulamium, 1–2, 89, 207
defences at, 87, 91, 92, 93
lararia at, 33, 34, 36, 38, 40, 43, 45
shops at, 33, 87
temple at, 251
Vespasian, 263, 266, 267, 268
Vetera, fortress at, 119

Vettius Severus, Q., 211, 213, 215, 218
Vetus Salina (Adony), fort at, 266
Via Appia, 122
Via Gabina, 61
Vichy:
    cauldron chain from, 134
    figurines from, 45
Viducius Placidus, L., 21–24
villas – see also individual sites
    agriculture at, 62, 63, 64, 244–247
    British, decline of, 240–241, 244–250, 252
    Gaulish, 163
    industry at, 58, 61, 63
    Italian, 56–64
Viminacium, fortress at, 262, 265, 269, 270, 274
Vindobona, fortress at, 270
Vindolanda, fort at, 99
Vindonissa, bronze hand from, 190
Vitellius, 259, 262, 265

Wacher, J.S., 36, 38, 84, 90
Wallingford, Saxon burh at, 300
Wanborough, defences at, 90
Wardlaw, fort at, 222
Ward-Perkins, J., 56
Wareham, Saxon burh at, 300
Watling Street, 33
Webster, G., 84, 90
Weeting, cauldron chain from, 147, 152
Welwyn, villa at, 247

Whateley, villa at, 247
Wheeler, Prof. Sir R.E.M., 2, 36, 91
Whitehouse, D., 62, 63
Widrig, Prof. W., 61
Wiggonholt Common, cauldron chain from, 138, 139, 152
Wilkes, Prof. J.J., 26
Williams, A., 1
Wilson, R., 101
Winchester:
    cauldron chain from, 142, 147, 148, 152
    defences at, 87, 92
Winterton, villa at, 244
Woodchester, villa at, 244
Worcester, defences at, 90
Wroxeter:
    defences at, 88
    temple at, 251

Xanten (Colonia Ulpia Traiana), 2, 210

York (Eboracum):
    defences at, 91
    gravestone from, 185
    inscription from, 20, 21, 22–24

Zana (Diana Veteranorum), 237
Zárybník, cauldron chain from, 132
Zopyrion, 255
Zugmantel, cauldron chain from, 134, 135